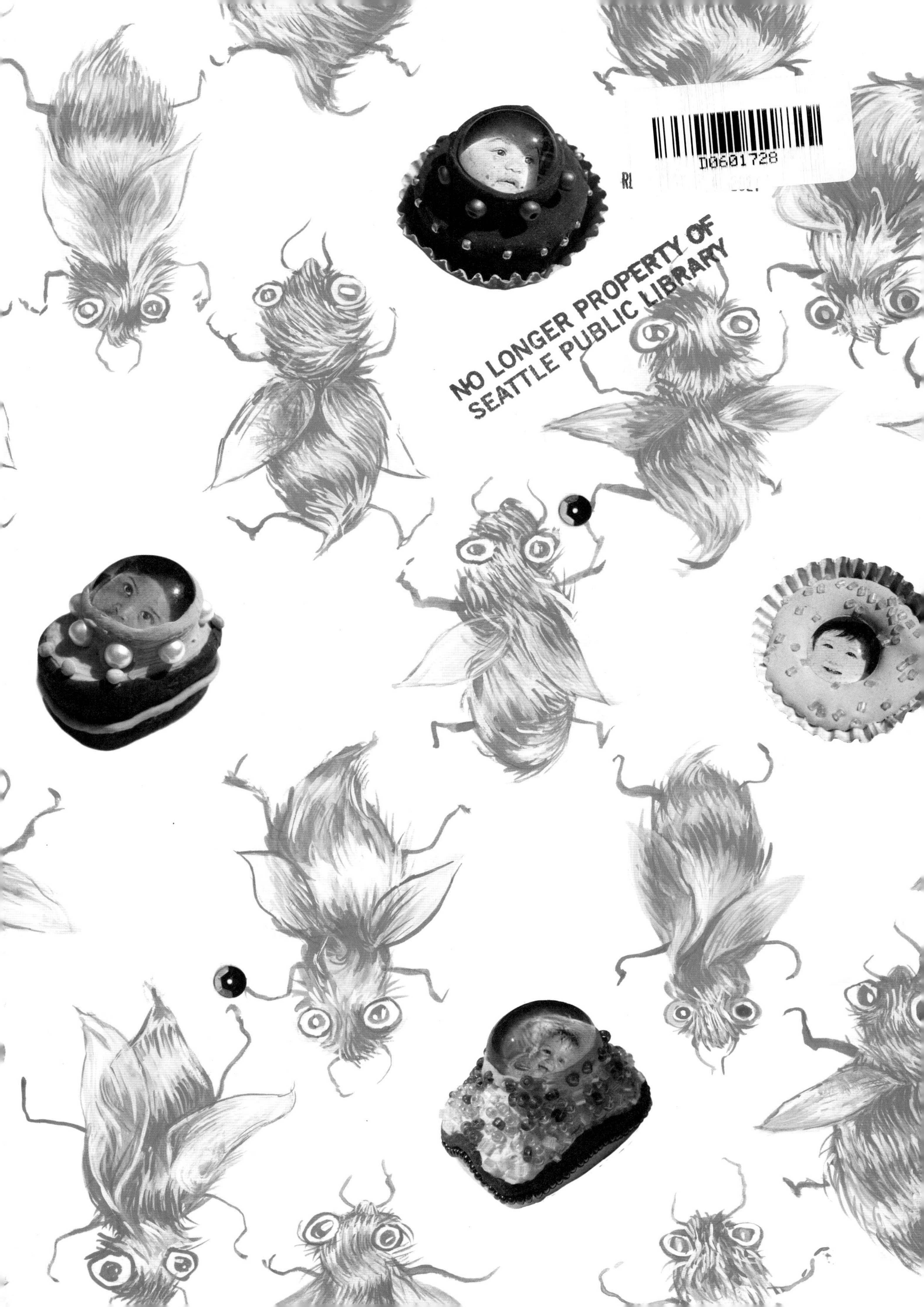

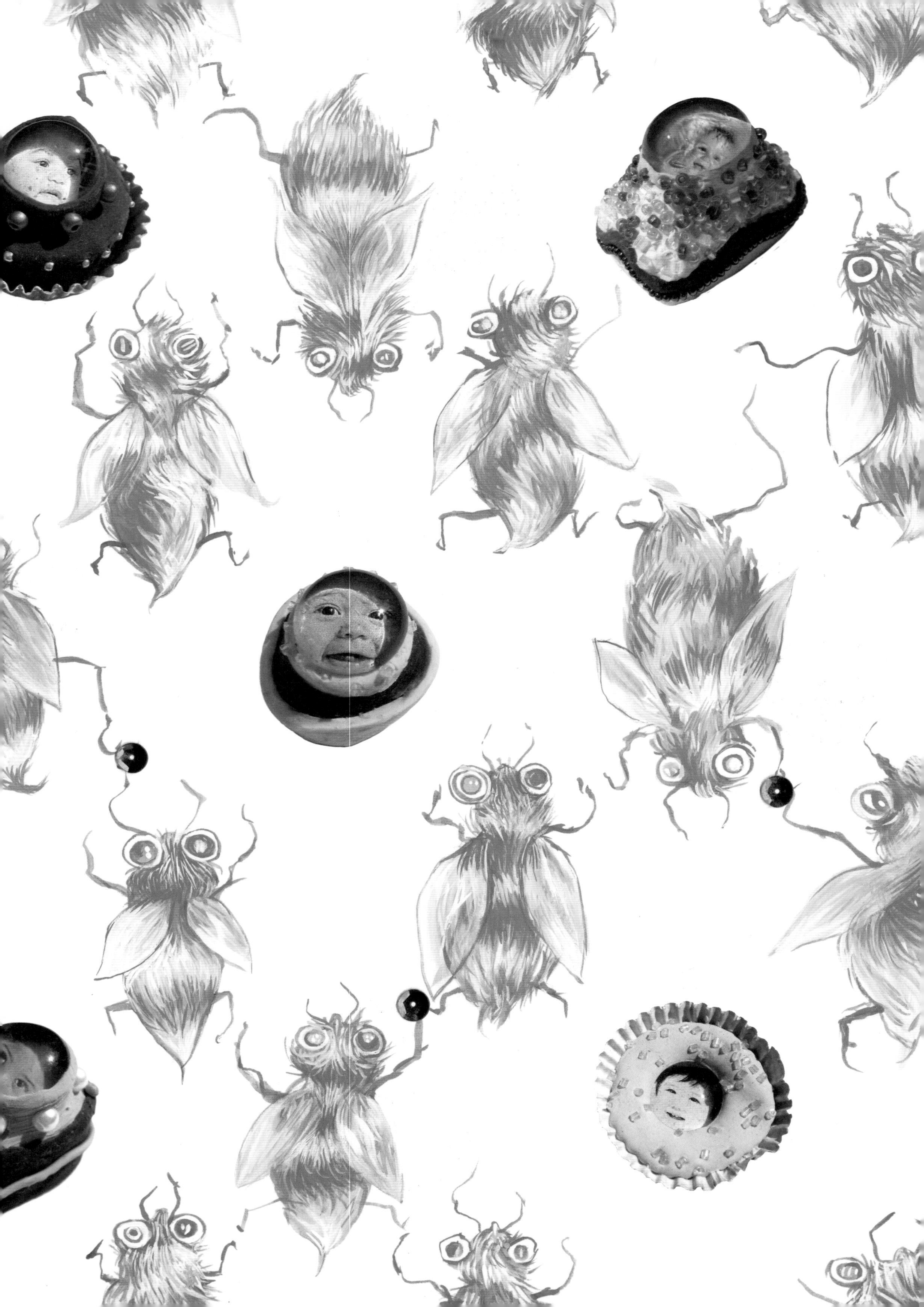

RED

ROCK

BABY

CANDY

For Rebecca

FANTAGRAPHICS 7563 Lake City Way • Seattle, Washington • 98115 •• Editor: Gary Groth •• Designer: Chelsea Wirtz •• Production: Christina Hwang •• Publisher: Gary Groth •• Associate Publisher: Eric Reynolds •• RED ROCK BABY CANDY. All comics, illustrations, and text is copyright © 2021 Shira Spector. This edition is copyright © 2021 Fantagraphics Books. All rights reserved. Published by Fantagraphics Books, 7563 Lake City Way, Seattle, WA 98115. Permission to reproduce for reviews and notices must be obtained from the publisher or the author. Our books may be viewed —and purchased— on our web site: fantagraphics.com @fantagraphics •• First Fantagraphics Books edition: April, 2021 •• ISBN 978-1-68396-404-9 •• Library of Congress Control Number 2020942302 •• Printed in Korea.

RED ROCK BABY CANDY

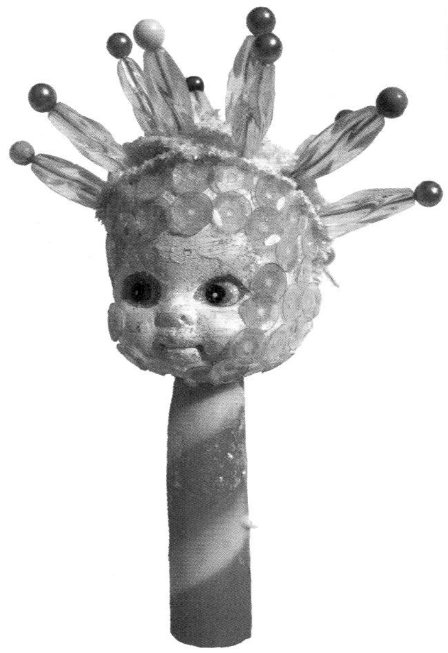

SHIRA
SPECTOR

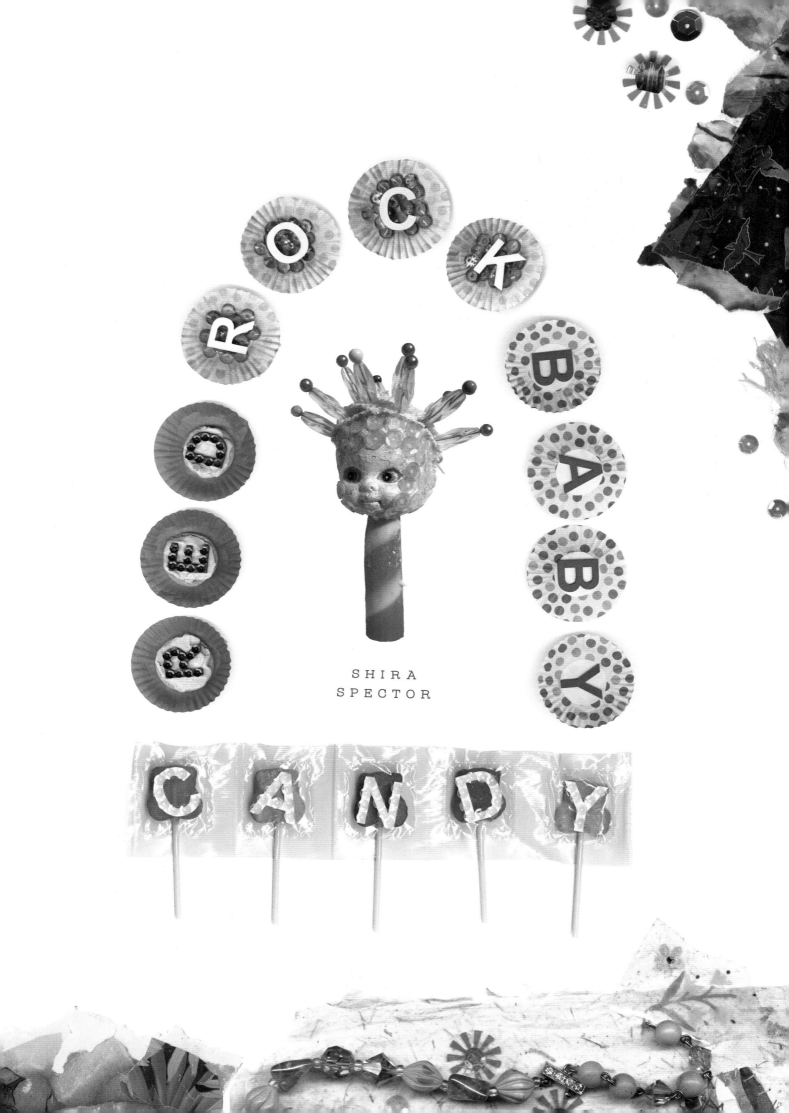

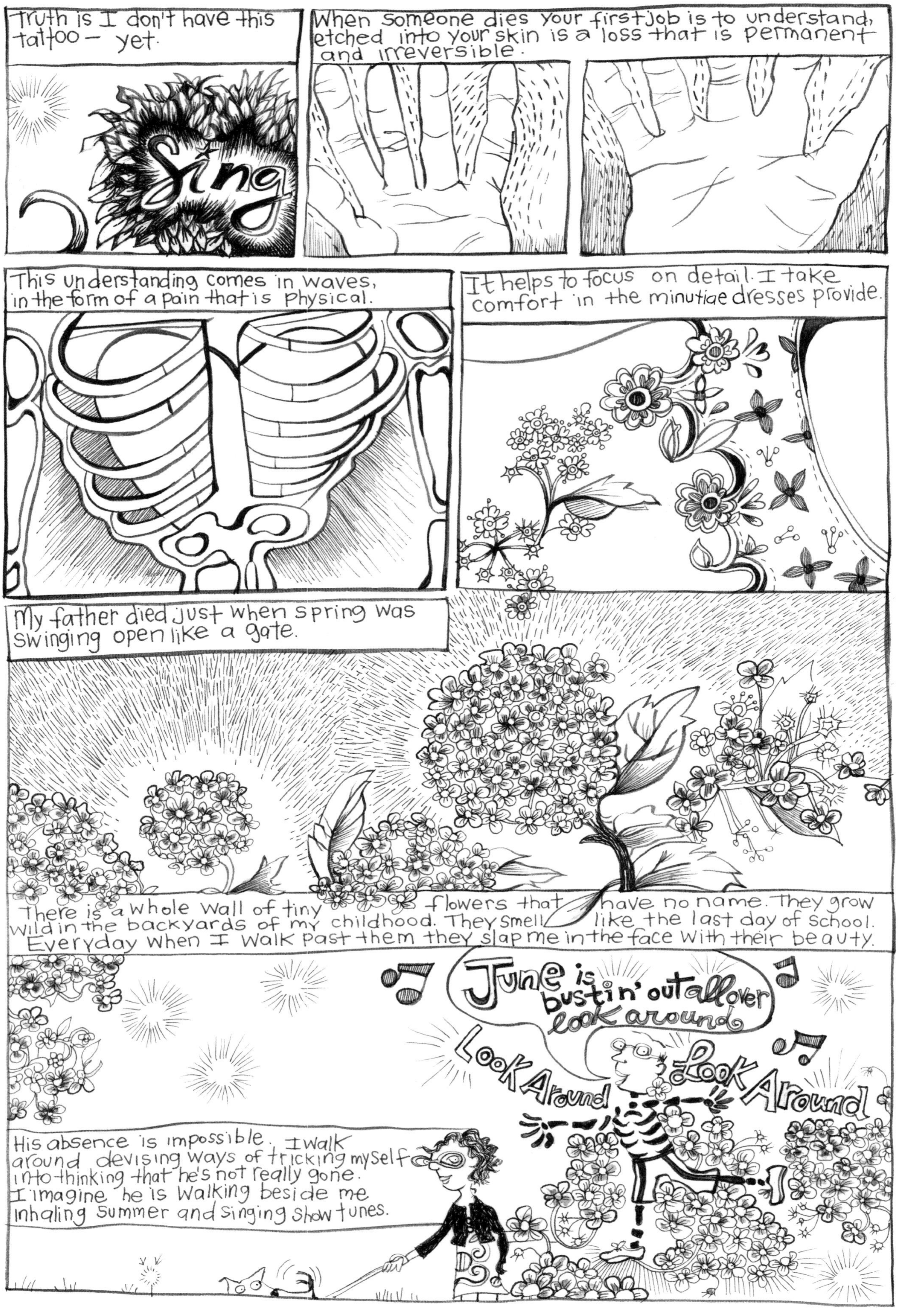
Truth is I don't have this tattoo — yet.
Sing
When someone dies your first job is to understand, etched into your skin is a loss that is permanent and irreversible.
This understanding comes in waves, in the form of a pain that is physical.
It helps to focus on detail. I take comfort in the minutiae dresses provide.
My father died just when spring was swinging open like a gate.
There is a whole wall of tiny flowers that have no name. They grow wild in the backyards of my childhood. They smell like the last day of school. Everyday when I walk past them they slap me in the face with their beauty.
June is bustin' out all over look around
Look Around Look Around
His absence is impossible. I walk around devising ways of tricking myself into thinking that he's not really gone. I imagine he is walking beside me inhaling summer and singing show tunes.

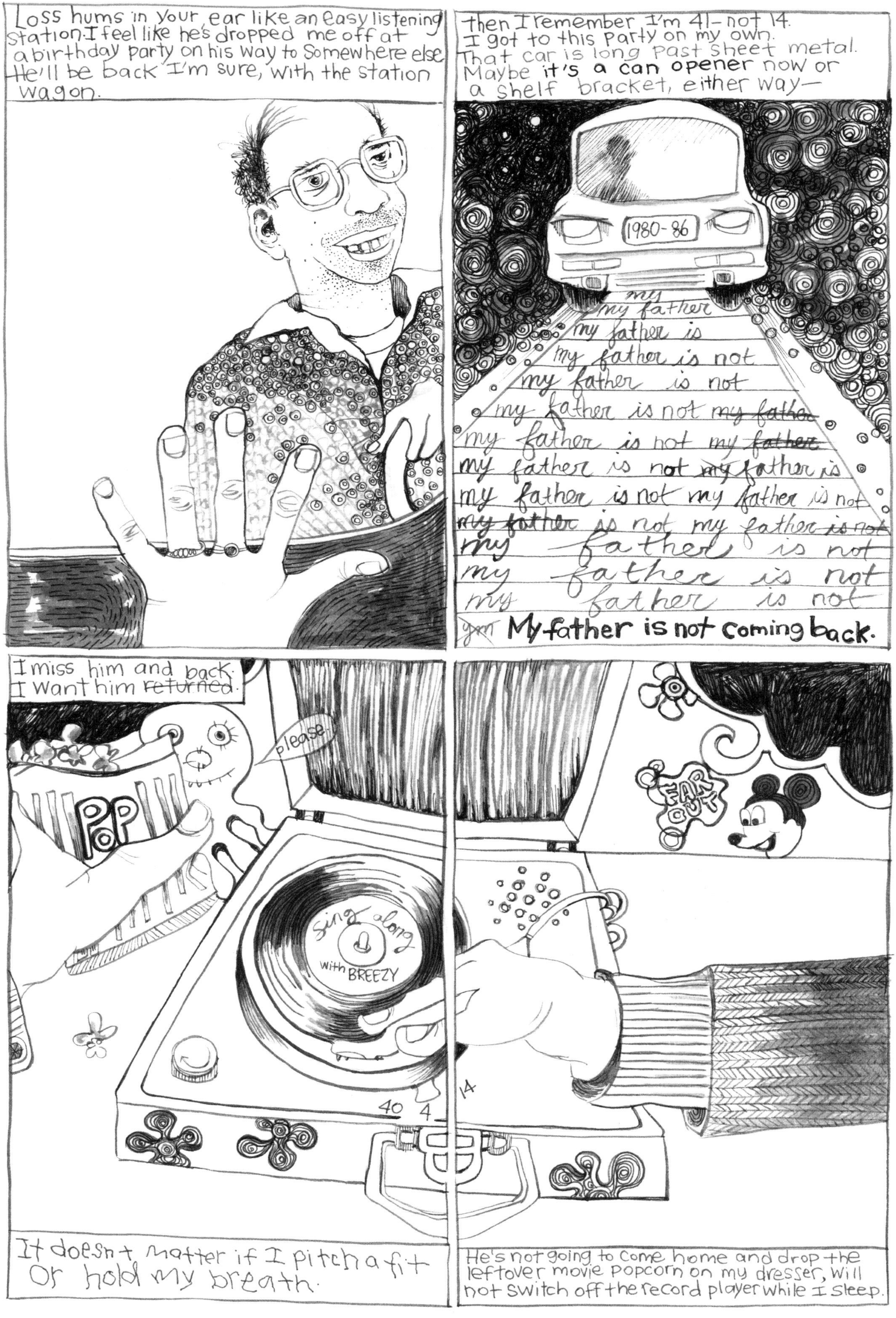
Loss hums in your ear like an easy listening station. I feel like he's dropped me off at a birthday party on his way to somewhere else. He'll be back I'm sure, with the station wagon.
Then I remember I'm 41 - not 14. I got to this party on my own. That car is long past sheet metal. Maybe it's a can opener now or a shelf bracket, either way—
1980-86
my
my father
my father is
my father is not
my father is not
my father is not ~~my father~~
my father is not my ~~father~~
my father is not ~~my~~ father is
my father is not my father is not
~~my father~~ is not my father ~~is not~~
my father is not
my father is not
my father is not
~~ym~~ My father is not coming back.
I miss him and back.
I want him ~~returned~~.
please.
POP
Sing along with BREEZY
40 4 14
FAR OUT
It doesn't matter if I pitch a fit or hold my breath.
He's not going to come home and drop the leftover movie popcorn on my dresser, will not switch off the record player while I sleep.

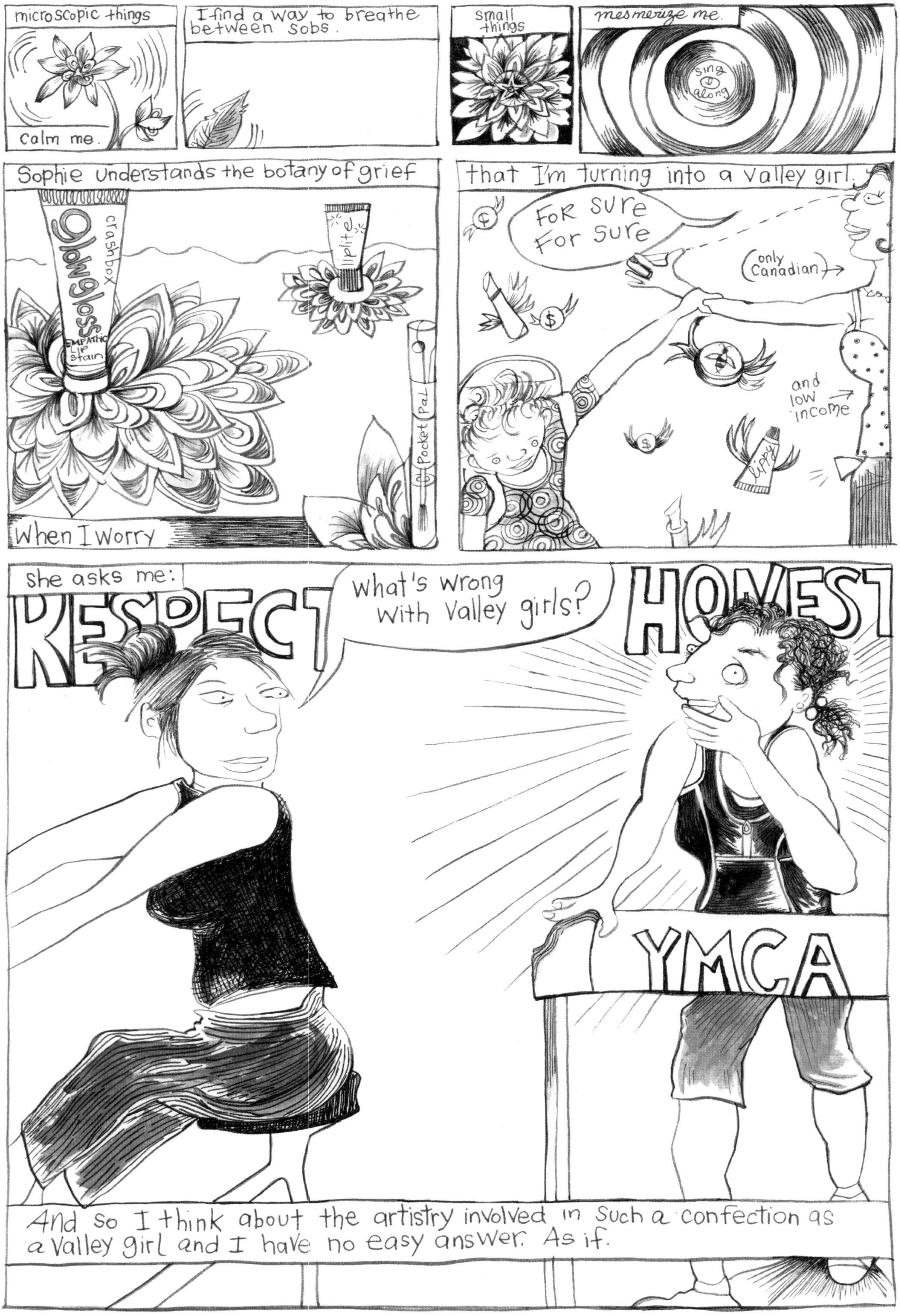
microscopic things
calm me.
I find a way to breathe between sobs.
small things
mesmerize me.
sing along
Sophie understands the botany of grief
glowgloss
crashbox
EMPATHIC LIP stain
iplite
Pocket PaL
When I worry
that I'm turning into a valley girl.
For sure For sure
(only Canadian)
and low income
lippy
she asks me:
RESPECT
What's wrong with Valley girls?
HONEST
YMCA
And so I think about the artistry involved in such a confection as a valley girl and I have no easy answer. As if.

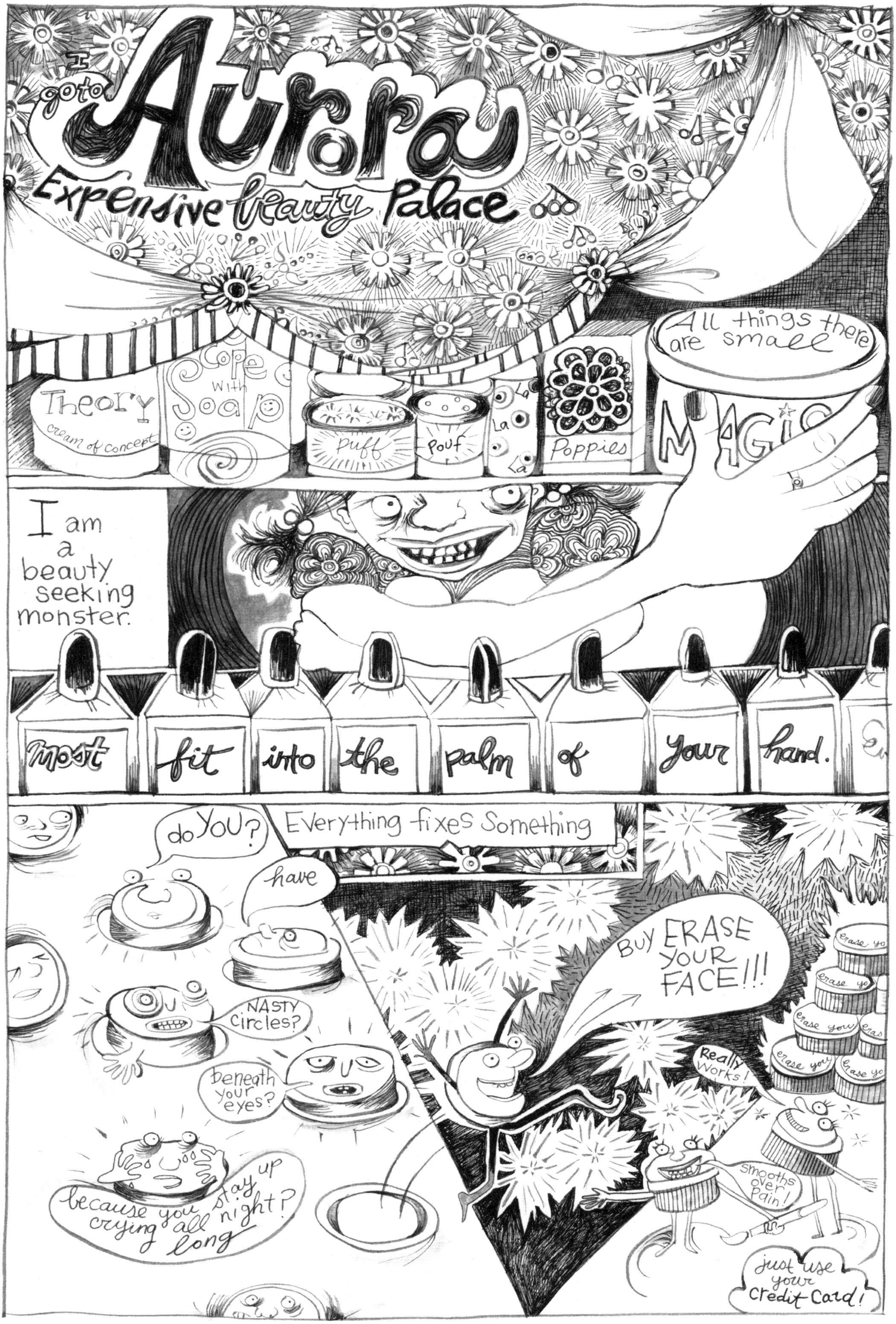

I go to Aurora Expensive Beauty Palace
All things there are small
Theory cream of concept
Cope with Soap
puff
pouf
La La La
Poppies
MAGIC
I am a beauty seeking monster.
most fit into the palm of your hand.
Everything fixes Something
do YOU?
have
NASTY circles?
beneath your eyes?
because you stay up crying all night long?
BUY ERASE YOUR FACE!!!
Really works!
smooths over pain!
just use your credit card!

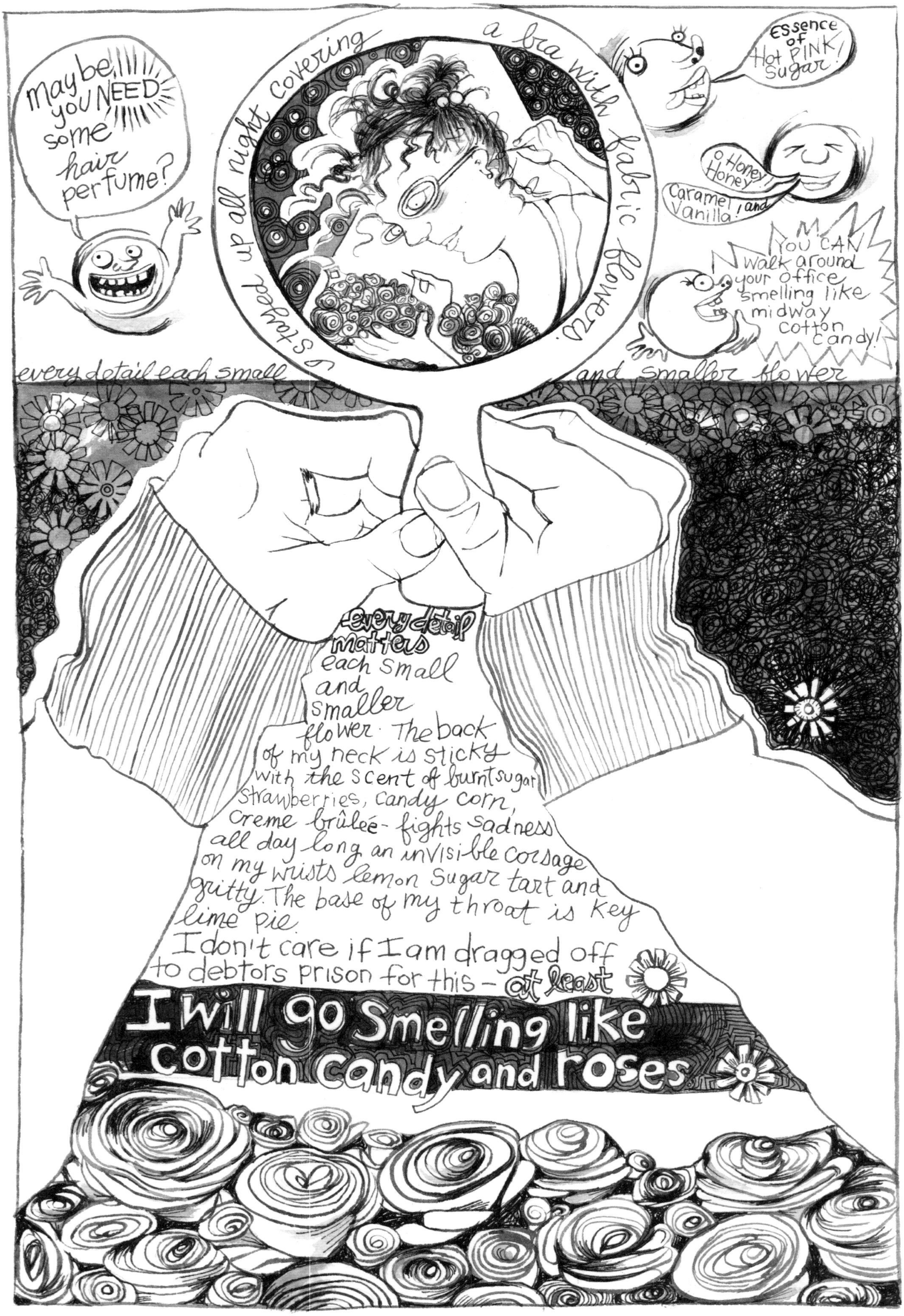

maybe you NEED some hair perfume?
I stayed up all night covering a bra with fabric flowers
Essence of Hot PINK Sugar!
O Honey Honey Caramel and Vanilla!
YOU CAN walk around your office smelling like midway cotton candy!
every detail each small and smaller flower
every detail matters each small and smaller flower. The back of my neck is sticky with the scent of burnt sugar strawberries, candy corn, creme brûlée- fights sadness all day long an invisible corsage on my wrists lemon sugar tart and gritty. The base of my throat is key lime pie.
I don't care if I am dragged off to debtors prison for this - at least
I will go smelling like cotton candy and roses.

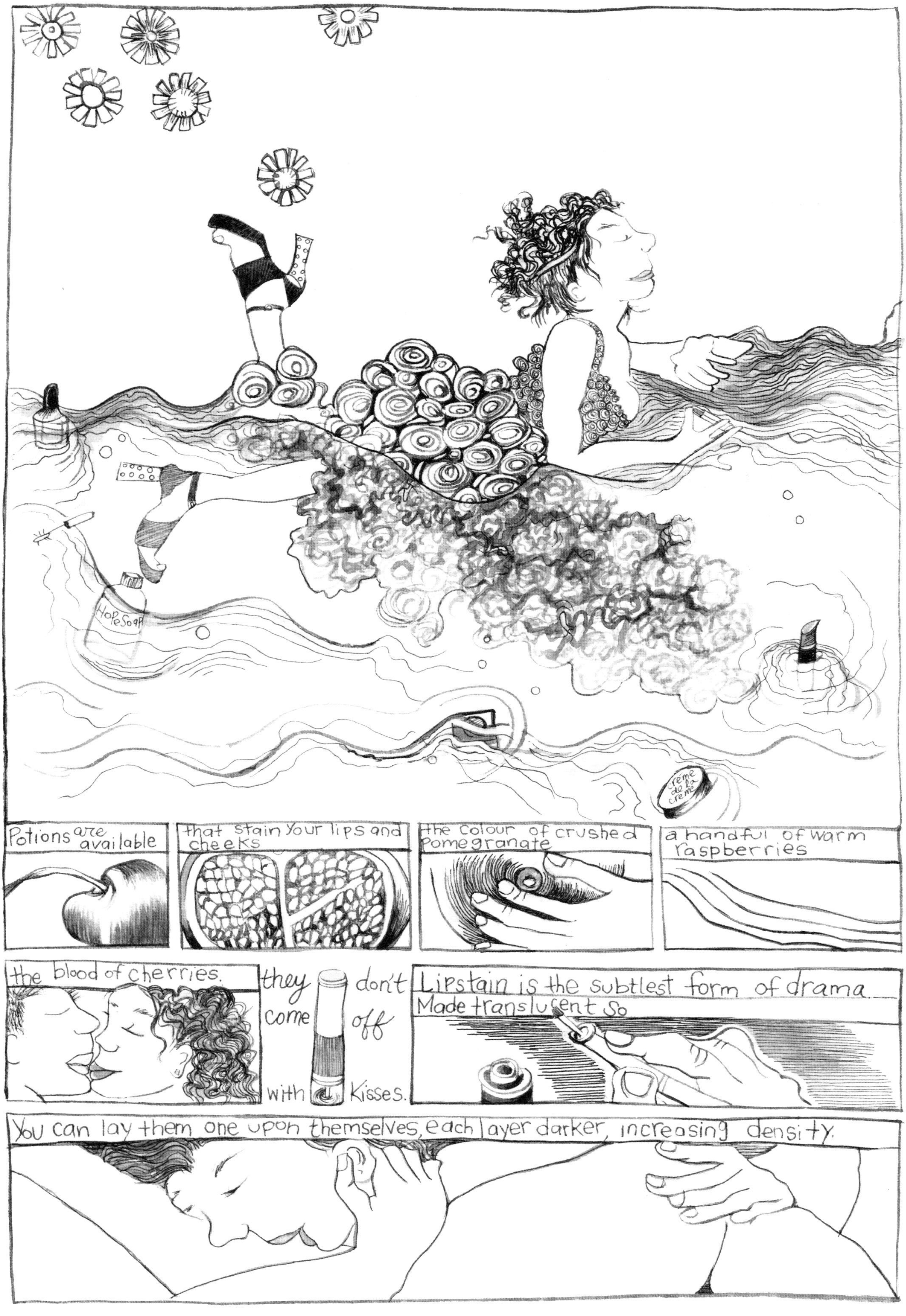

Hope Soap
creme de la creme
Potions are available
that stain your lips and cheeks
the colour of crushed pomegranate
a handful of warm raspberries
the blood of cherries.
they don't come off with kisses.
Lipstain is the subtlest form of drama.
Made translucent so
You can lay them one upon themselves, each layer darker, increasing density.

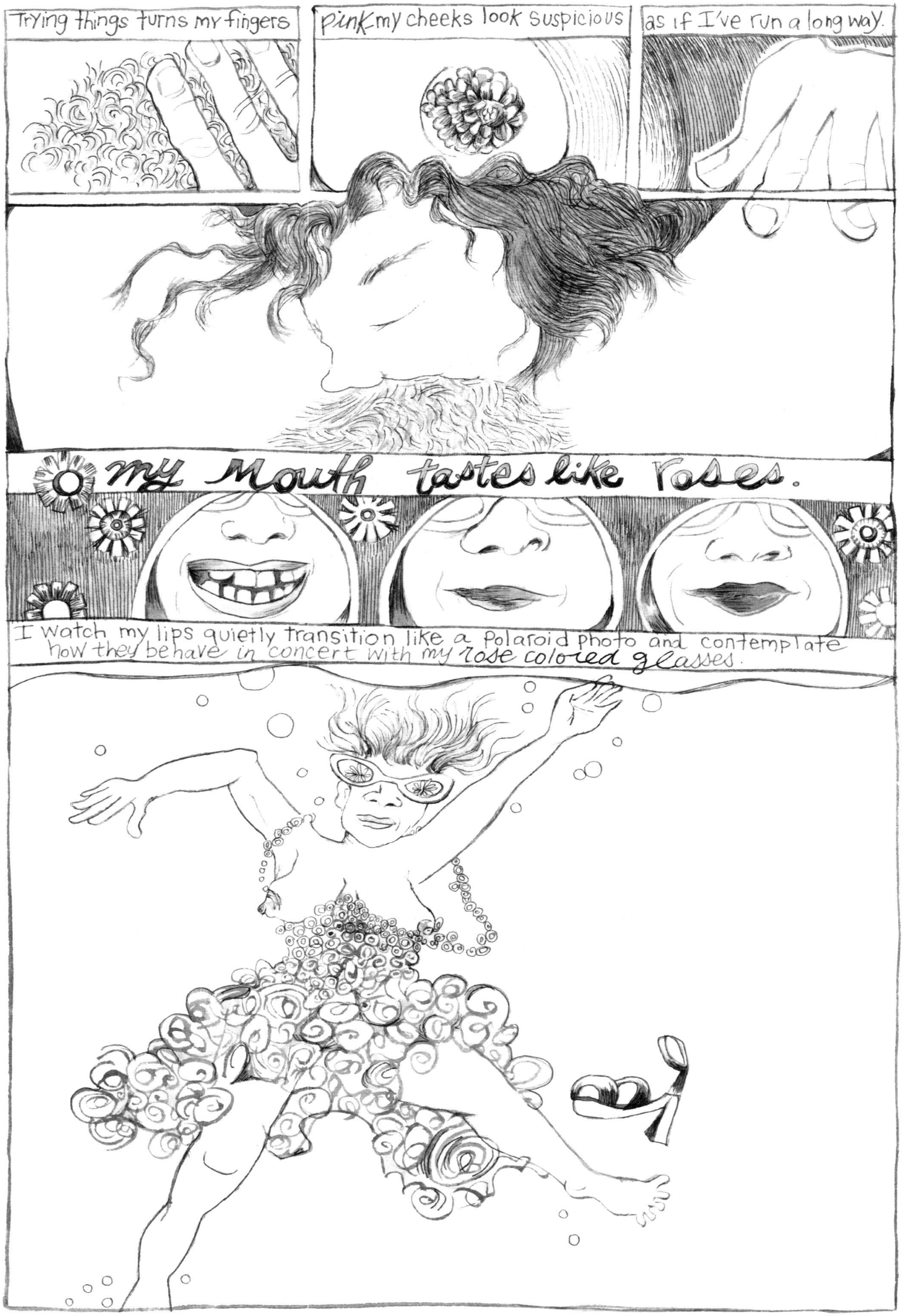
Trying things turns my fingers
pink my cheeks look suspicious
as if I've run a long way.
my mouth tastes like roses.
I watch my lips quietly transition like a polaroid photo and contemplate how they behave in concert with my rose colored glasses.

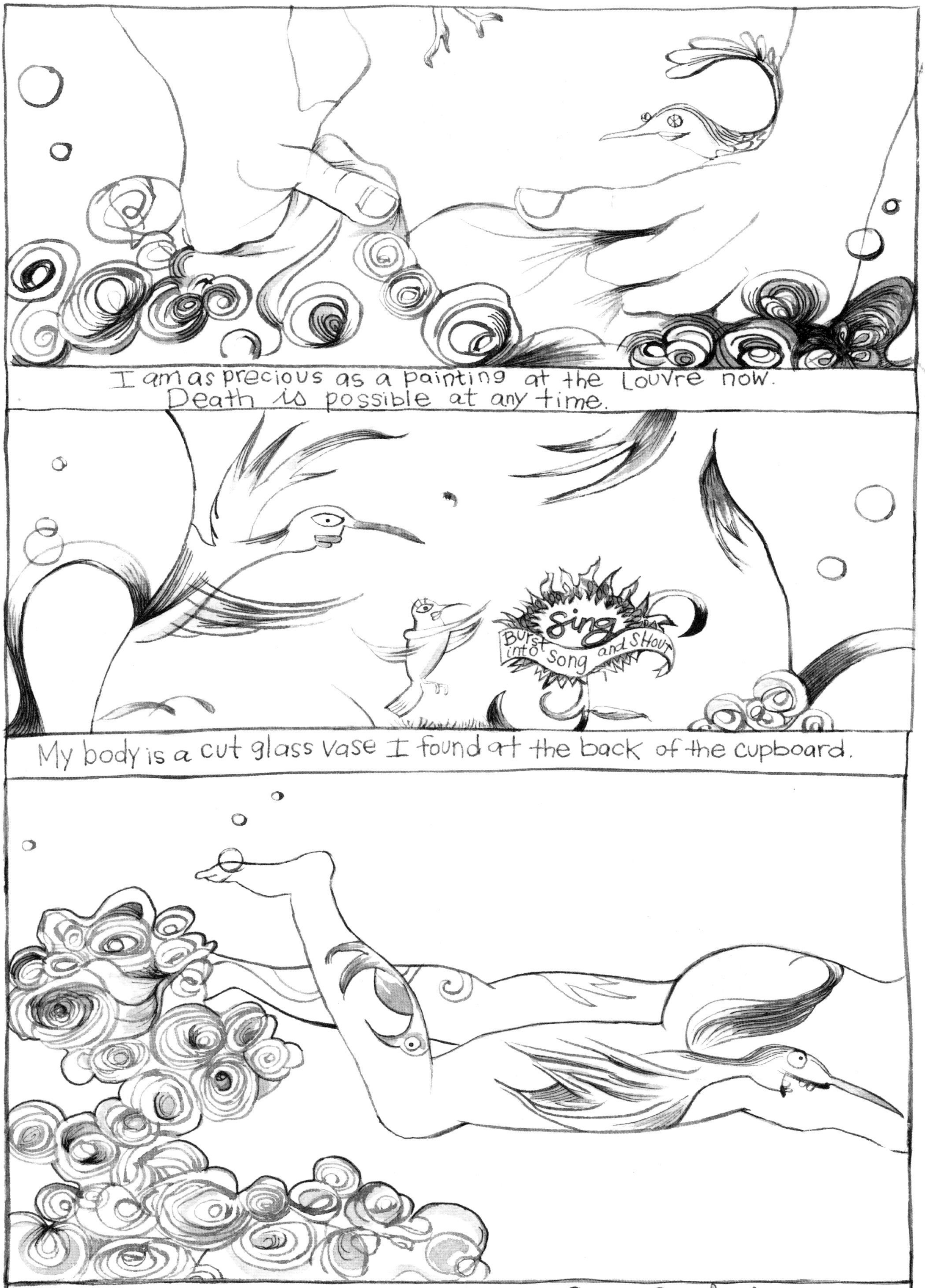
I am as precious as a painting at the Louvre now.
Death is possible at any time.
Sing
Burst into song and shout
My body is a cut glass vase I found at the back of the cupboard.
I am washing the dust off in sunlight.

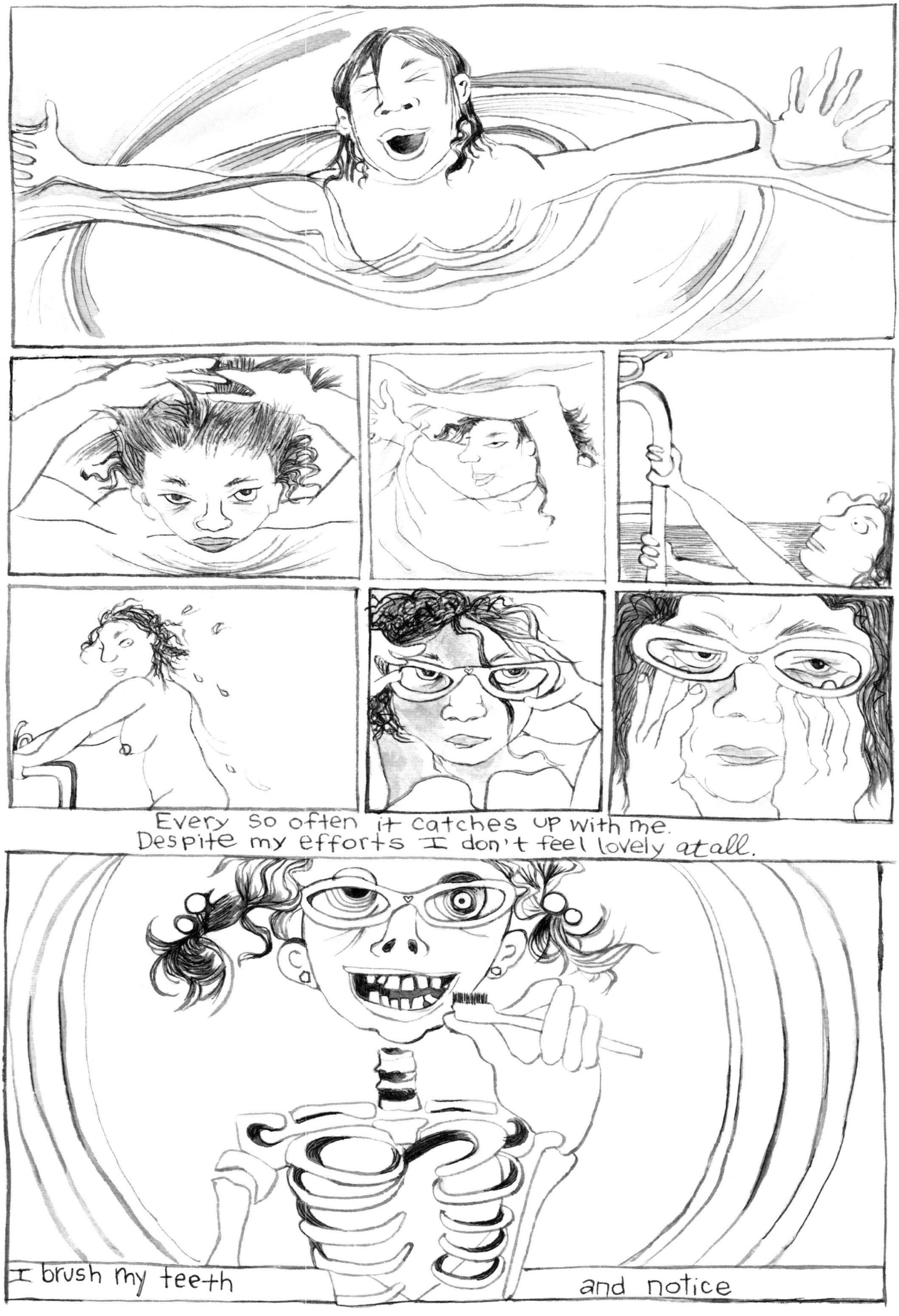

Every so often it catches up with me.
Despite my efforts I don't feel lovely at all.
I brush my teeth
and notice

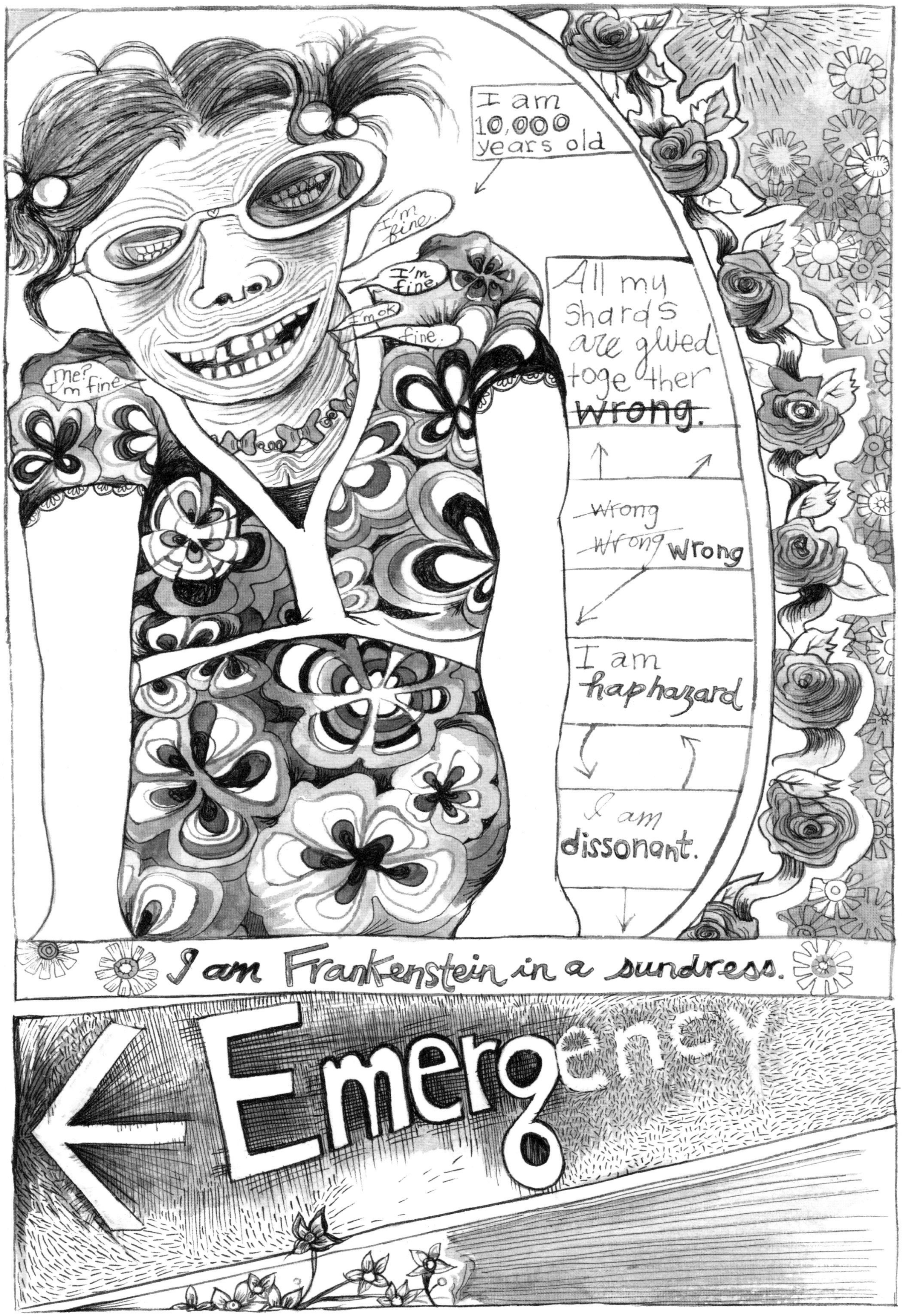
I am 10,000 years old
I'm fine.
I'm fine.
I'm ok
fine.
Me? I'm fine
All my shards are glued together wrong.
wrong
wrong wrong
I am haphazard
I am dissonant.
I am Frankenstein in a sundress.
Emergency

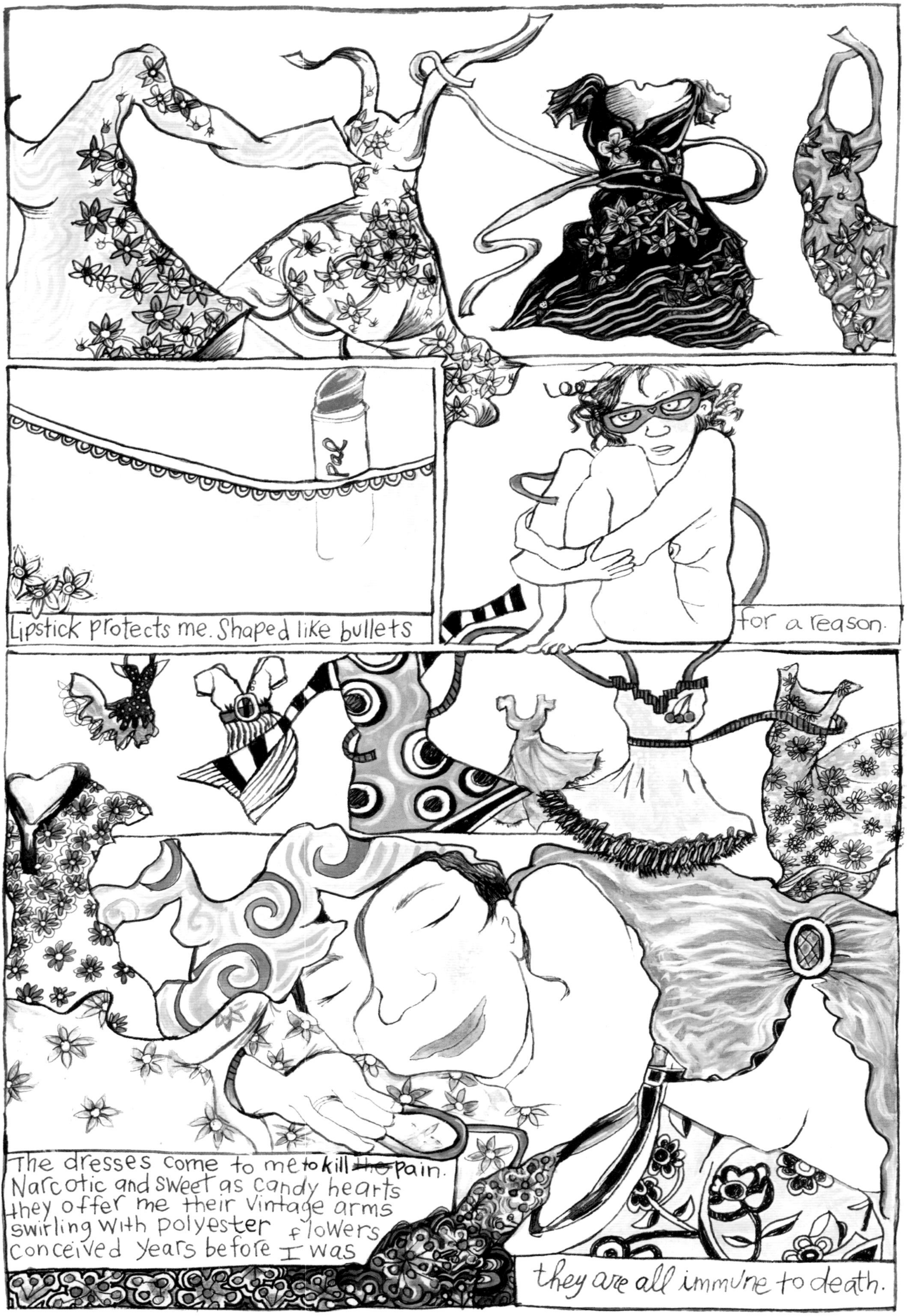
Lipstick protects me. Shaped like bullets
for a reason.
The dresses come to me to kill ~~the~~ pain.
Narcotic and sweet as candy hearts
they offer me their vintage arms
swirling with polyester flowers
conceived years before I was
they are all immune to death.

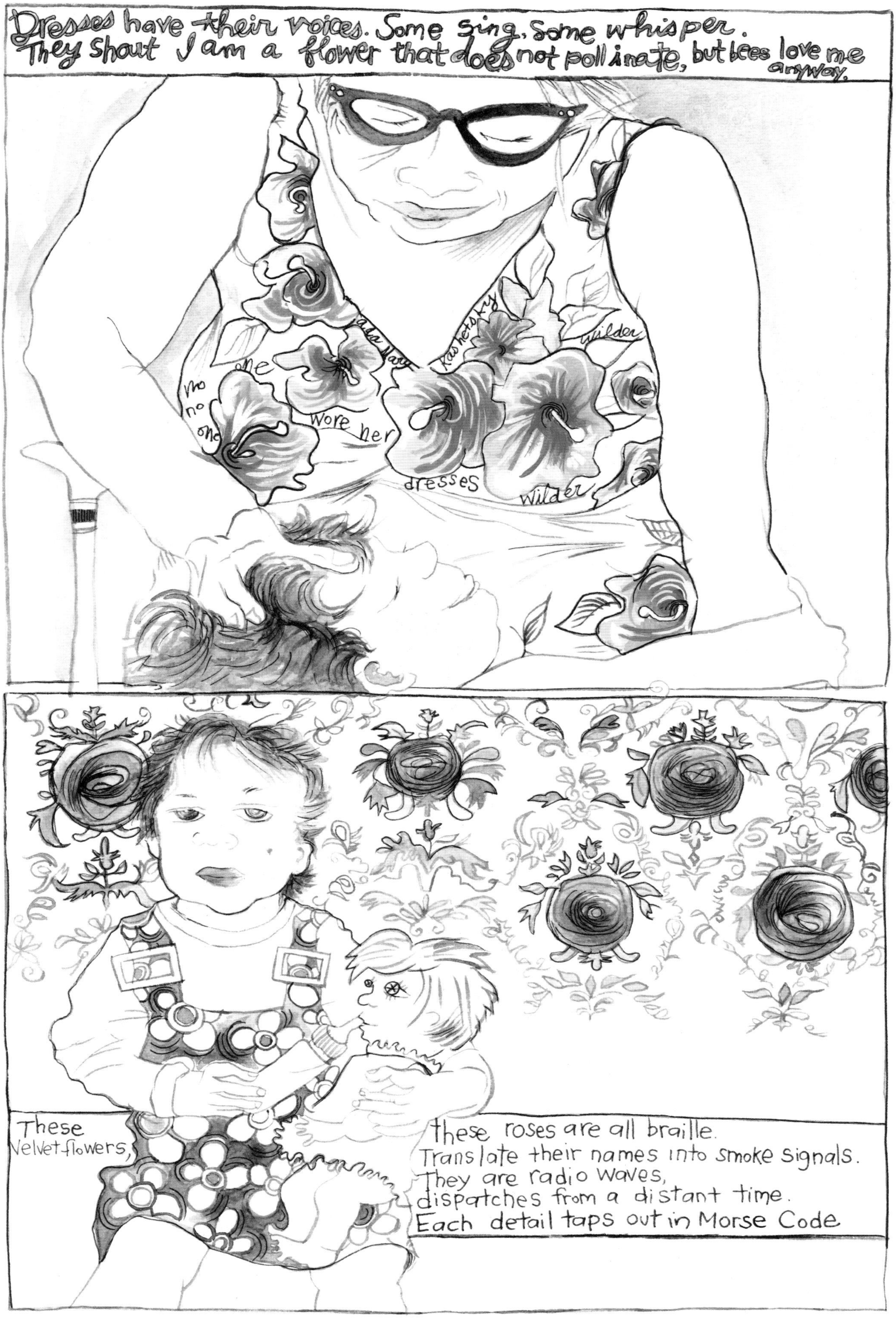
Dresses have their voices. Some sing, some whisper.
They shout I am a flower that does not pollinate, but bees love me anyway.
Ada May
Kashetsky
wilder
one
no
no
one
wore her
dresses
wilder
These
Velvet flowers,
these roses are all braille.
Translate their names into smoke signals.
They are radio waves,
dispatches from a distant time.
Each detail taps out in Morse Code

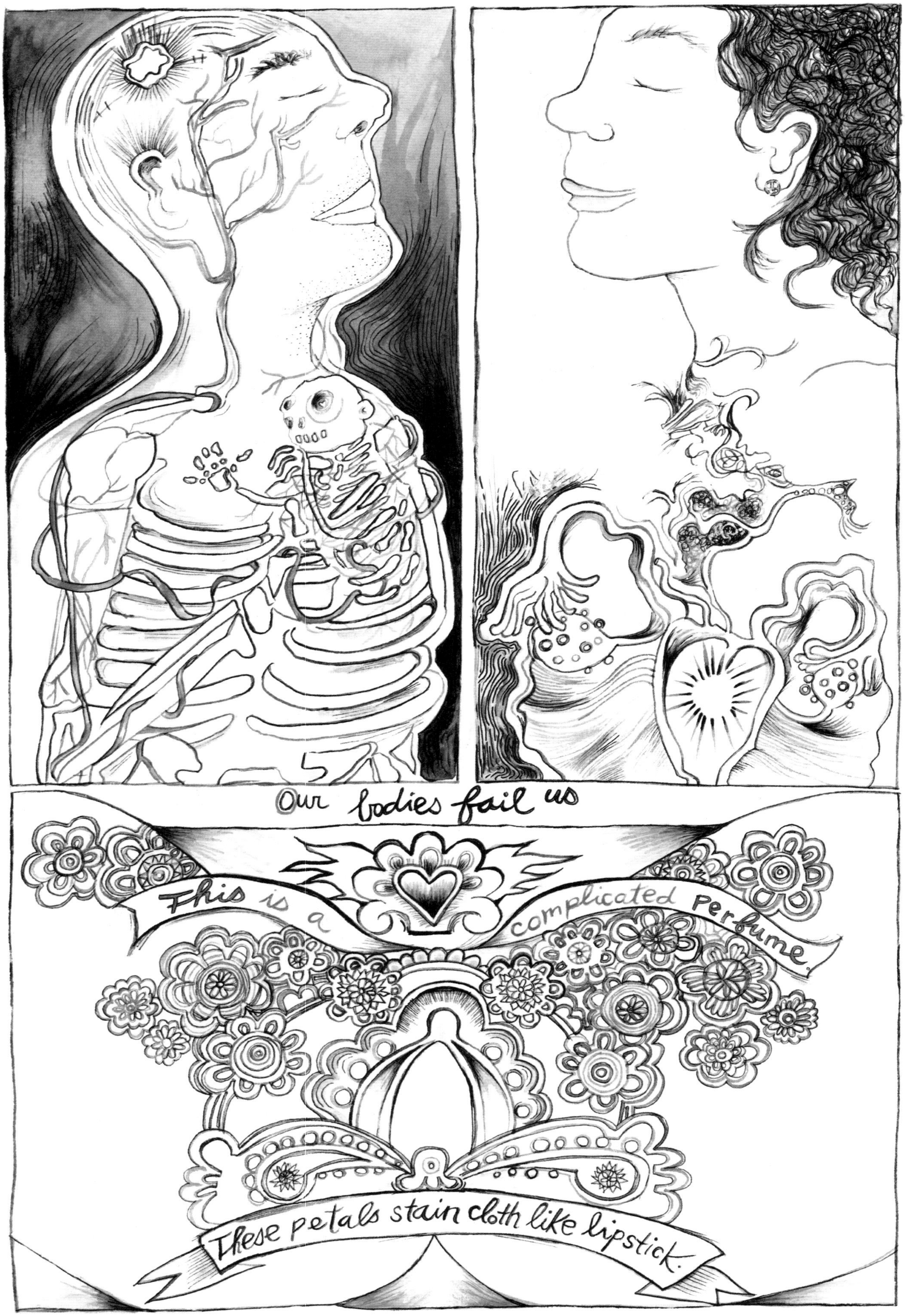
Our bodies fail us
This is a complicated perfume.
These petals stain cloth like lipstick.

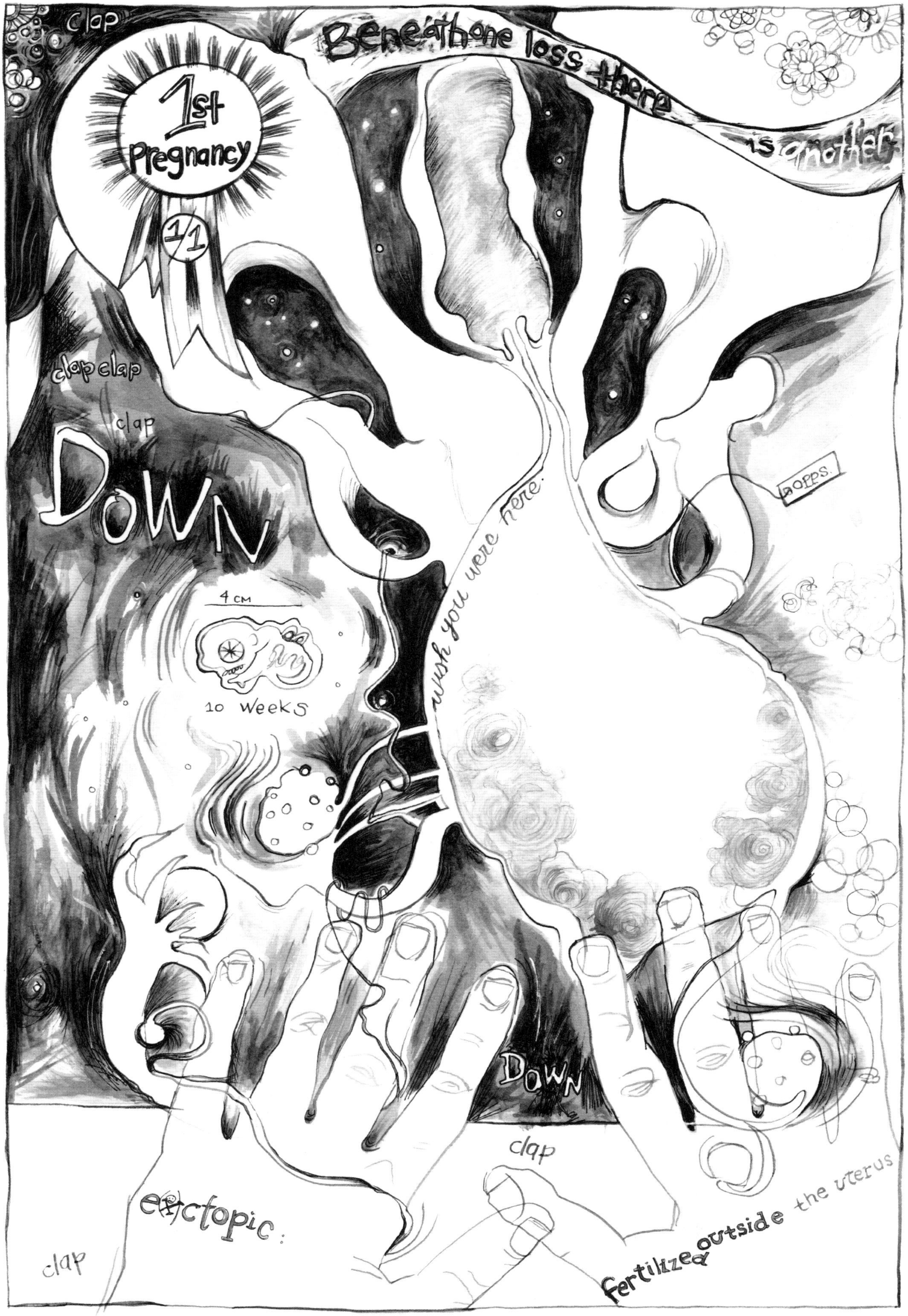
clap
Beneath one loss there is another
1st Pregnancy
1/1
clap clap
clap
DOWN
4 CM
10 WEEKS
wish you were here.
oops.
DOWN
clap
ectopic:
fertilized outside the uterus
clap

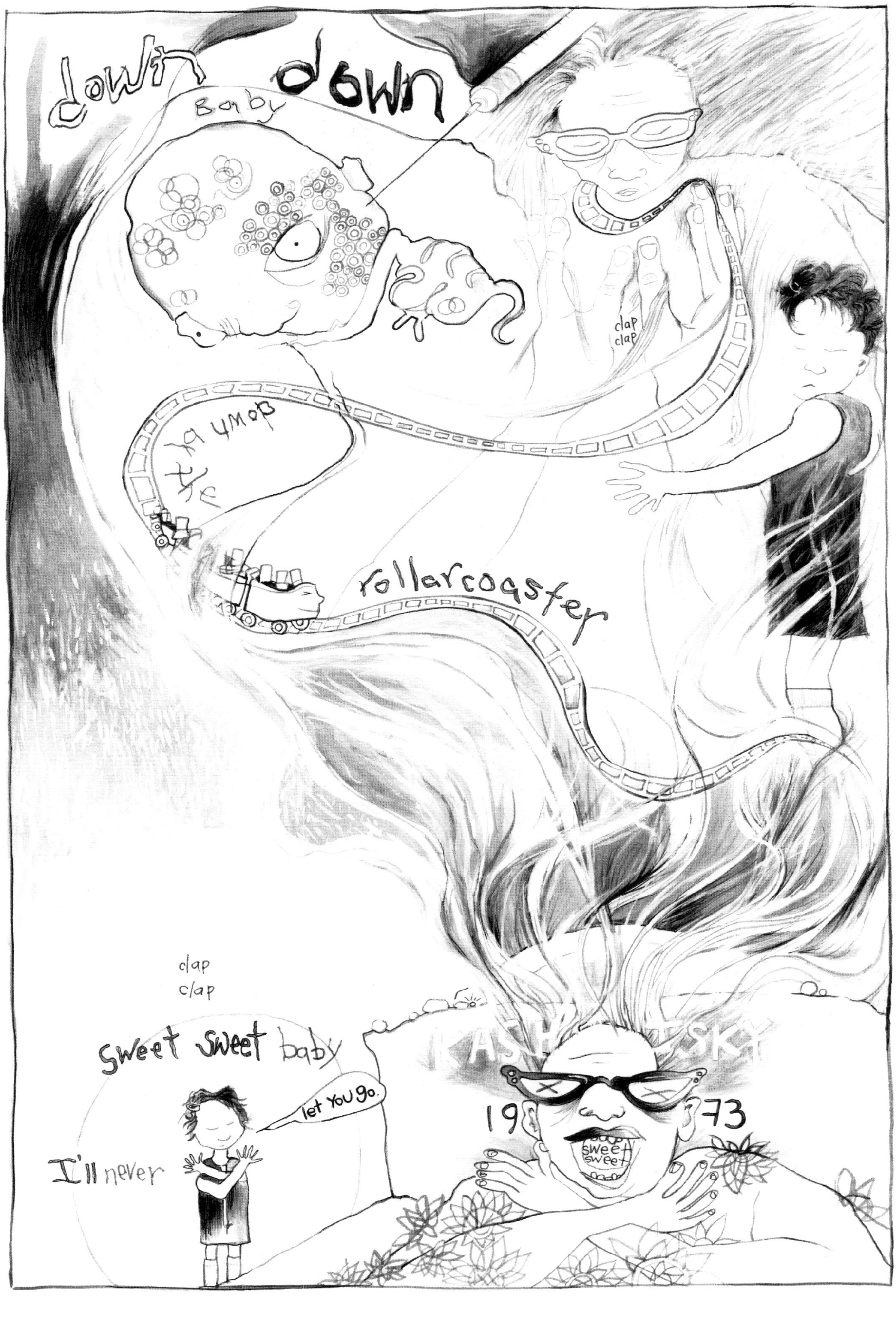
down down
Baby
down by the
rollarcoaster
clap
clap
clap
clap
sweet sweet baby
I'll never
let YOU go.
19 73
sweet sweet

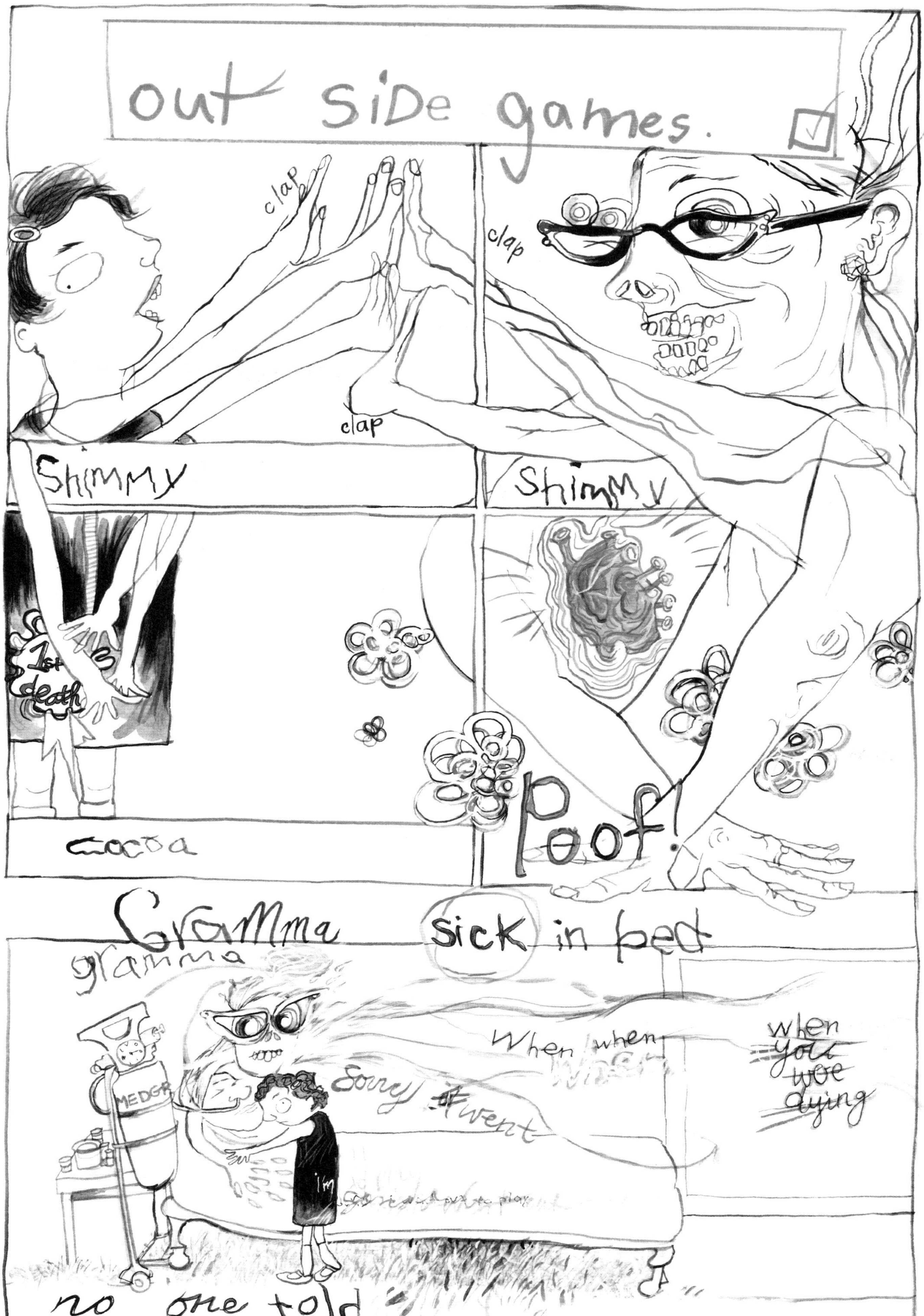
out side games.
clap
clap
clap
Shimmy
Shimmy
1st death
cocoa
Poof!
Gramma
sick in bed
gramma
MEDGR
When when
Sorry
went
when you woe dying
i'm
no one told

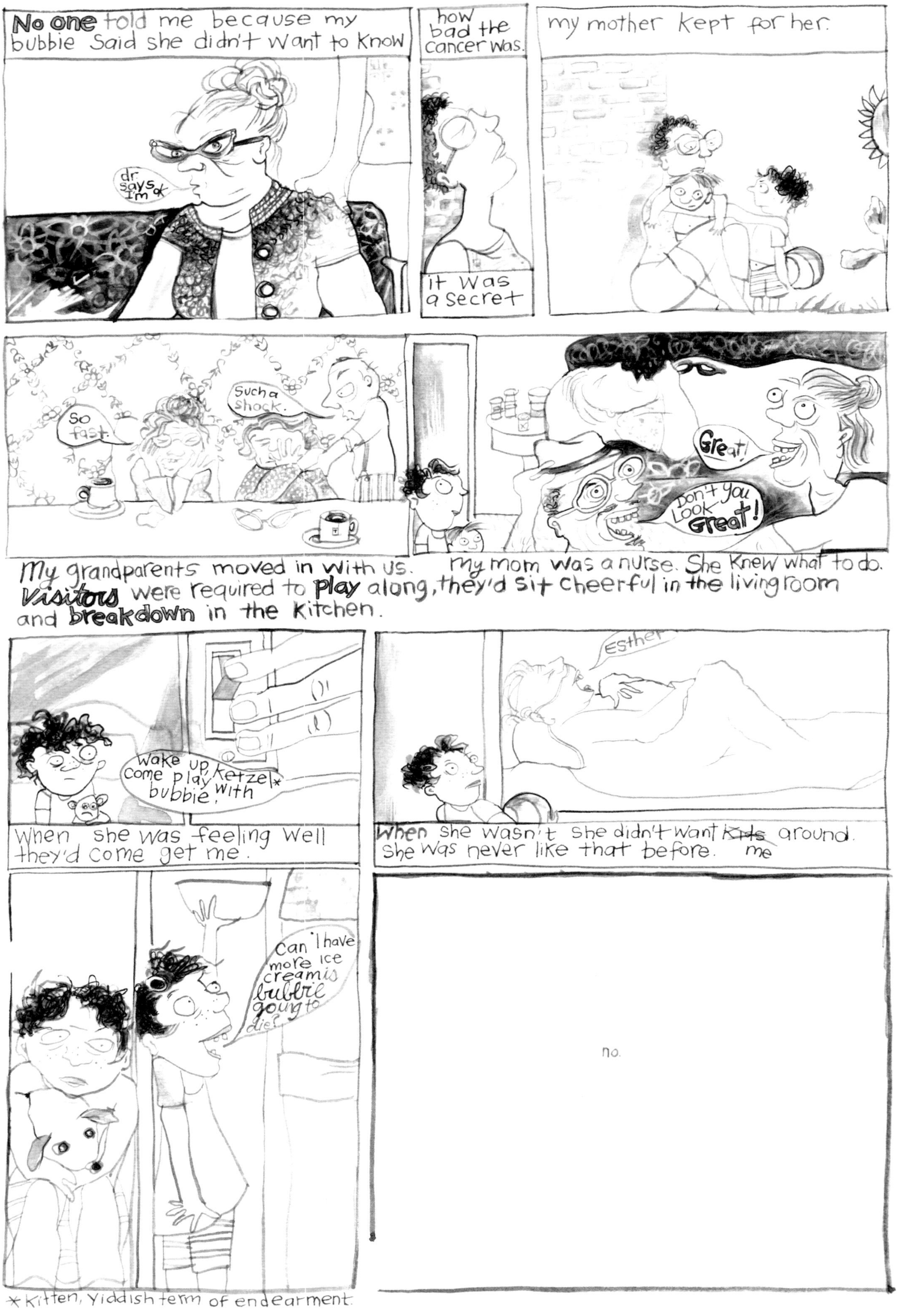
No one told me because my bubbie said she didn't want to know
how bad the cancer was.
dr. says I'm ok
it was a secret
my mother kept for her.
So fast.
Such a shock.
Great!
Don't you look Great!
My grandparents moved in with us. my mom was a nurse. She knew what to do. Visitors were required to play along, they'd sit cheerful in the living room and breakdown in the kitchen.
wake up, ketzel* come play with bubbie.
When she was feeling well they'd come get me.
Esther
When she wasn't she didn't want ~~Kids~~ me around.
She was never like that before.
Can I have more ice cream is bubbie going to die?
no.
*Kitten, Yiddish term of endearment.

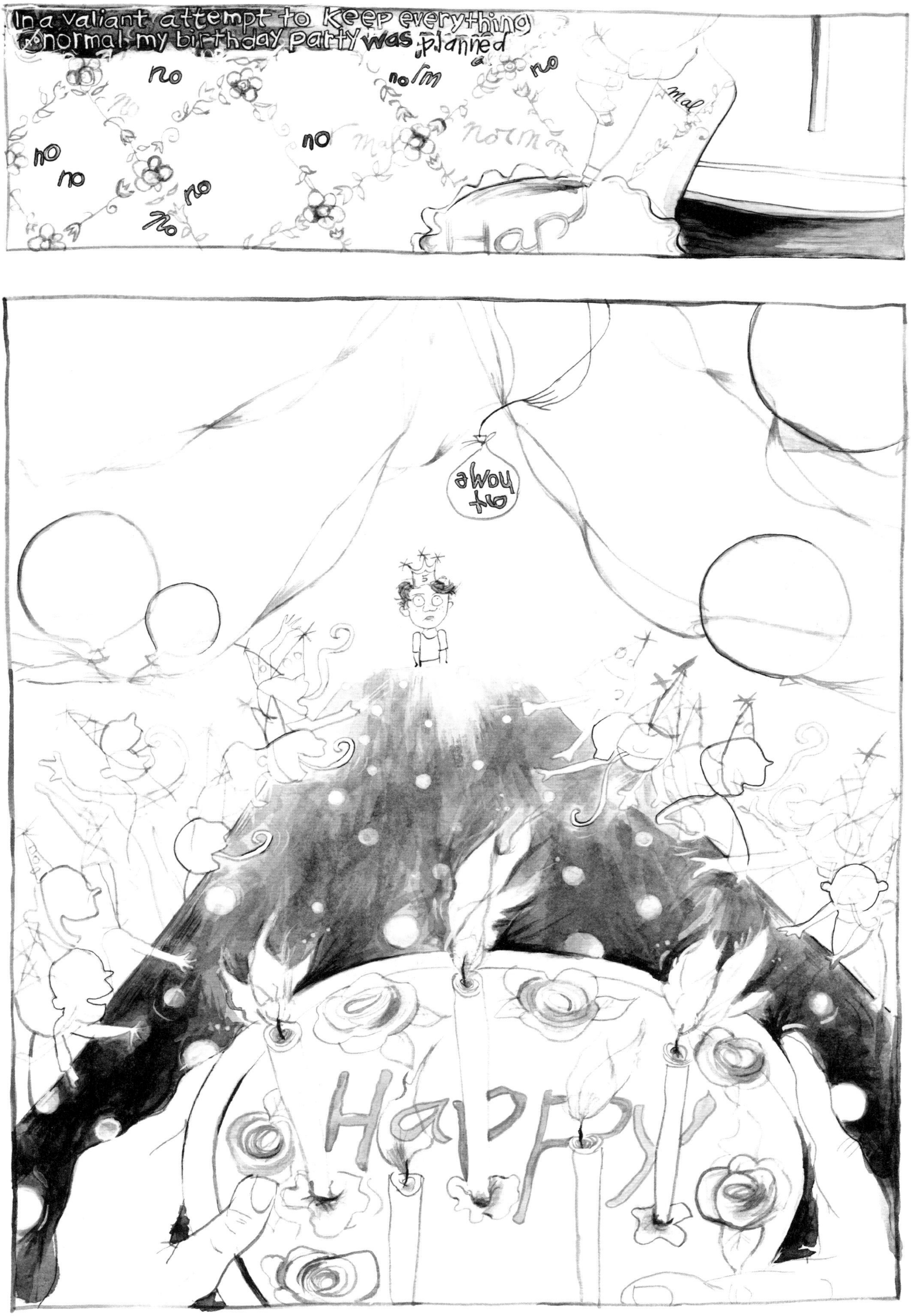
In a valiant attempt to keep everything normal, my birthday party was planned
no
no
no
no
no
no
no
Hap
Happy

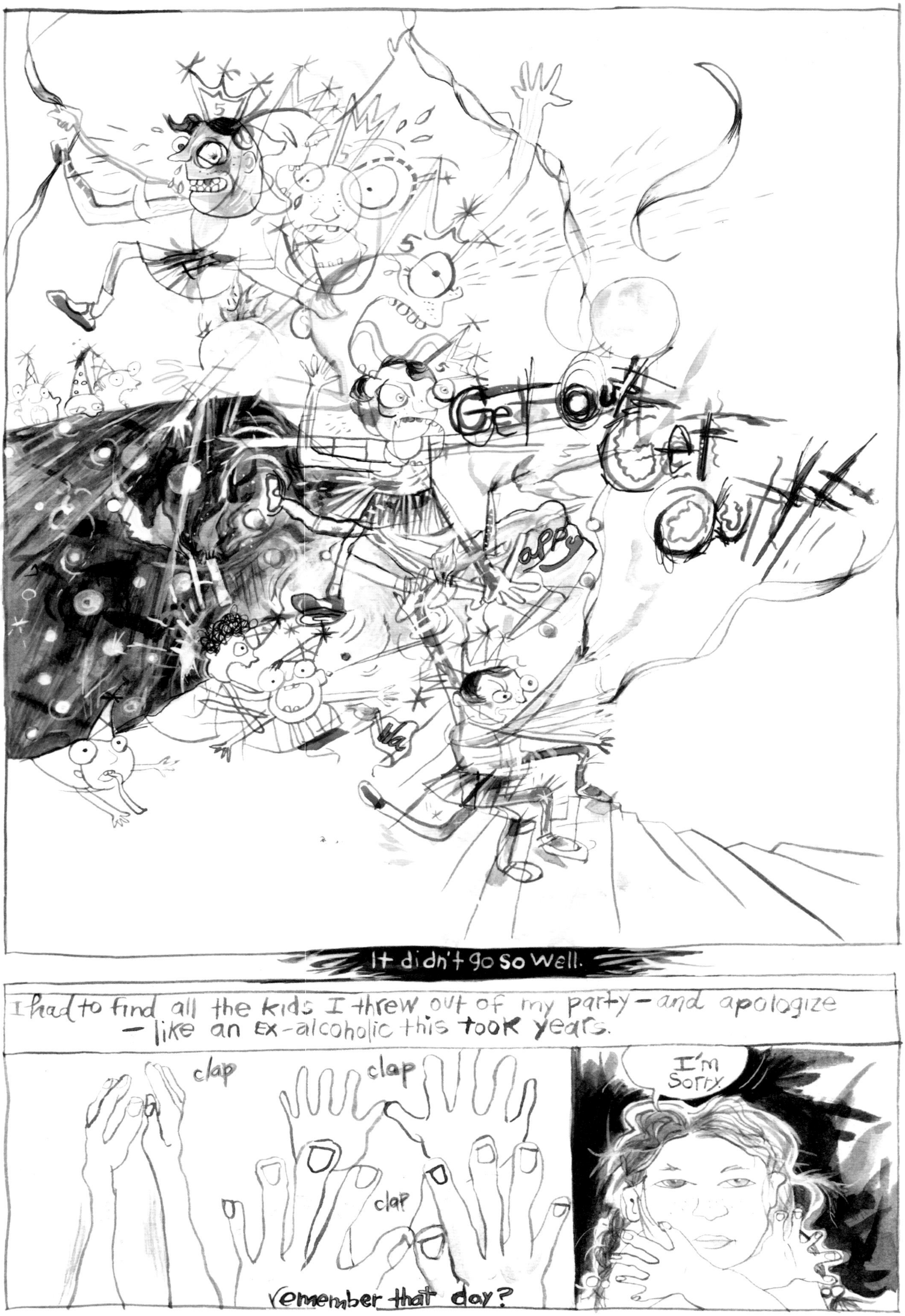
Get Out
Get Out
It didn't go so well.
I had to find all the kids I threw out of my party — and apologize — like an ex-alcoholic this took years.
clap
clap
clap
remember that day?
I'm Sorry.

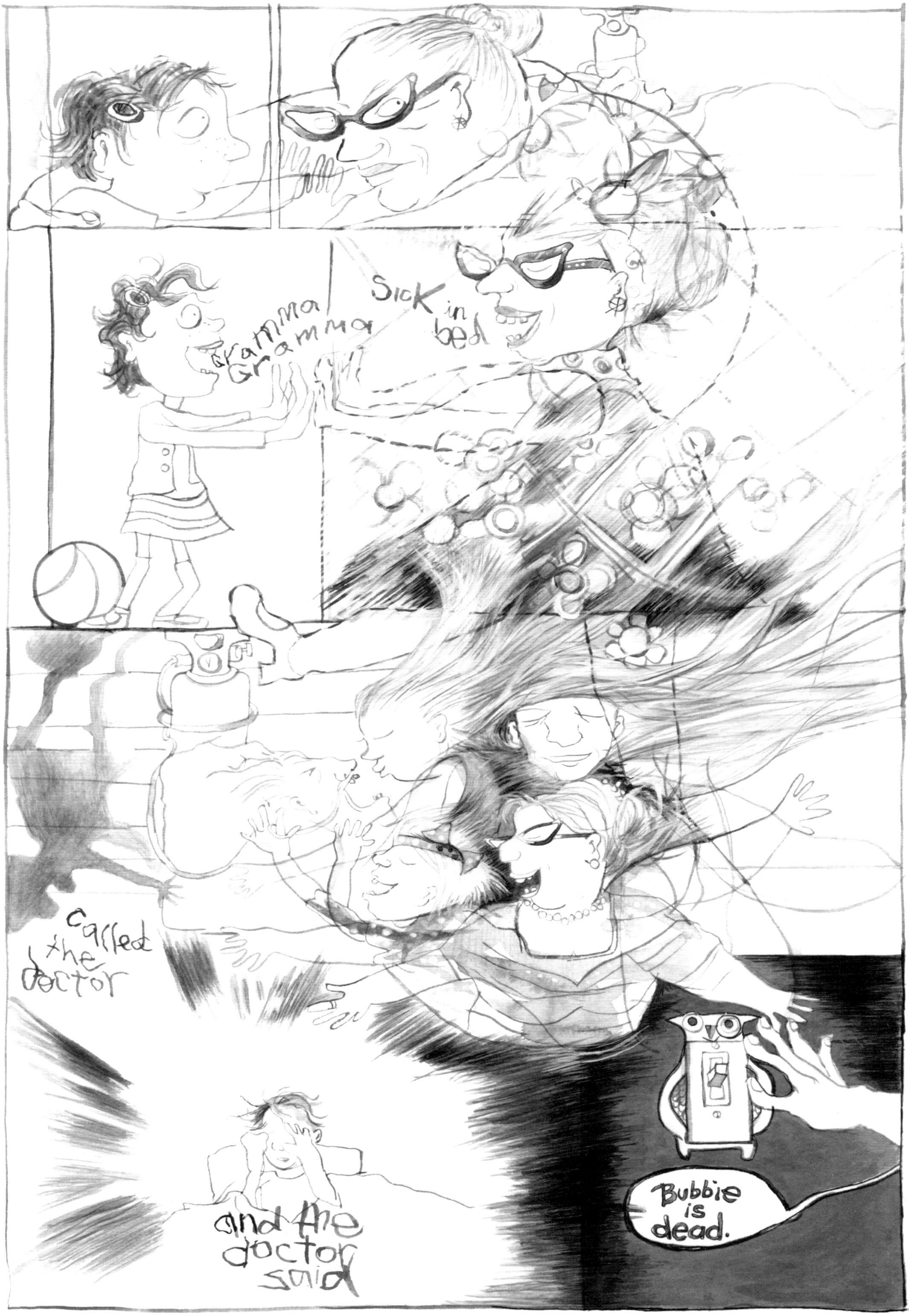
Gramma Gramma
Sick in bed
called the doctor
and the doctor said
Bubbie is dead.

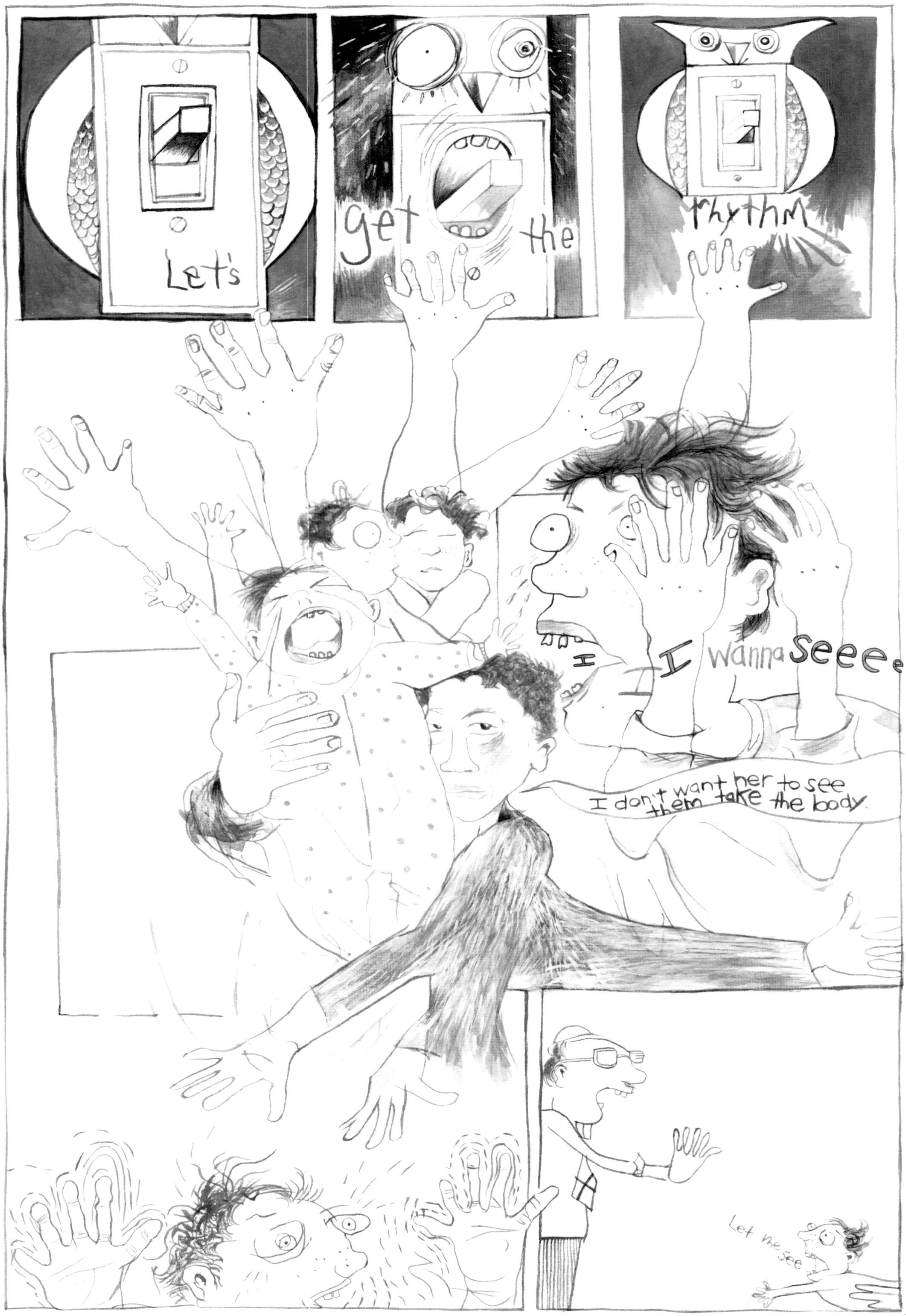
Let's
get the
rhythm
I wanna Seeee
I don't want her to see them take the body.
Let me see

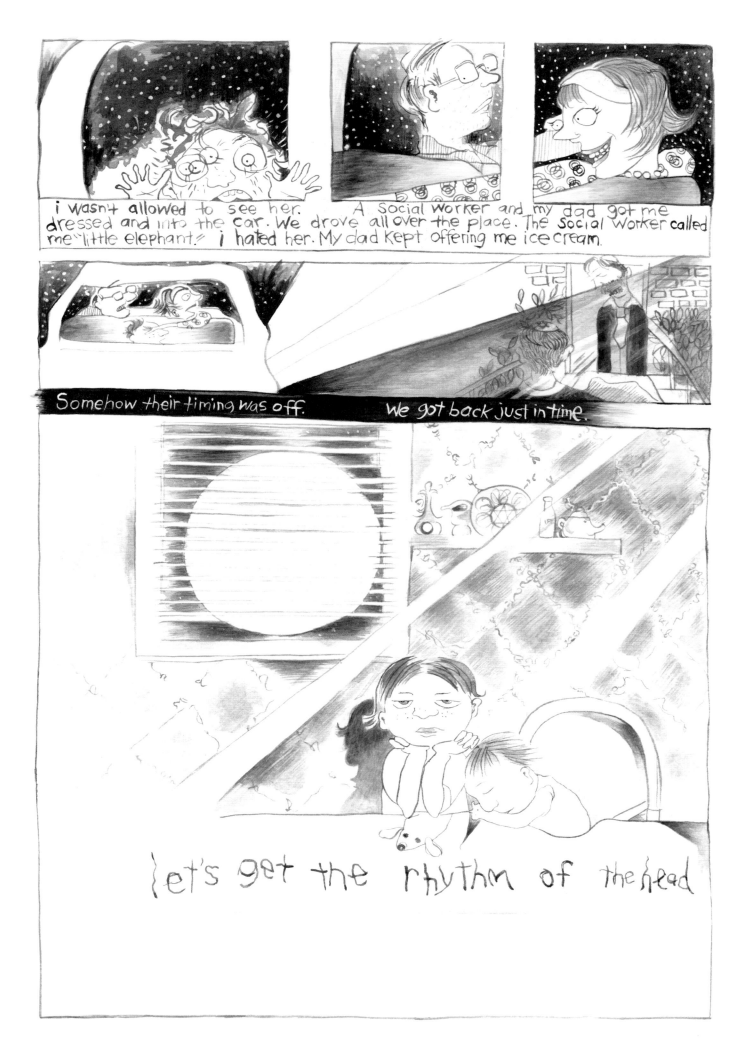

i wasn't allowed to see her. A social worker and my dad got me dressed and into the car. We drove all over the place. The social worker called me "little elephant." i hated her. My dad kept offering me ice cream.

Somehow their timing was off.   We got back just in time.

let's get the rhythm of the head

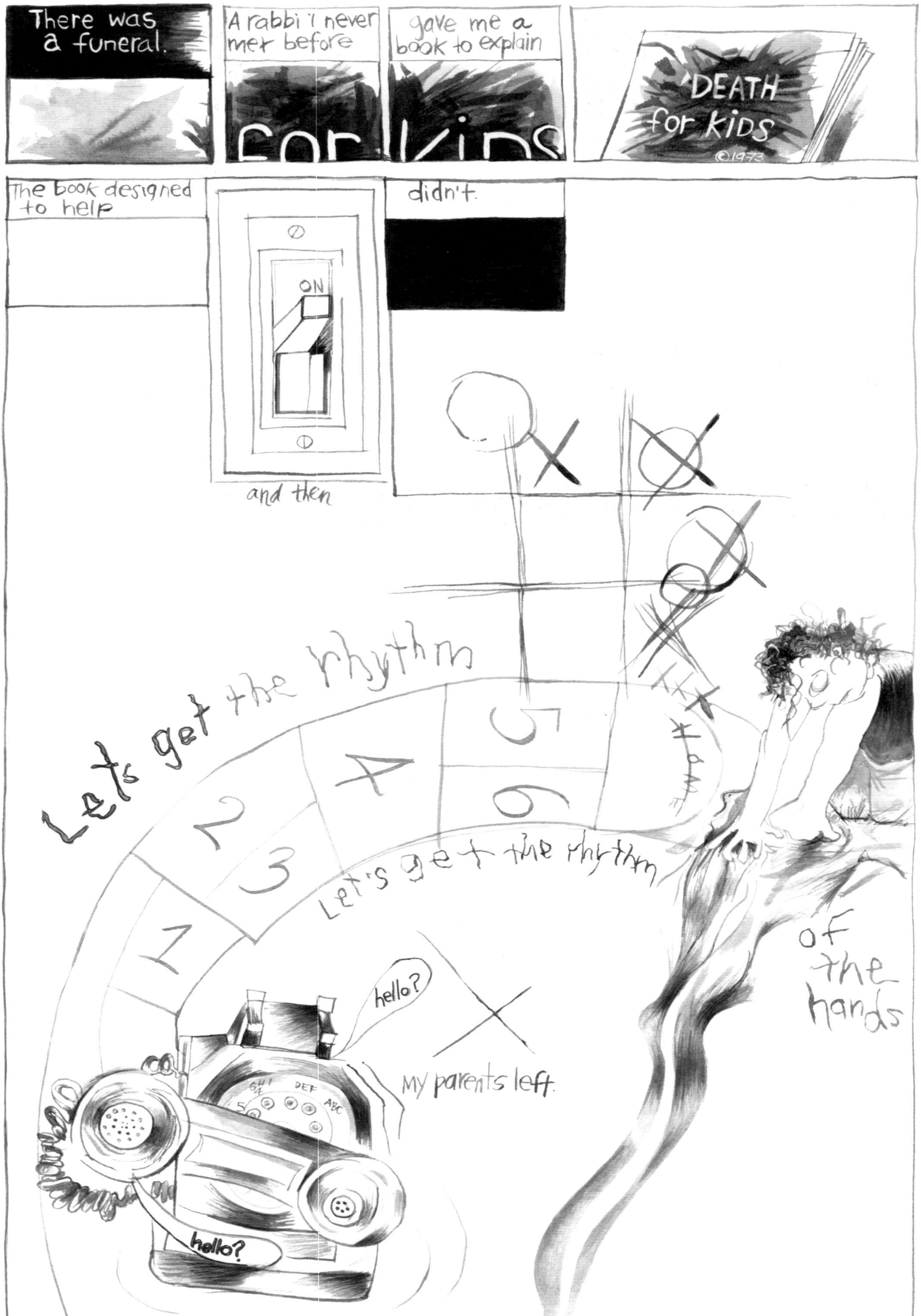

There was a funeral.
A rabbi i never met before
gave me a book to explain
for kids
'DEATH for KIDS
©1973
The book designed to help
and then
didn't.
Lets get the rhythm
1
2
3
4
5
6
Let's get the rhythm
of the hands
hello?
My parents left.
hello?

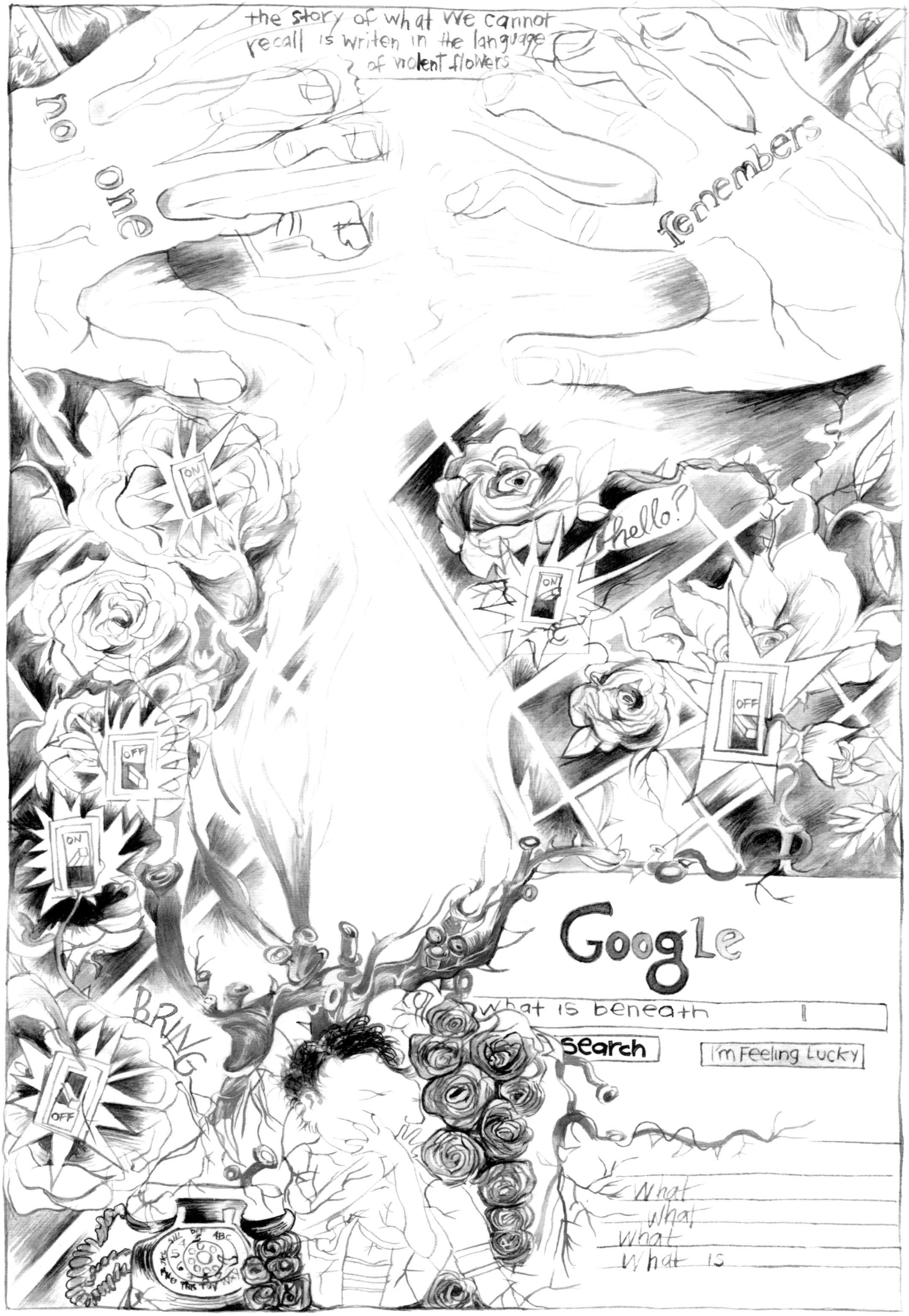
the story of what we cannot recall is writen in the language of violent flowers
no one
remembers
ON
hello?
ON
OFF
OFF
ON
BRING
OFF
Google
what is beneath
Search
I'm Feeling Lucky
What
what
What
What is

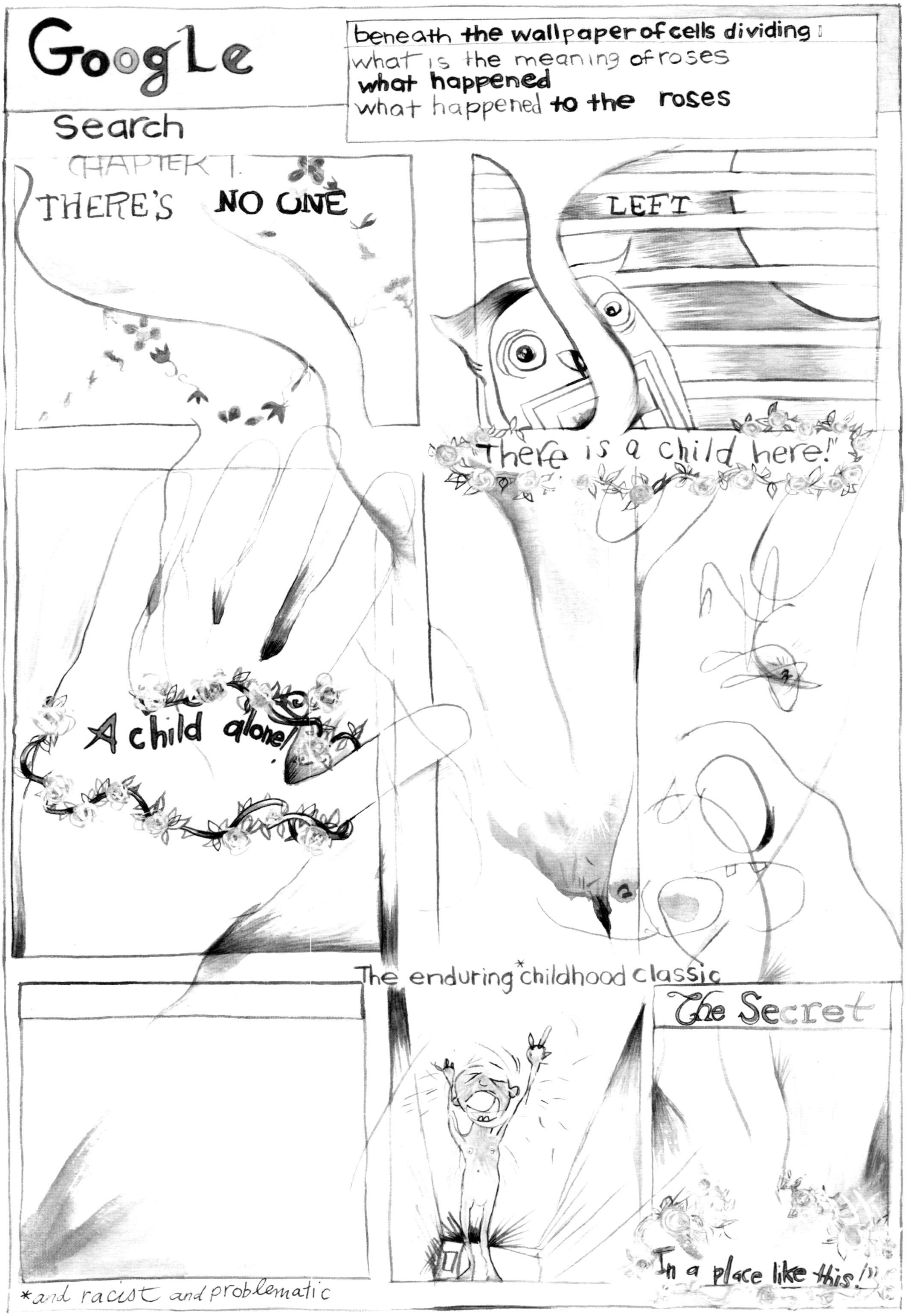
Google
beneath the wallpaper of cells dividing :
what is the meaning of roses
what happened
what happened to the roses
Search
CHAPTER I.
THERE'S NO ONE
LEFT
"There is a child here!"
A child alone!
The enduring* childhood classic
The Secret
In a place like this!"
*and racist and problematic

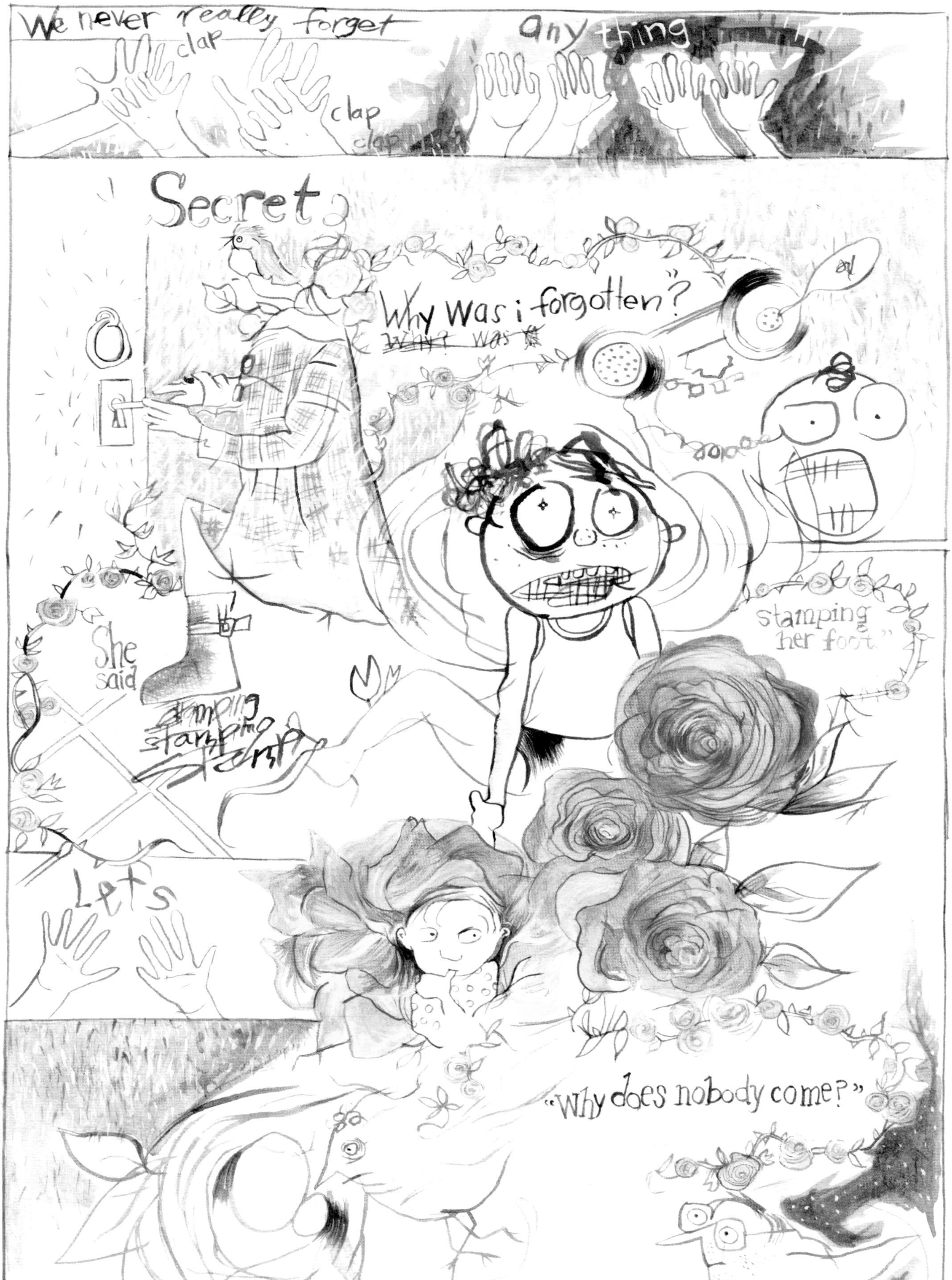
We never really forget
clap
clap
clap
any thing
Secret
Why was i forgotten?
Why? was
She said
stamping stamping stamp
stamping her foot."
Let's
"Why does nobody come?"
Let's get the rhthym of the heart

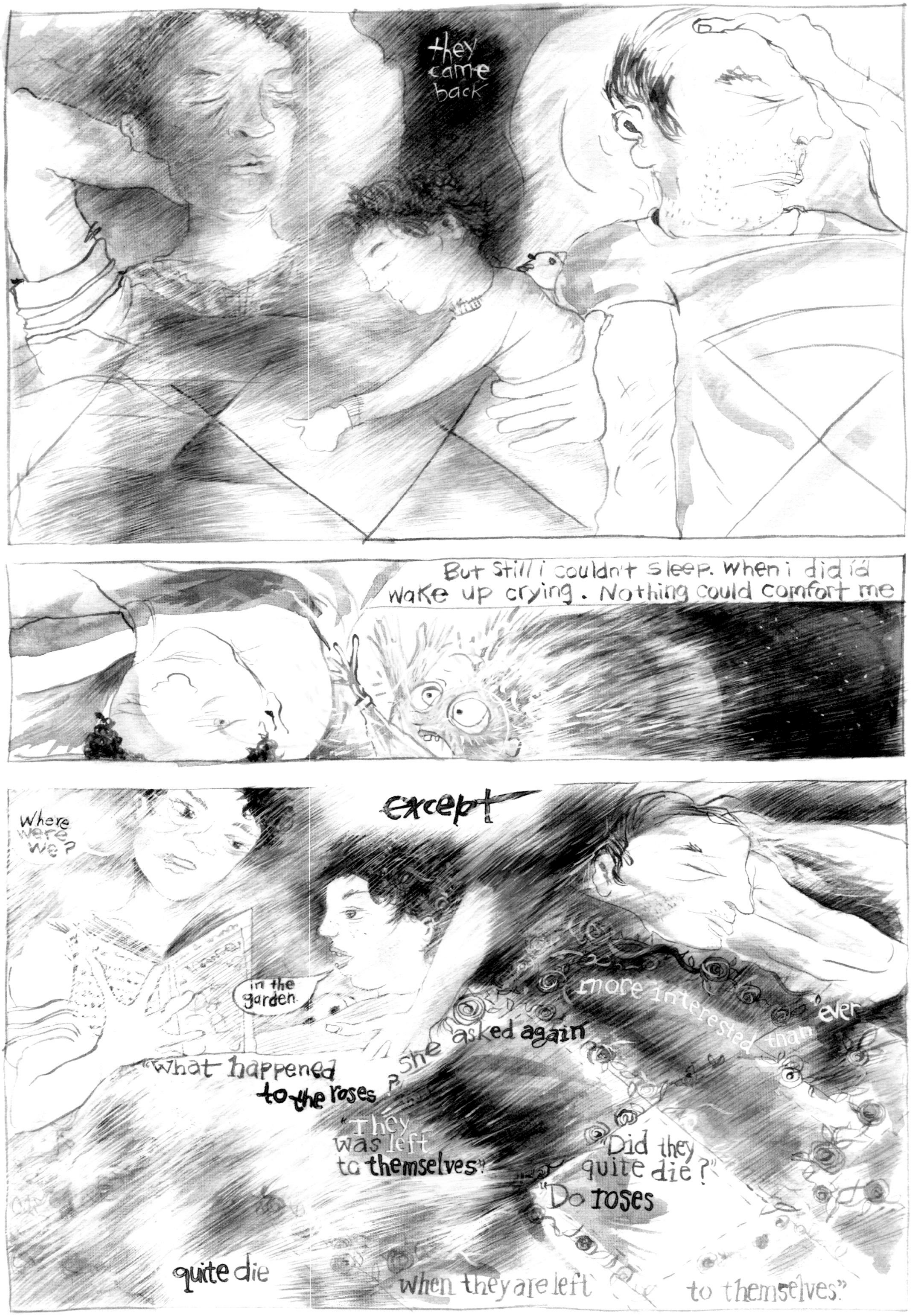
they came back
But still i couldn't sleep. when i did i'd wake up crying. Nothing could comfort me
except
Where were we?
in the garden.
"What happened to the roses?"
she asked again
more interested than ever
"They was left to themselves."
"Did they quite die?"
"Do roses
quite die
when they are left
to themselves."

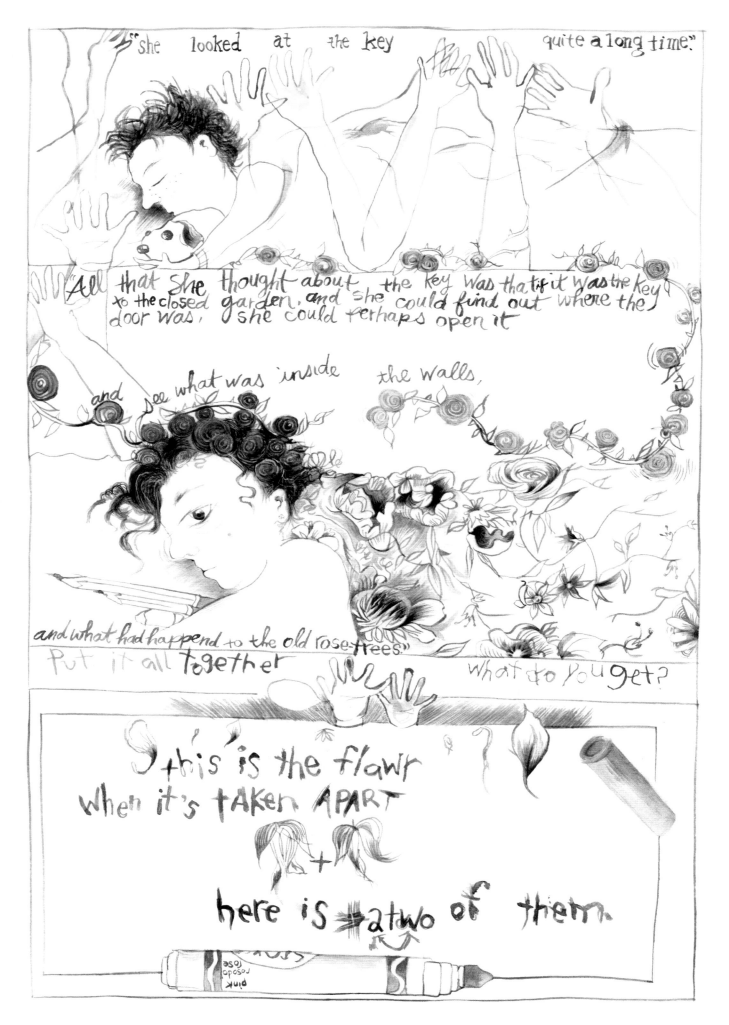

"she looked at the key quite a long time"

"All that she thought about the key was that if it was the key to the closed garden, and she could find out where the door was, she could perhaps open it

and see what was inside the walls,

and what had happend to the old rose-trees"

Put it all together what do you get?

this is the flawr
when it's tAKen APART

+

here is a two of them.

pink rosopos

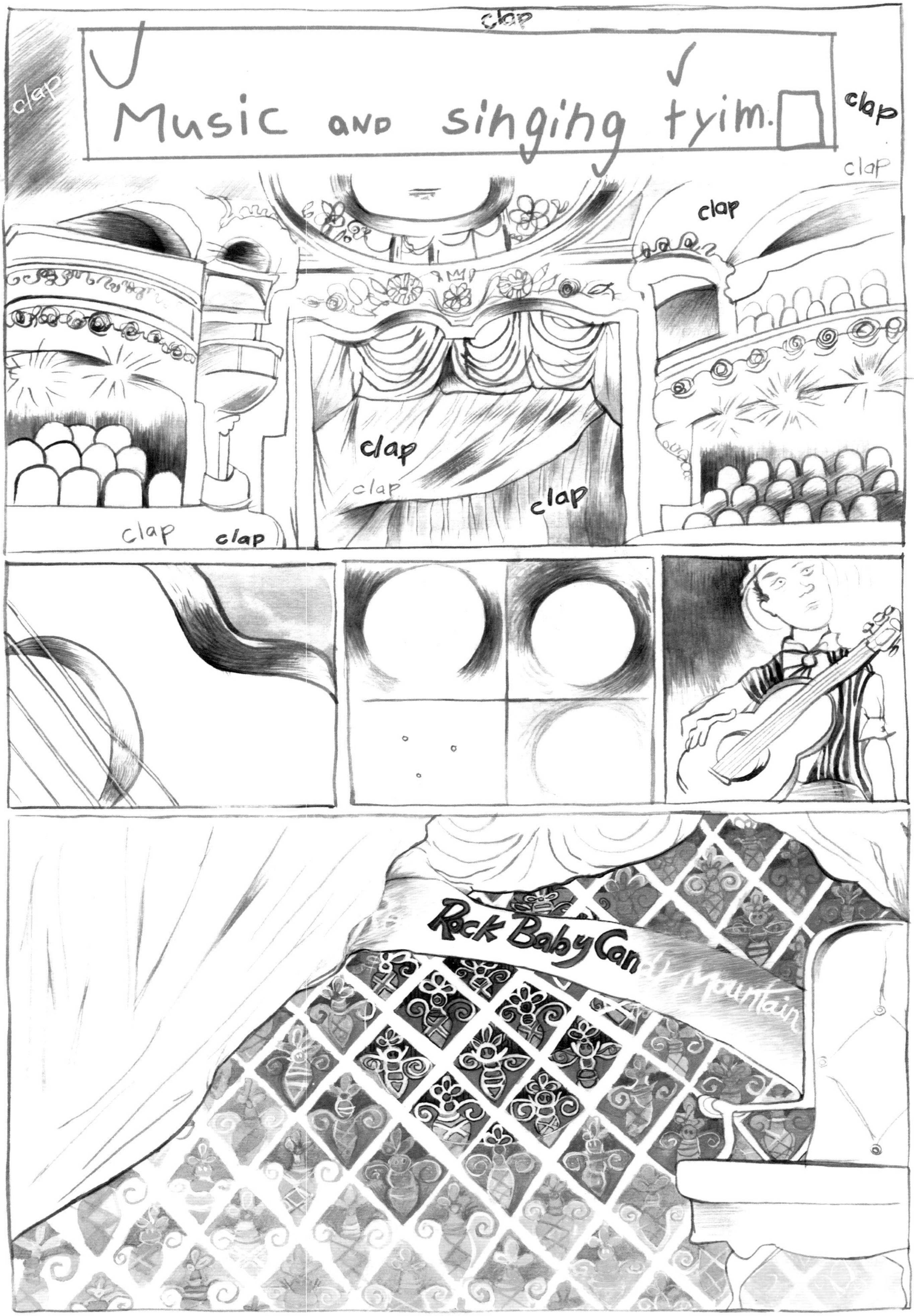
Music and singing tyim.
clap
clap
clap
clap
clap
clap
clap
clap
clap
clap
Rock Baby Candy Mountain

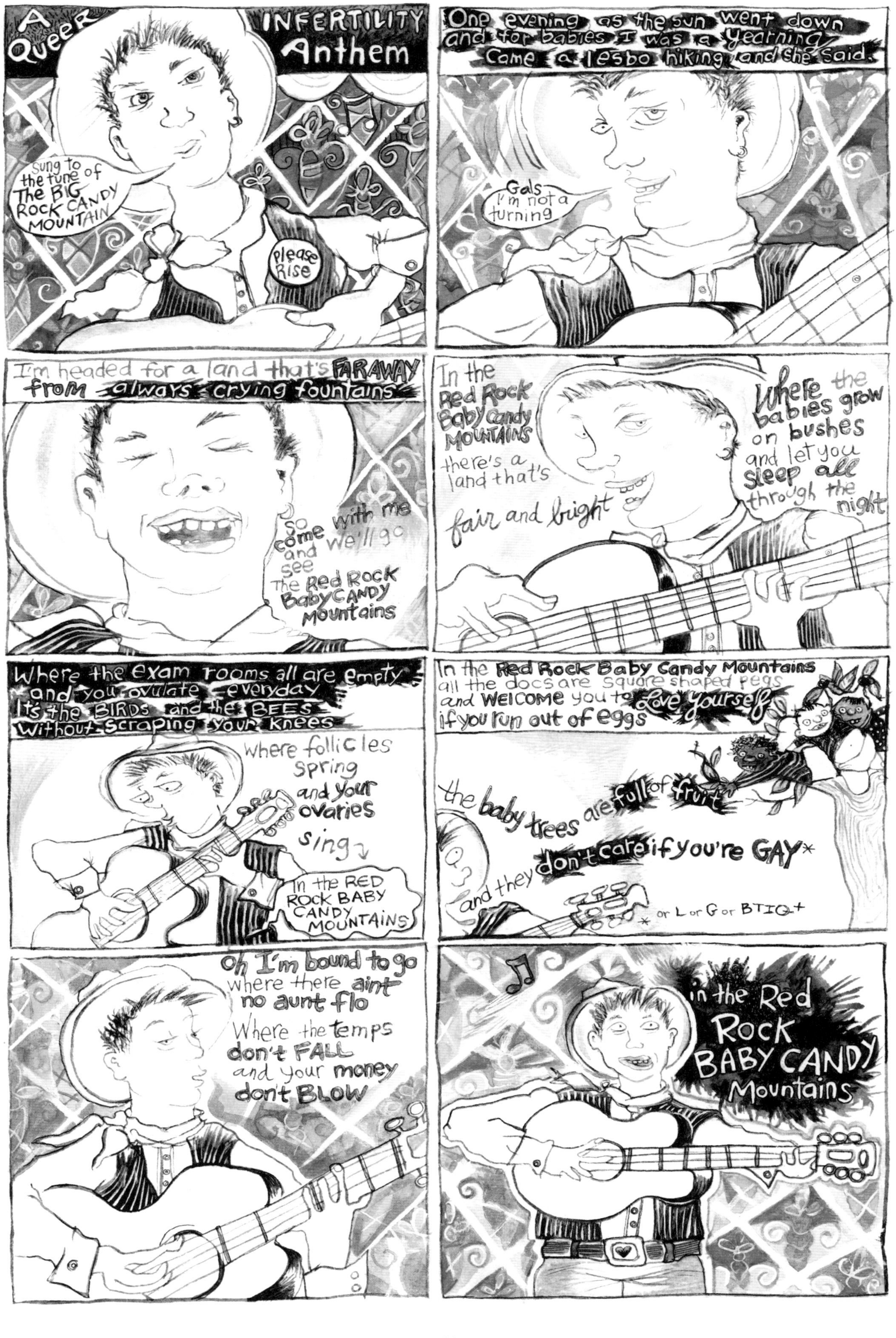
A Queer INFERTILITY Anthem
Sung to the tune of The BIG ROCK CANDY MOUNTAIN
Please Rise
One evening as the sun went down and for babies I was a yearning Came a lesbo hiking and she said.
Gals I'm not a turning
I'm headed for a land that's FARAWAY from always crying fountains
so come with me and we'll go see The Red Rock Baby CANDY Mountains
In the Red Rock Baby candy MOUNTAINS there's a land that's fair and bright
Where the babies grow on bushes and let you sleep all through the night
Where the exam rooms all are empty and you ovulate everyday It's the BIRDS and the BEES without scraping your knees
where follicles spring and your ovaries sing
In the RED ROCK BABY CANDY MOUNTAINS
In the Red Rock Baby Candy Mountains all the docs are square shaped pegs and WELCOME you to Love yourself if you run out of eggs
the baby trees are full of fruit and they don't care if you're GAY*
* or L or G or BTIQ+
oh I'm bound to go where there aint no aunt flo Where the temps don't FALL and your money don't BLOW
in the Red ROCK BABY CANDY Mountains

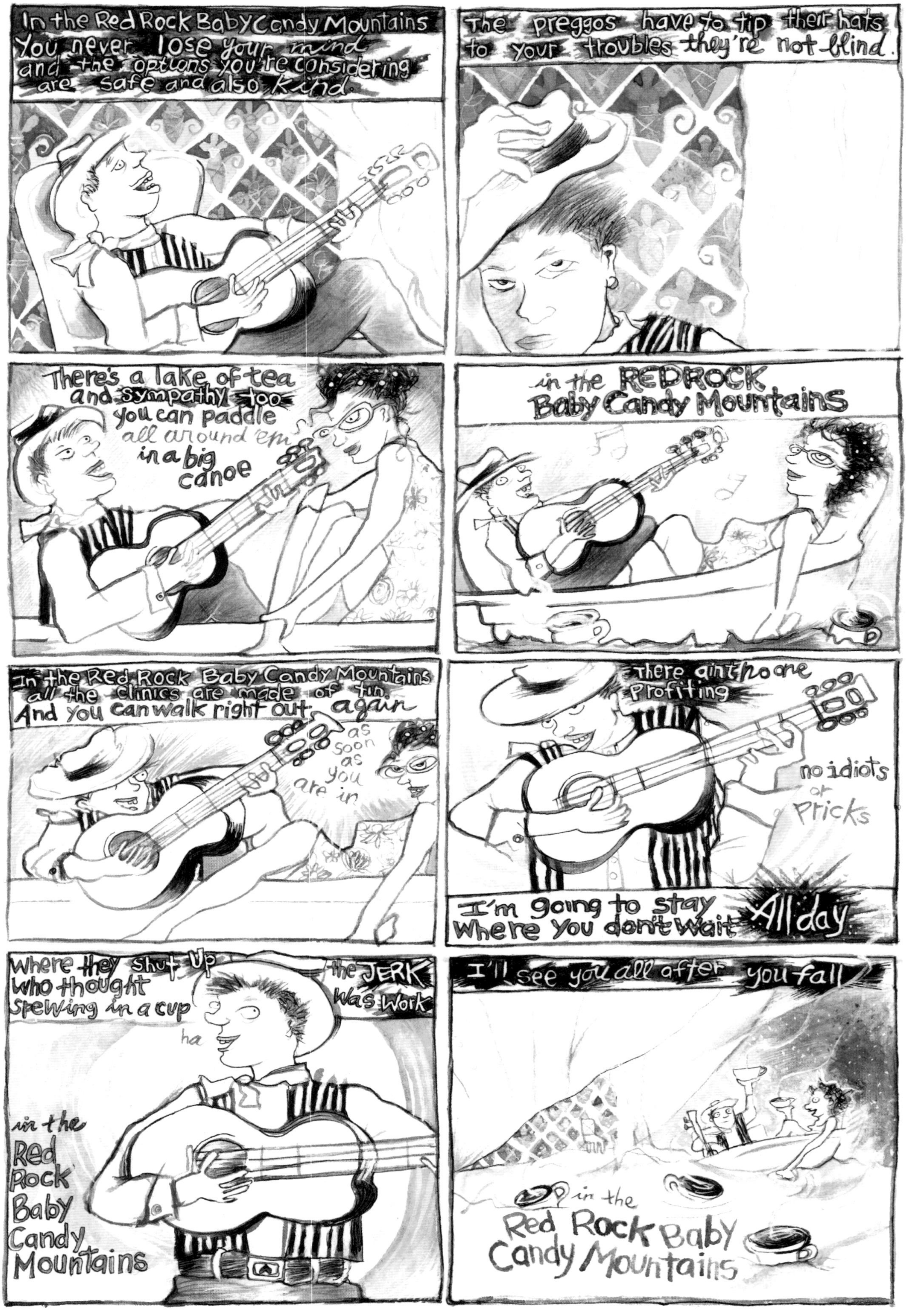

In the Red Rock Baby Candy Mountains
You never lose your mind
and the options you're considering
are safe and also kind.
The preggos have to tip their hats
to your troubles they're not blind.
There's a lake of tea
and sympathy too
you can paddle
all around 'em
in a big
canoe
in the REDROCK
Baby Candy Mountains
In the Red Rock Baby Candy Mountains
all the clinics are made of tin.
And you can walk right out again
as soon as you are in
There ain't no one profiting
no idiots or Pricks
I'm going to stay
Where you don't wait All day.
Where they shut up
who thought
spewing in a cup
the JERK
was work
ha
in the
Red
Rock
Baby
Candy
Mountains
I'll see you all after you fall
in the
Red Rock Baby
Candy Mountains

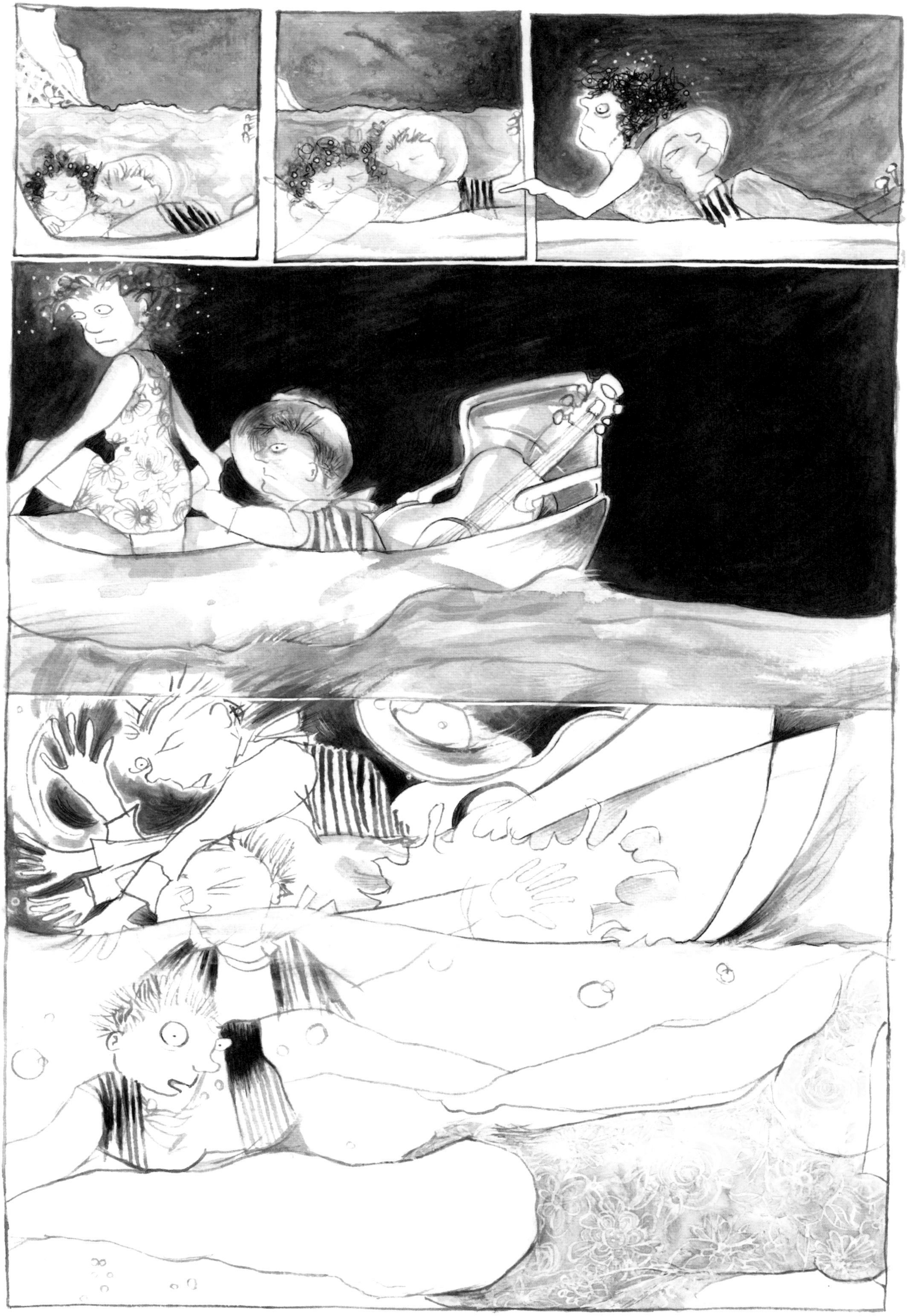

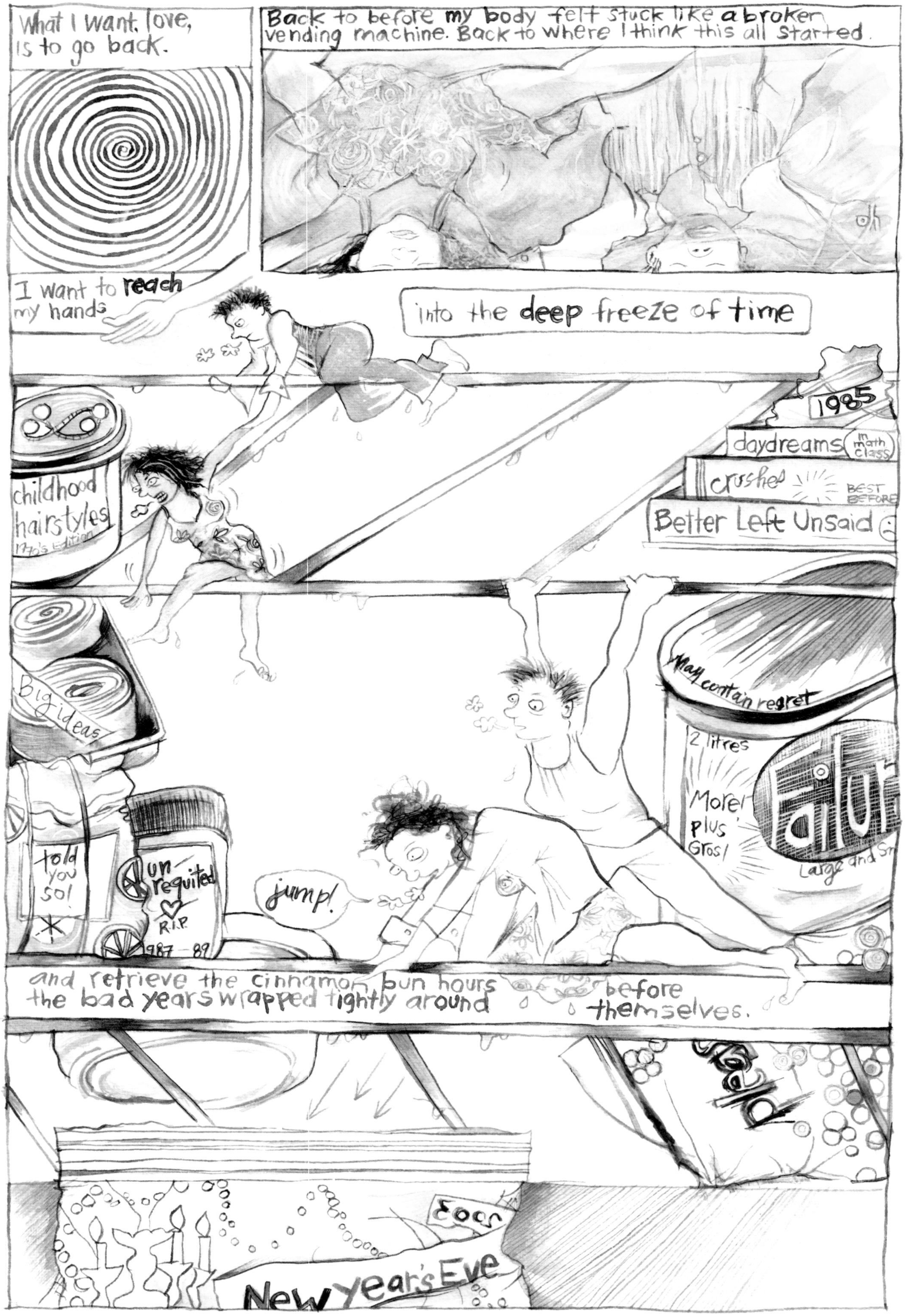
What I want, love, is to go back.
Back to before my body felt stuck like a broken vending machine. Back to where I think this all started.
I want to reach my hands
into the deep freeze of time
1985
daydreams
in math class
crushes
BEST BEFORE
Better Left Unsaid
childhood hairstyles
1970's Edition
Big ideas
May contain regret
2 litres
More! plus Gros!
Failur
Large and Sm
told you so!
un-requited
R.I.P.
1987 – 89
jump!
and retrieve the cinnamon bun hours before the bad years wrapped tightly around themselves.
2003
New Year's Eve

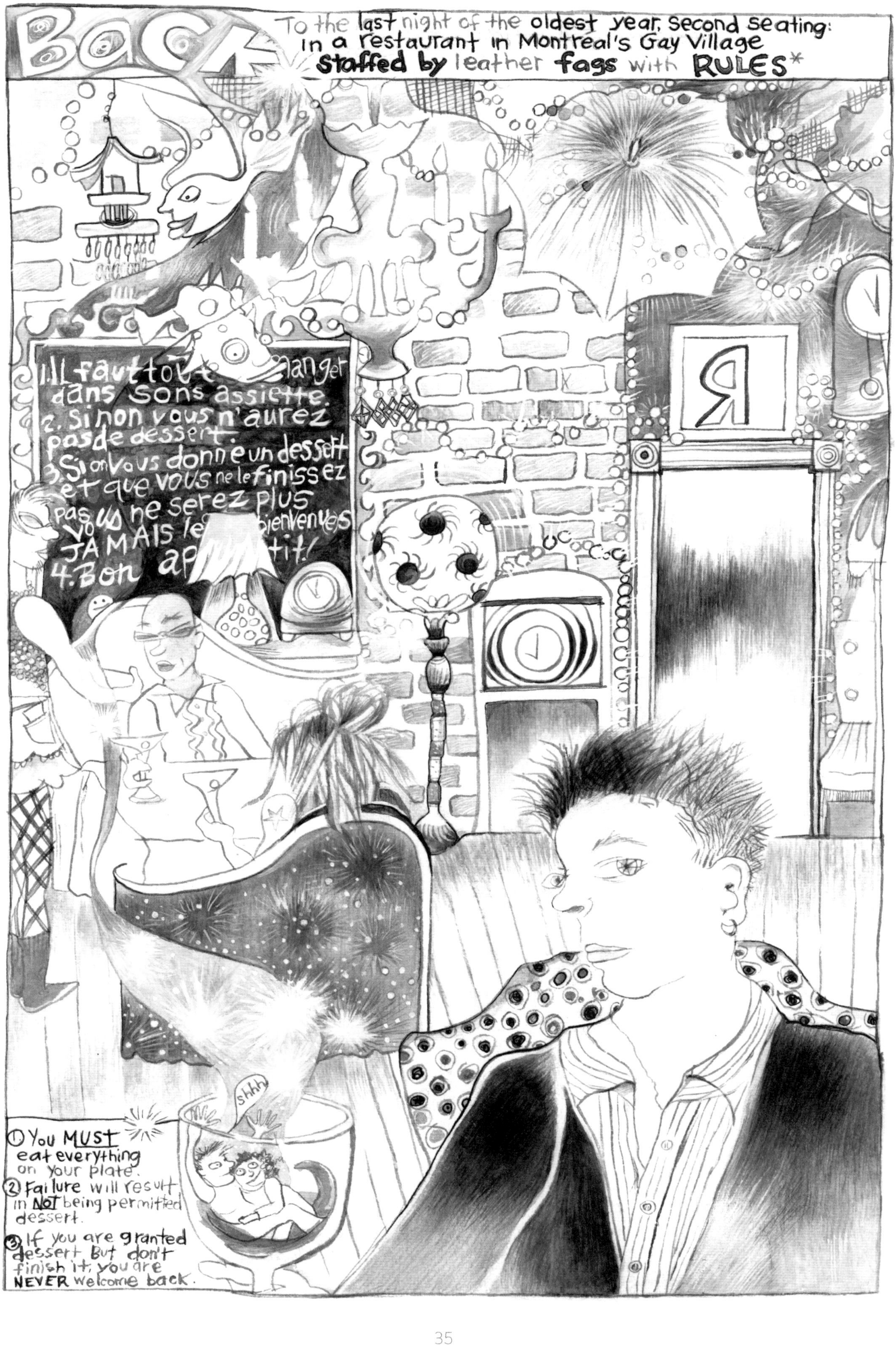
BACK
To the last night of the oldest year, second seating: in a restaurant in Montreal's Gay Village staffed by leather fags with RULES*
1. IL faut tou manger
dans sons assiette.
2. Si non vous n'aurez
pas de dessert.
3. Si on vous donne un dessert
et que vous ne le finissez
pas vous ne serez plus
JAMAIS le bienvenu(e)s
4. Bon ap tit!
shhh
① You MUST eat everything on your plate.
② Failure will result in NOT being permitted dessert.
③ If you are granted dessert But don't finish it, you are NEVER welcome back.

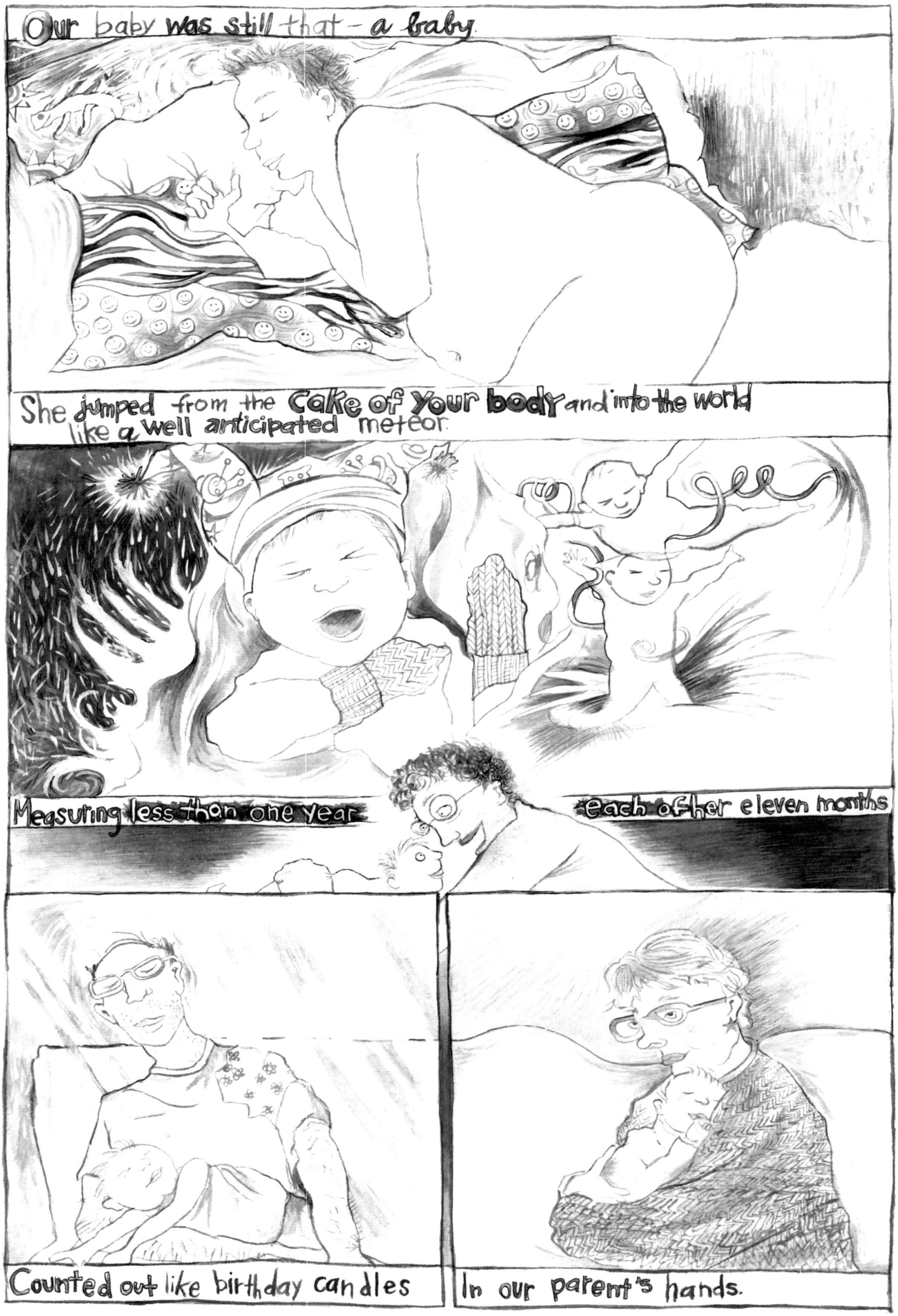
Our baby was still that - a baby.
She jumped from the cake of your body and into the world like a well anticipated meteor.
Measuring less than one year
each of her eleven months
Counted out like birthday candles
In our parent's hands.

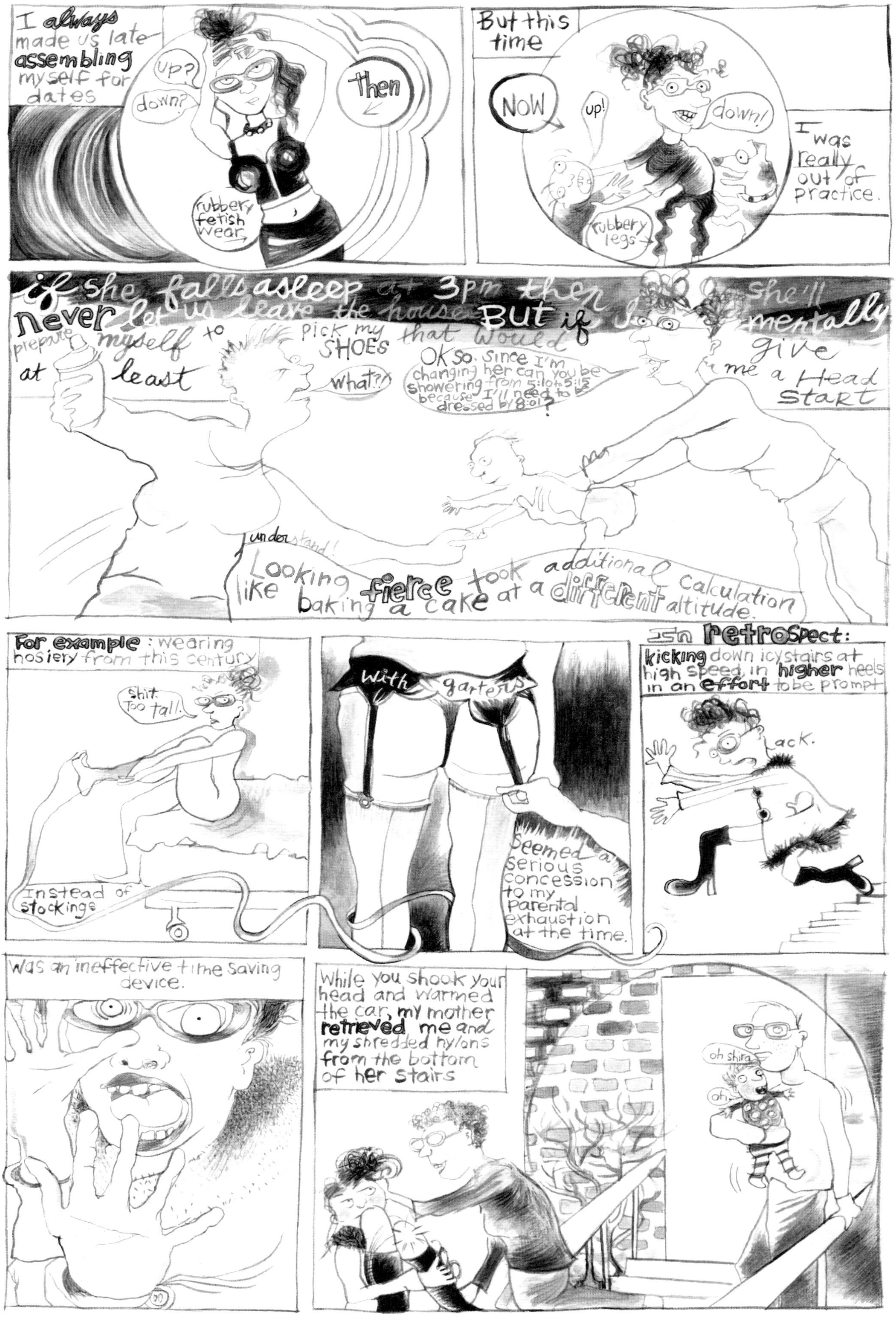

I always made us late assembling myself for dates
up?
down?
then
rubbery fetish wear
But this time
NOW
up!
down!
I was really out of practice.
rubbery legs
if she falls asleep at 3pm then she'll never let us leave the house BUT if I mentally prepare myself to pick my SHOES that would at least give me a Head Start
what?!
OK so. Since I'm changing her can you be showering from 5:10 to 5:15 because I'll need to be dressed by 8:01?
understand!
Looking fierce took additional calculation like baking a cake at a different altitude.
For example: wearing hosiery from this century
shit. Too tall.
Instead of stockings
with garters
Seemed a serious concession to my parental exhaustion at the time.
In retrospect: kicking down icy stairs at high speed, in higher heels in an effort to be prompt
ack.
Was an ineffective time saving device.
While you shook your head and warmed the car, my mother retrieved me and my shredded nylons from the bottom of her stairs
oh shira
oh.

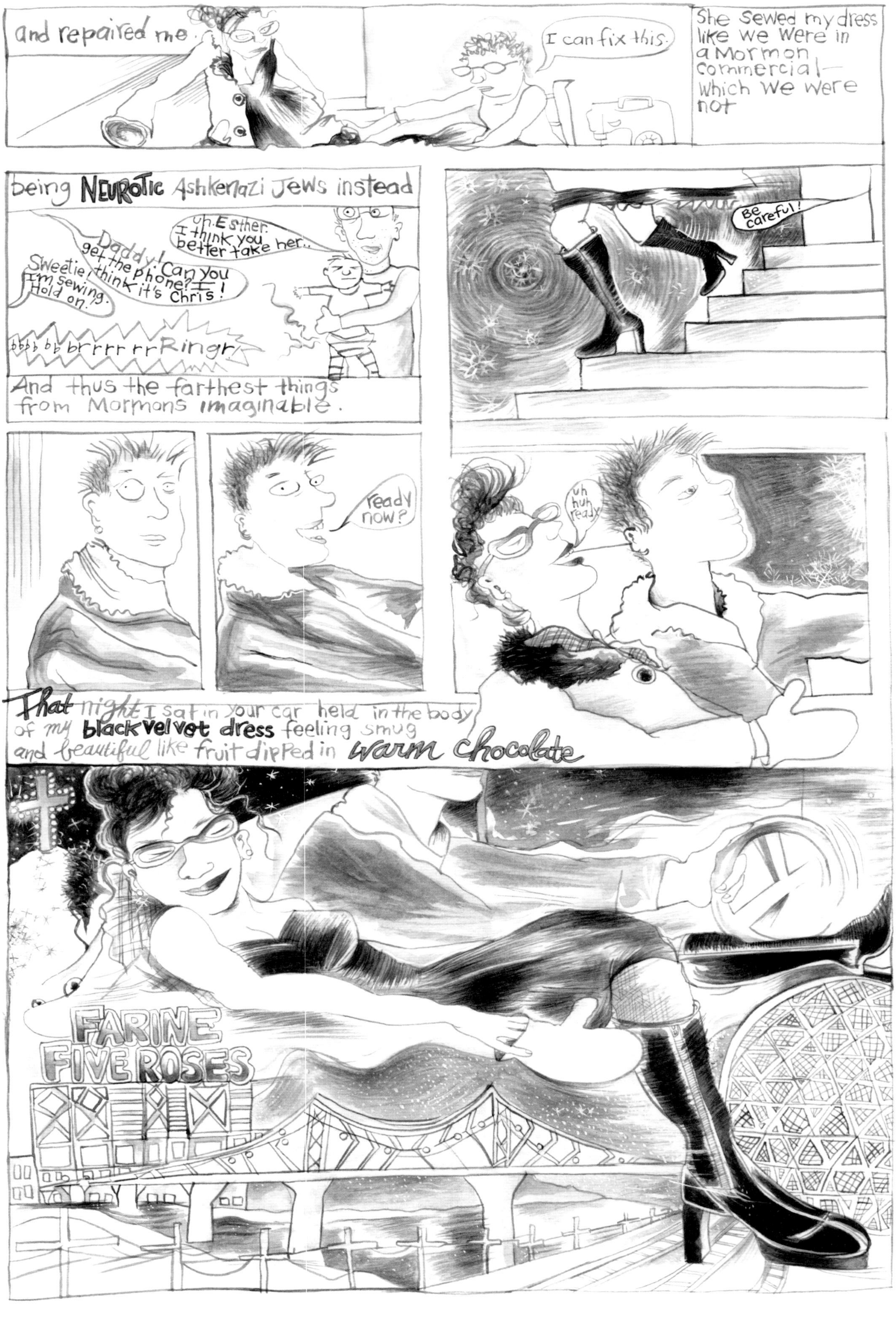

and repaired me.
I can fix this.
She sewed my dress like we were in a Mormon commercial — which we were not
being NEUROTIC Ashkenazi Jews instead
uh. Esther. I think you better take her..
Daddy! Can you get the phone? I think it's Chris!
Sweetie, I'm sewing. Hold on.
bbbb bb brrrrr rrRingr
And thus the farthest things from Mormons imaginable.
Be careful!
ready now?
uh huh ready
That night I sat in your car held in the body of my black velvet dress feeling smug and beautiful like fruit dipped in warm chocolate
FARINE FIVE ROSES

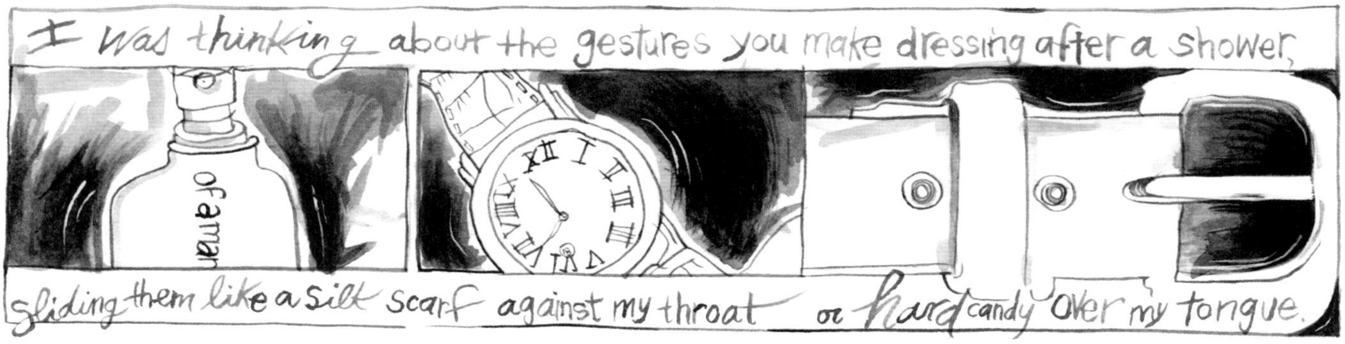
I was thinking about the gestures you make dressing after a shower,
of a man
sliding them like a silk scarf against my throat or hard candy over my tongue.

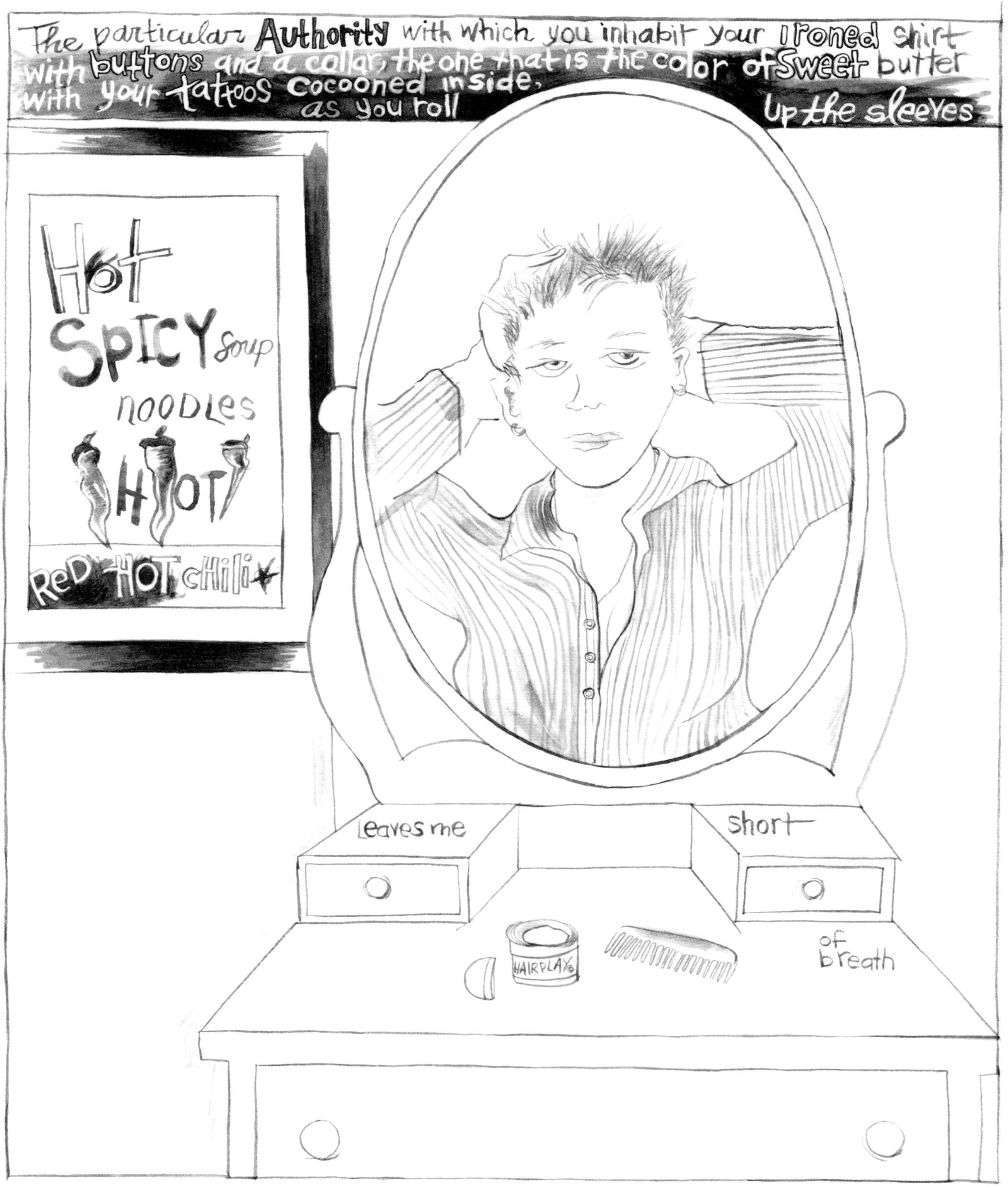
The particular Authority with which you inhabit your ironed shirt with buttons and a collar, the one that is the color of sweet butter with your tattoos cocooned inside, as you roll up the sleeves
Hot SPICY soup noodles HOT
RED HOT CHILI
leaves me
short
of breath
HAIRPLAY

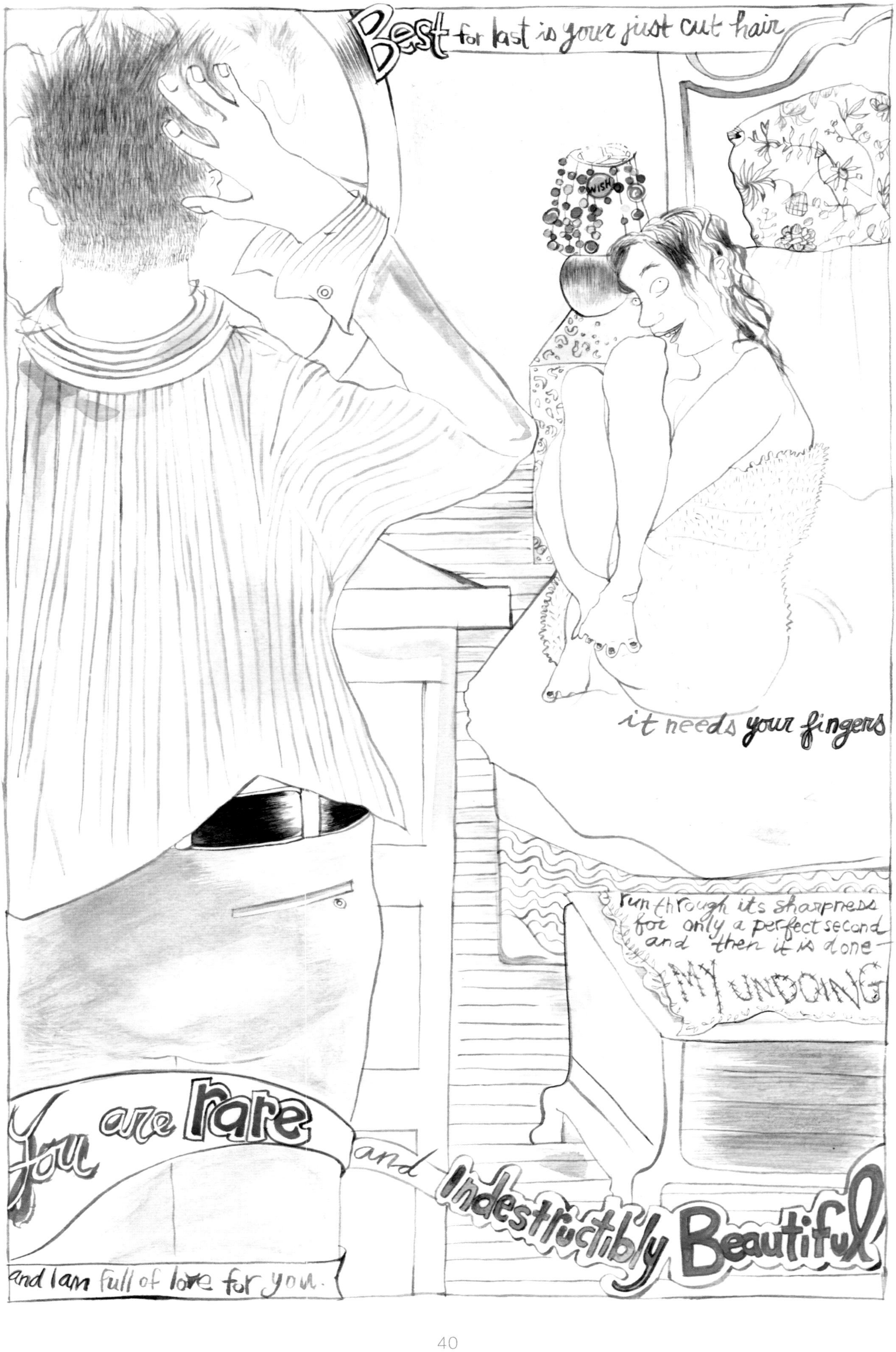
Best for last is your just cut hair
WISH
it needs your fingers
run through its sharpness
for only a perfect second
and then it is done—
MY UNDOING
You are rare and Indestructibly Beautiful
and I am full of love for you.

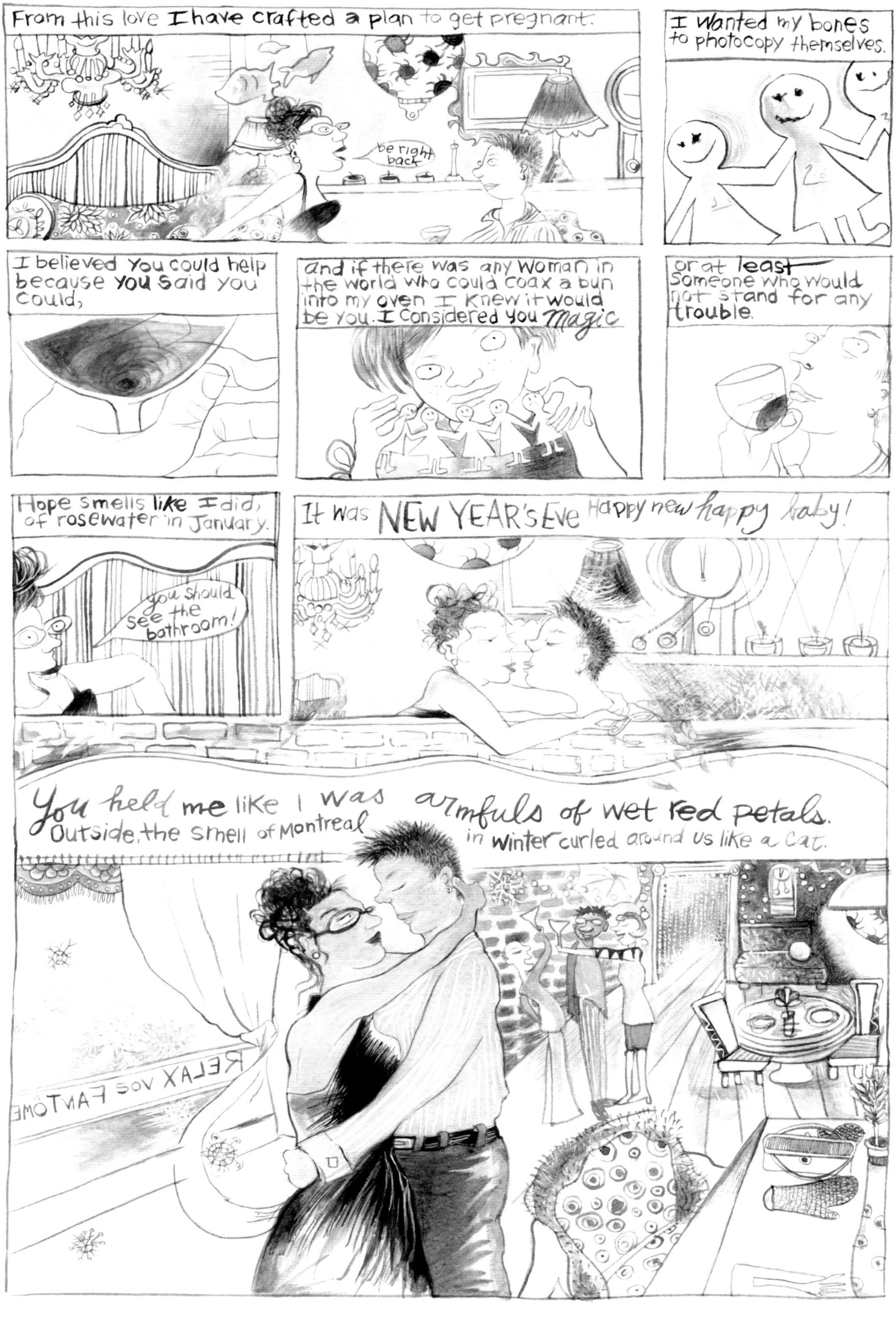
From this love I have crafted a plan to get pregnant.
be right back
I wanted my bones to photocopy themselves.
I believed you could help because you said you could,
and if there was any woman in the world who could coax a bun into my oven I knew it would be you. I considered you magic
or at least someone who would not stand for any trouble.
Hope smells like I did, of rosewater in January.
you should see the bathroom!
It was NEW YEAR's Eve Happy new happy baby!
You held me like I was armfuls of wet red petals.
Outside, the smell of Montreal in winter curled around us like a cat.
RELAX vos FANTOME

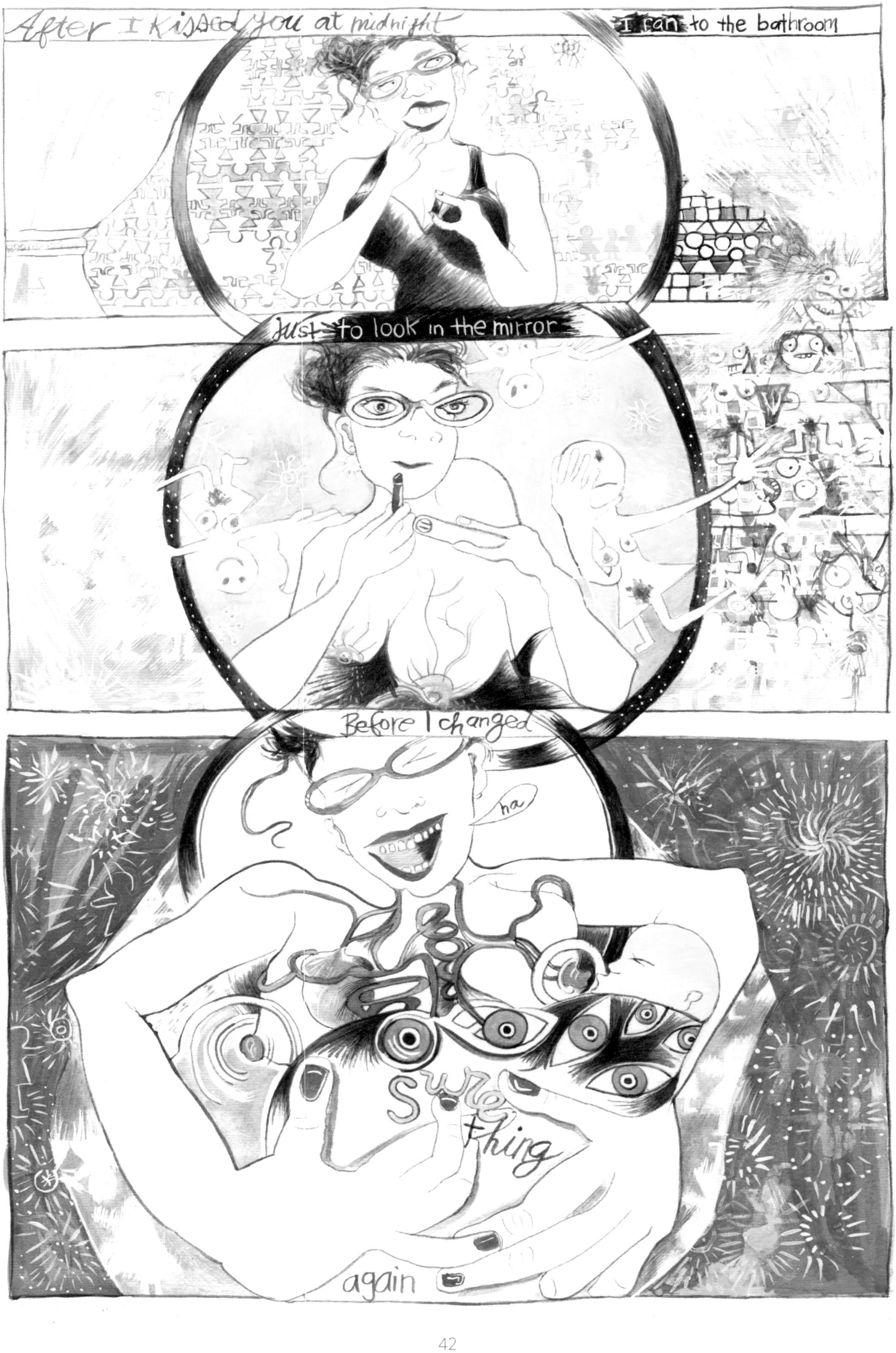
After I kissed you at midnight
I ran to the bathroom
Just to look in the mirror
Before I changed
ha
sure
thing
again

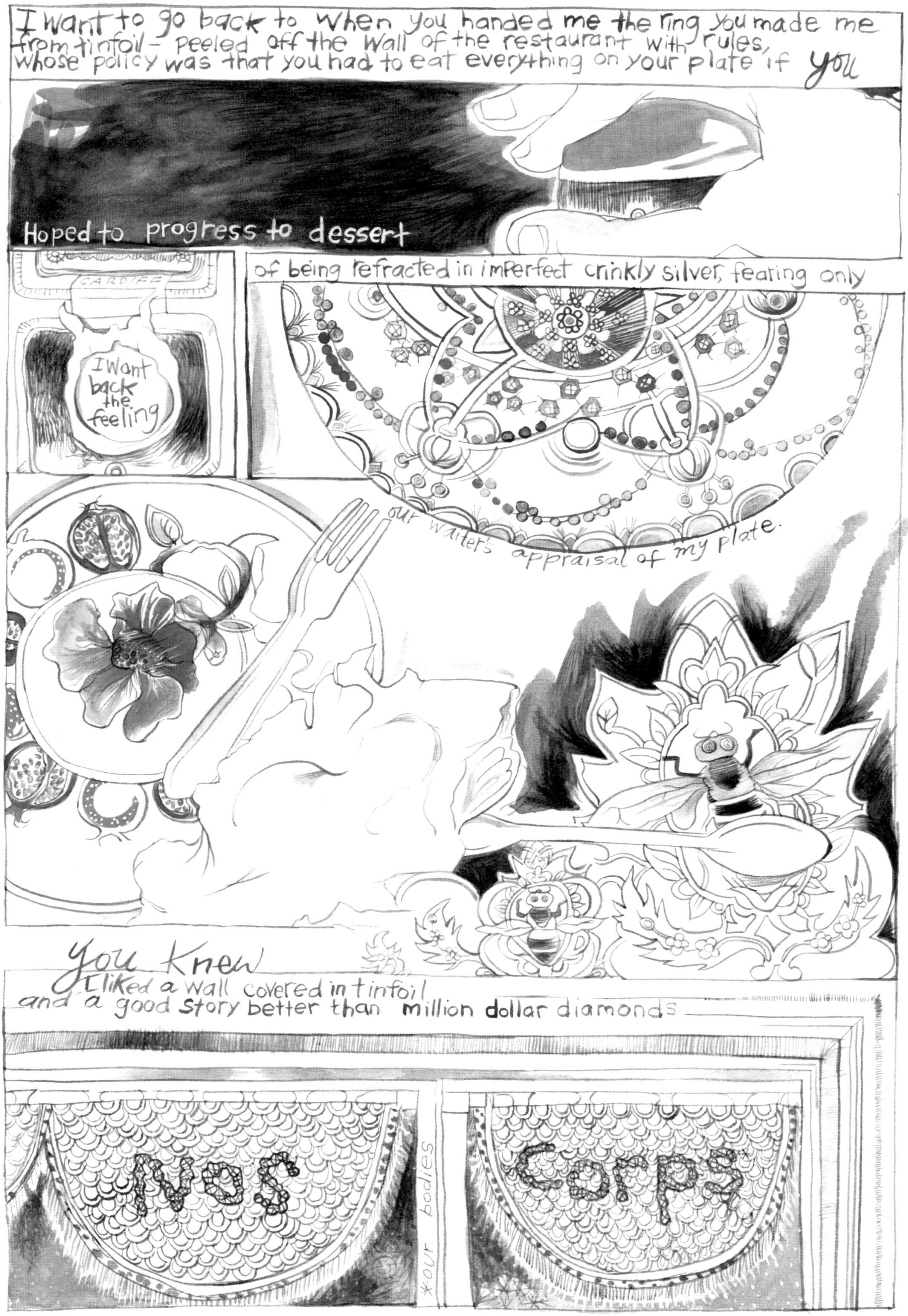

I want to go back to when you handed me the ring you made me from tinfoil – peeled off the wall of the restaurant with rules, whose policy was that you had to eat everything on your plate if you
Hoped to progress to dessert
CARDIFF
I want back the feeling
of being refracted in imperfect crinkly silver, fearing only
our waiter's appraisal of my plate.
You knew I liked a wall covered in tinfoil and a good story better than million dollar diamonds
Nos Corps*
*our bodies

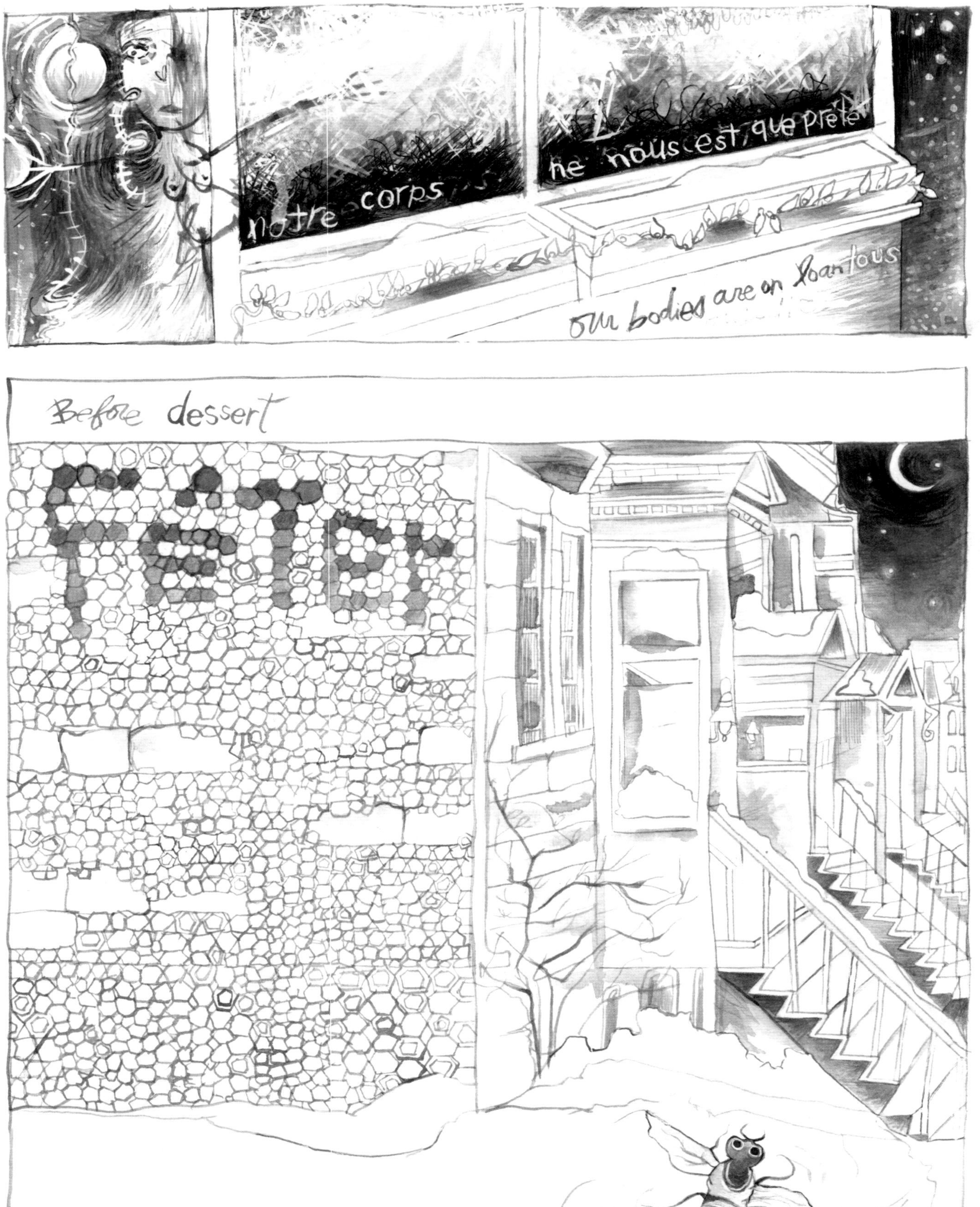
notre corps
ne nous est que prêté
Our bodies are on loan to us
Before dessert
Fêter
You asked me to marry you.

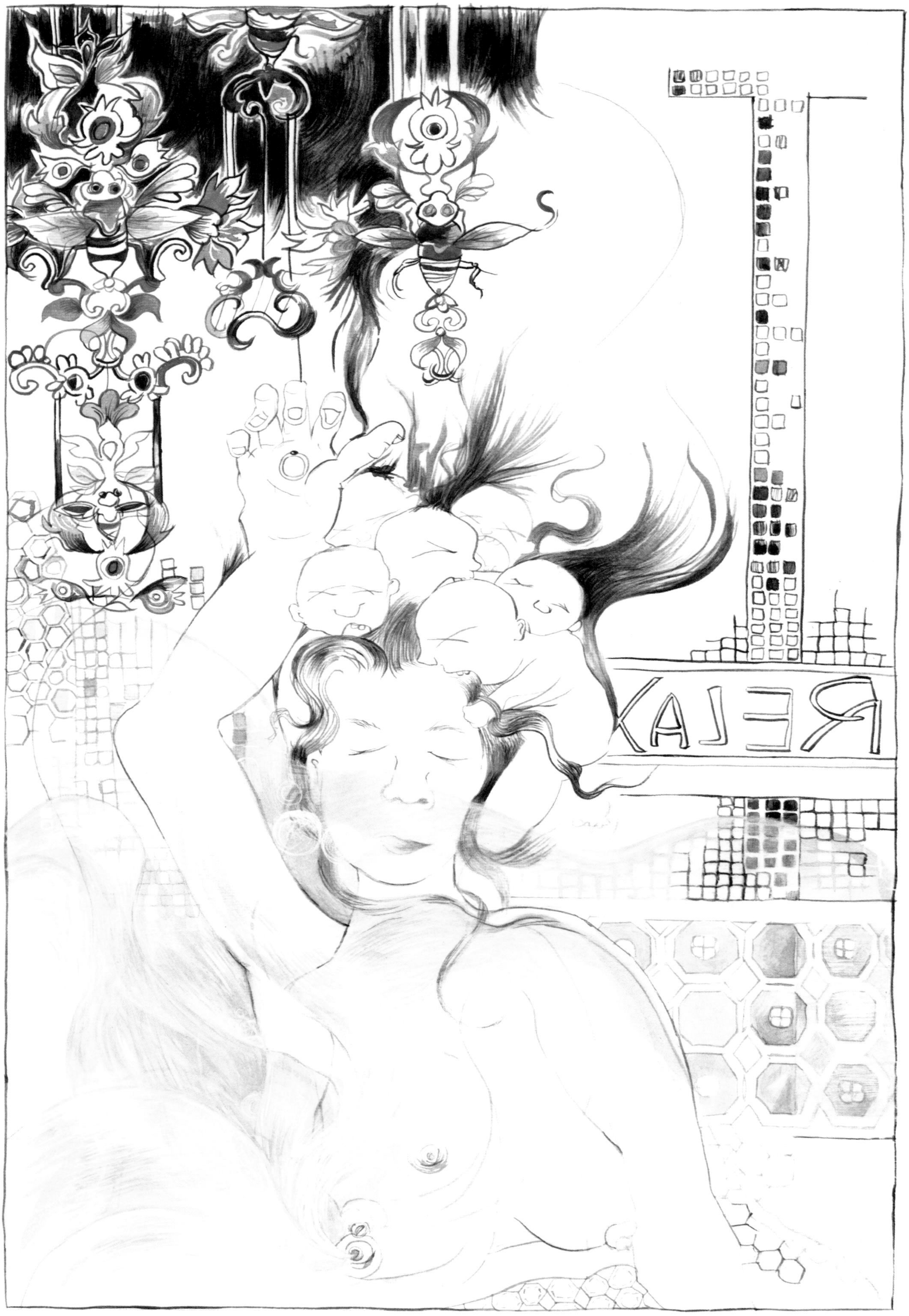
RELAX

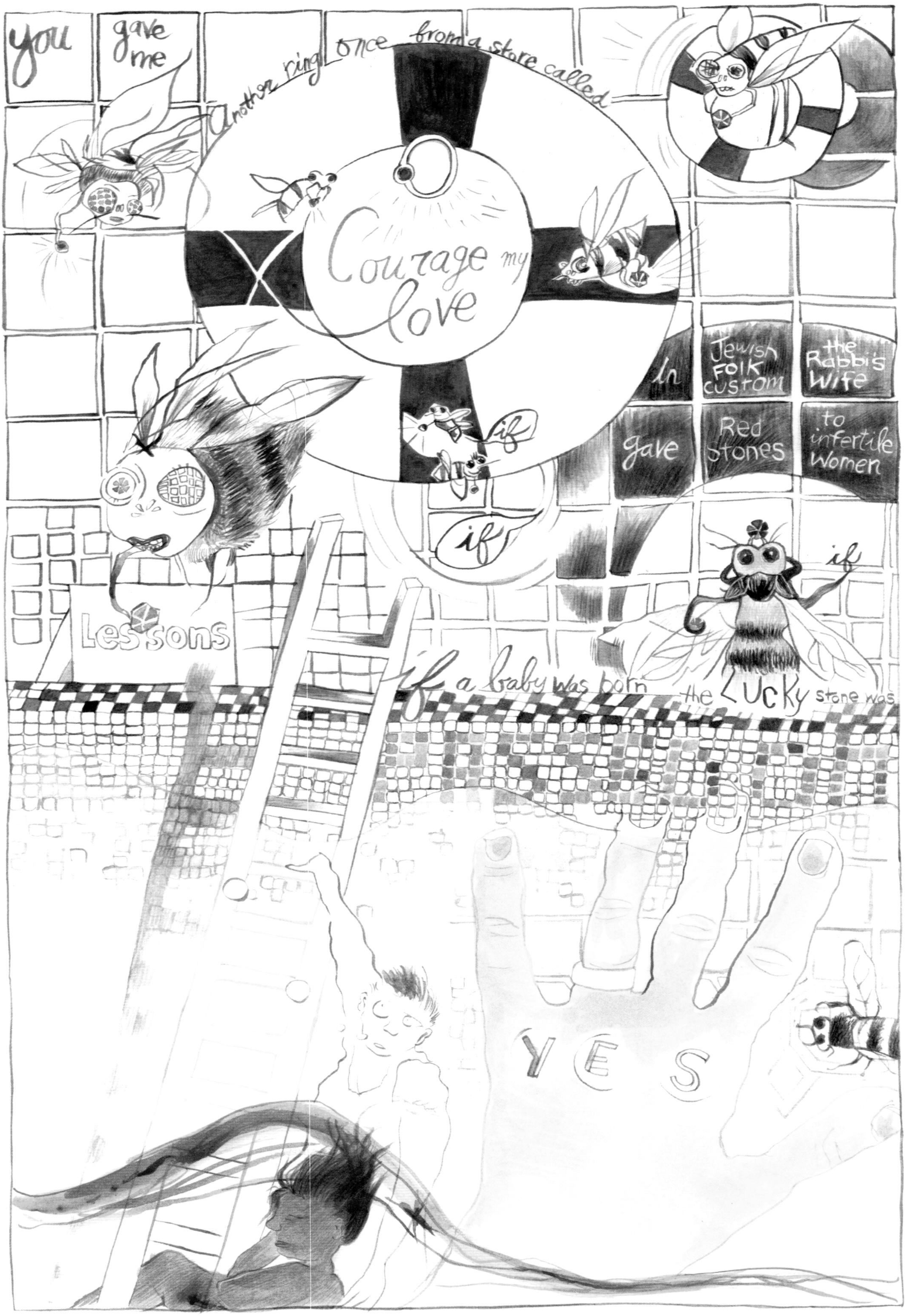
you
gave me
Another ring once from a store called
Courage my love
In Jewish folk custom the Rabbi's wife gave Red stones to infertile women
if
if
if
Lessons
if a baby was born the Lucky stone was
YES

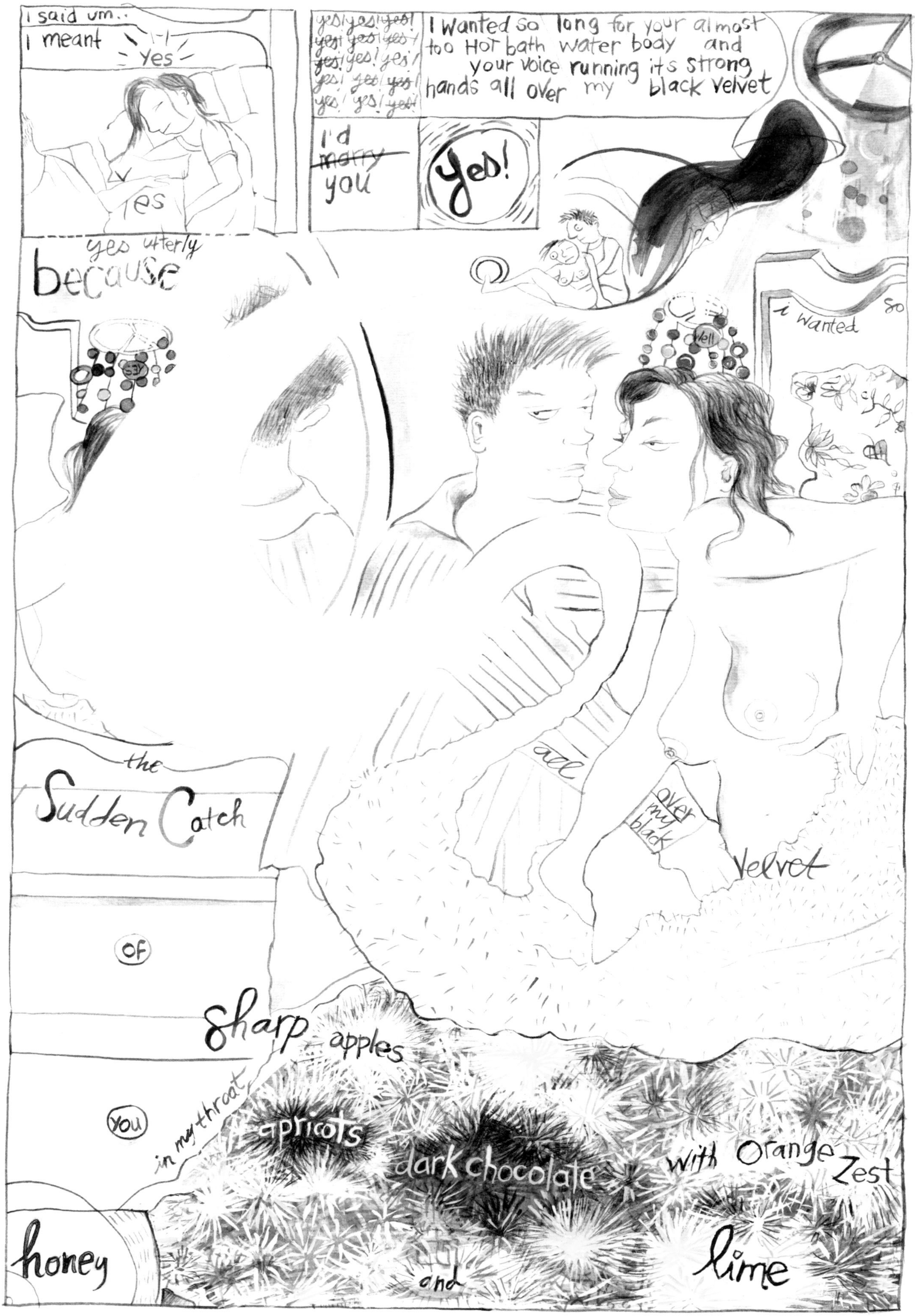

I said um..
I meant Yes
Yes
yes! yes! yes! yes! yes! yes! yes! yes! yes! yes! yes! yes! yes! yes! yes!
I wanted so long for your almost too HOT bath water body and your voice running its strong hands all over my black velvet
I'd marry you
Yes!
yes utterly
because
say
well
i wanted so
the Sudden Catch
all over my black velvet
of
sharp apples
you
in my throat
apricots
dark chocolate
with Orange Zest
honey
and
lime

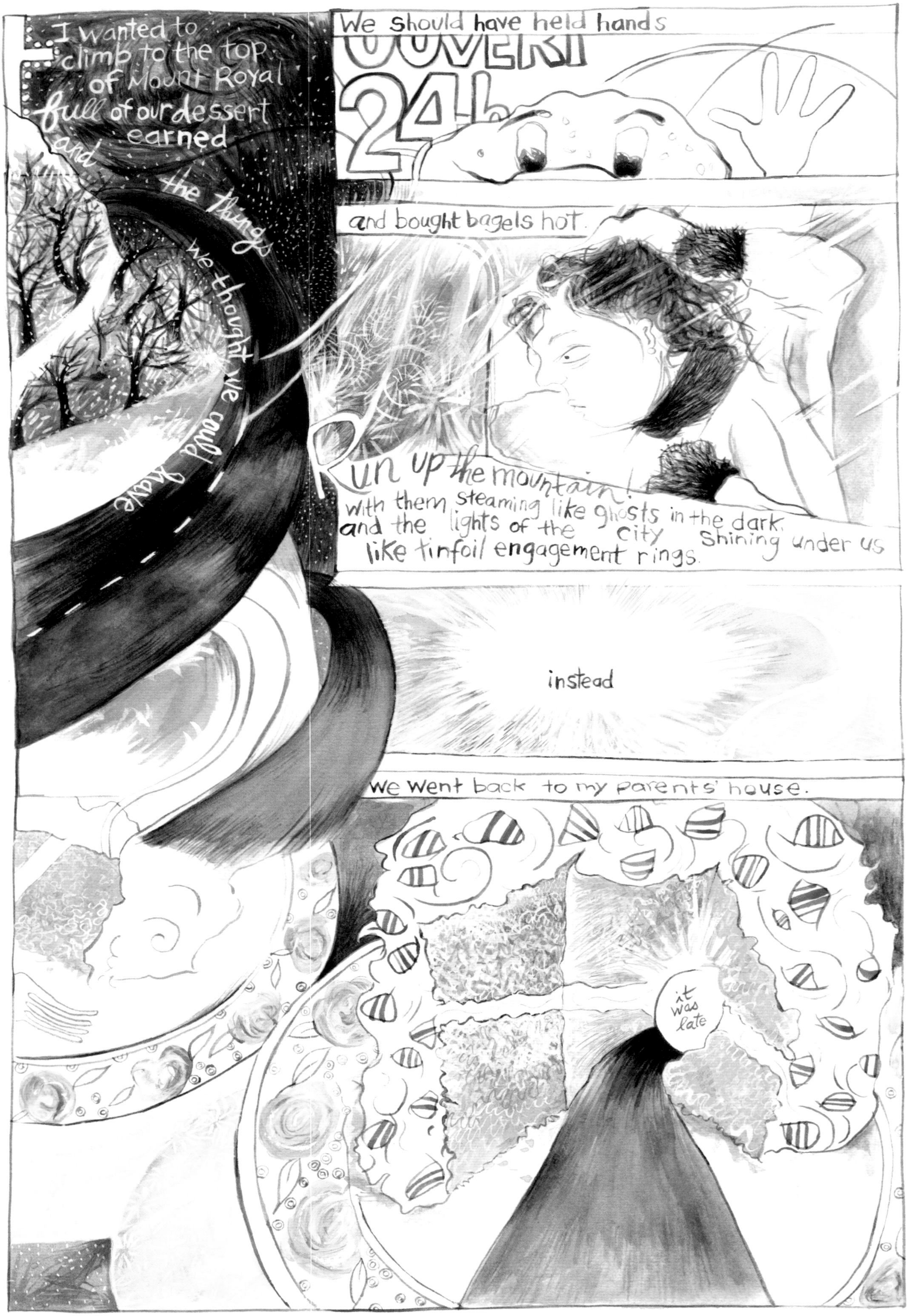
I wanted to climb to the top of Mount Royal full of our dessert earned
and the things we thought we could have
We should have held hands
OUVERT 24h
and bought bagels hot.
Run up the mountain!
with them steaming like ghosts in the dark
and the lights of the city shining under us like tinfoil engagement rings.
instead
we went back to my parents' house.
it was late

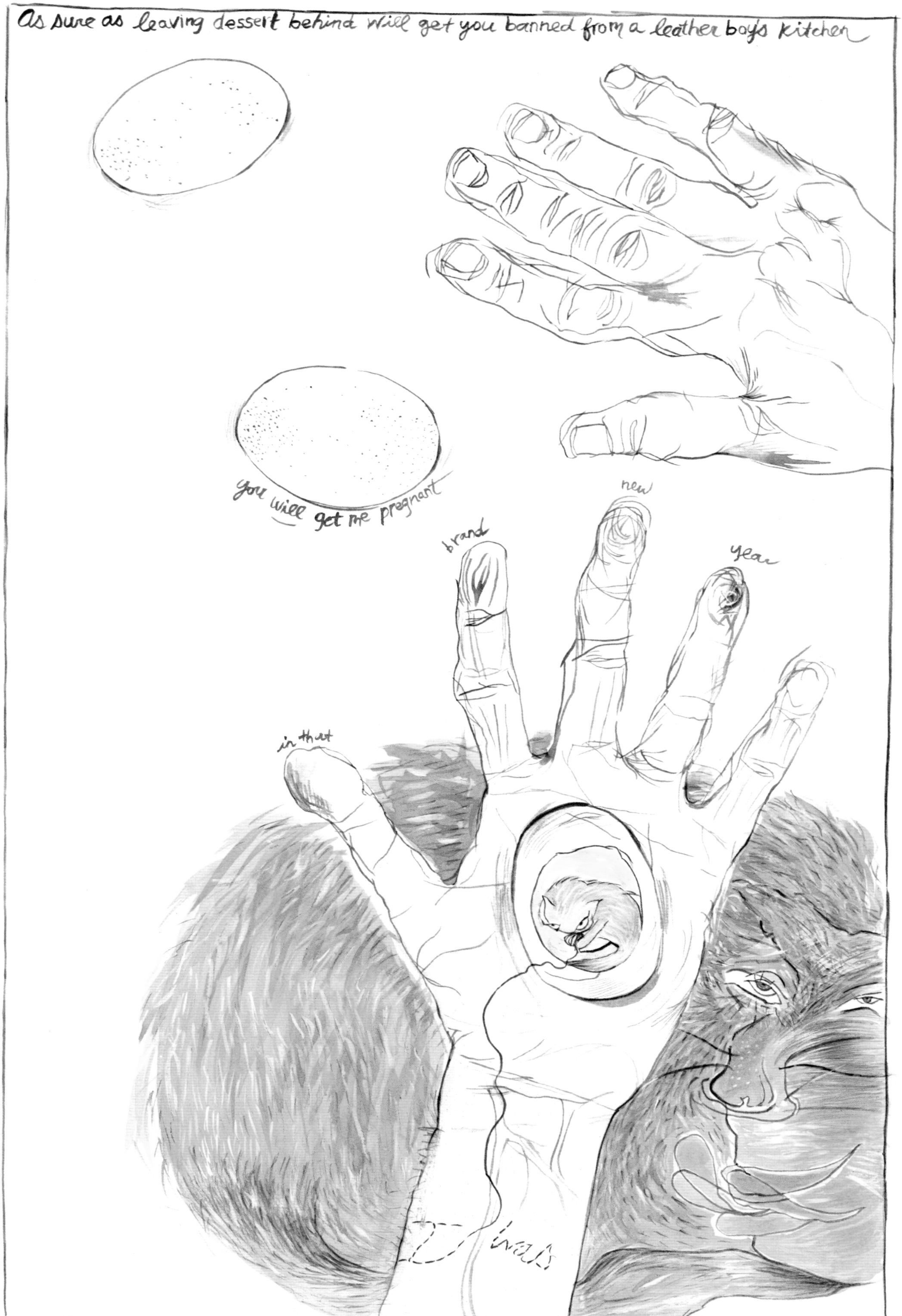
As sure as leaving dessert behind will get you banned from a leather boy's kitchen
you will get me pregnant
brand
new
year
in that

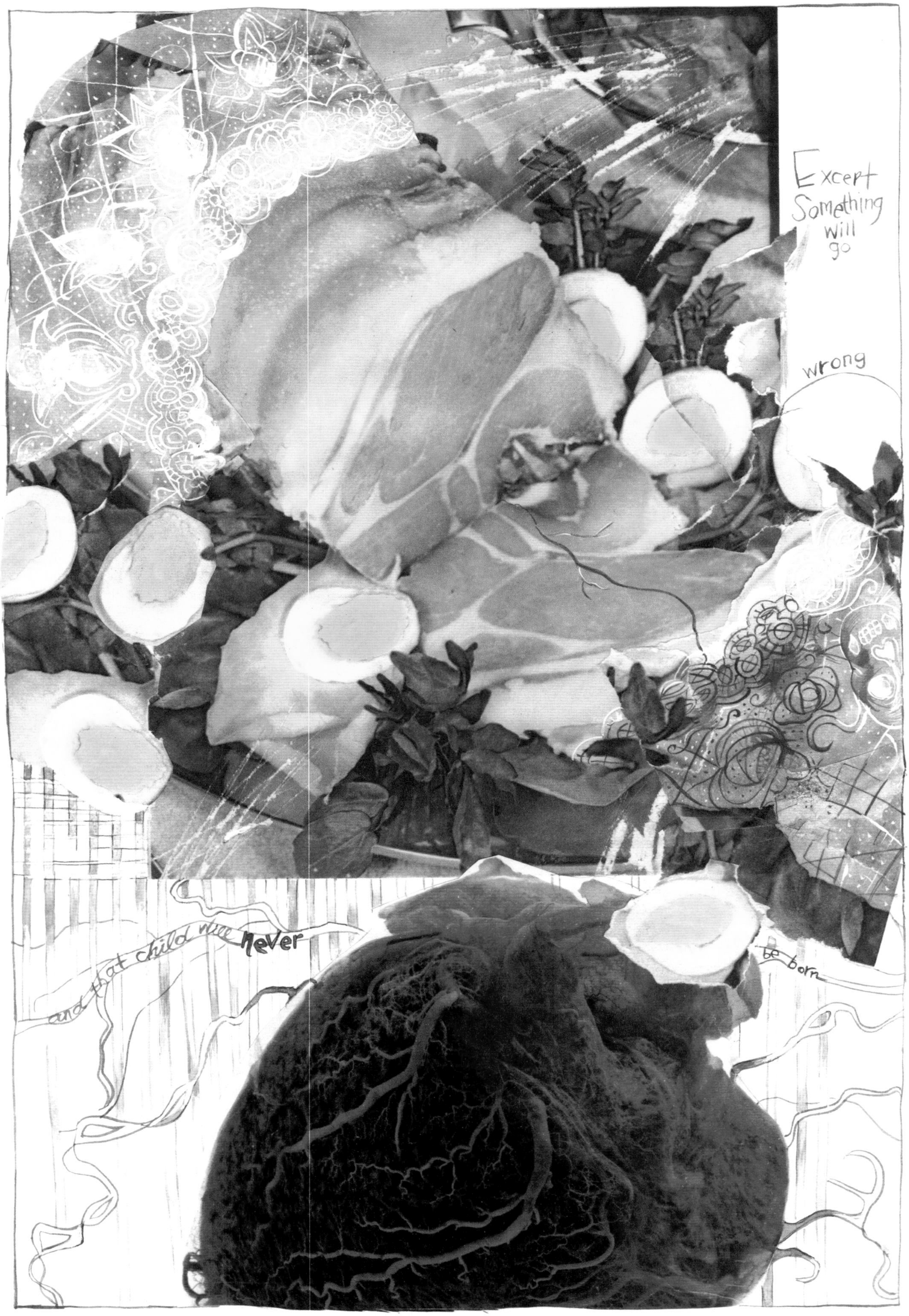
Except Something will go
wrong
and that child will never
be born

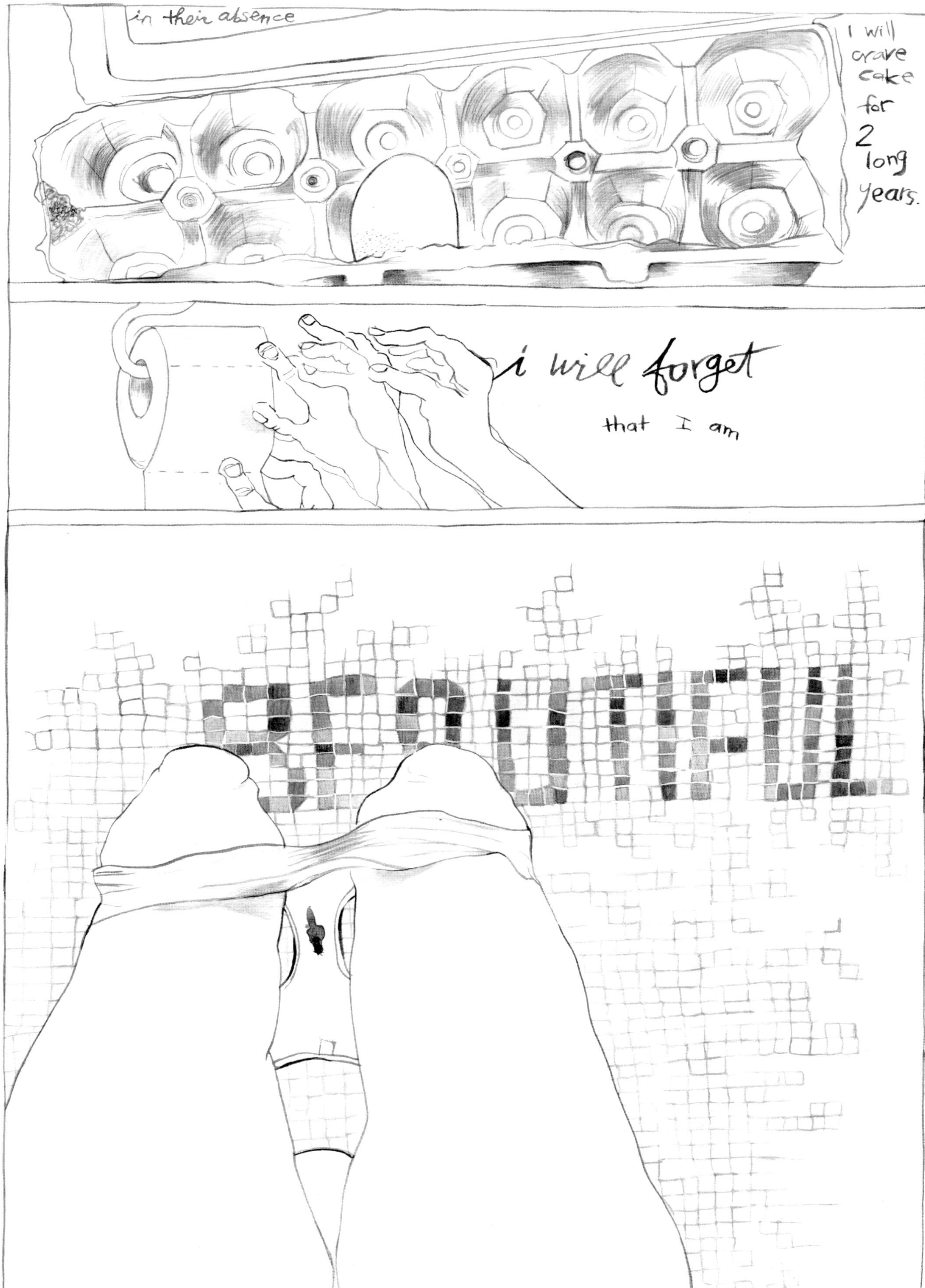
in their absence
I will crave cake for 2 long years.
i will forget
that I am

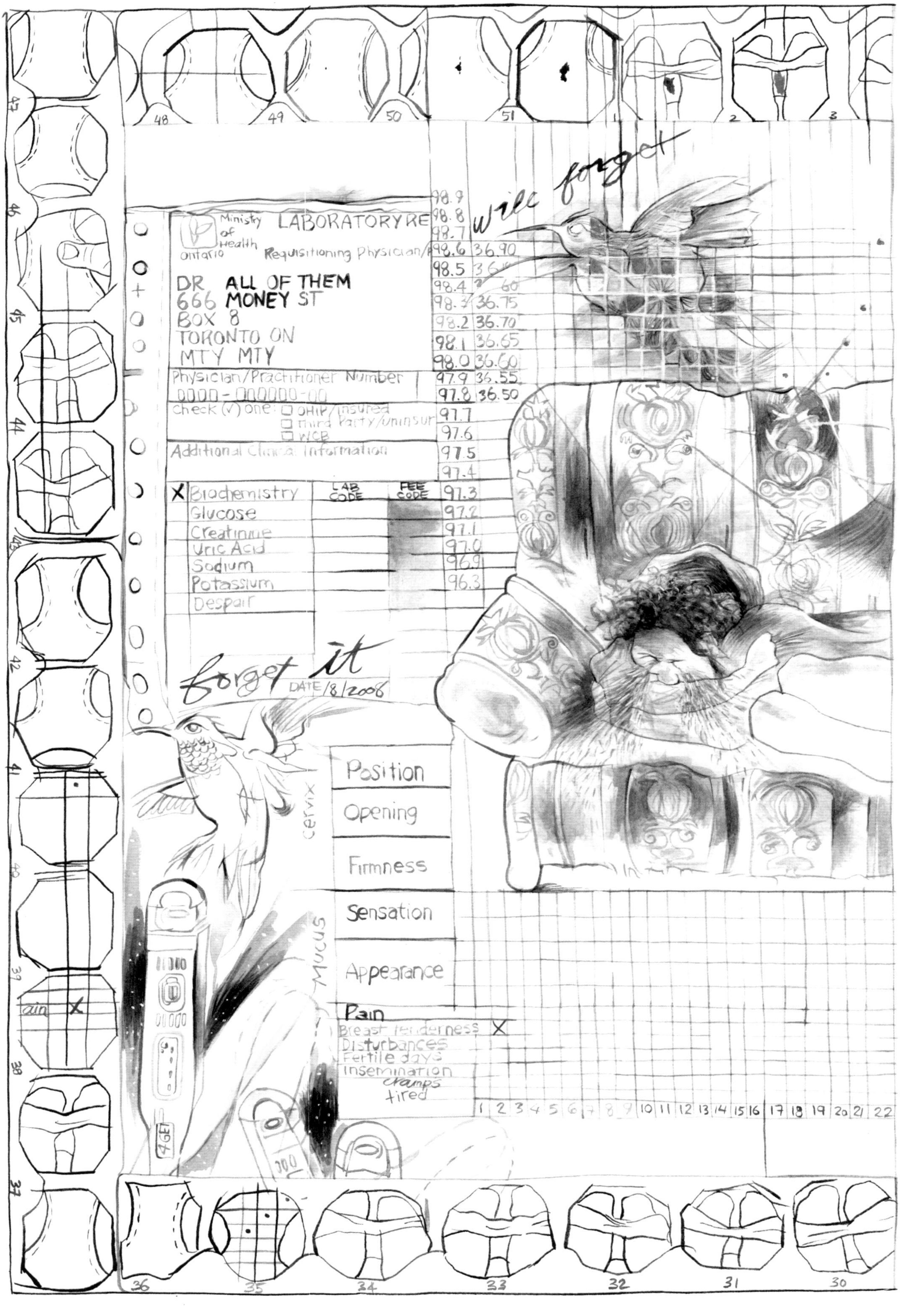

will forget
Ministry of Health Ontario
LABORATORY RE
Requisitioning Physician/
DR ALL OF THEM
666 MONEY ST
BOX 8
TORONTO ON
MTY MTY
Physician/Practitioner Number
0000-000000-00
Check (✓) one: OHIP/Insured Third Party/Uninsur WCB
Additional Clinical Information
Biochemistry
Glucose
Creatinine
Uric Acid
Sodium
Potassium
Despair
LAB CODE
FEE CODE
98.9
98.8
98.7
98.6 36.90
98.5
98.4
98.3 36.75
98.2 36.70
98.1 36.65
98.0 36.60
97.9 36.55
97.8 36.50
97.7
97.6
97.5
97.4
97.3
97.2
97.1
97.0
96.9
96.3
forget it
DATE /8/2008
Position
Opening
Firmness
cervix
Sensation
Appearance
Mucus
Pain
Breast tenderness
Disturbances
Fertile days
Insemination
cramps
tired
1 2 3 4 5 6 7 8 9 10 11 12 13 14 15 16 17 18 19 20 21 22

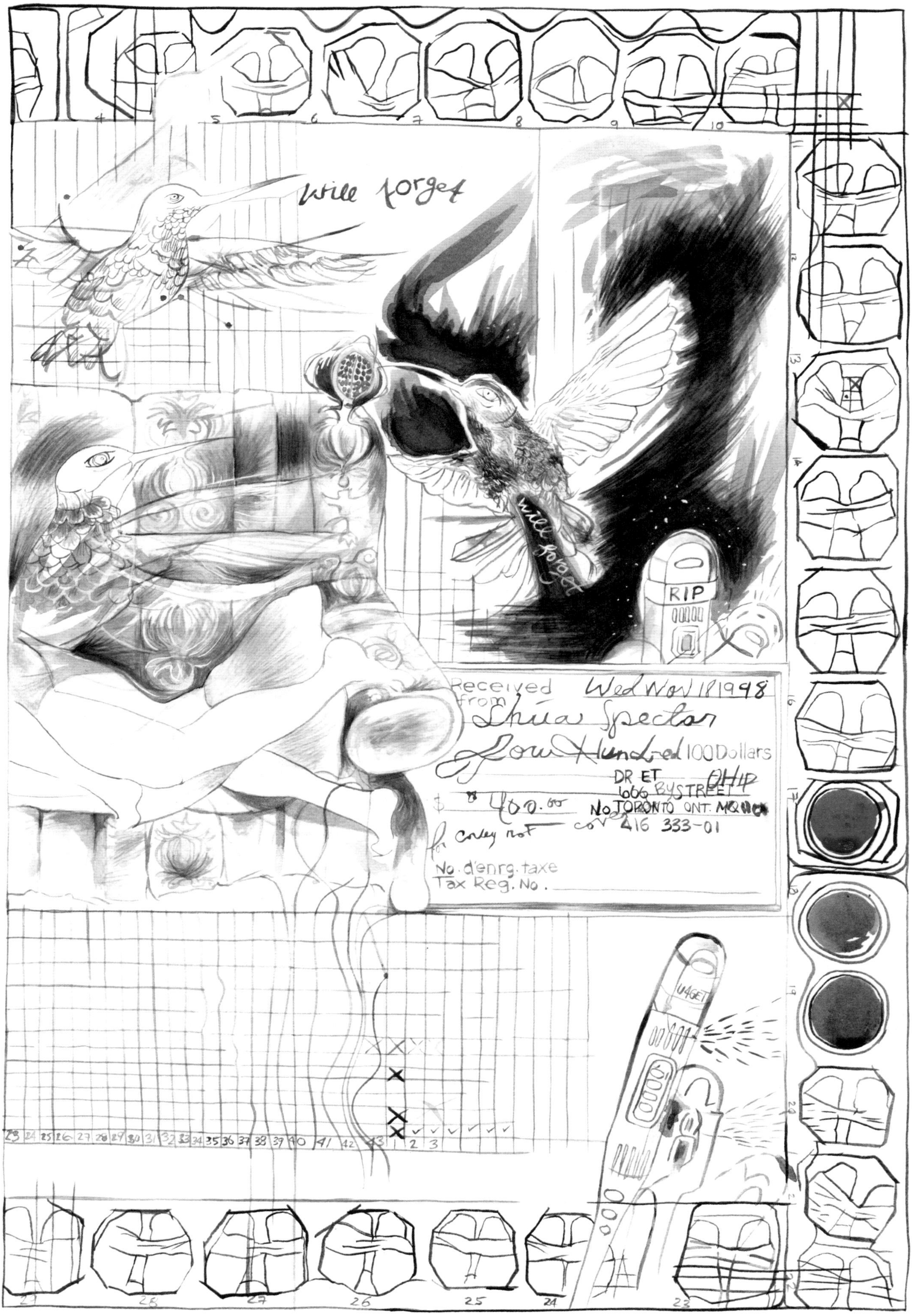
will forget
RIP
Received
from
Wed Nov 18 1998
Four Hundred 100 Dollars
DR ET
606 BYSTREET
OHIP
TORONTO ONT.
$ 400.00
416 333-01
No. d'enrg. taxe
Tax Reg. No.
U4GET

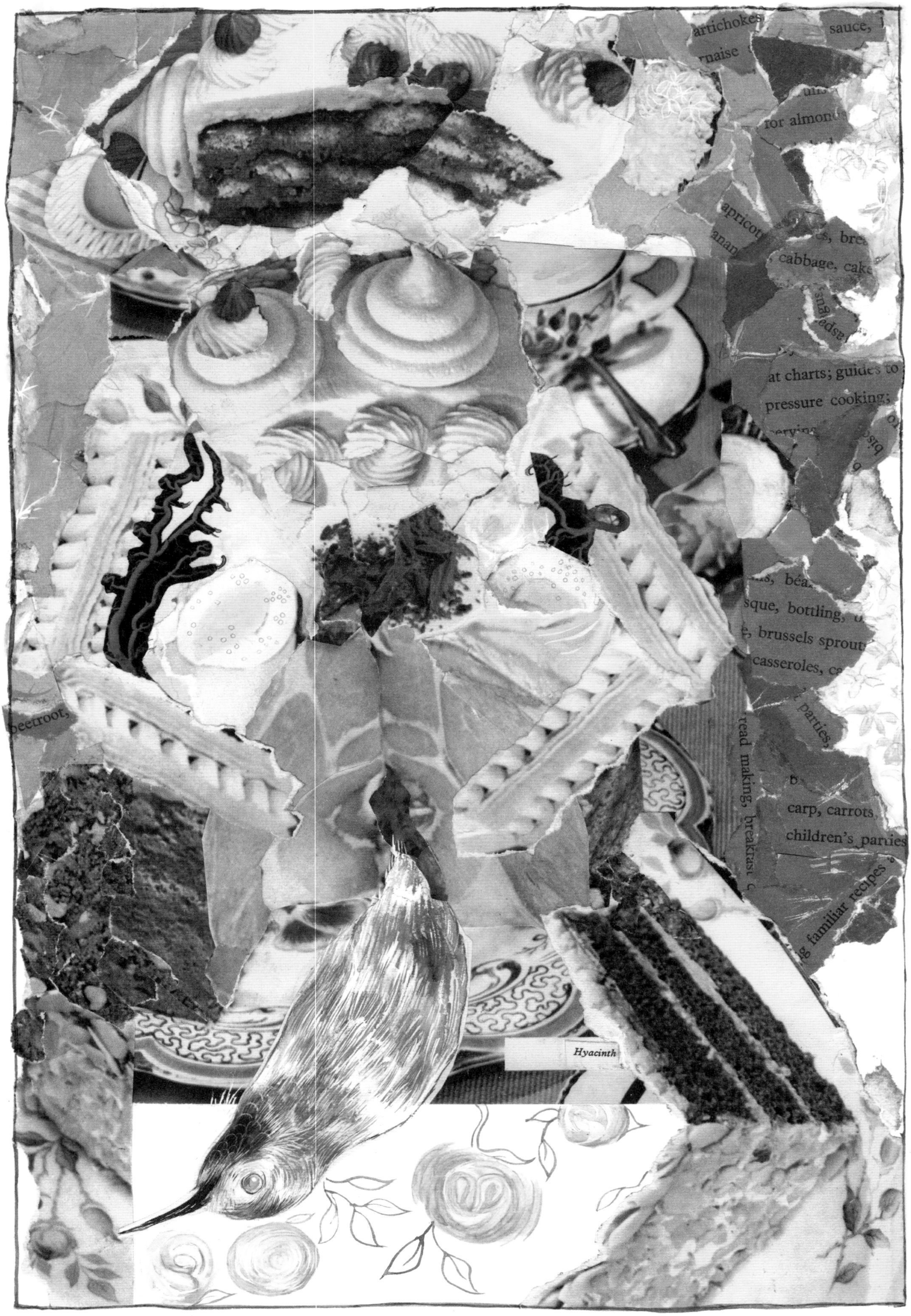
artichokes
sauce,
for almon
apricot
cabbage, cak
at charts; guides to
pressure cooking;
sque, bottling,
brussels sprout
casseroles,
beetroot,
read making, breakfast
parties,
carp, carrots,
children's parties
familiar recipes
Hyacinth

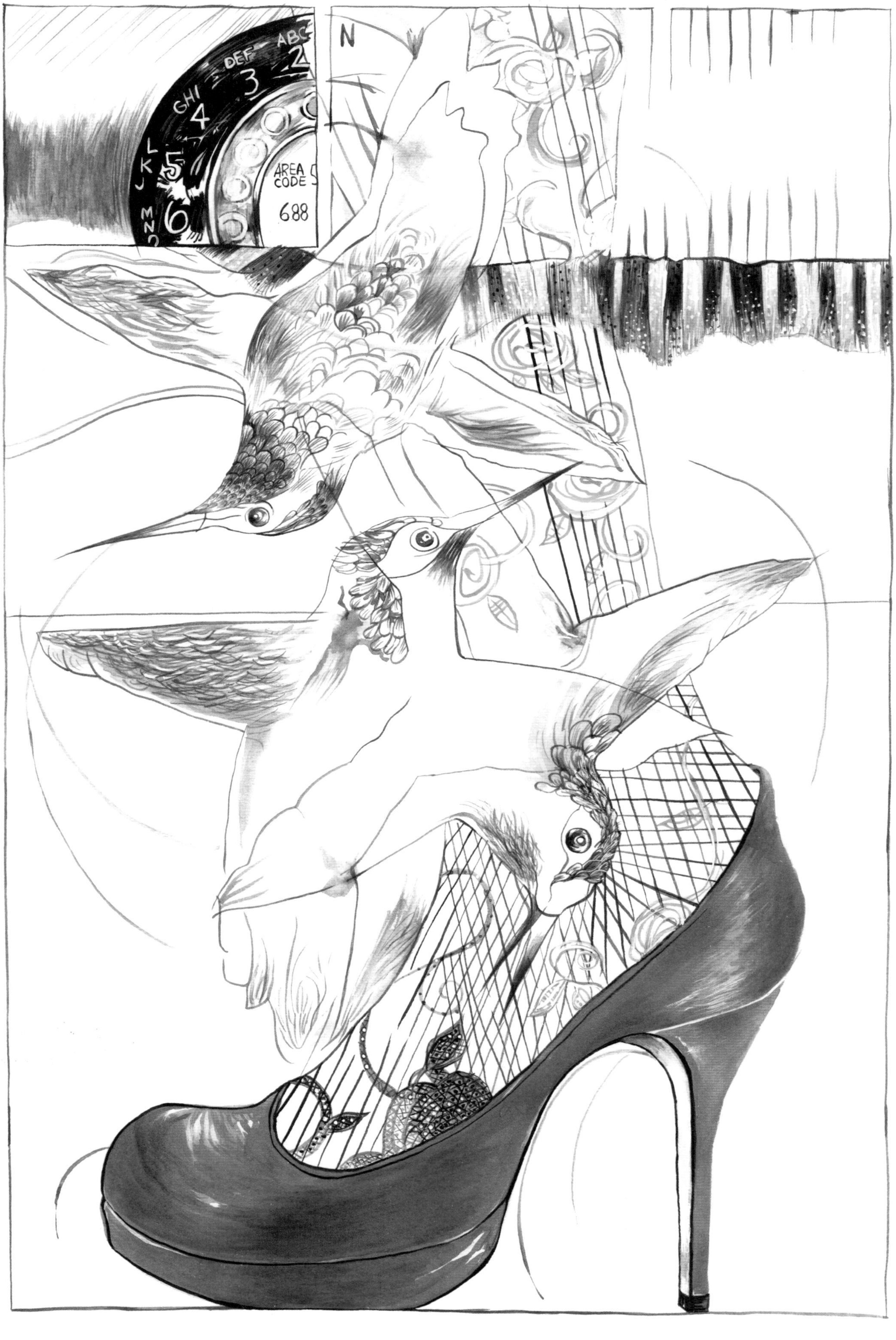
N
ABC 2
DEF 3
GHI 4
JKL 5
MNO 6
AREA CODE
688

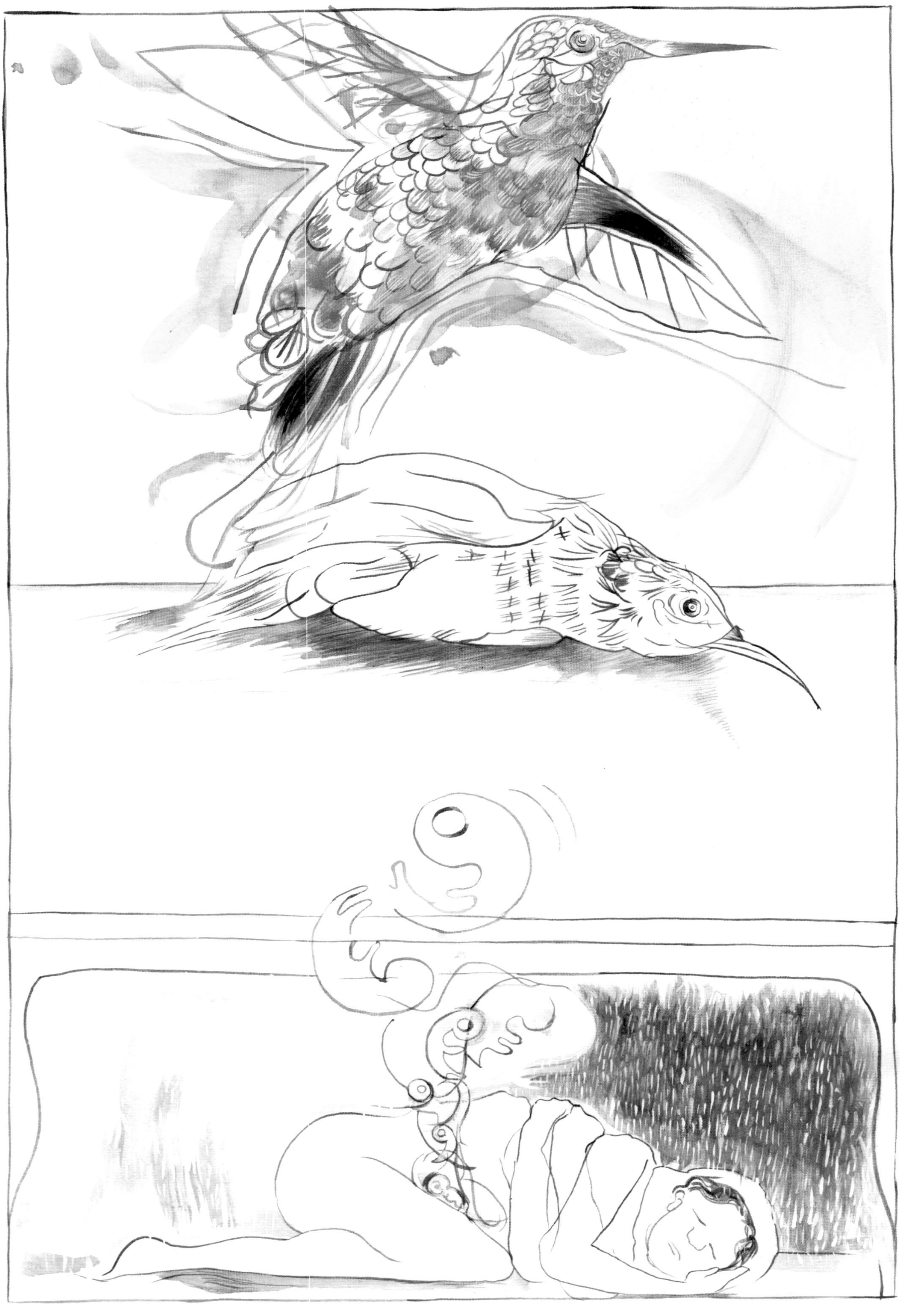

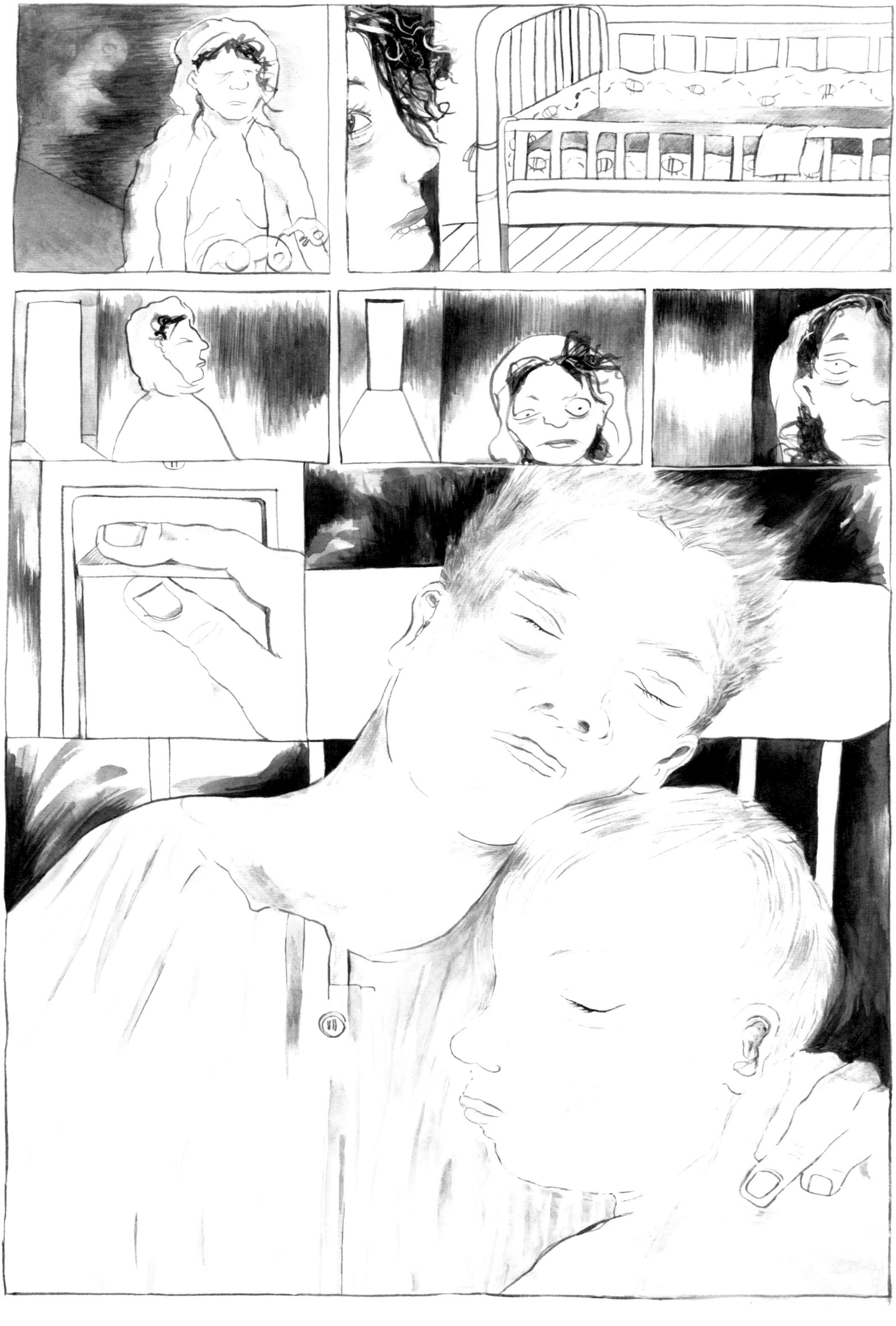

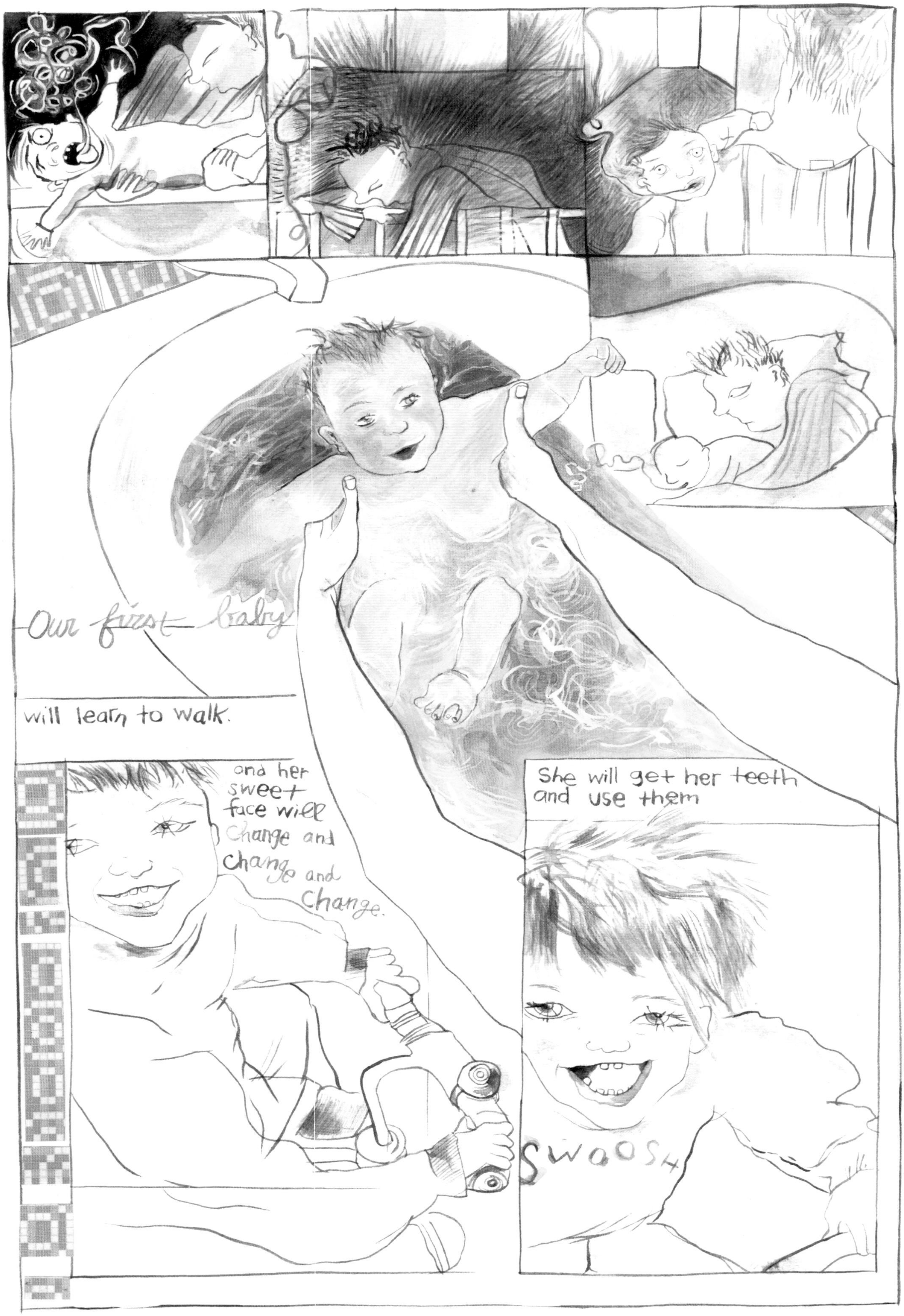
Our first baby
will learn to walk.
and her sweet face will change and change and change.
She will get her teeth and use them
SWOOSH

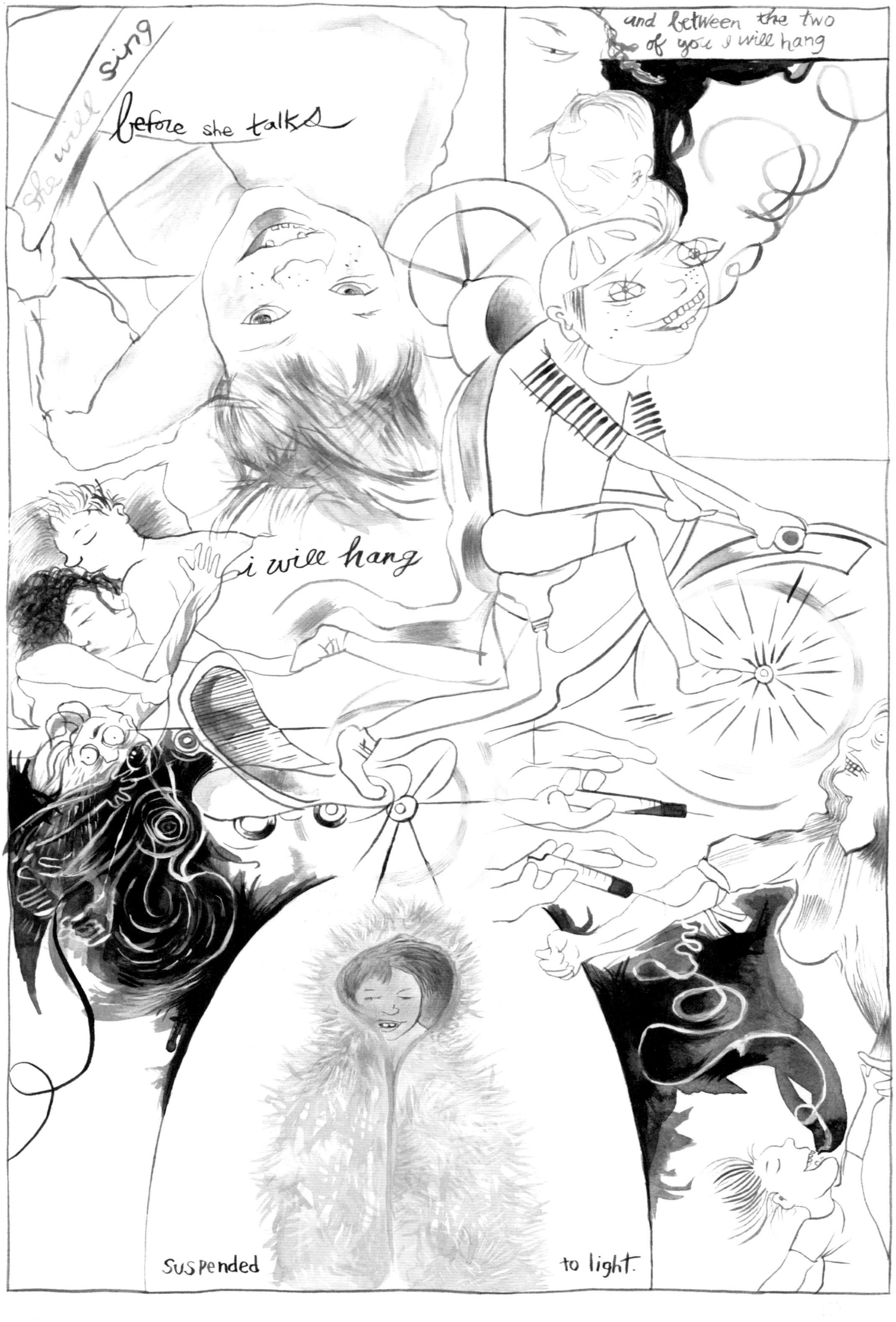
She will sing
before she talks
and between the two of you I will hang
i will hang
suspended
to light.

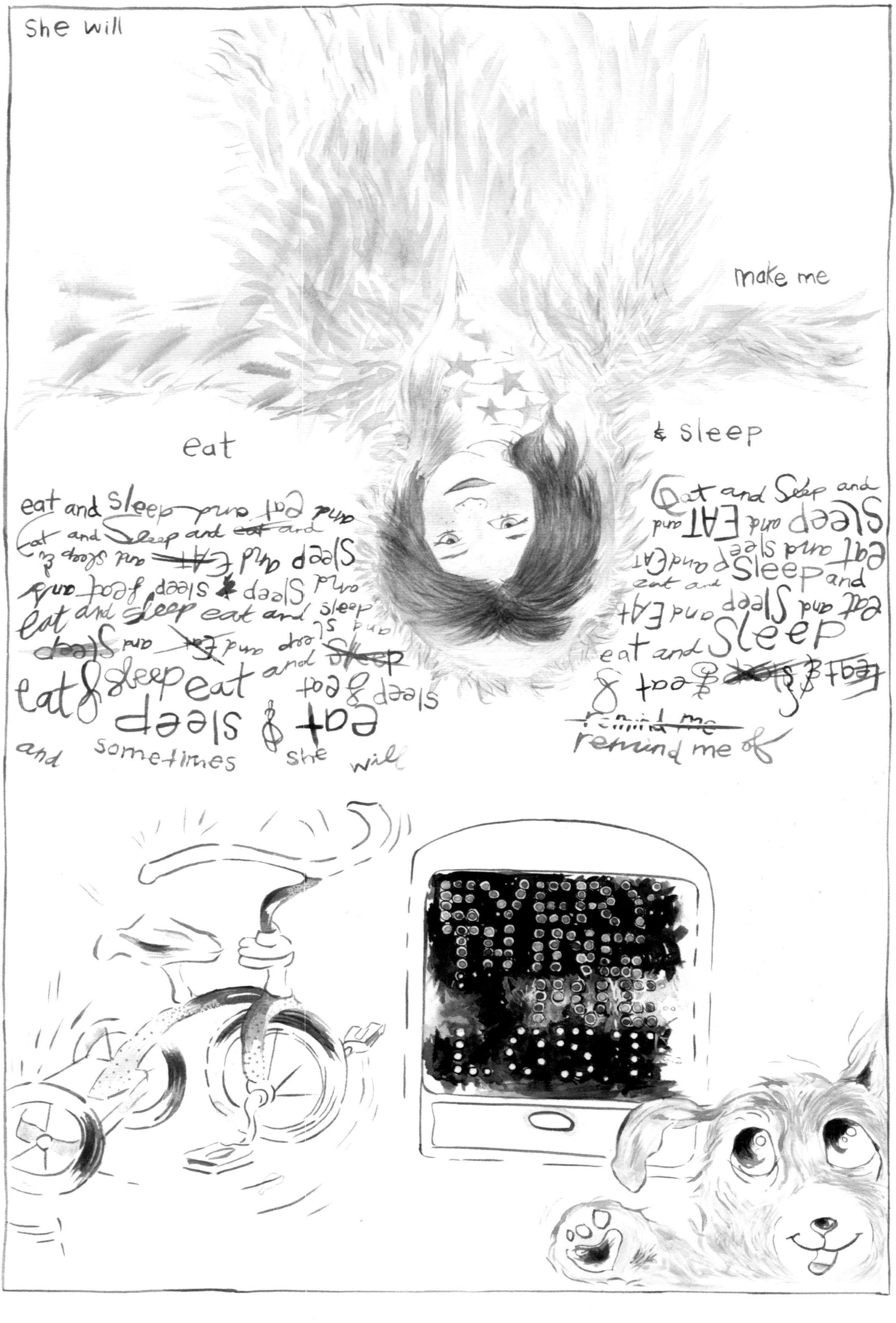
she will
make me
eat
& sleep
eat and sleep
eat and sleep and
eat and sleep eat and sleep
eat & sleep eat and
and sometimes she will
eat and sleep and
sleep and
eat and sleep
remind me
remind me of

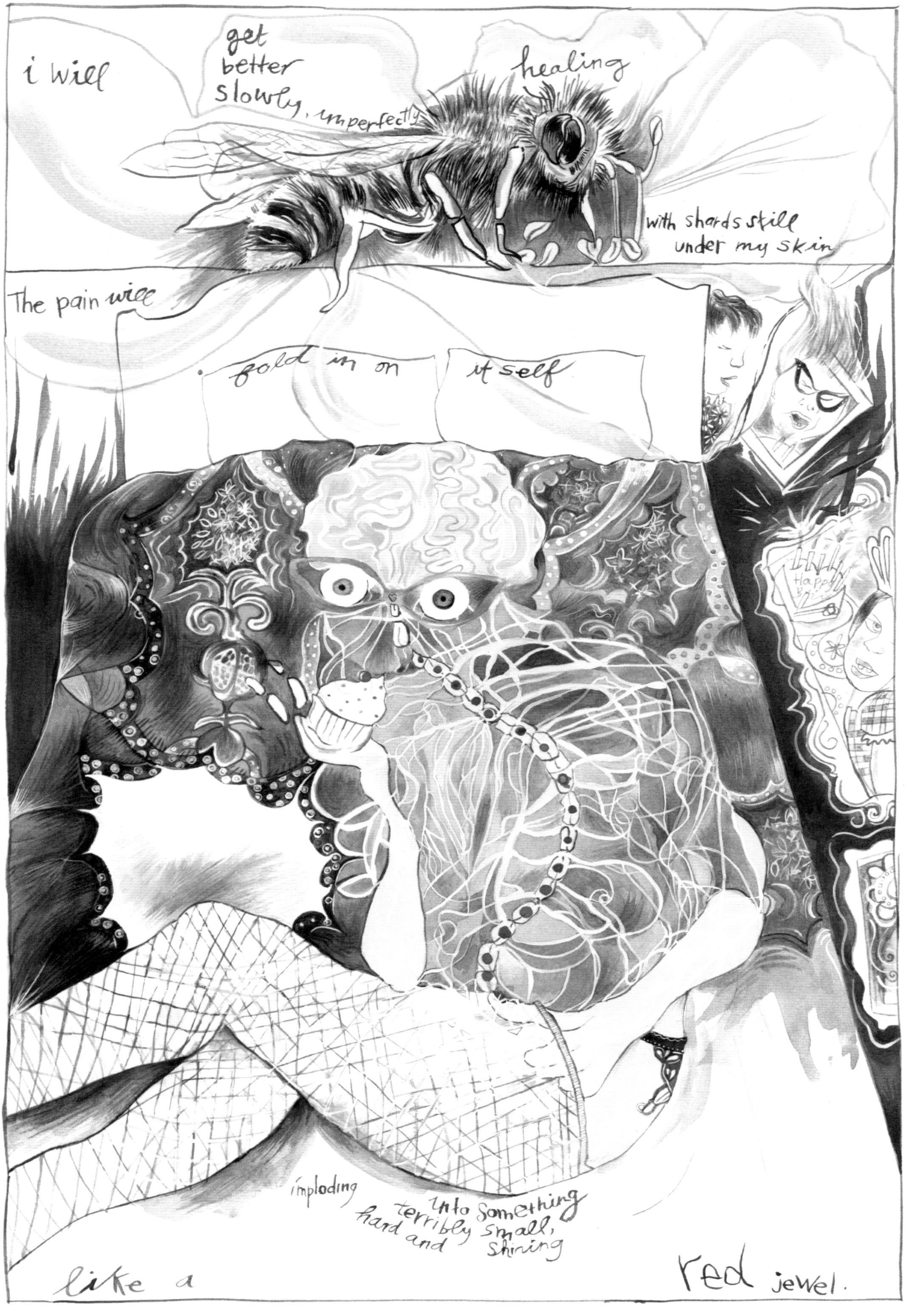
i will
get better slowly, imperfectly
healing
with shards still under my skin
The pain will
fold in on itself
imploding
into something terribly small, hard and shining
like a red jewel.

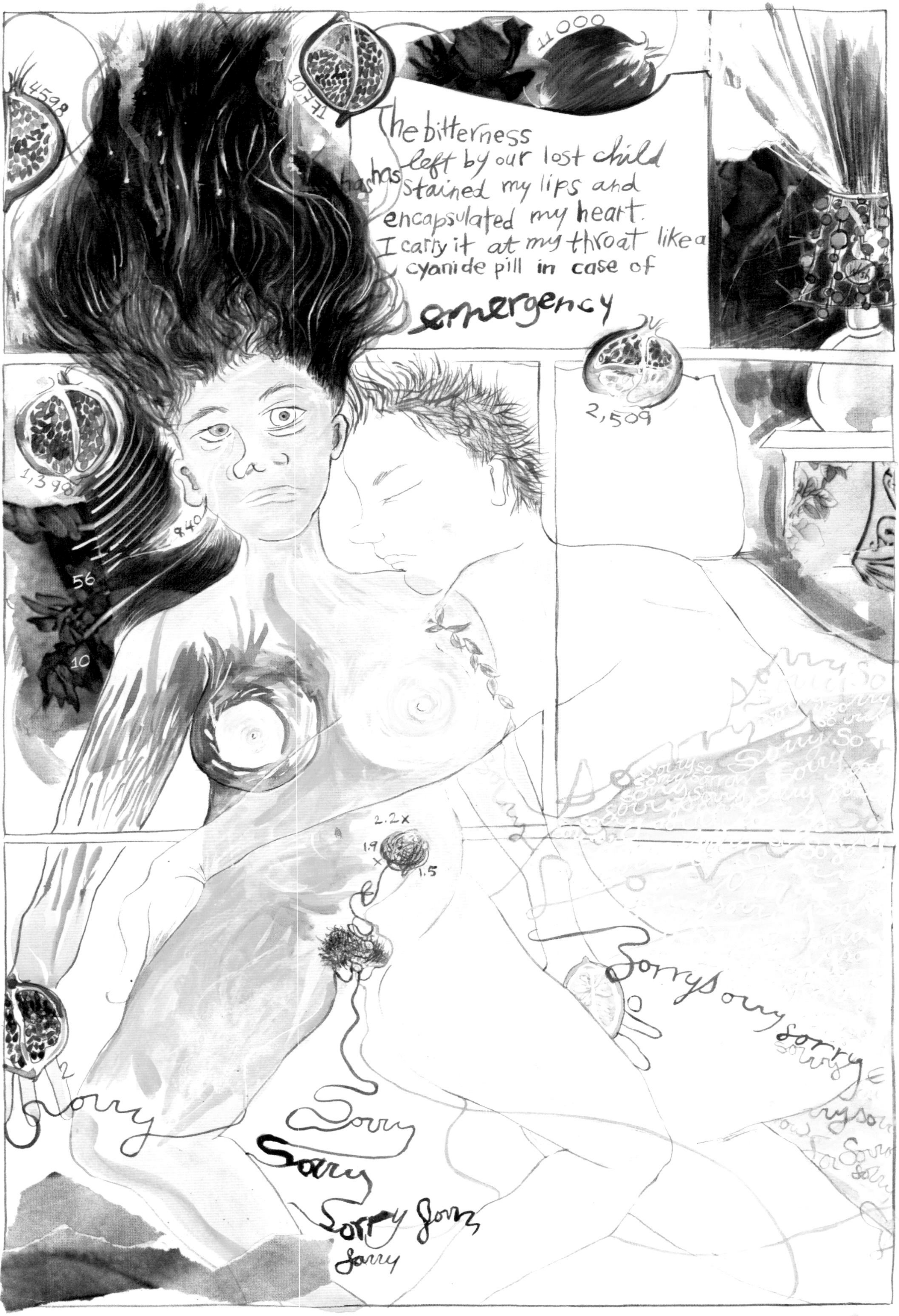
4598
10,771
11,000
The bitterness left by our lost child has stained my lips and encapsulated my heart. I carry it at my throat like a cyanide pill in case of
emergency
1,398
2,509
8.40
56
10
2.2x
1.9
1.5
Sorry
Sorry
Sorry
Sorry
Sorry
Sorry
SorrySorrySorry

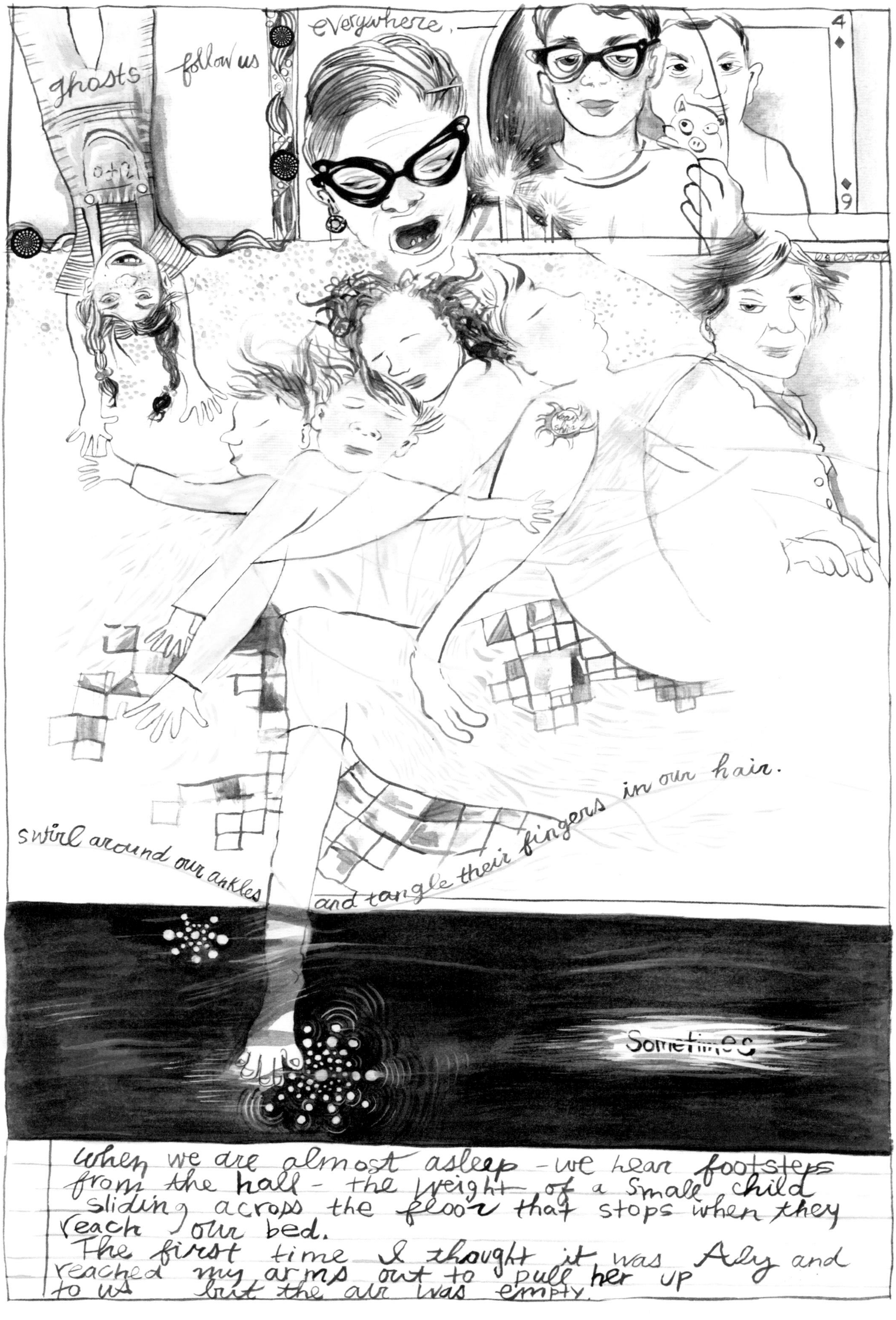
ghosts follow us everywhere.
swirl around our ankles and tangle their fingers in our hair.
Sometimes
when we are almost asleep - we hear footsteps from the hall - the weight of a small child sliding across the floor that stops when they reach our bed.
The first time I thought it was Aly and reached my arms out to pull her up to us but the air was empty.

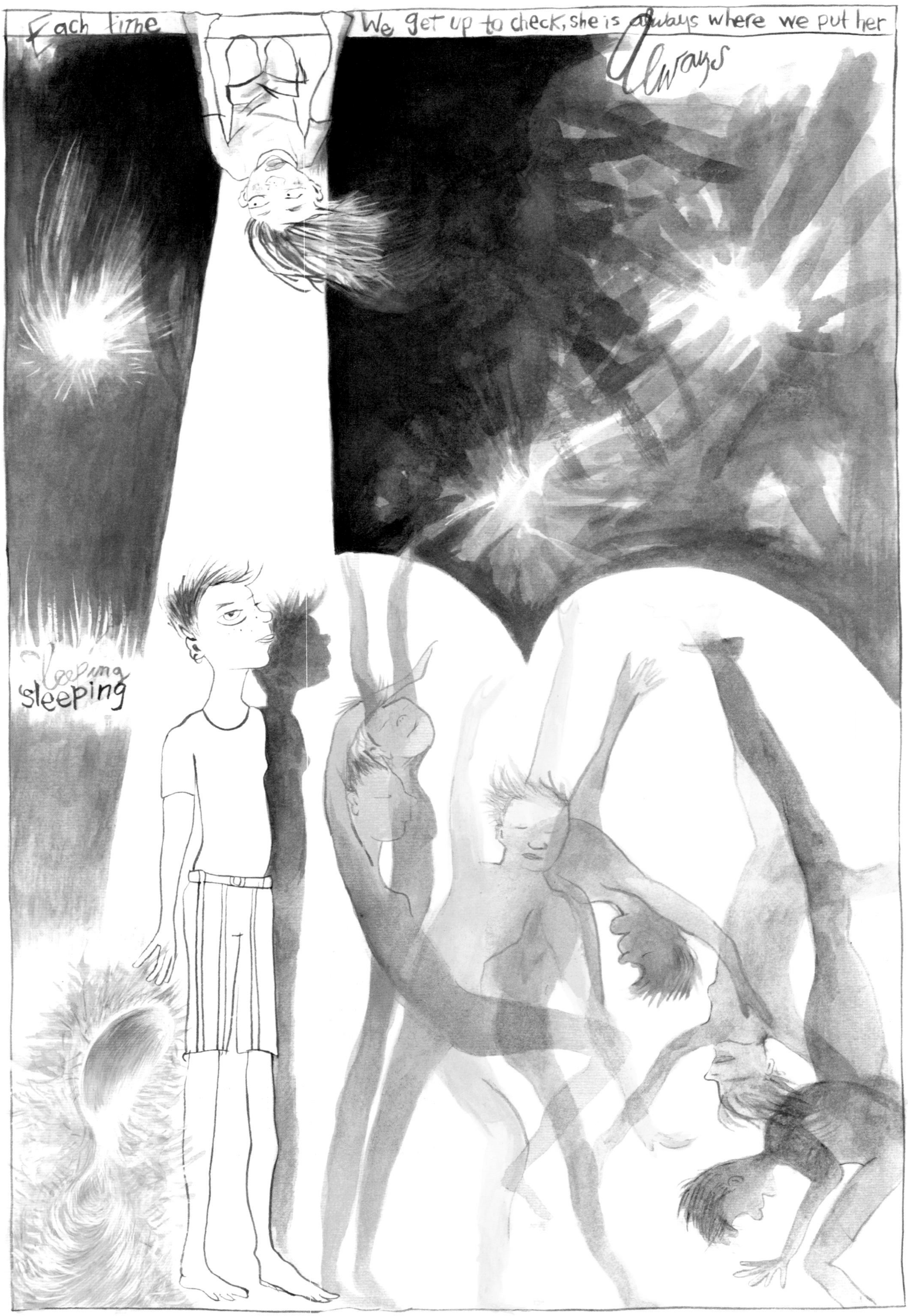
Each time
We get up to check, she is always where we put her
Always
Sleeping
sleeping

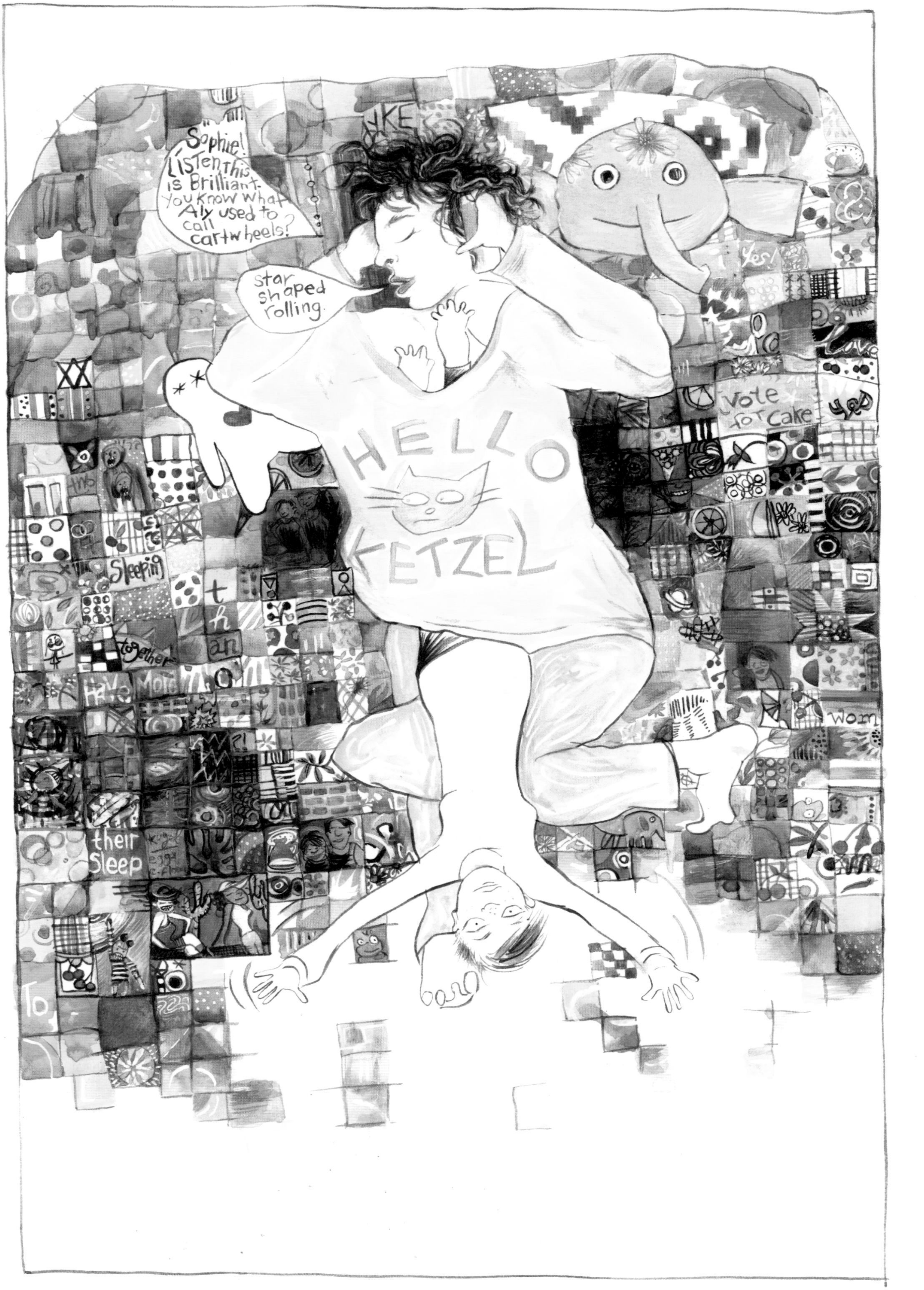
Sophie! LISTEN this is Brilliant. You know what Aly used to call cartwheels?
star shaped rolling.
HELLO KETZEL

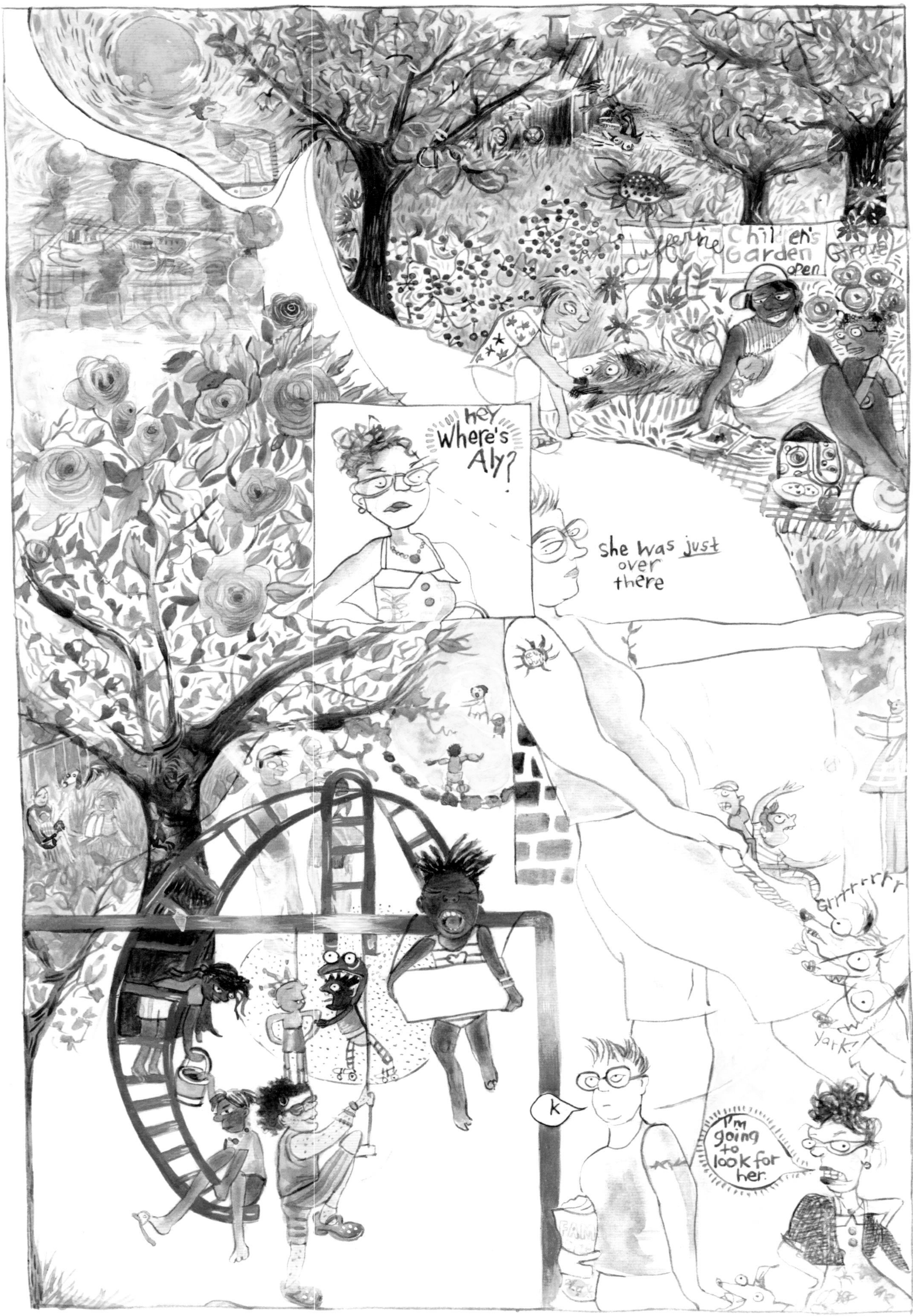
Garden
open
hey
Where's
Aly?
she was just
over
there
Grrrrrrr
yark!
k
I'm
going
to
look for
her.

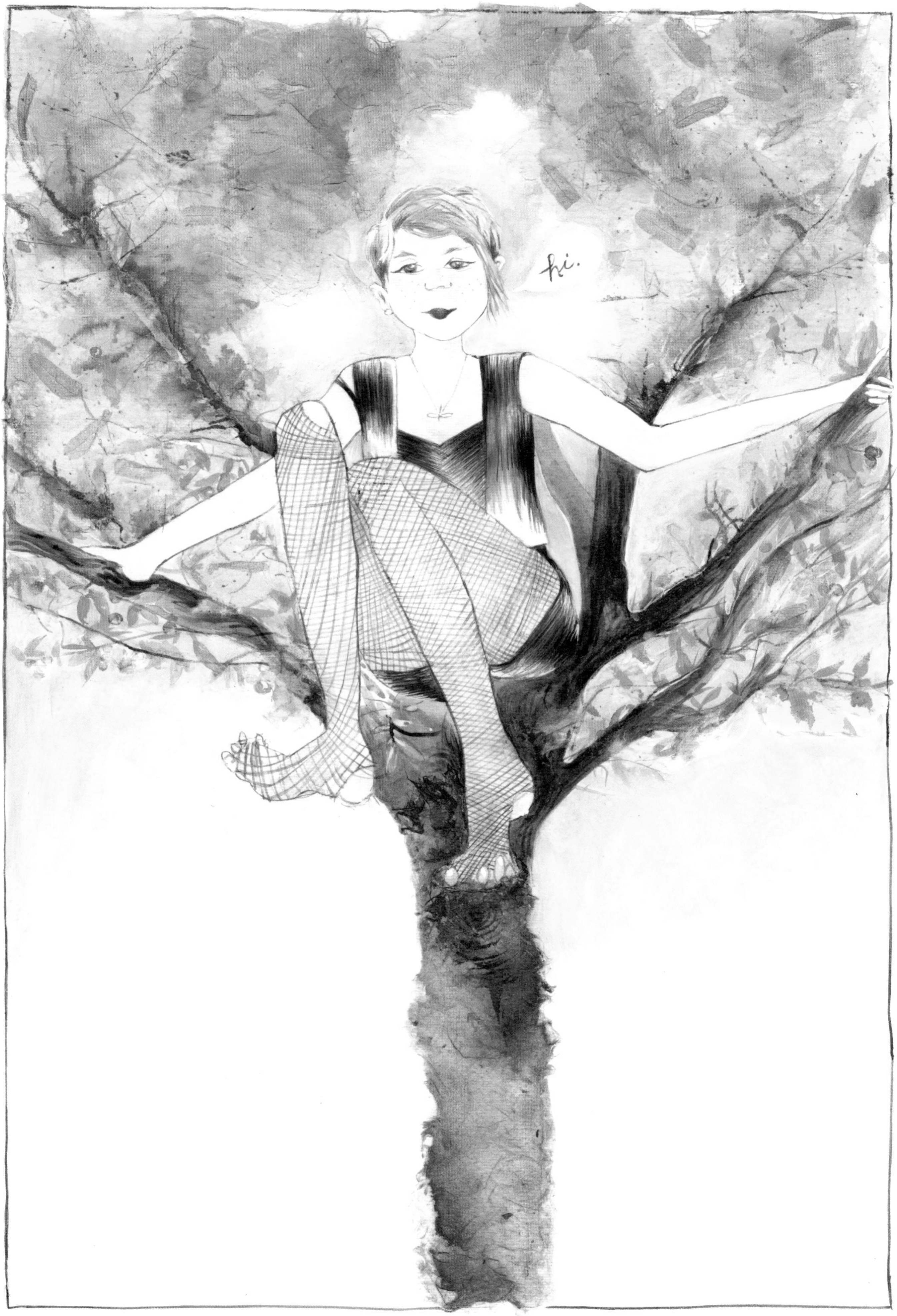
hi.

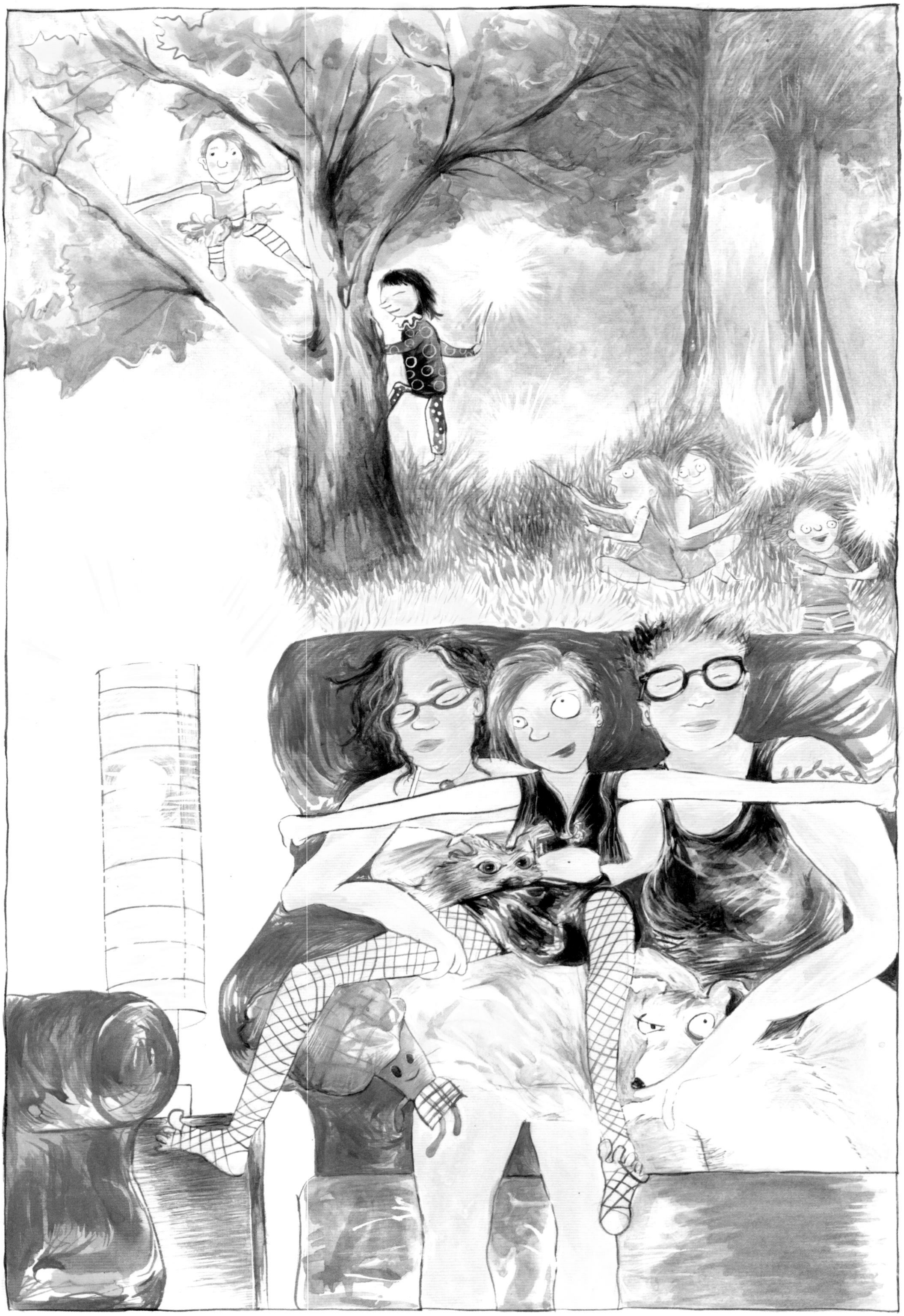

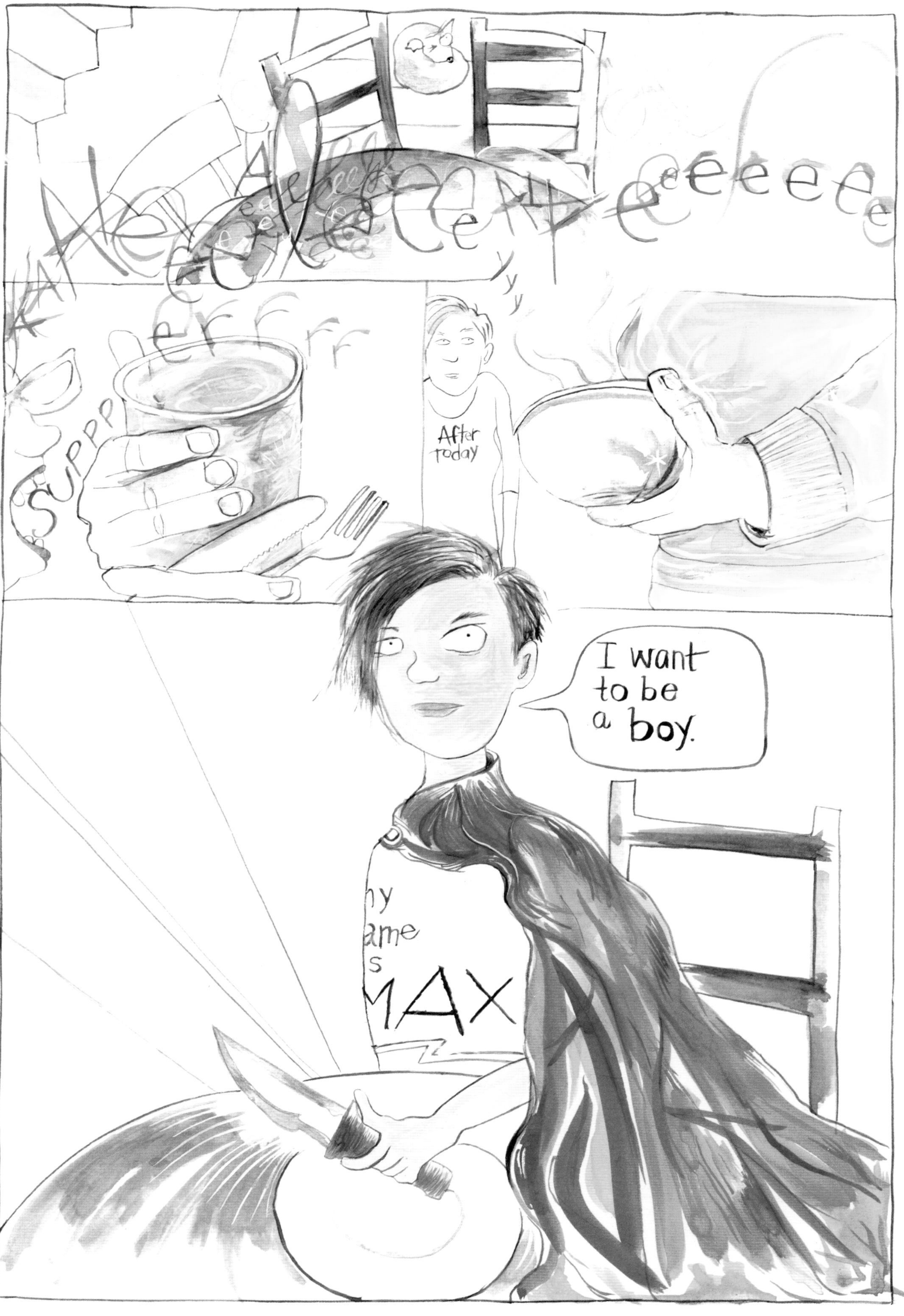
After today
I want to be a boy.
my name is MAX

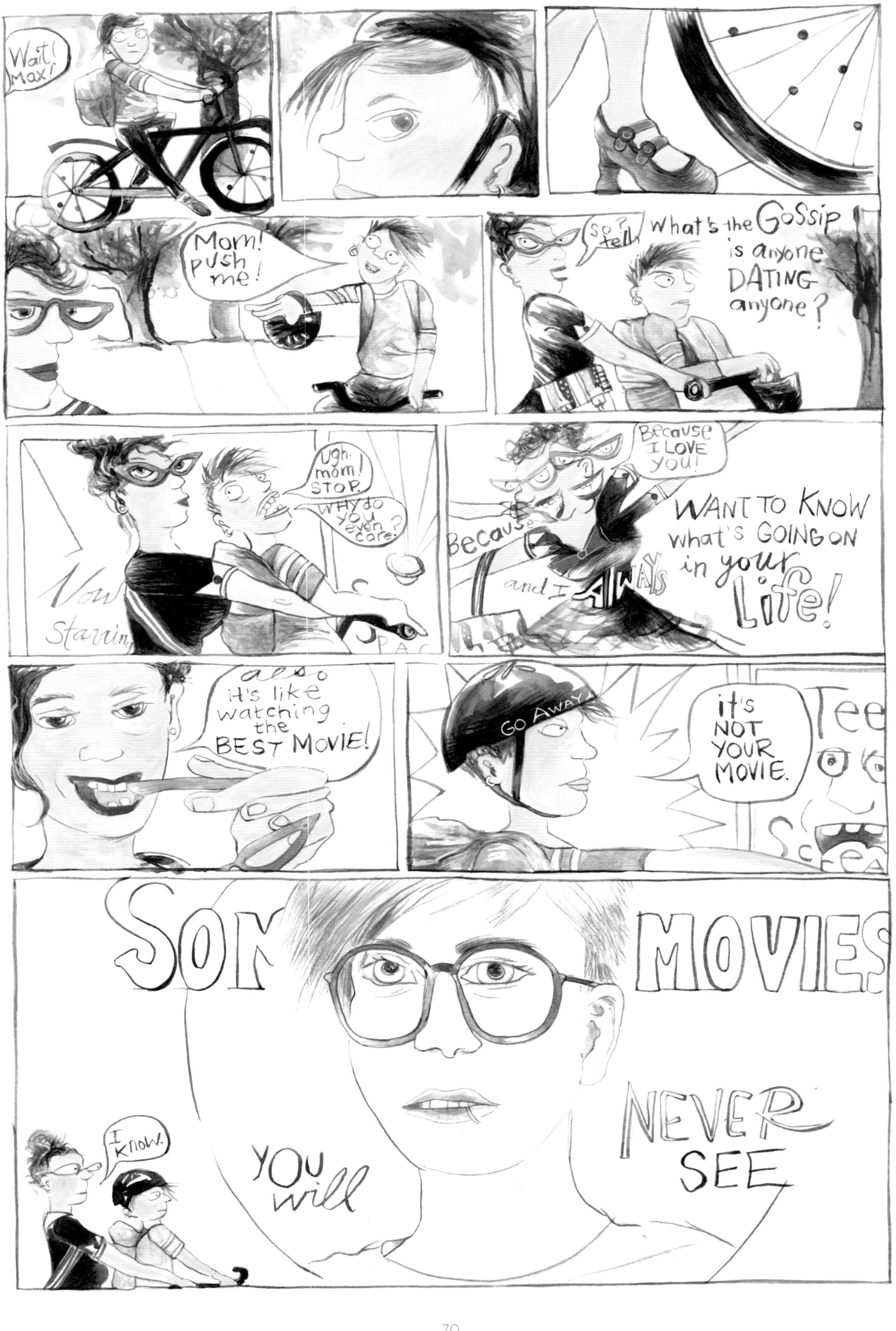
Wait! Max!
Mom! push me!
So? tell!
What's the GOSSIP is anyone DATING anyone?
Ugh. mom! STOP.
WHY do you even care?
Because I LOVE you!
Because
WANT TO KNOW what's GOING ON in your Life!
and I ALWAYS
also it's like watching the BEST MOVIE!
GO AWAY
it's NOT YOUR MOVIE.
SOME MOVIES
YOU will
NEVER SEE
I know.

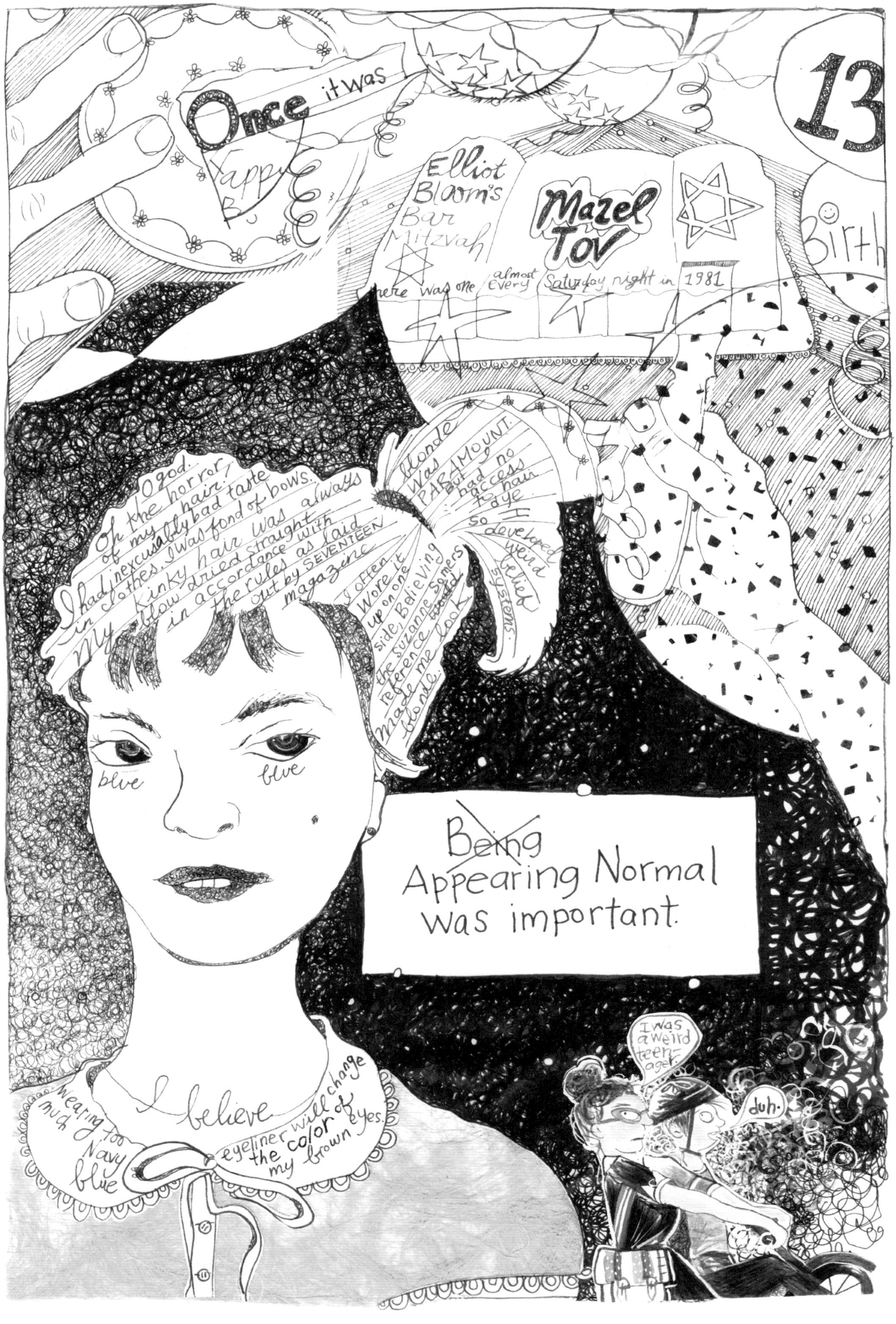
Once it was
13
Elliot Bloom's Bar Mitzvah
Mazel Tov
There was one almost every Saturday night in 1981
Birth
O god.
Oh the horror of my hair!
I had inexcusably bad taste in clothes. I was fond of bows.
My kinky hair was always blow dried straight in accordance with the rules as laid out by SEVENTEEN magazine
blonde was PARAMOUNT. But I had no access to hair dye
so I developed weird belief systems.
I often wore it up on one side, Believing the Suzanne Somers reference would made me look blonde.
blue
blue
~~Being~~ Appearing Normal was important.
I believe wearing too much Navy blue eyeliner will change the color of my brown eyes.
I was a weird teen-ager.
duh.

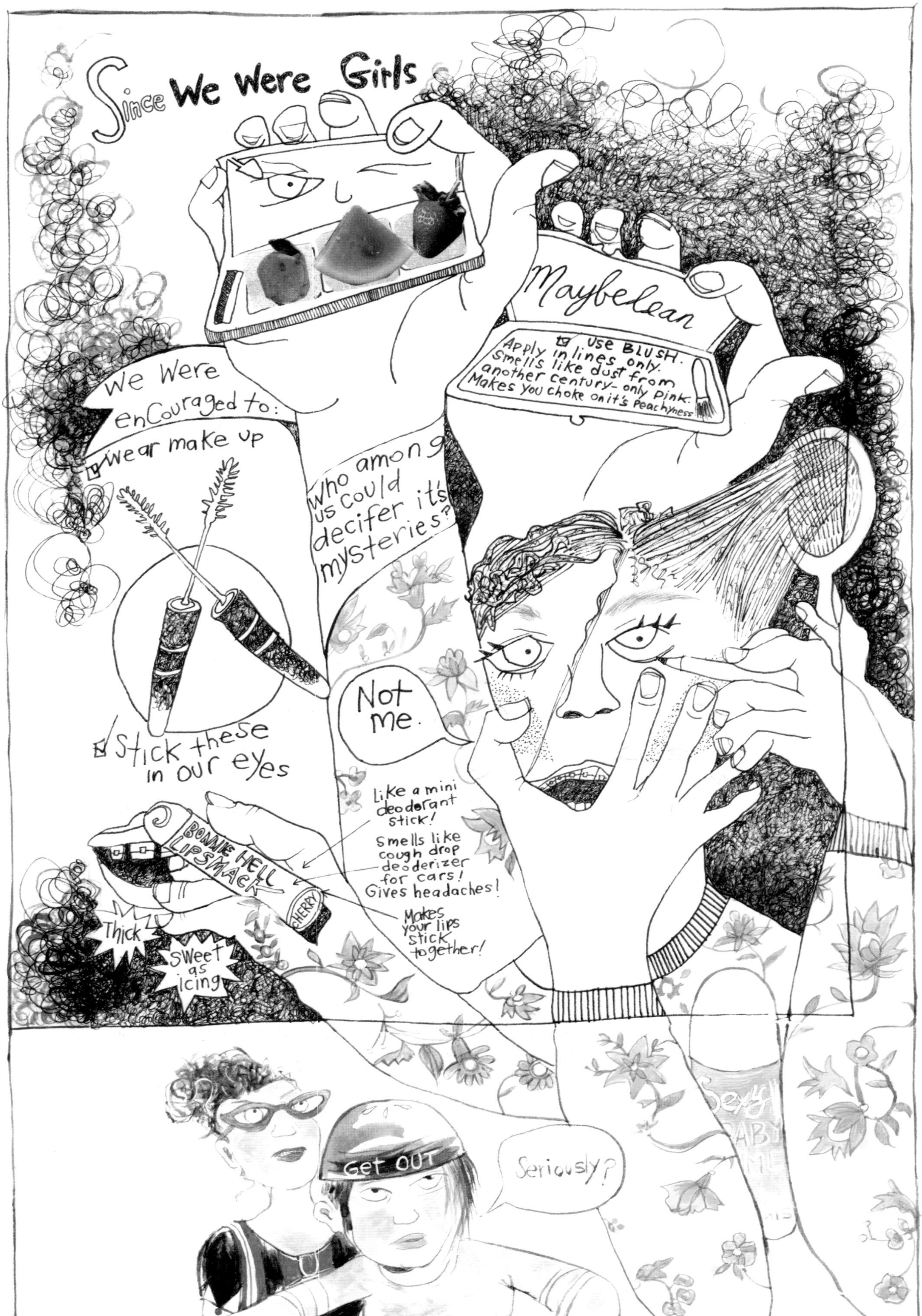
Since We Were Girls
Maybelean
USE BLUSH.
Apply in lines only.
Smells like dust from another century- only pink.
Makes you choke on it's Peachyness
We Were enCouraged to:
wear make up
Who among us could decifer it's mysteries?
Stick these in our eyes
Not me.
BONNIE HELL LIPSMACK
CHERRY
Like a mini deodorant stick!
Smells like cough drop deoderizer for cars! Gives headaches!
Makes your lips stick together!
Thick
SWeet as icing
GET OUT
Seriously?

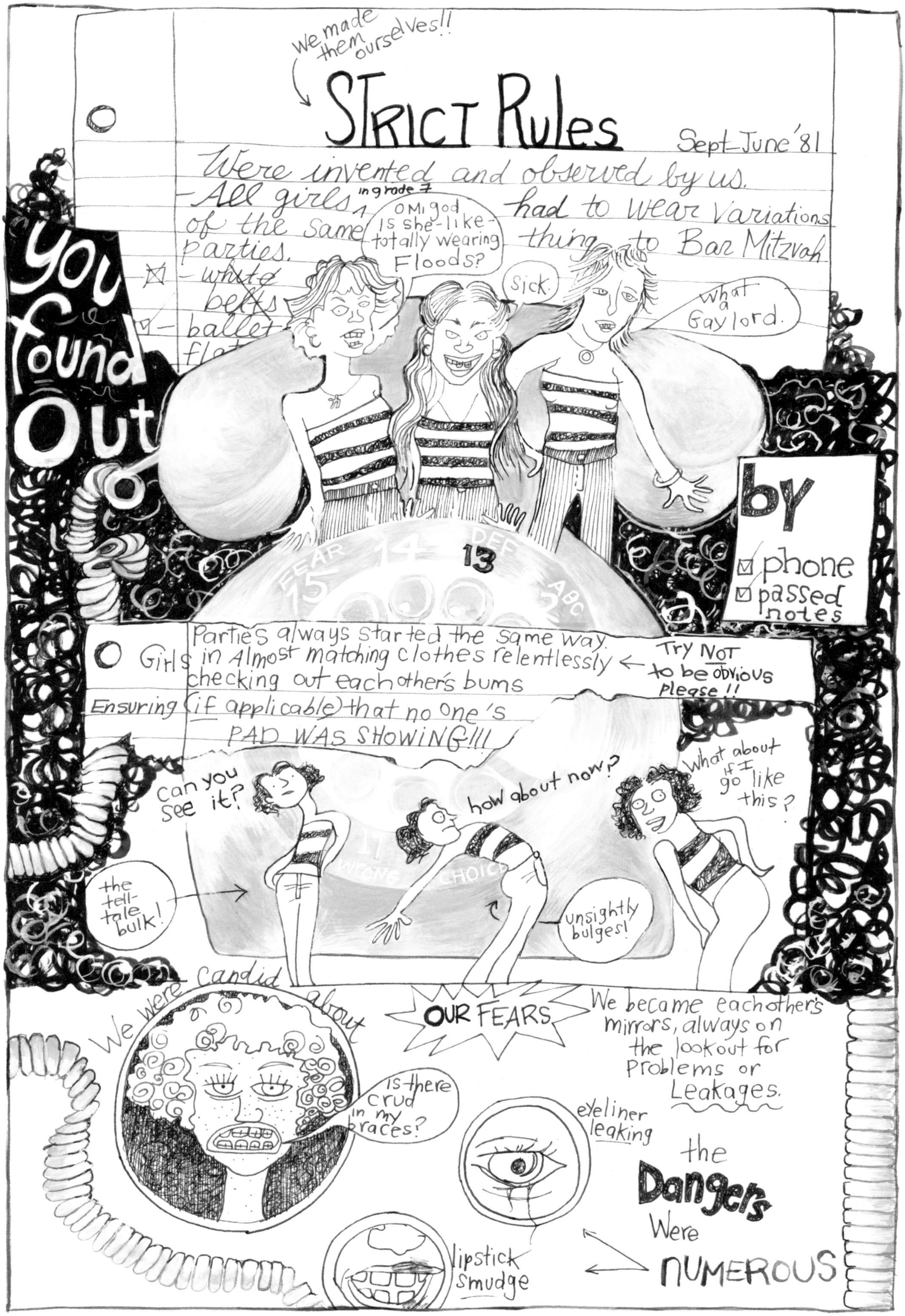
we made them ourselves!!
STRICT Rules
Sept-June '81
Were invented and observed by us.
- All girls in grade 7 had to wear variations of the same thing to Bar Mitzvah parties.
- white belts
- ballet flats
OMigod is she-like-totally wearing Floods?
Sick.
what a Gaylord.
You found Out
by
phone
passed notes
FEAR 15
14
DEF 13
ABC 2
Parties always started the same way.
Girls in Almost matching clothes relentlessly checking out each other's bums
Ensuring (if applicable) that no one's PAD WAS SHOWING!!!
Try NOT to be obvious please!!
can you see it?
how about now?
what about if I go like this?
the tell-tale bulk!
unsightly bulges!
WRONG CHOICE
We were candid about
OUR FEARS
We became eachother's mirrors, always on the lookout for Problems or Leakages.
is there crud in my braces?
eyeliner leaking
lipstick smudge
the Dangers Were NUMEROUS

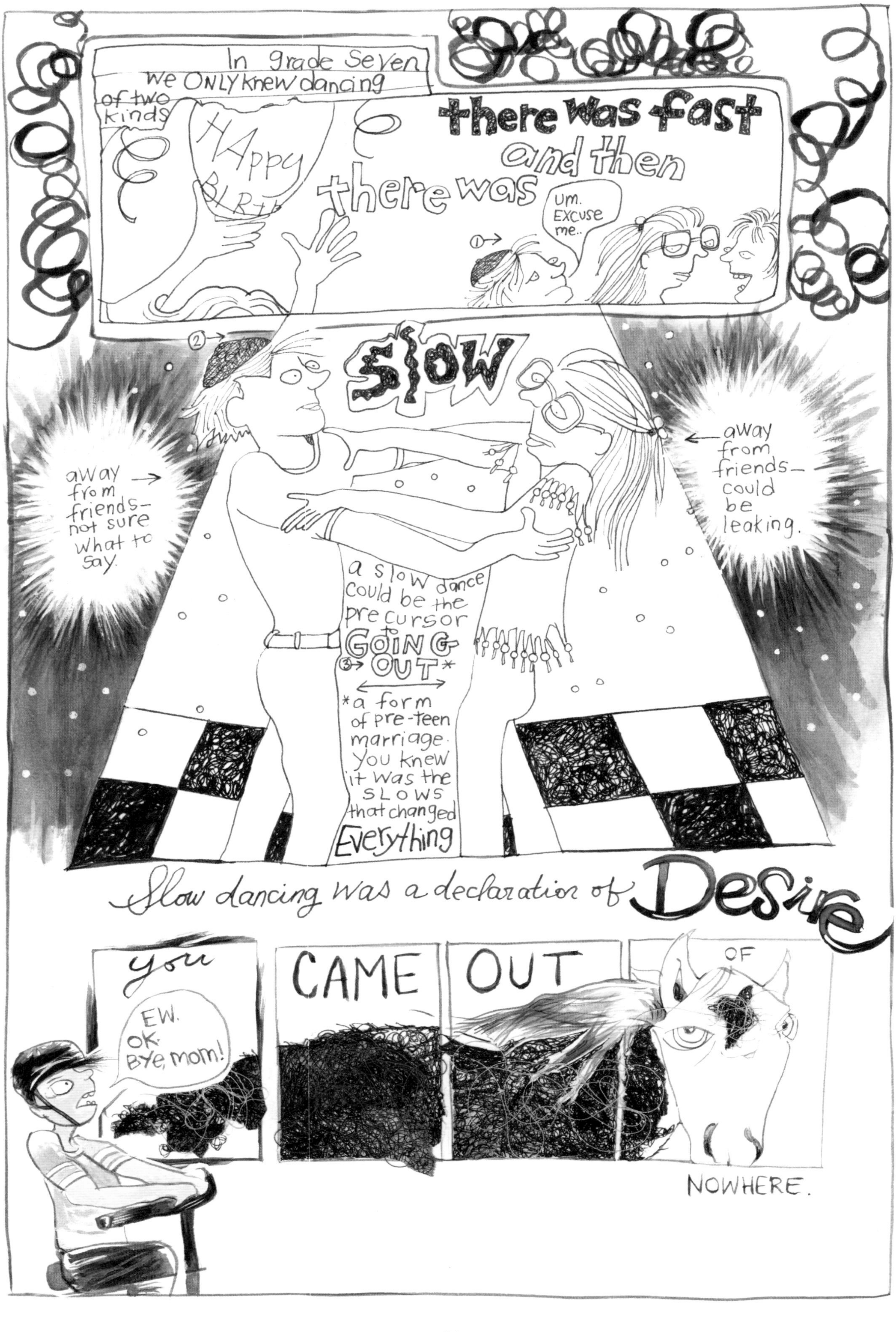
In grade seven we ONLY knew dancing of two kinds
HAppy BIRth
there was fast
and then there was
Um. EXCUSE me..
SLOW
away from friends- not sure what to say.
away from friends- could be leaking.
a slow dance could be the precursor to GOING OUT*
*a form of pre-teen marriage. You knew it was the SLOWS that changed EVERYTHING
Slow dancing was a declaration of Desire
you
EW. OK. BYE, mom!
CAME
OUT
OF
NOWHERE.

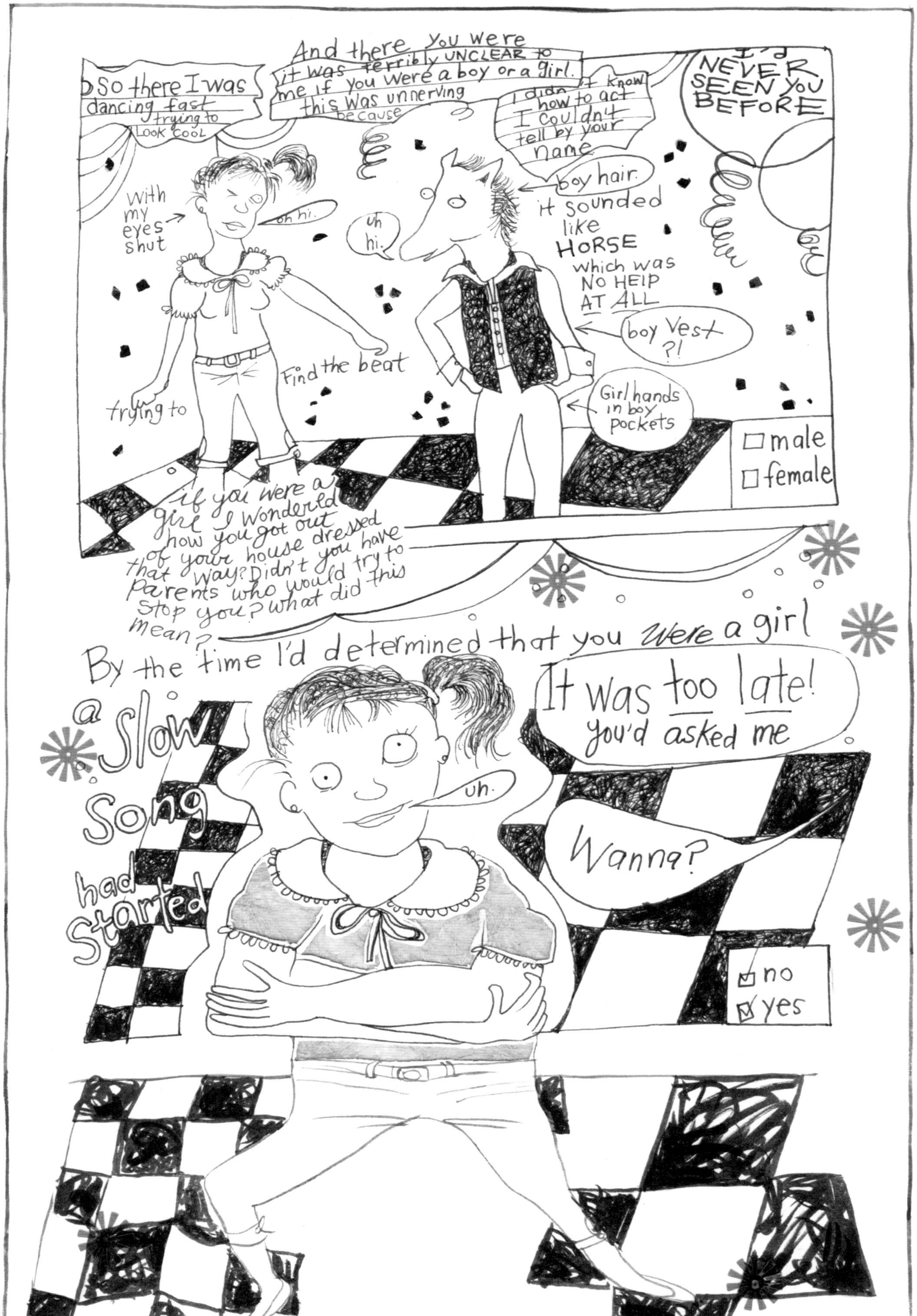
So there I was dancing fast trying to look cool
And there you were
It was terribly UNCLEAR to me if you were a boy or a girl. this was unnerving because
I didn't know how to act I couldn't tell by your name
I'd NEVER SEEN YOU BEFORE
with my eyes shut
oh hi.
uh hi.
boy hair.
it sounded like HORSE which was NO HELP AT ALL
boy Vest ?!
Find the beat
trying to
Girl hands in boy pockets
male
female
if you were a girl I wondered how you got out of your house dressed that way? Didn't you have parents who would try to stop you? what did this mean?
By the time I'd determined that you were a girl
It was too late! you'd asked me
a slow song had started
uh.
Wanna?
no
yes

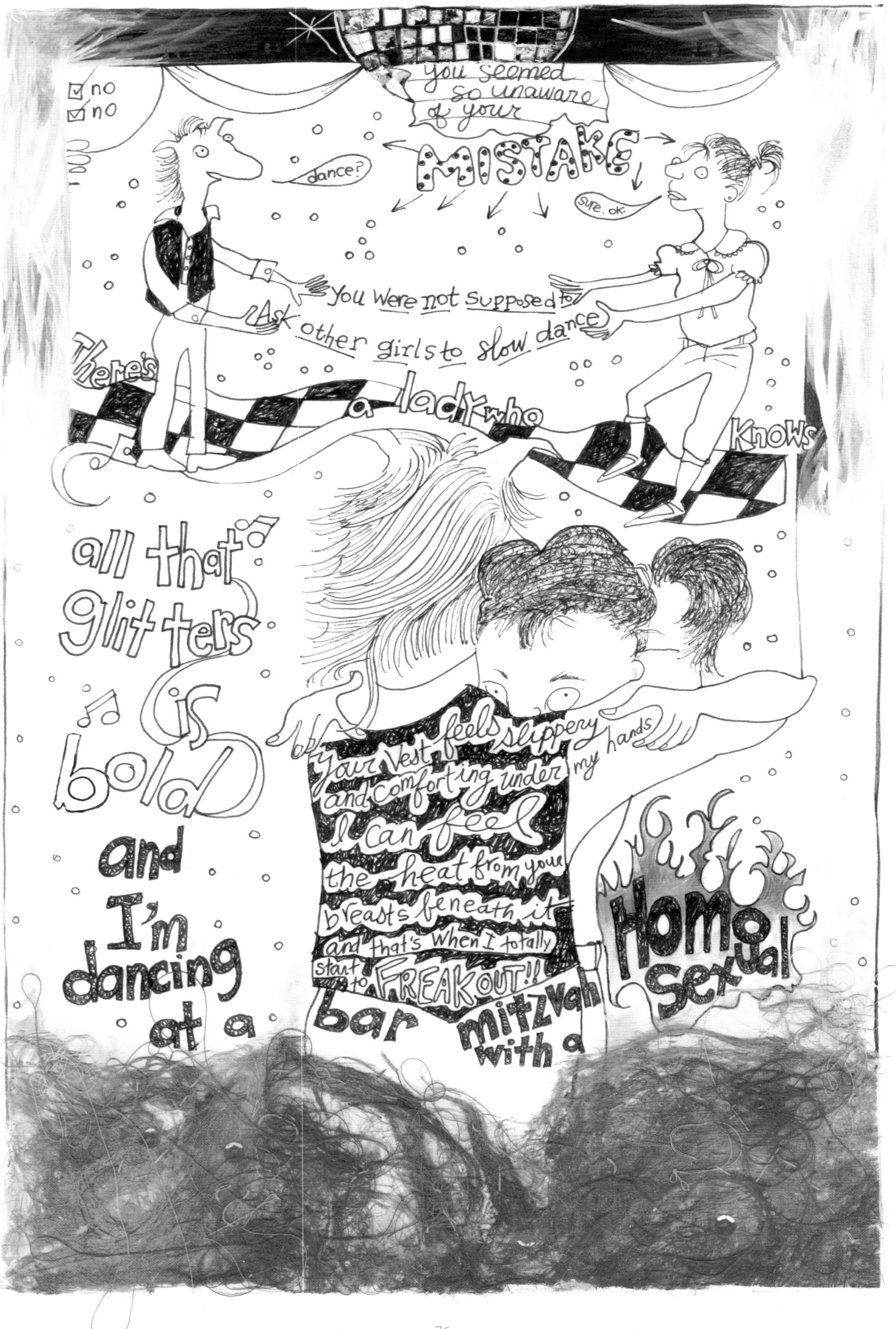

no
no
you seemed so unaware of your
MISTAKE
dance?
sure. ok.
you were not supposed to ask other girls to slow dance
There's a lady who knows
all that glitters is gold
and I'm dancing at a bar mitzvah with a
your vest feels slippery and comforting under my hands
I can feel the heat from your breasts beneath it and that's when I totally start to FREAK OUT!!
Homosexual

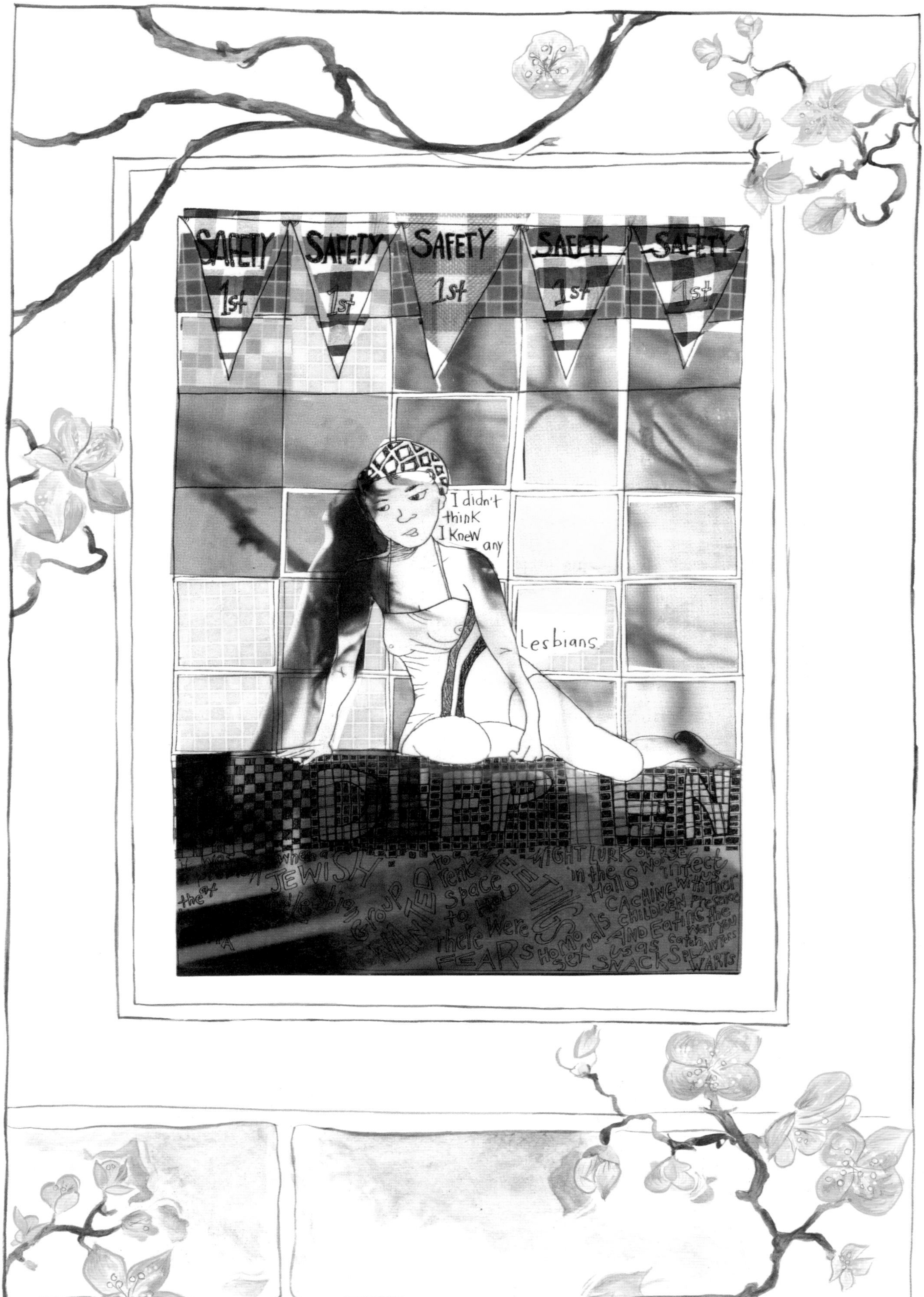
SAFETY 1st
SAFETY 1st
SAFETY 1st
SAFETY 1st
SAFETY 1st
I didn't think I knew any
Lesbians.

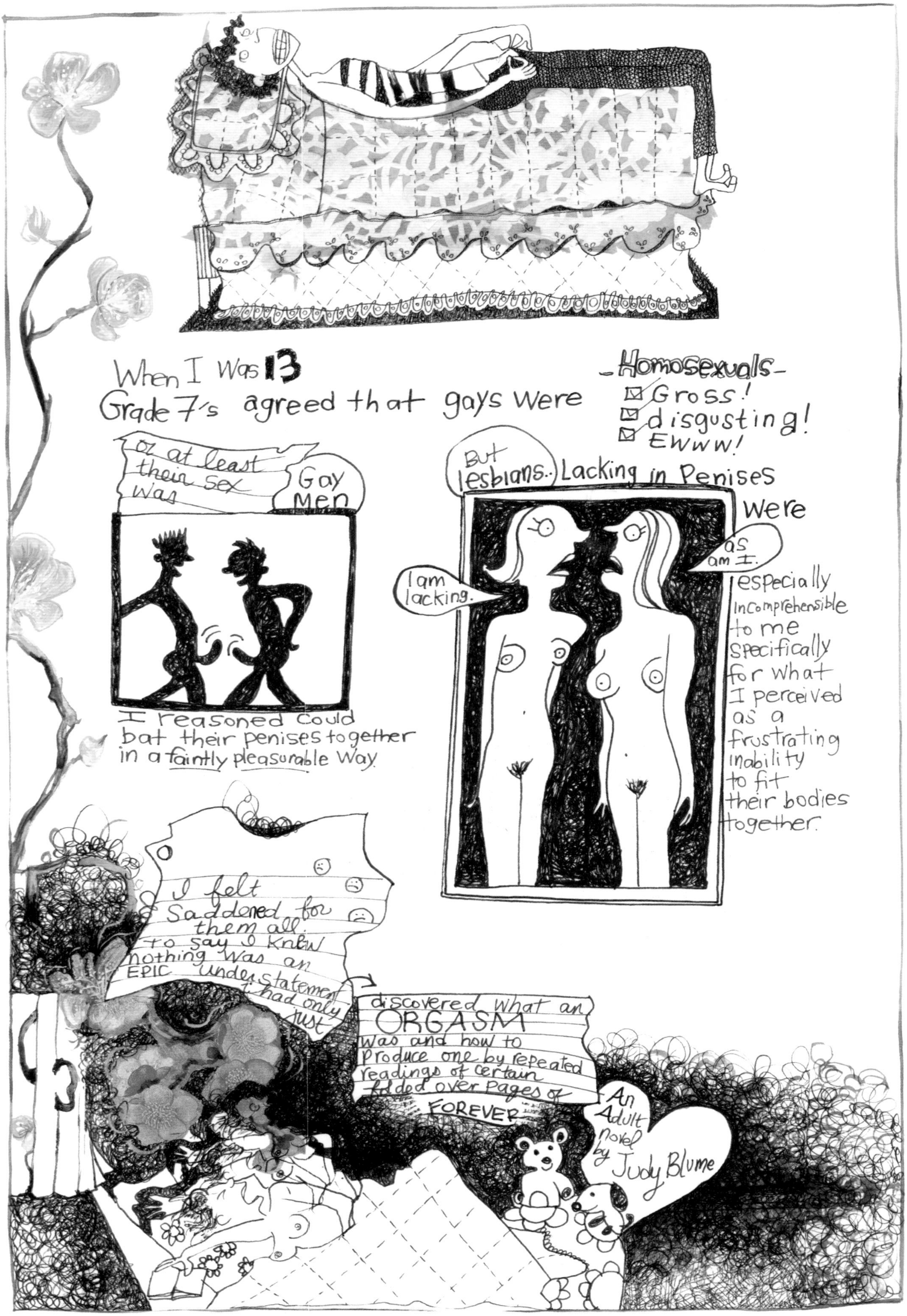
When I Was 13
Grade 7's agreed that gays were
-Homosexuals-
Gross!
disgusting!
Ewww!
or at least their sex was
Gay Men
I reasoned could bat their penises together in a faintly pleasurable way.
But lesbians.. Lacking in Penises
I am lacking.
as am I.
were
especially incomprehensible to me specifically for what I perceived as a frustrating inability to fit their bodies together.
I felt saddened for them all.
to say I knew nothing was an EPIC understatement
I had only just
discovered what an ORGASM was and how to produce one by repeated readings of certain folded over pages of FOREVER
An Adult novel by Judy Blume

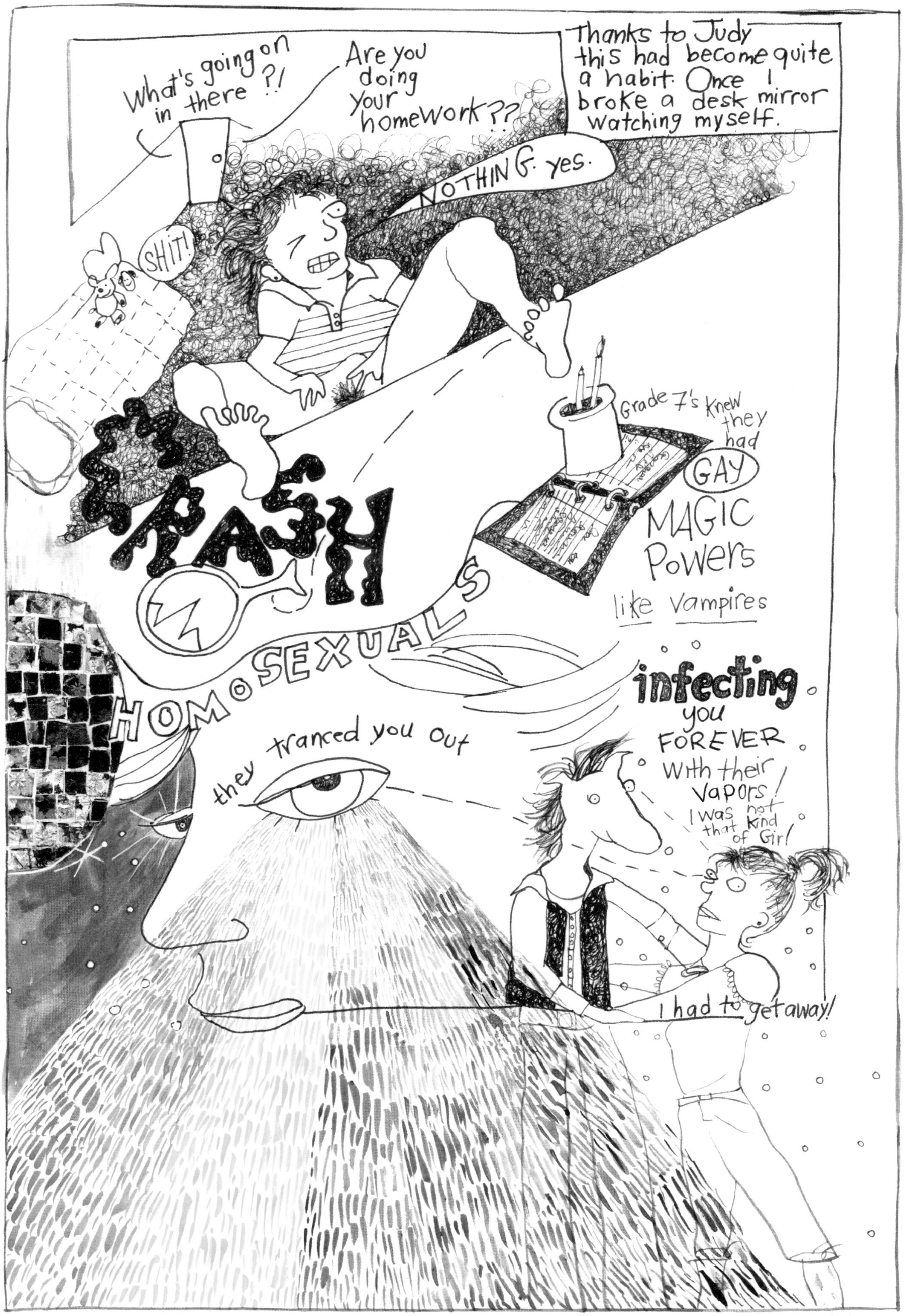

What's going on in there ?!
Are you doing your homework??
Thanks to Judy this had become quite a habit. Once I broke a desk mirror watching myself.
NOTHING. yes.
SHIT!
CRASH
Grade 7's knew they had
GAY
MAGIC Powers
like vampires
HOMOSEXUALS
infecting you FOREVER with their vapors!
they tranced you out
I was not that kind of Girl!
I had to get away!

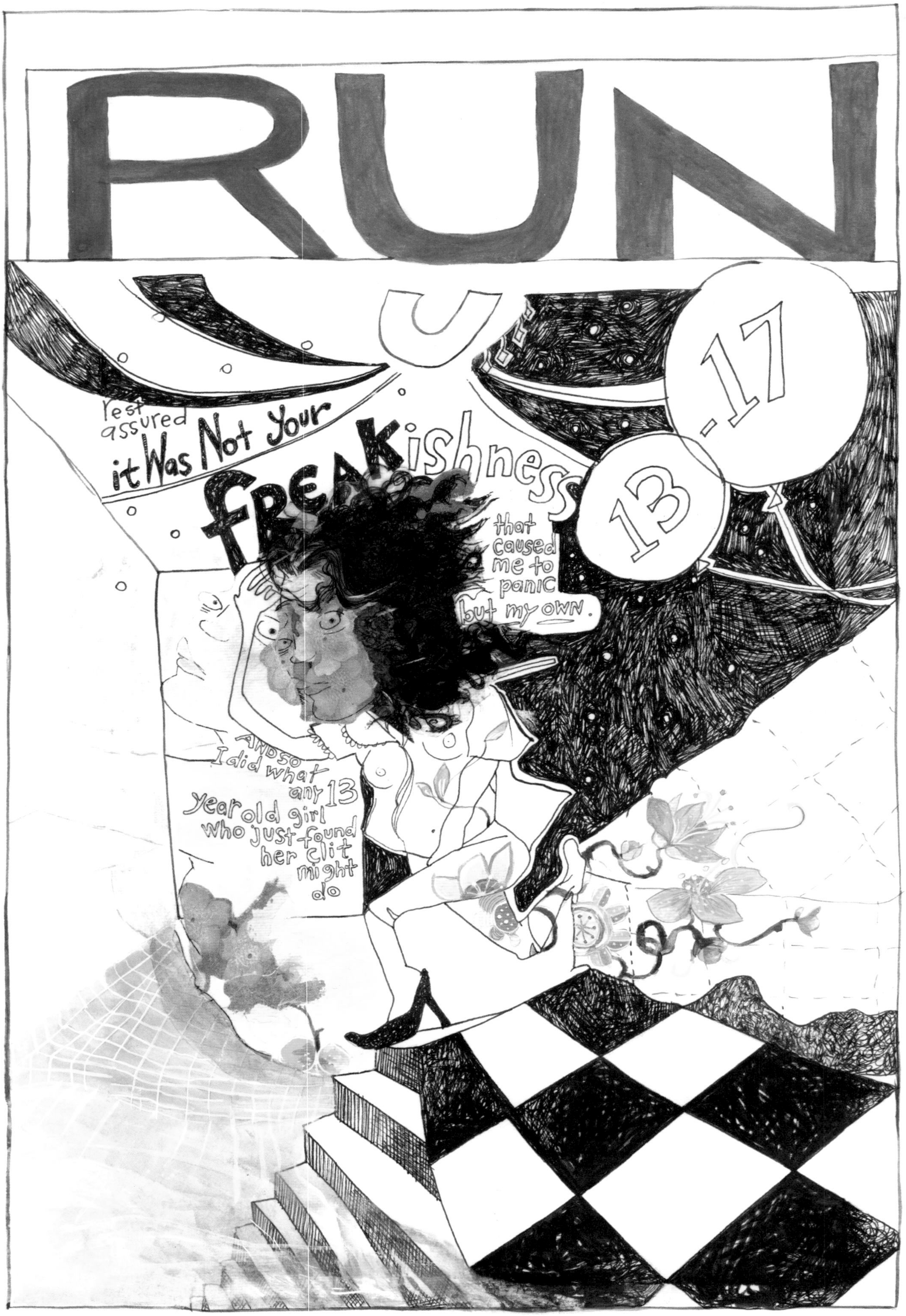
RUN
rest assured it Was Not your
fREAKishness
that caused me to panic but my OWN.
13
17
AND SO I did what any 13 year old girl who just found her clit might do

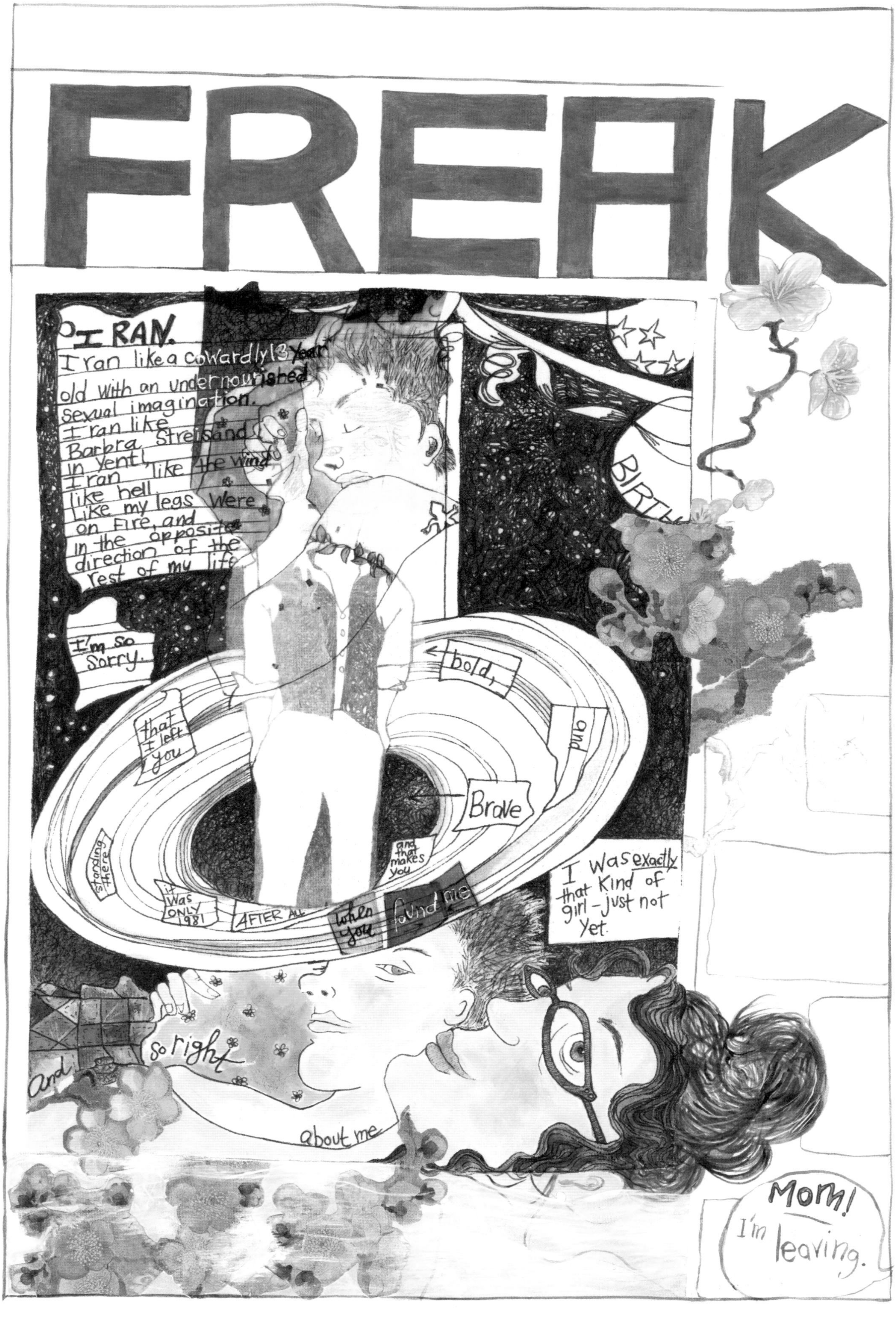

FREAK
I RAN.
I ran like a cowardly 13 year old with an undernourished sexual imagination.
I ran like Barbra Streisand in Yentl, like the wind
I ran like hell.
Like my legs were on Fire, and in the opposite direction of the rest of my life
I'm so sorry.
that I left you
bold,
and
Brave
standing there
it was only 1981
AFTER ALL
and that makes you
when you
found me
I was exactly that kind of girl - just not yet.
And
so right
about me
Mom! I'm leaving.

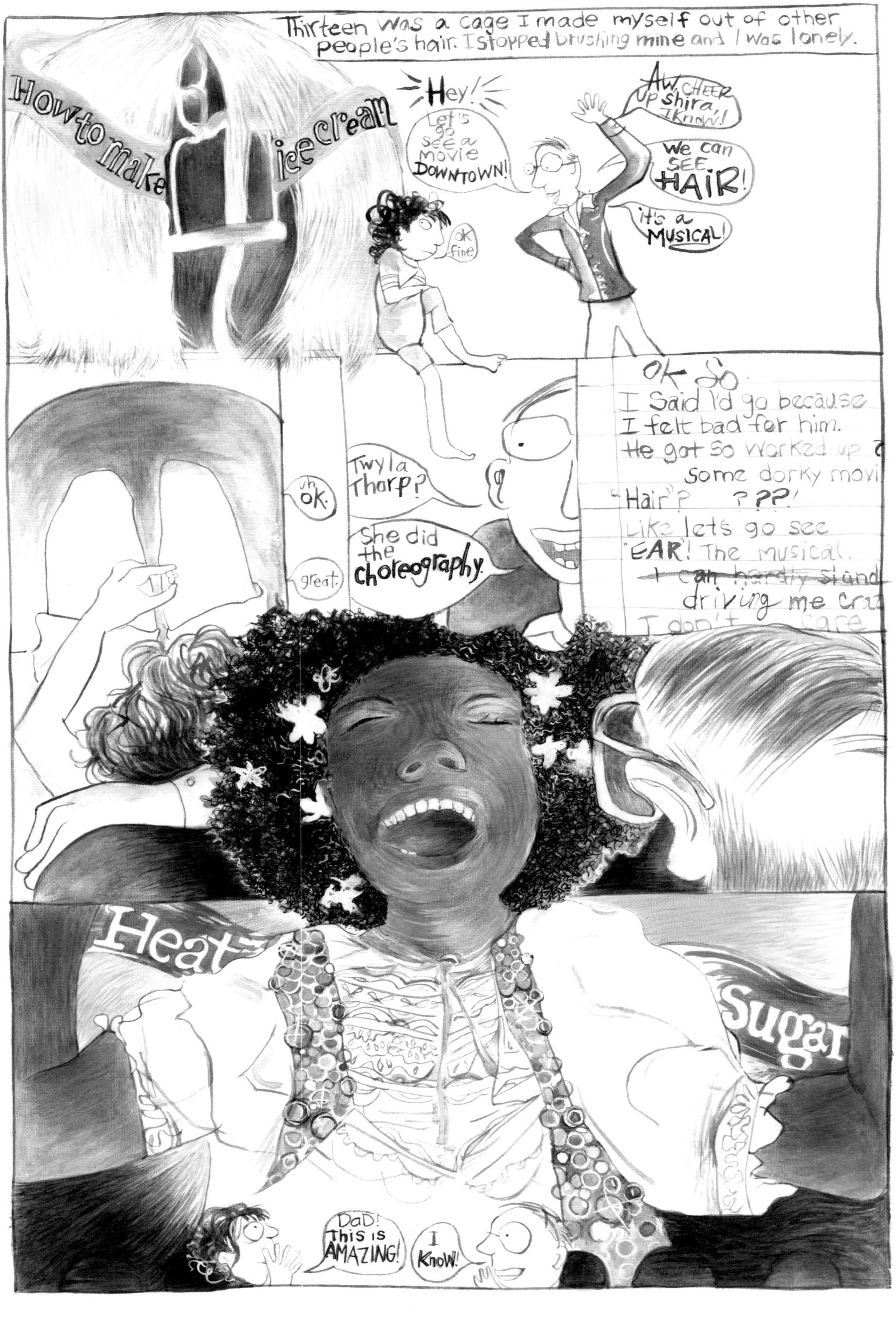

Thirteen was a cage I made myself out of other people's hair. I stopped brushing mine and I was lonely.
How to make ice cream
Hey! Let's go see a movie DOWNTOWN!
ok fine
Aw, CHEER UP Shira, I know!
We can SEE HAIR!
it's a MUSICAL!
Twyla Tharp?
uh ok.
She did the choreography.
great.
ok So
I Said I'd go because
I felt bad for him.
He got So worked up
Some dorky movi
"Hair"? ???!
Like let's go see
"EAR"! The musical.
I can hardly stand
driving me cra
I don't care
Heat
Sugar
DaD! This is AMAZING!
I KNOW!

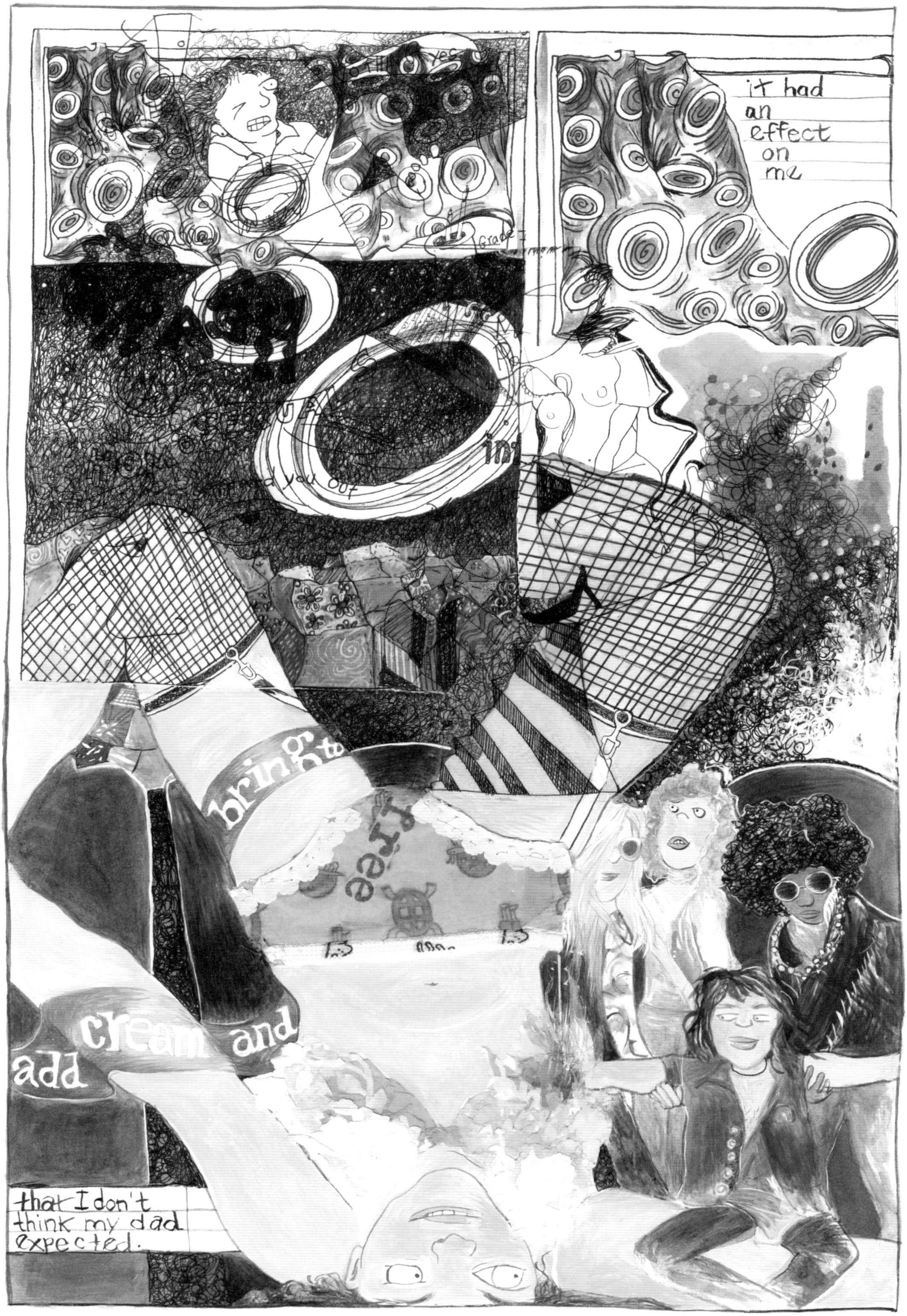
it had an effect on me
bring
add cream and
that I don't think my dad expected.

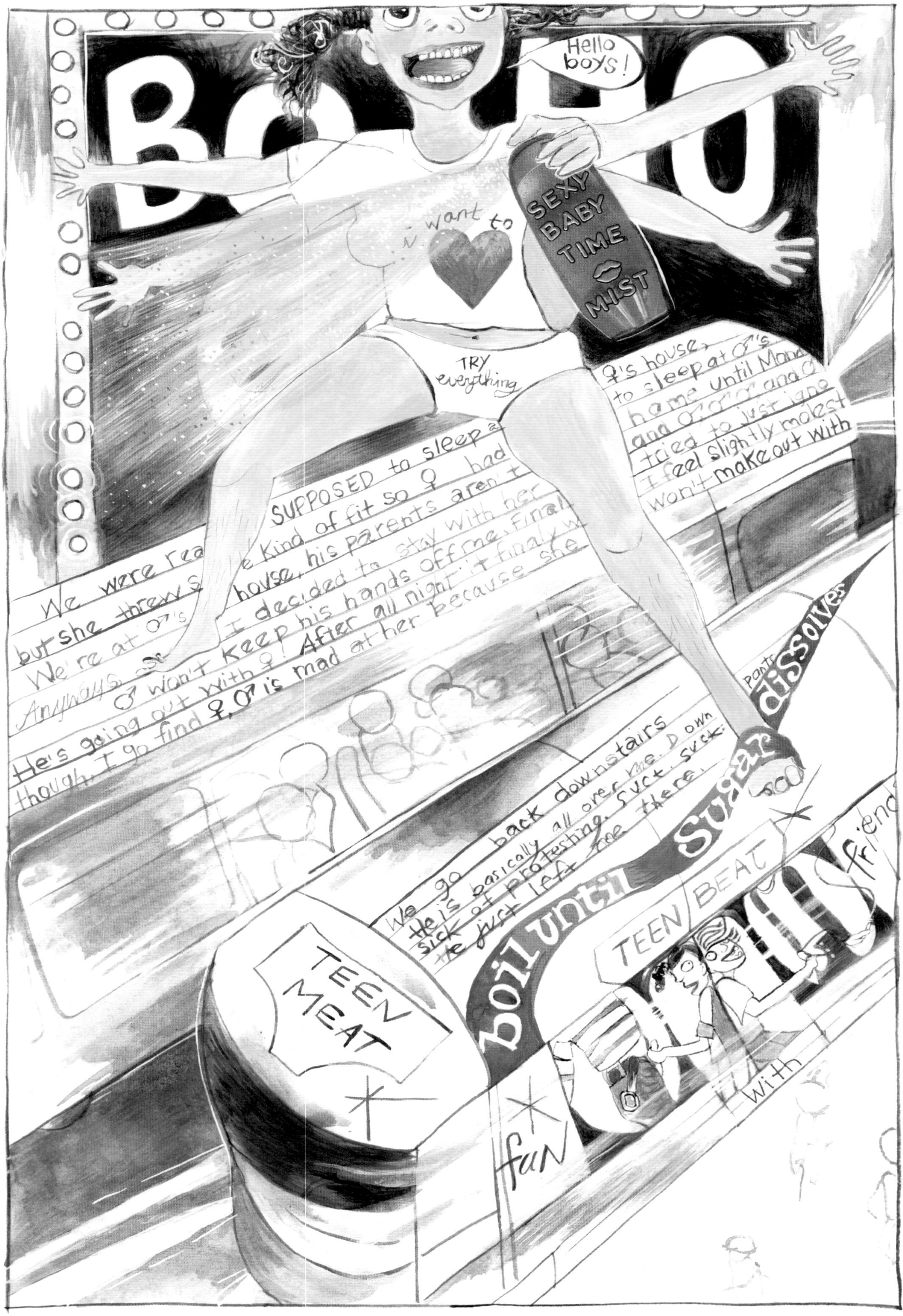
Hello boys!
I want to ♥ to
SEXY BABY TIME MIST
TRY everything
♀'s house,
to sleep at ♂'s
home until Mond
and ♂♀♂ and ♂
tried to just igno
I feel slightly molest
won't make out with
SUPPOSED to sleep a
kind of fit so ♀ had
his parents aren't
to stay with her
off me, final
it finaly w
We were rea
but she threw s
house,
We're at ♂'s
I decided
Anyways,
♂ won't keep his hands
He's going out with ♀! After all night
though. I go find ♀, ♂ is mad at her because she
pants dissolves
Sugar
We go back downstairs
He is basically all over me. Down
sick of protesting. Suck. Suck.
he just left me there.
boil until
TEEN BEAT
TEEN BEAT
friends
TEEN MEAT
fun
with

On My First Fingering.

By Shira Spector

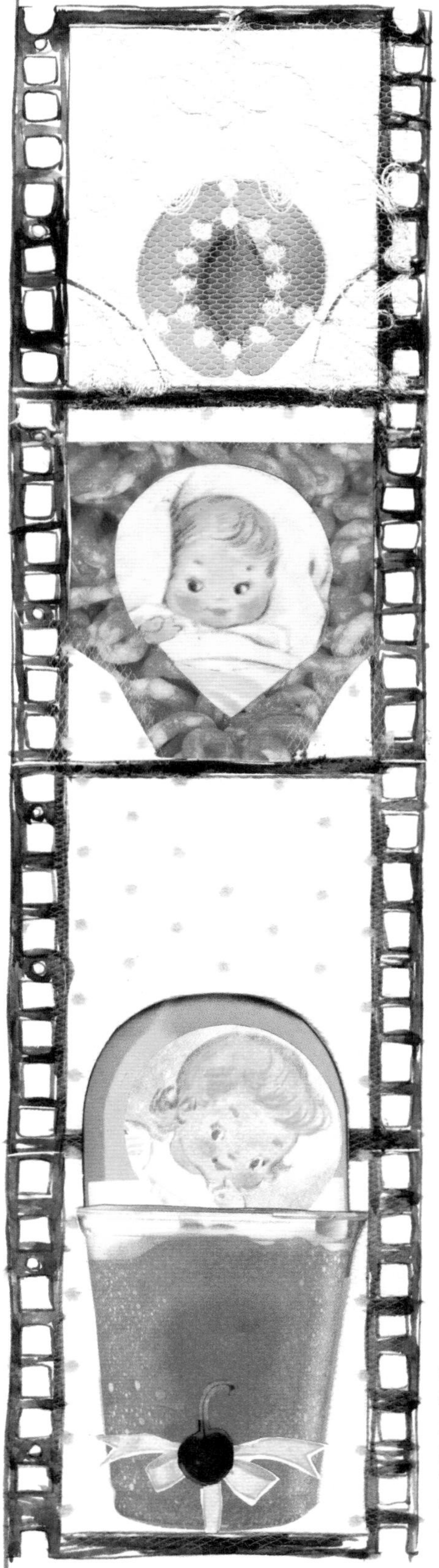

Actually, my first time being groped was when I was four years old, in nursery school. This kid kept crawling his hands into the V of my pants and crashing his digits into me like I was a piano. He didn't know how to play. I asked my mom what to do, and she talked to the teacher *and* the kid about it. Way to go, mom! But the next day he just did it again. Nothing changed! It made me cry. I don't remember what happened after that. My pediatrician also used his fingers to separate the lips of my vulva at the end of every check up, like he was looking to see if I was hiding something. When he was satisfied, they would snap shut.
I sort of looked forward to that part because it felt interesting, plus I always passed the test. Phew! I could never put my finger on the reason for this procedure, but he always did it with my mother right there so I knew it must be standard.

I don't really consider that my first time being groped. But it's an uncomfortable story. Naturally, I'd dreamed a lot about my first *real* GROPING. I wanted to be ready for that moment. Sweet as barfed up diet soda, and also romantic! Wearing a pretty bra not shoved up around my neck, underwear too, but not yanked down around my ankles. It felt important to smell just right, compliant and uncomplicated, like a freshly ironed bed sheet.

I wanted my first grope to be perfect. Either outdoors, or on a movie set, with my best friend directing. Not in some kid's basement with his parents gone until Monday, predatory teenage boys lurking in every room, waiting like velociraptors. I didn't want to waste my first groping on some guy I never even fooled around with; I wanted it to be meaningful. But when you're a teenage girl, getting molested in someone else's basement is just practicing. *Mazel tov!*
Being the first guy to actually sexually assault me was special. It was a very long time ago. I have never told anyone the details. I just kept them stuffed up in myself like a tampon I forgot about for thirty-five years.

It was just me and him down there. We were not on a date. I guess I'm a bit old fashioned, I thought there would be some talking at least, he would plead for a hand job or just push my head down to his crotch. I enjoy starting out slow. I slip right into a semi coma. I like cuddling! It felt nice at that moment and I almost fell asleep, just like how hypothermia sets in. After awhile, his digits had another idea. That's how my clothes came off, I think. I couldn't catch up because I was so busy freezing solid. I was used to saying "no" and being *convinced,* but he never even asked me. I was so easy to break into. His hands lost all their kindness. He stabbed into the core of me with his butter knife fingers in absolute silence.

Sure, I'm an artist and a writer and you probably think now that I'm fifty years old, a grown up woman, a mom of a teenager even, that I'd be able to tell this story easily, but I can't. I do like to smell good. I'm just a normal girl.

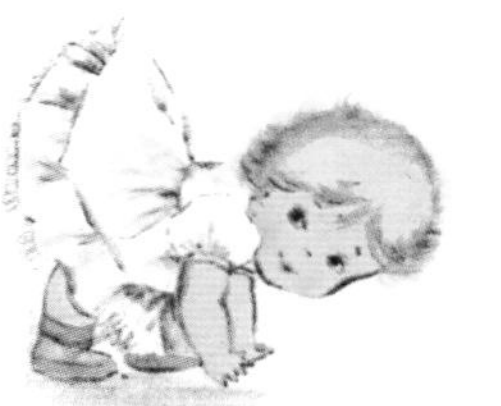

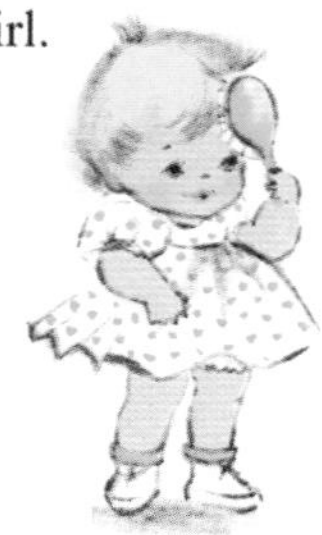

I do *really* like to smell good. I do not like to smell like panic
and my cunt in popsicle shards on the claw
of some teenage dinosaur
who was never invited to the party
that hadn't even started in my pants.
Boys like the way babies smell. Brand new
and vulnerable. Clean.
Yummy. So delicious they want to ruin
them.

That's why I love *Sexy Baby Time Perfume.* It's pink
and soft and normal. Like my vagina that is sore
and mangled in a place that never
felt like anything much at all.
It's for that first awful assault. It's for those moments.
When you realize you are not even considered a person.
When you just know.
You are a slut, and it is all your fault for letting it get this far.

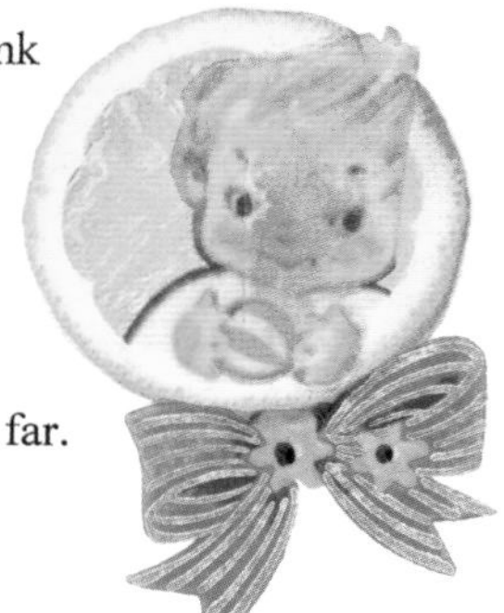

Sexy Baby Times Body Mist.
The perfume for the moments of just knowing you're fucked

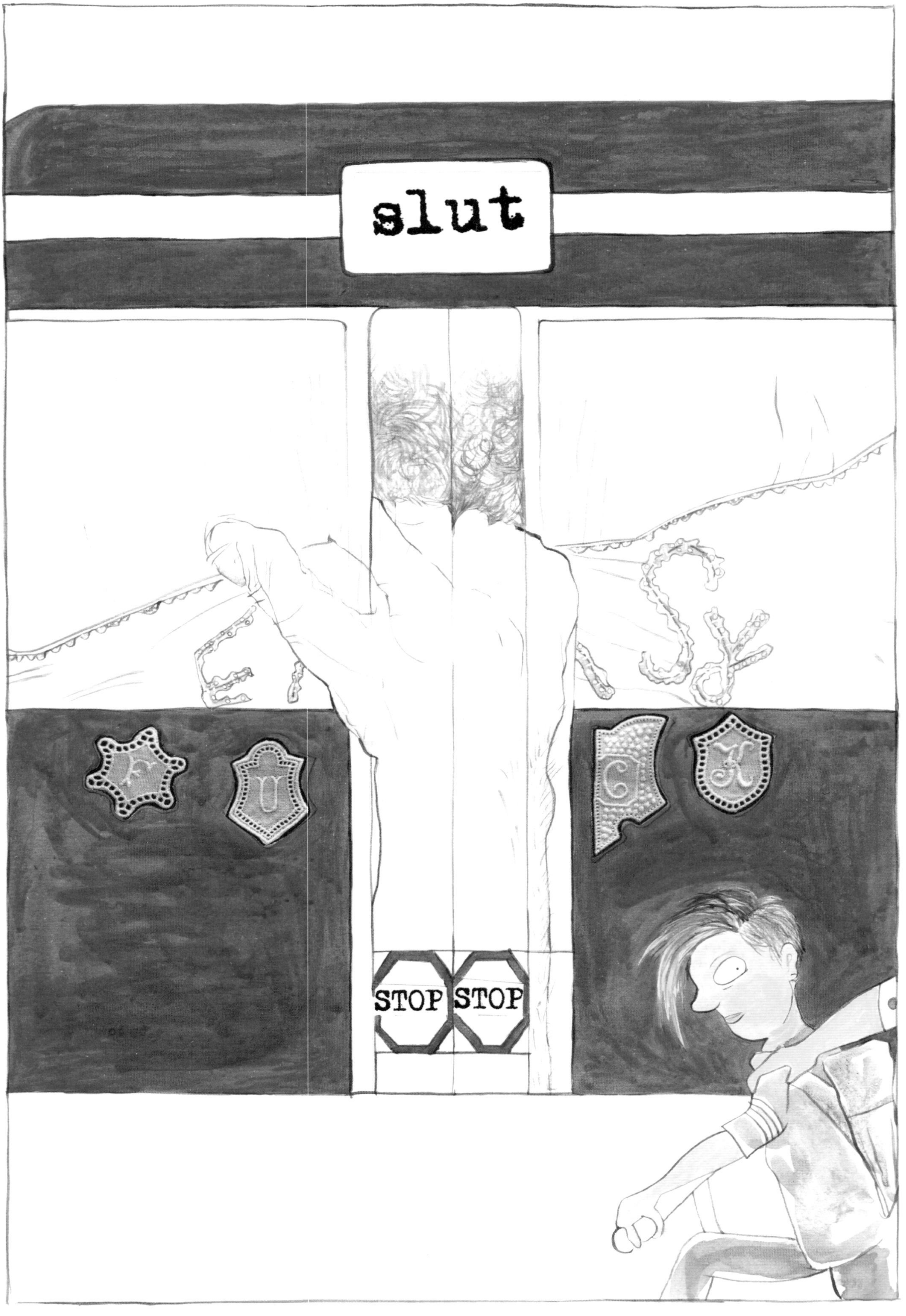
slut
F U C K
STOP STOP

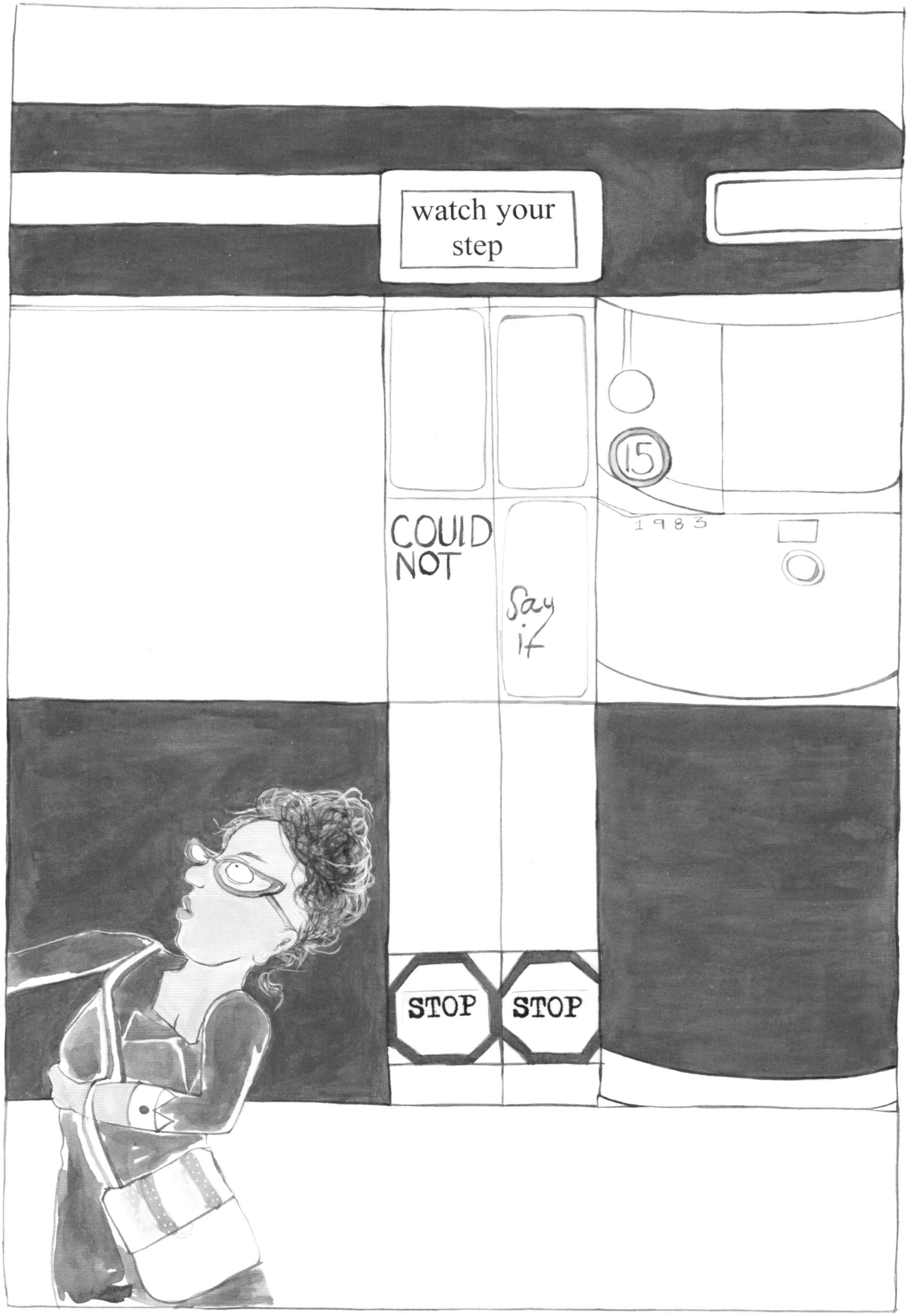
watch your step
15
COULD NOT
Say it
1983
STOP
STOP

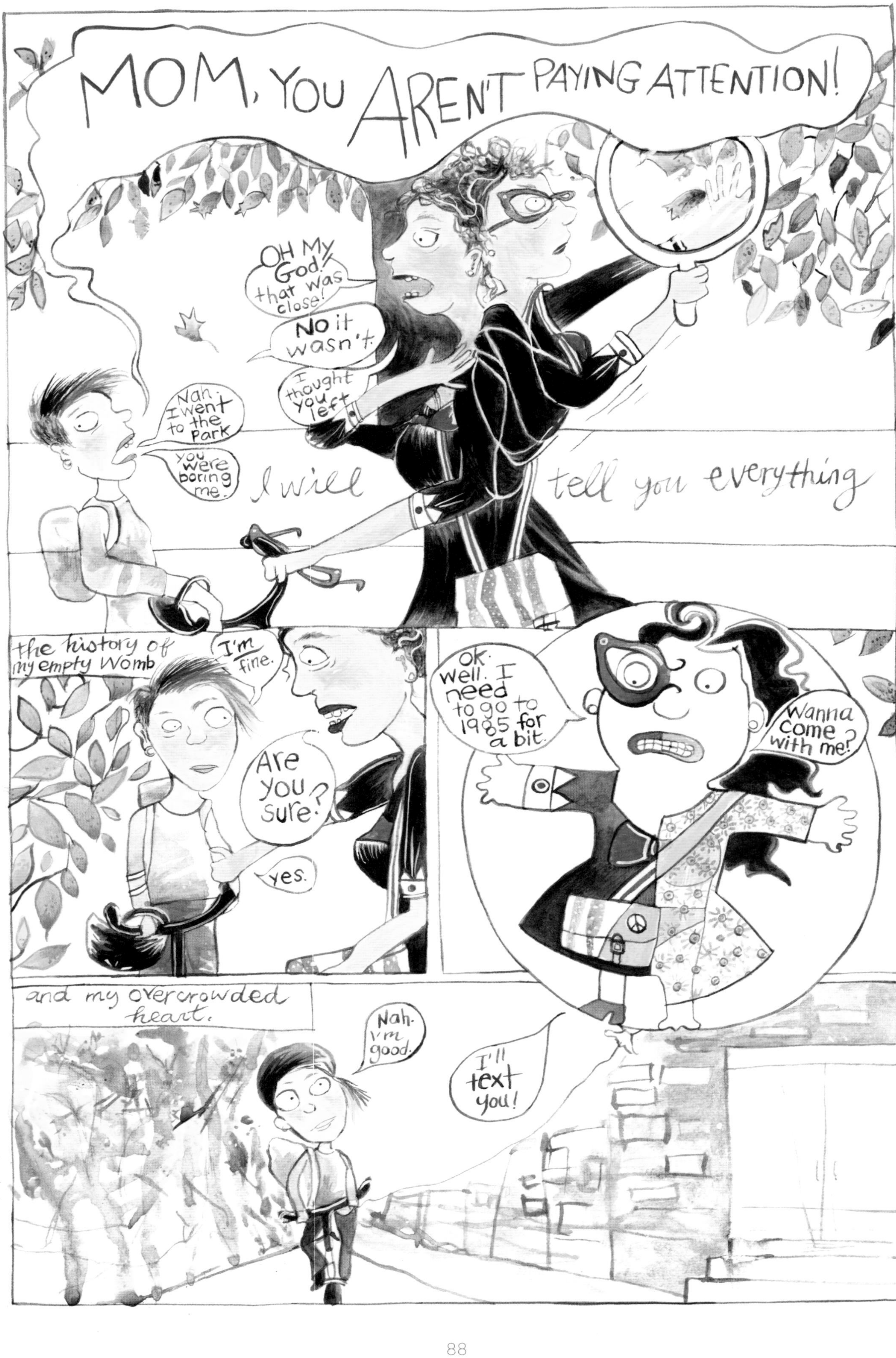
MOM, YOU AREN'T PAYING ATTENTION!
OH My God! that was close!
No it wasn't.
I thought you left
Nah. I went to the park
you were boring me.
I will tell you everything
the history of my empty Womb
I'm fine.
Are you sure?
yes.
Ok. Well. I need to go to 1985 for a bit.
Wanna come with me?
and my overcrowded heart.
Nah. I'm good.
I'll text you!

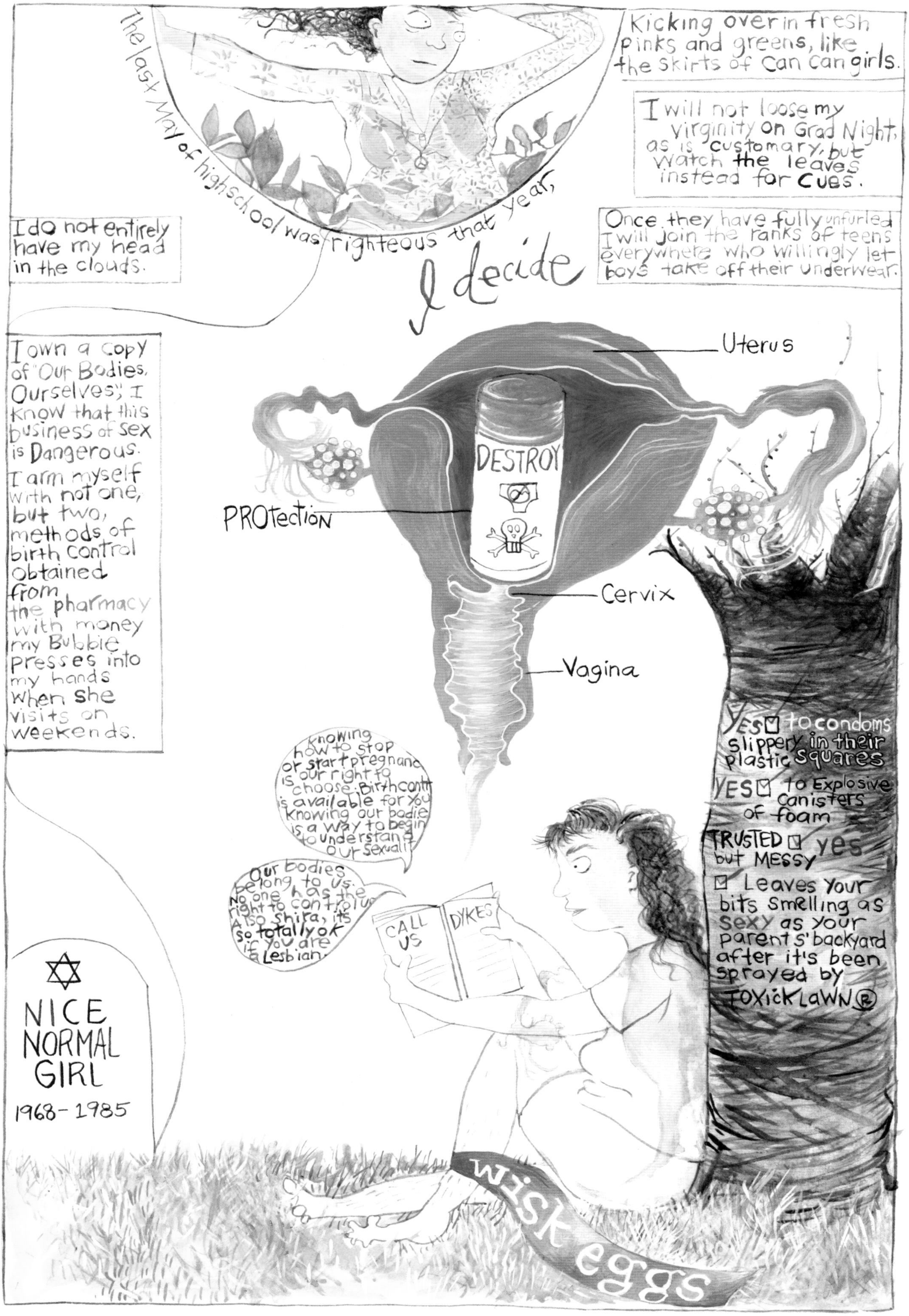

the last May of highschool was righteous that year,
I do not entirely have my head in the clouds.
Kicking over in fresh pinks and greens, like the skirts of can can girls.
I will not loose my virginity on Grad Night, as is customary, but watch the leaves instead for cues.
Once they have fully unfurled I will join the ranks of teens everywhere who willingly let boys take off their underwear.
I decide
I own a copy of "Our Bodies, Ourselves," I know that this business of sex is Dangerous. I arm myself with not one, but two, methods of birth control obtained from the pharmacy with money my Bubbie presses into my hands when she visits on weekends.
Uterus
DESTROY
PROtection
Cervix
Vagina
Knowing how to stop or start pregnanc is our right to choose. Birthcontr is available for you Knowing our bodie is a way to begin to understand our sexuali
Our bodies belong to us. No one has the right to control us. Also Shira, it's so totally ok if you are a Lesbian.
CALL US
DYKES
YES ☑ to condoms slippery in their plastic squares
YES ☑ to Explosive canisters of foam
TRUSTED ☑ yes but MESSY
☑ Leaves your bits smelling as sexy as your parents' backyard after it's been sprayed by TOXICKLAWN®
NICE NORMAL GIRL
1968-1985
wisk eggs

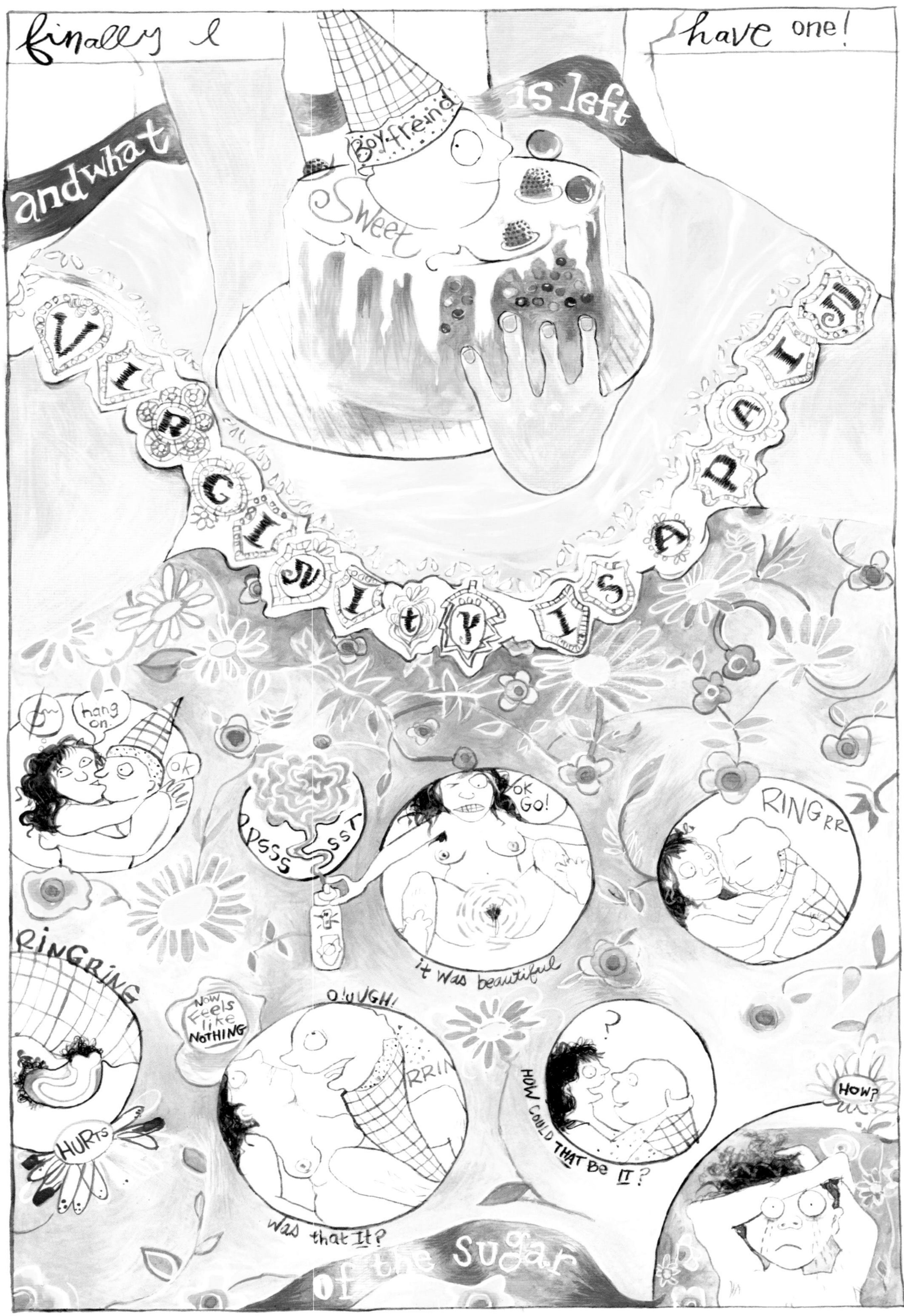

finally I
have one!
and what
is left
Boyfreind
Sweet
VIRGINITY IS A PAIN
hang on.
ok
PSSSSST
OK GO!
it was beautiful
RINGRR
RINGRING
Now Feels like NOTHING
O!UUGH!
RRIN
?
HOW COULD THAT Be IT?
HOW?
HURTS
was that IT?
of the sugar

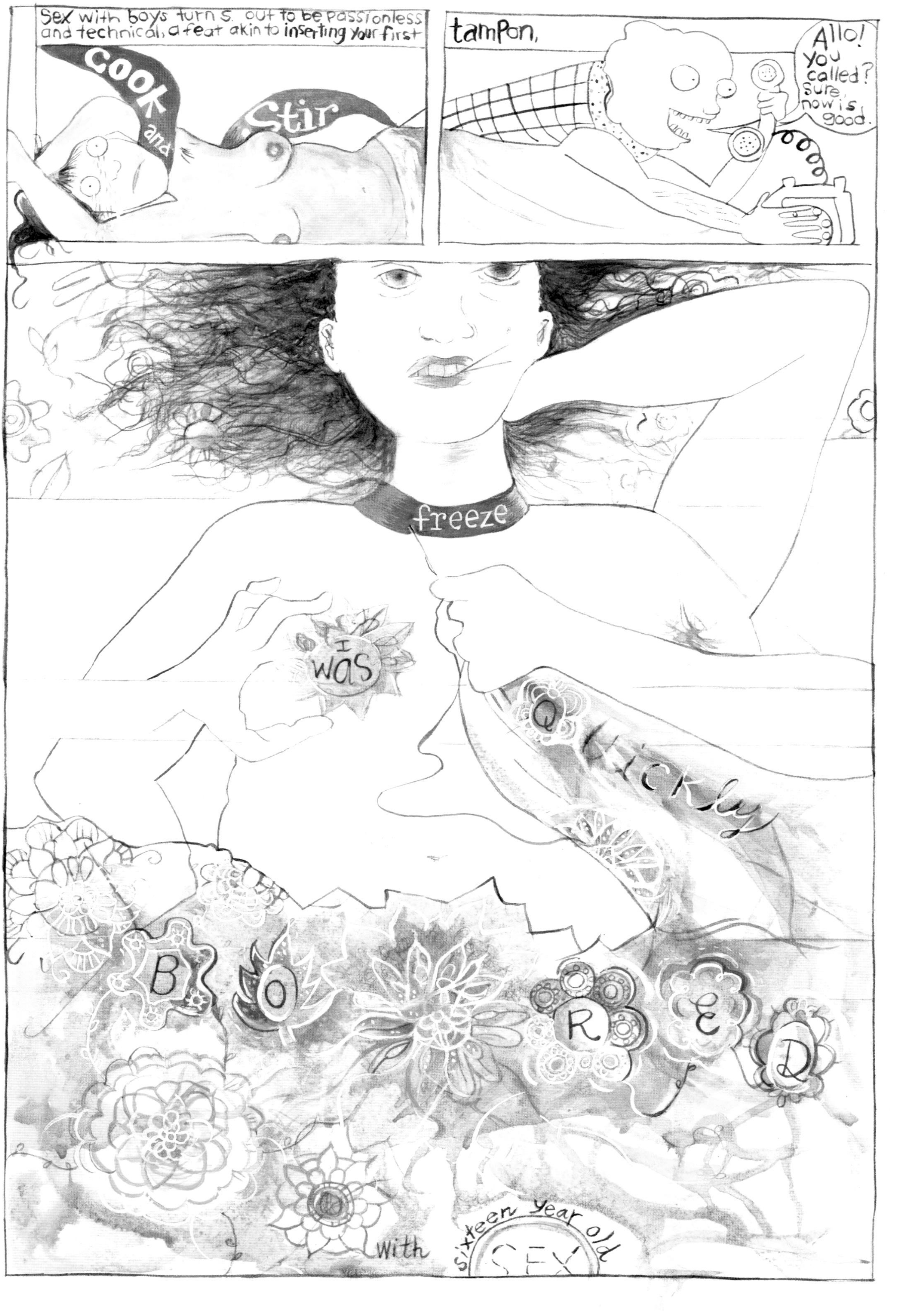
Sex with boys turns out to be passionless and technical, a feat akin to inserting your first
cook and stir
tampon,
Allo! you called? sure, now is good.
freeze
I was
quickly
BORED
with sixteen year old SEX

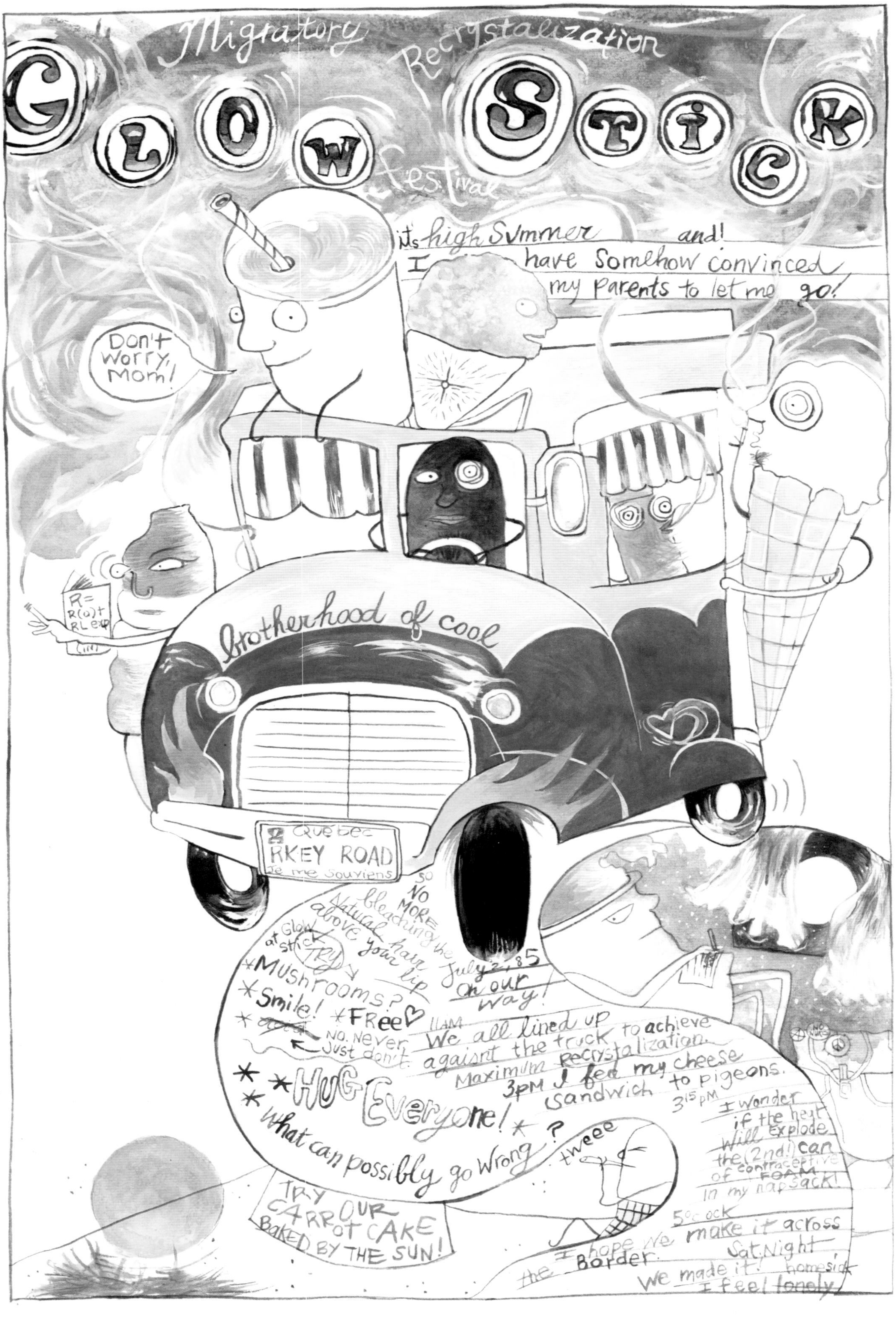
Migratory Recrystalization
GLOW STICK festival
it's high Summer and! I have somehow convinced my parents to let me go!
Don't worry, Mom!
R= R(a)+ RL exp
brotherhood of cool
Québec
RKEY ROAD
Je me souviens
so No MORE bleaching the Natural hair above your lip
at Glow stick TRY
*Mushrooms?
*Smile!
*Free♡
No. Never. Just don't.
**HUG Everyone!
*What can possibly go Wrong?
July 2, 85 on our way!
11AM We all lined up against the truck to achieve Maximum recrystalization.
3PM I fed my cheese sandwich to pigeons.
3:15 PM I wonder if the heat will explode the (2nd!) can of contraceptive FOAM in my napsack!
tweee
TRY OUR CARROT CAKE BAKED BY THE SUN!
5 o'clock I hope we make it across the Border.
Sat. Night We made it! homesick I feel lonely

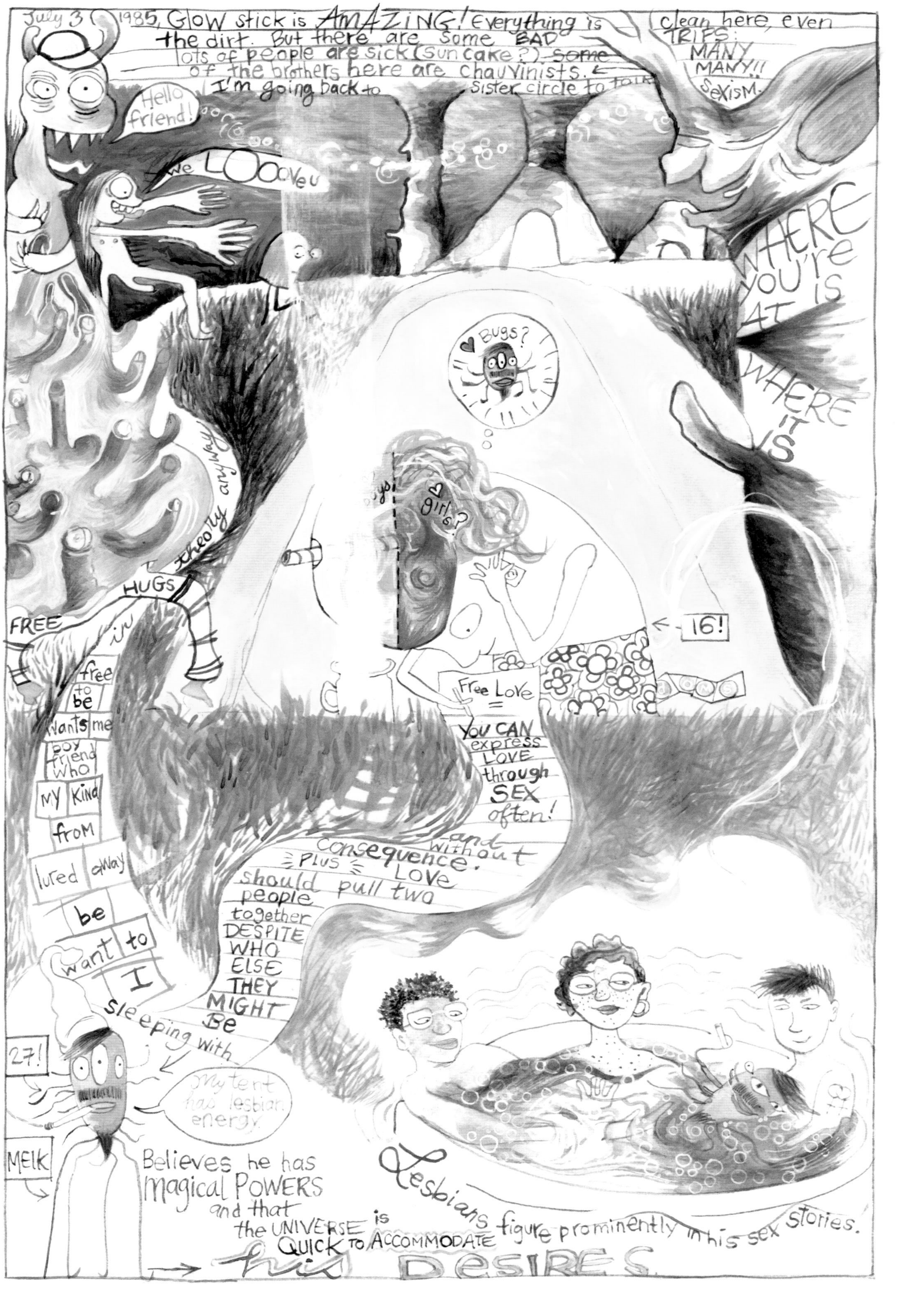
July 3 1985, Glow stick is AMAZING! Everything is clean here, even
the dirt. But there are some BAD
TRIPS:
MANY
MANY!!
lots of people are sick (sun cake?) Some
of the brothers here are chauvinists. ←
I'm going back to sister circle to talk
SeXisM.
Hello friend!
we LOOOOveu
WHERE YOU'RE AT IS
WHERE IT IS
Bugs?
boys
girls?
16!
FREE HUGS
in theory anyway
free
to
be
wants me
boy friend
who
my kind
from
lured away
be
want to
I
Free Love =
YOU CAN
express
LOVE
through
SEX
often!
and without
consequence.
PLUS LOVE
should pull two
people
together
DESPITE
WHO
ELSE
THEY
MIGHT
Be
sleeping with
27!
My tent has lesbian energy.
MELK
Believes he has
magical POWERS
and that
the UNIVERSE is
QUICK TO ACCOMMODATE
his
DESIRES.
Lesbians figure prominently in his sex stories.

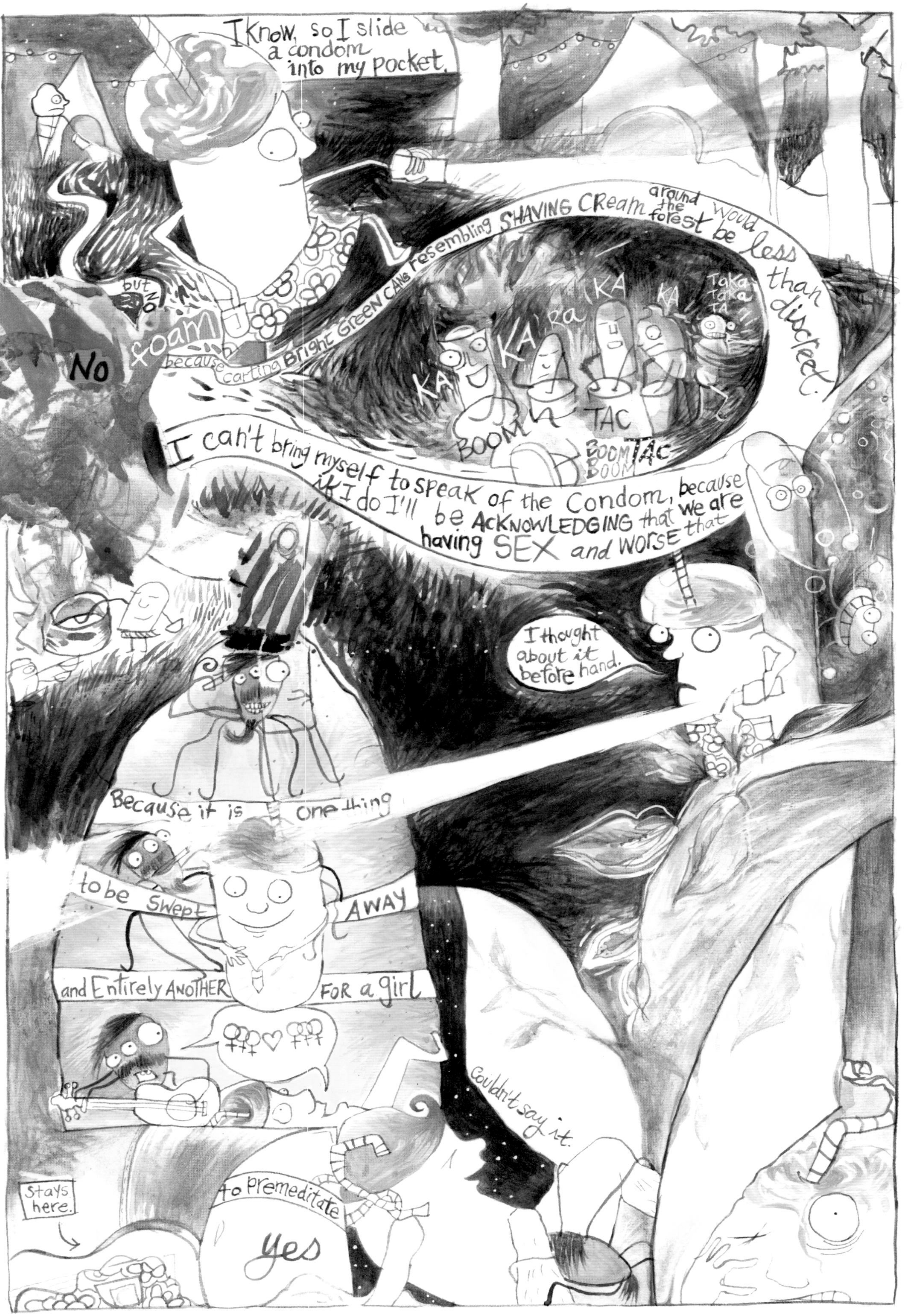
I know, so I slide a condom into my pocket.
No foam
but no
because carting BRIGHT GREEN CANS resembling SHAVING CReam around the forest would be less than discreet.
KA
KA
Ka
KA
KA
TAKA TAKA TA
BOOM
TAC
BOOM BOOM TAC
I can't bring myself to speak of the Condom, because if I do I'll be ACKNOWLEDGING that we are having SEX and WORSE that
I thought about it before hand.
Because it is one thing
to be Swept AWAY
and Entirely ANOTHER FOR a girl
Couldn't say it.
Stays here.
to premeditate
yes

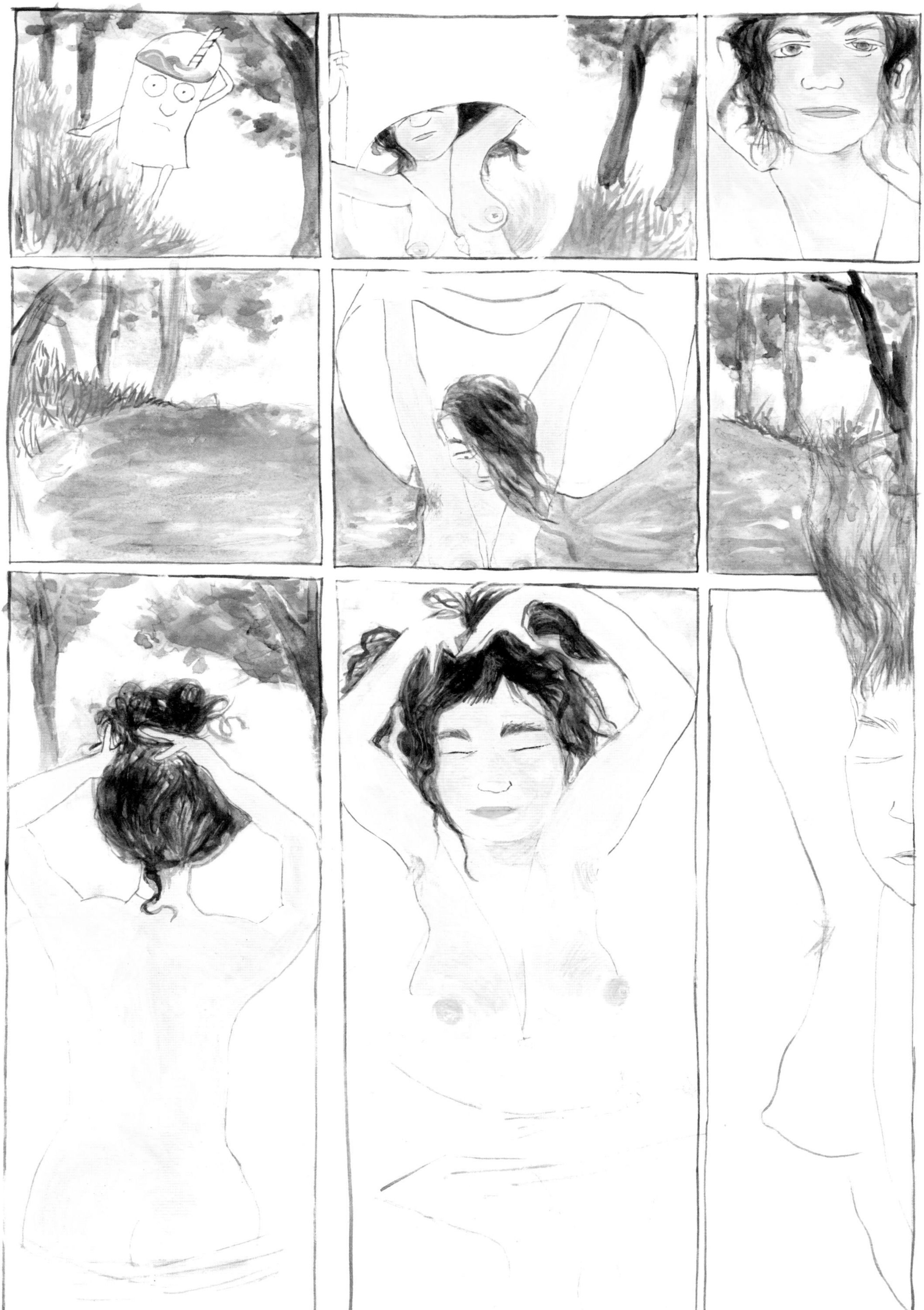

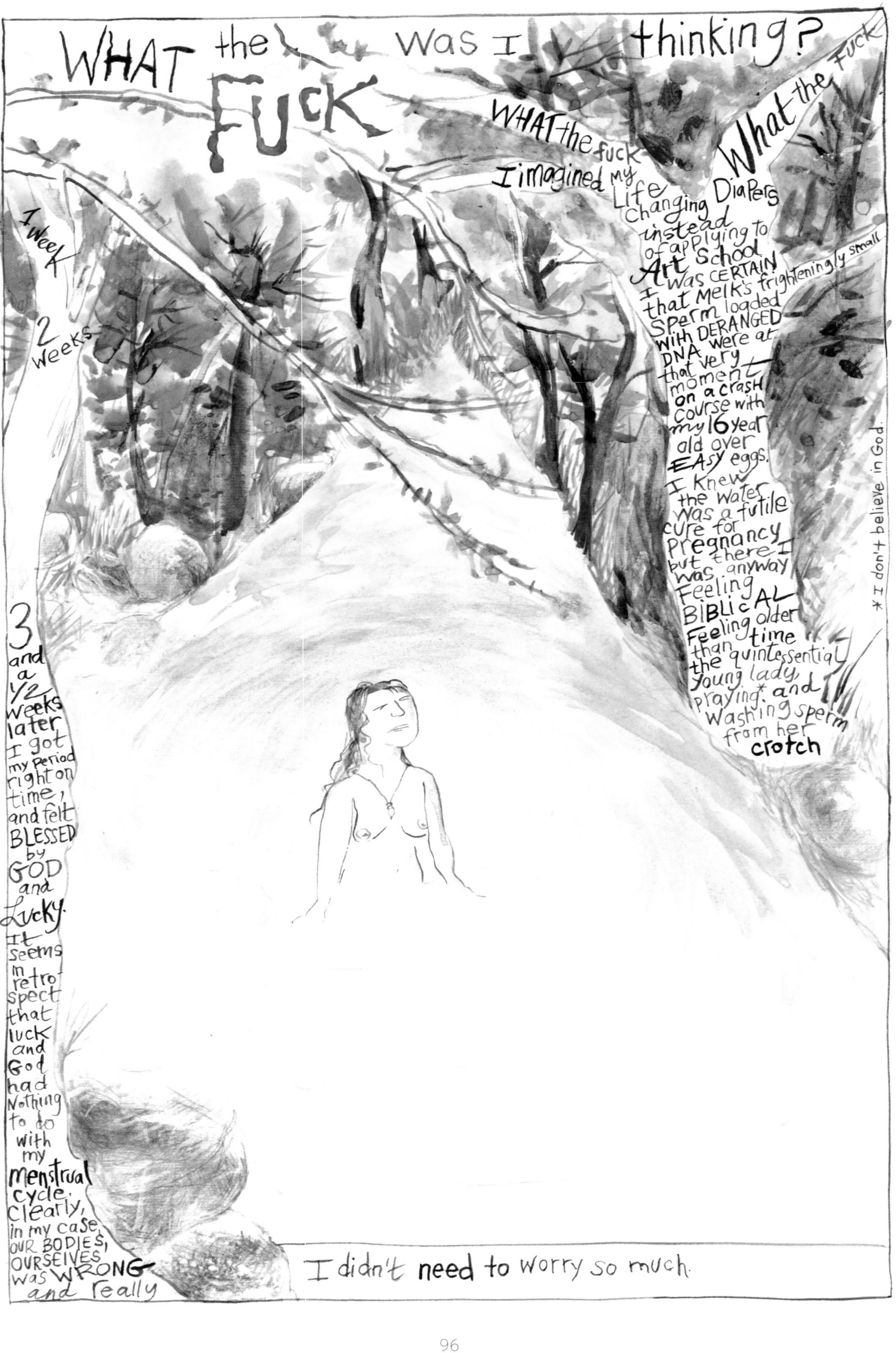
WHAT the FUCK was I thinking?
WHAT the fuck
What the FUCK
I imagined my Life Changing Diapers instead of applying to Art School
I was CERTAIN that Melk's frighteningly small sperm loaded with DERANGED DNA were at that very moment on a crash course with my 16 year old over EASY eggs.
I knew the water was a futile cure for Pregnancy but there I was anyway Feeling BIBLICAL Feeling older than time the quintessential young lady, praying* and washing sperm from her crotch
1 week
2 weeks
3 and a 1/2 weeks later I got my period right on time, and felt BLESSED by GOD and Lucky.
It seems in retrospect that luck and God had nothing to do with my menstrual cycle. clearly, in my case, OUR BODIES, OURSELVES was WRONG and really
I didn't need to worry so much.
* I don't believe in God.

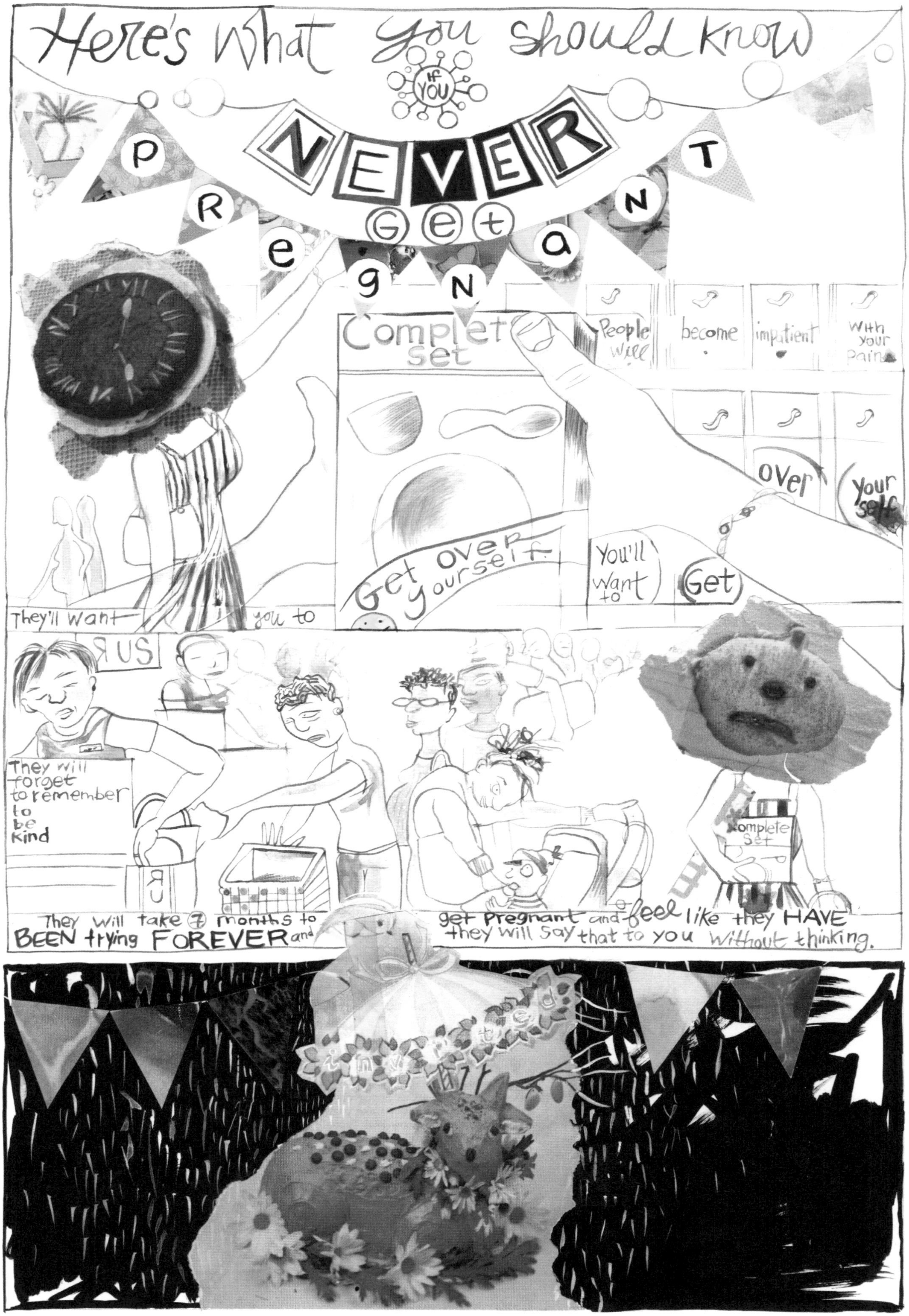

Here's What You should know
IF YOU
NEVER
Get
Pregnant
Complete set
People will
become
impatient
with your pain
over
yourself
Get over yourself
You'll want to
Get
They'll want
you to
RUS
They will forget to remember to be kind
Complete Set
They will take 7 months to get pregnant and feel like they HAVE BEEN trying FOREVER and they will say that to you without thinking.
invited

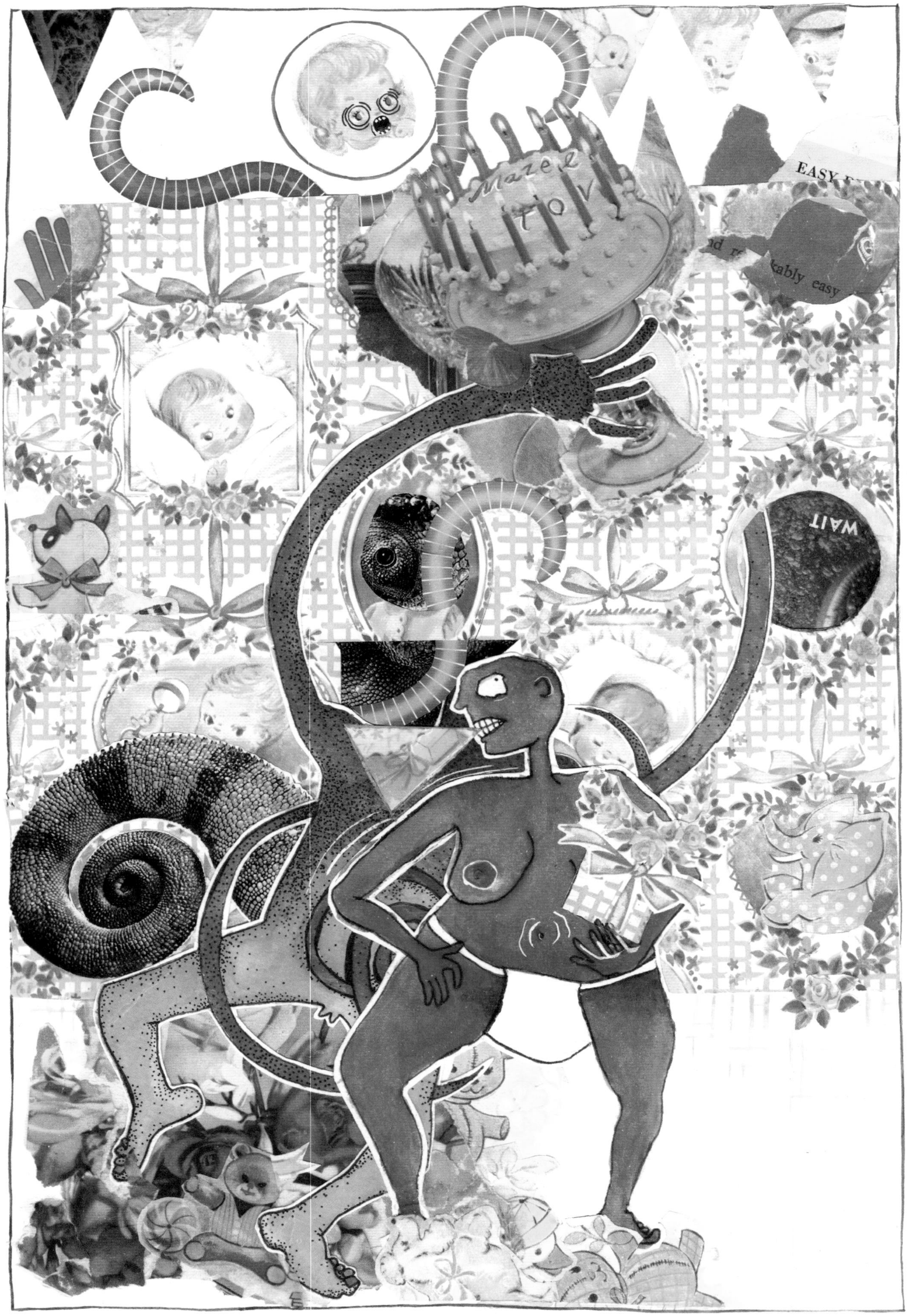
Mazel Tov
EASY
kably easy
WAIT

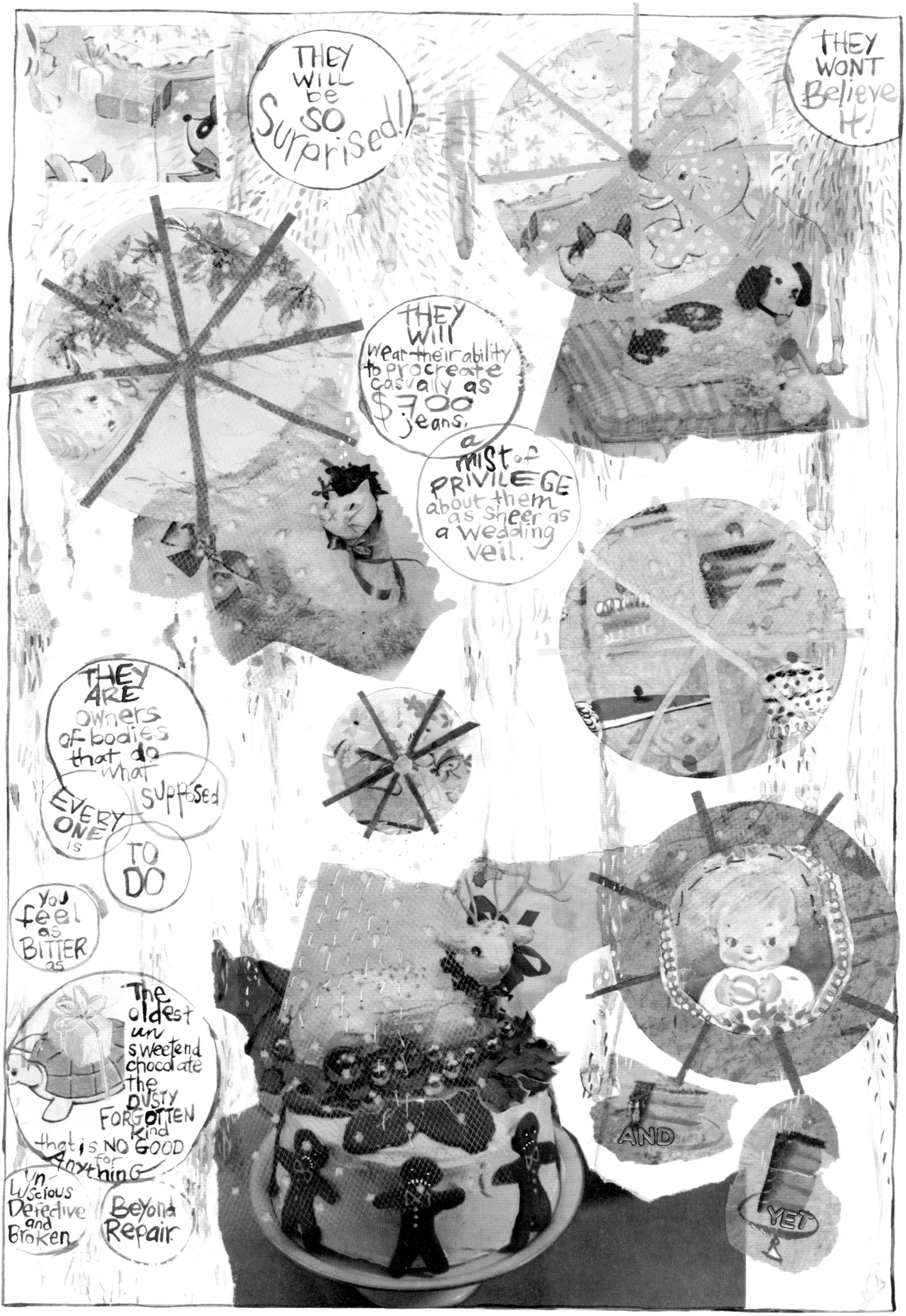
THEY WILL be SO Surprised!
THEY WONT Believe It!
THEY WILL wear their ability to procreate casually as $700 jeans,
a mist of PRIVILEGE about them as sheer as a wedding veil.
THEY ARE owners of bodies that do what
EVERY ONE is
supposed
TO DO
You feel as BITTER as
The oldest un sweetend chocolate the DUSTY FORGOTTEN kind that is NO GOOD for Anything
Un-Luscious Defective and Broken
Beyond Repair.
AND
YET

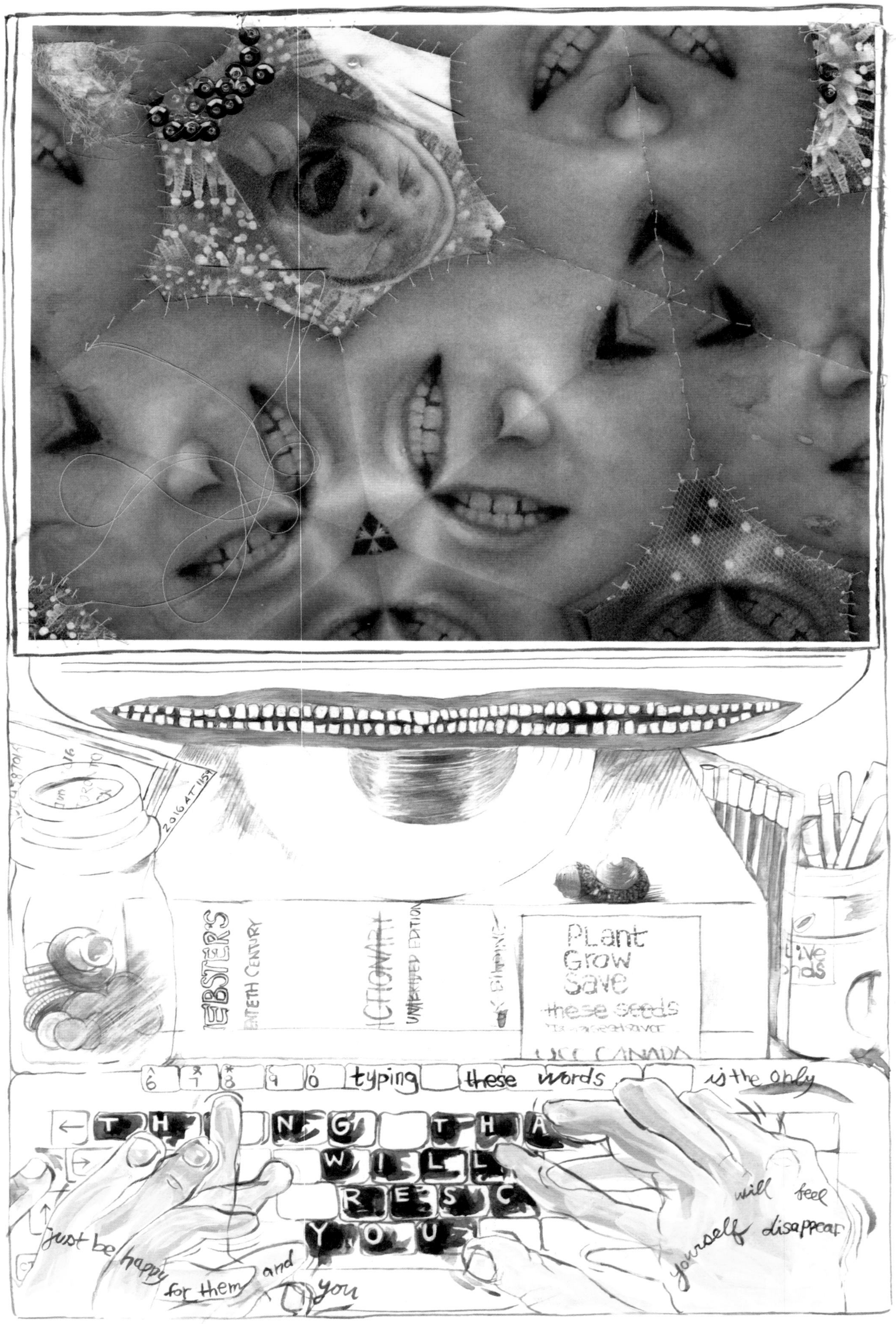
EBSTERS
NTIETH CENTURY
ICTIONARY
UNABRIDGED EDITION
Plant
Grow
Save
these seeds
USC CANADA
typing these words is the only
T H N G T H A
W I L L
R E S C
Y O U
just be happy for them and you
will feel yourself disappear

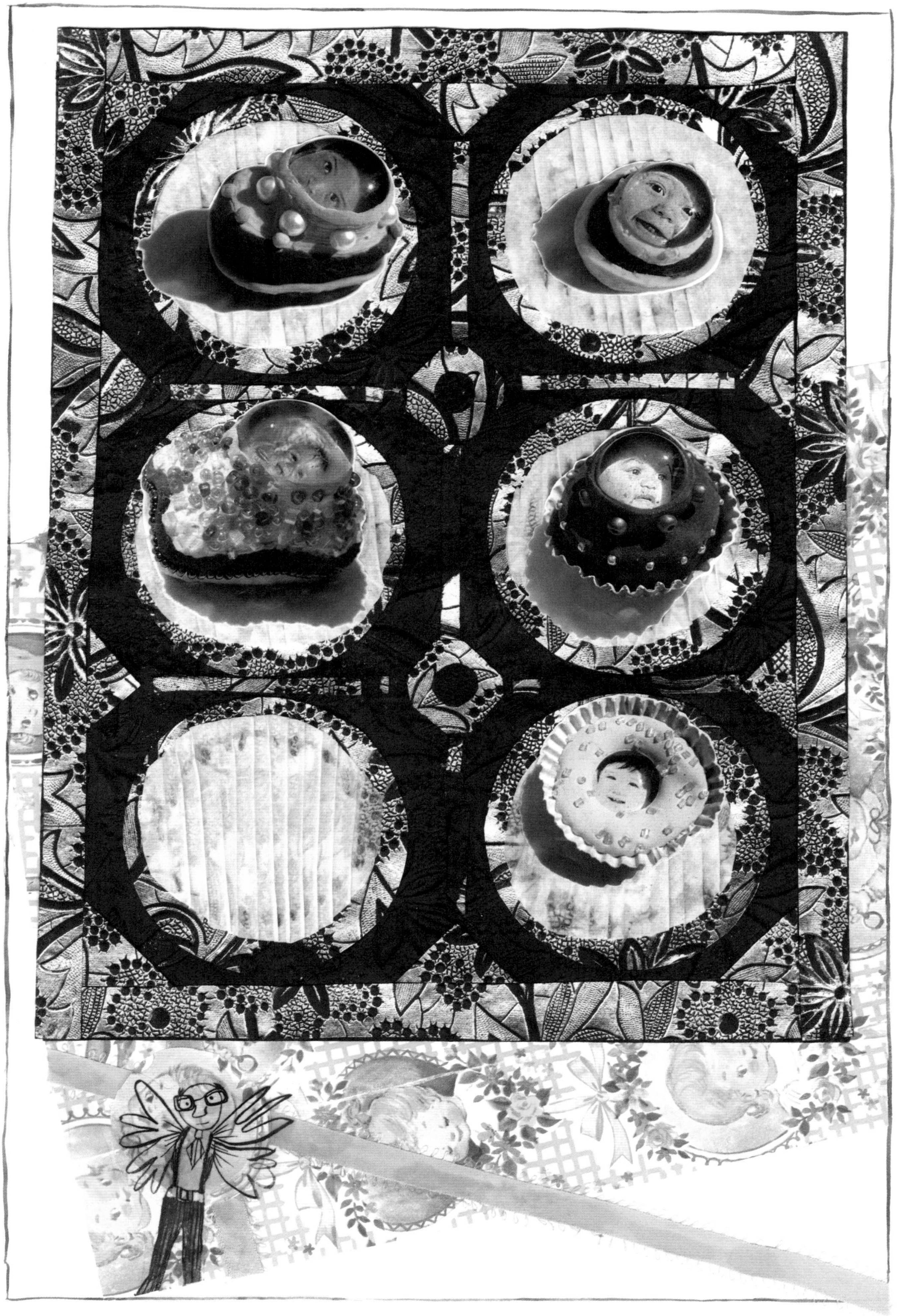

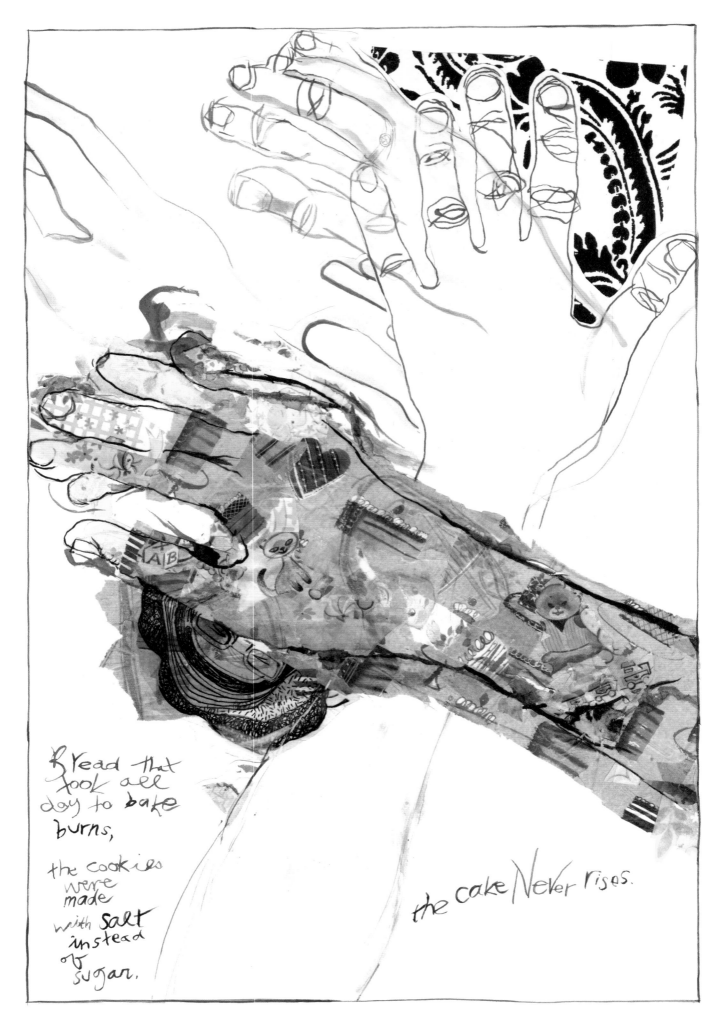

I read that
took all
day to bake
burns,

the cookies
were
made
with salt
instead
of sugar.

the cake Never rises.

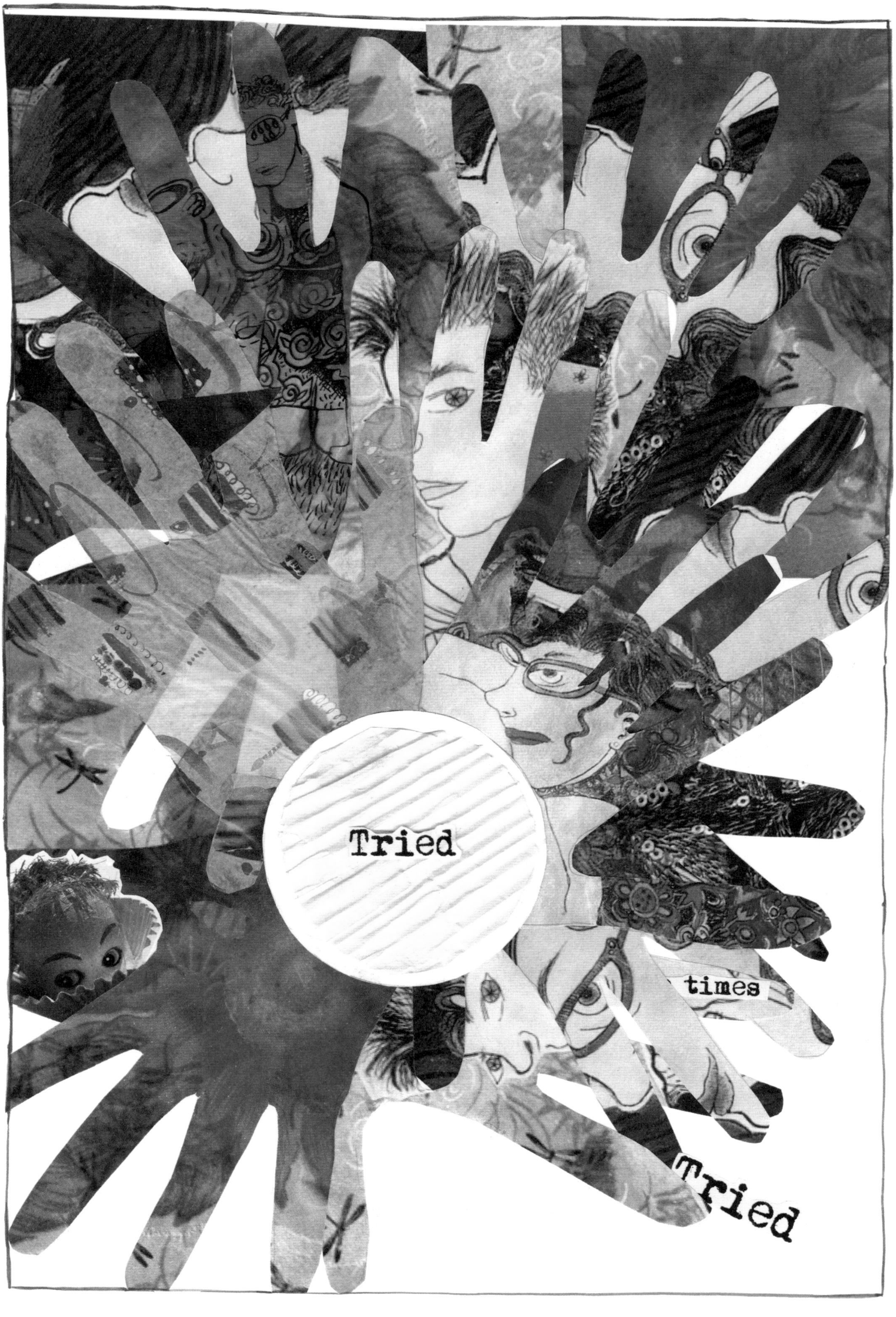
Tried
times
Tried

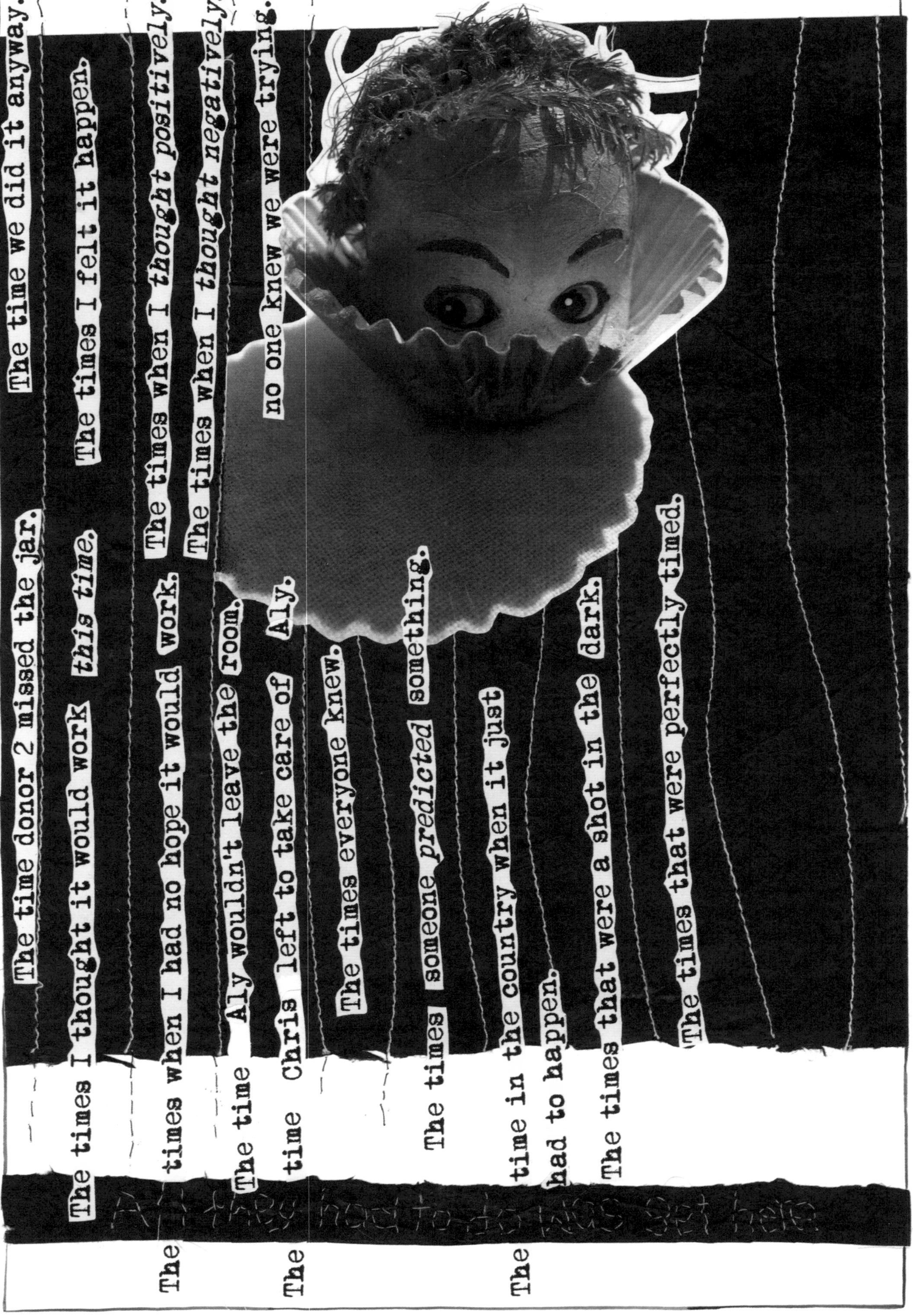
The time donor 2 missed the jar. The time we did it anyway.
The times I thought it would work this time. The times I felt it happen.
The times when I had no hope it would work. The times when I *thought positively.*
The time Aly wouldn't leave the room. The times when I *thought negatively.*
The time Chris left to take care of Aly. no one knew we were trying.
The times everyone knew.
The times someone *predicted* something.
The time in the country when it just had to happen.
The times that were a shot in the dark.
The times that were perfectly timed.
All they had to do was get here

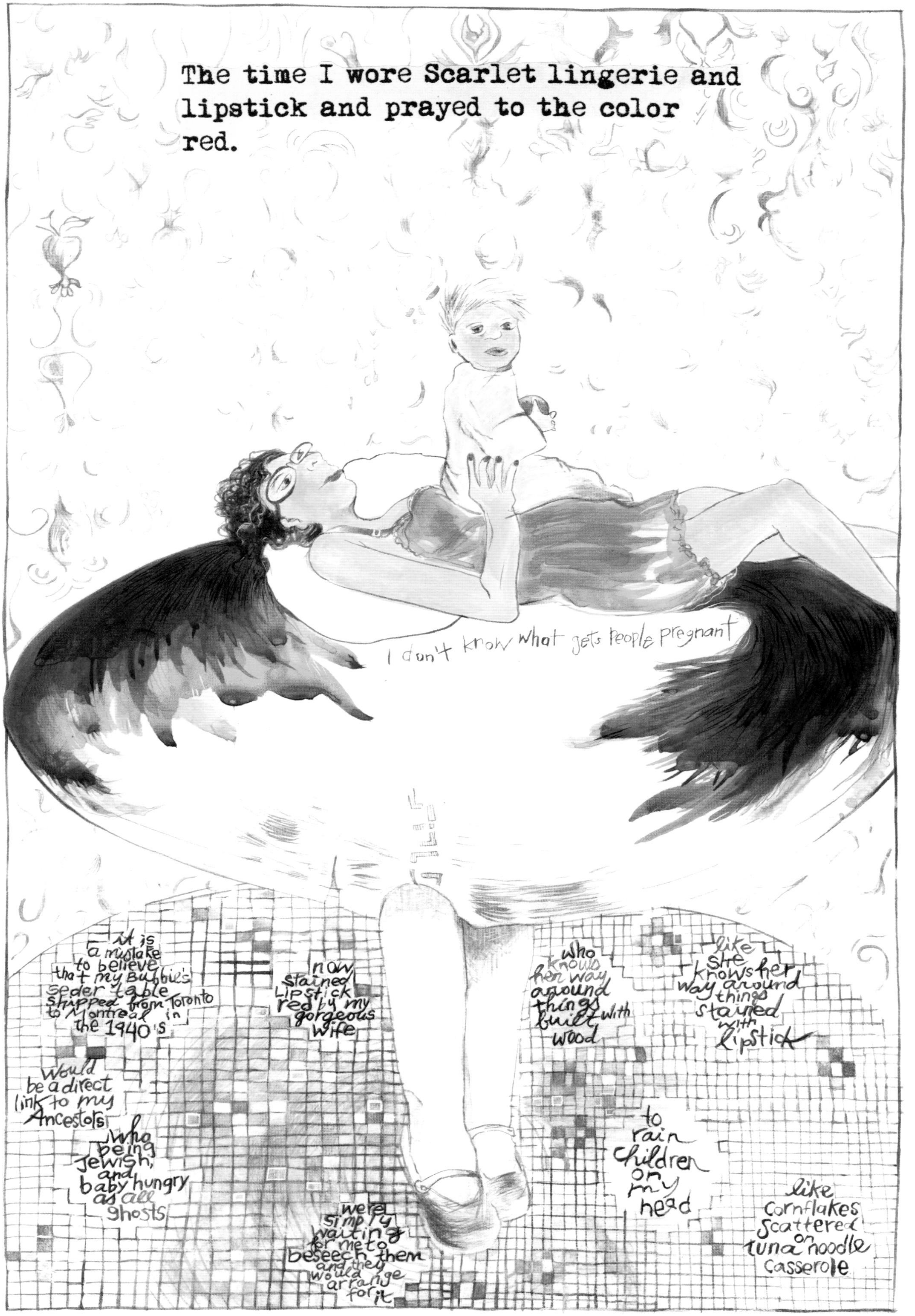
The time I wore Scarlet lingerie and lipstick and prayed to the color red.
I don't know what gets people pregnant
it is a mistake to believe that my Bubbie's seder table shipped from Toronto to Montreal in the 1940's
now stained Lipstick red by my gorgeous wife
who knows her way around things built with wood
like she knows her way around things stained with lipstick
would be a direct link to my Ancestors
who being Jewish, and baby hungry as all ghosts
were simply waiting for me to beseech them and they would arrange for it
to rain children on my head
like cornflakes scattered on tuna noodle casserole

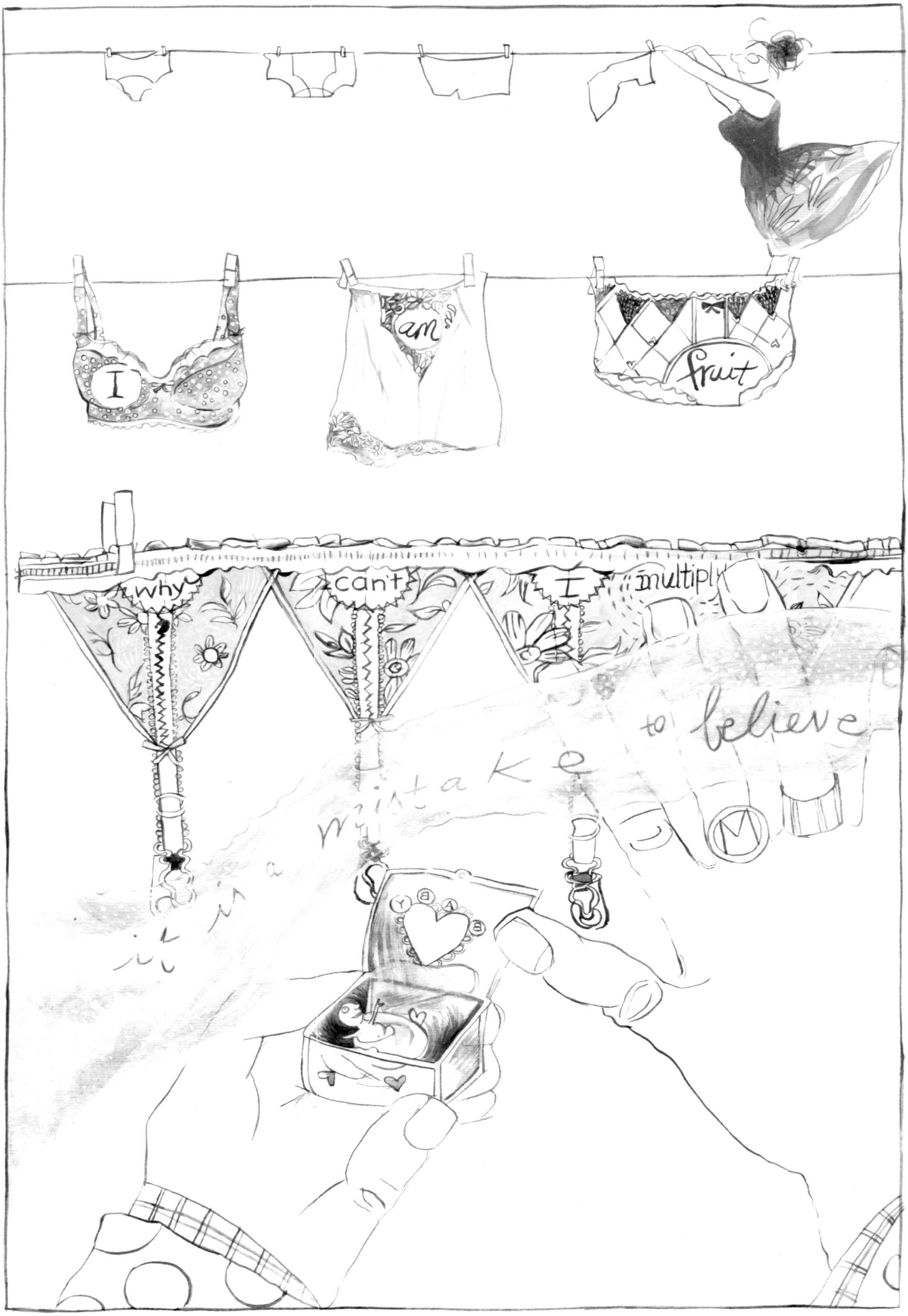
I
am
fruit
why
can't
I
multipl
it is a mistake
to believe

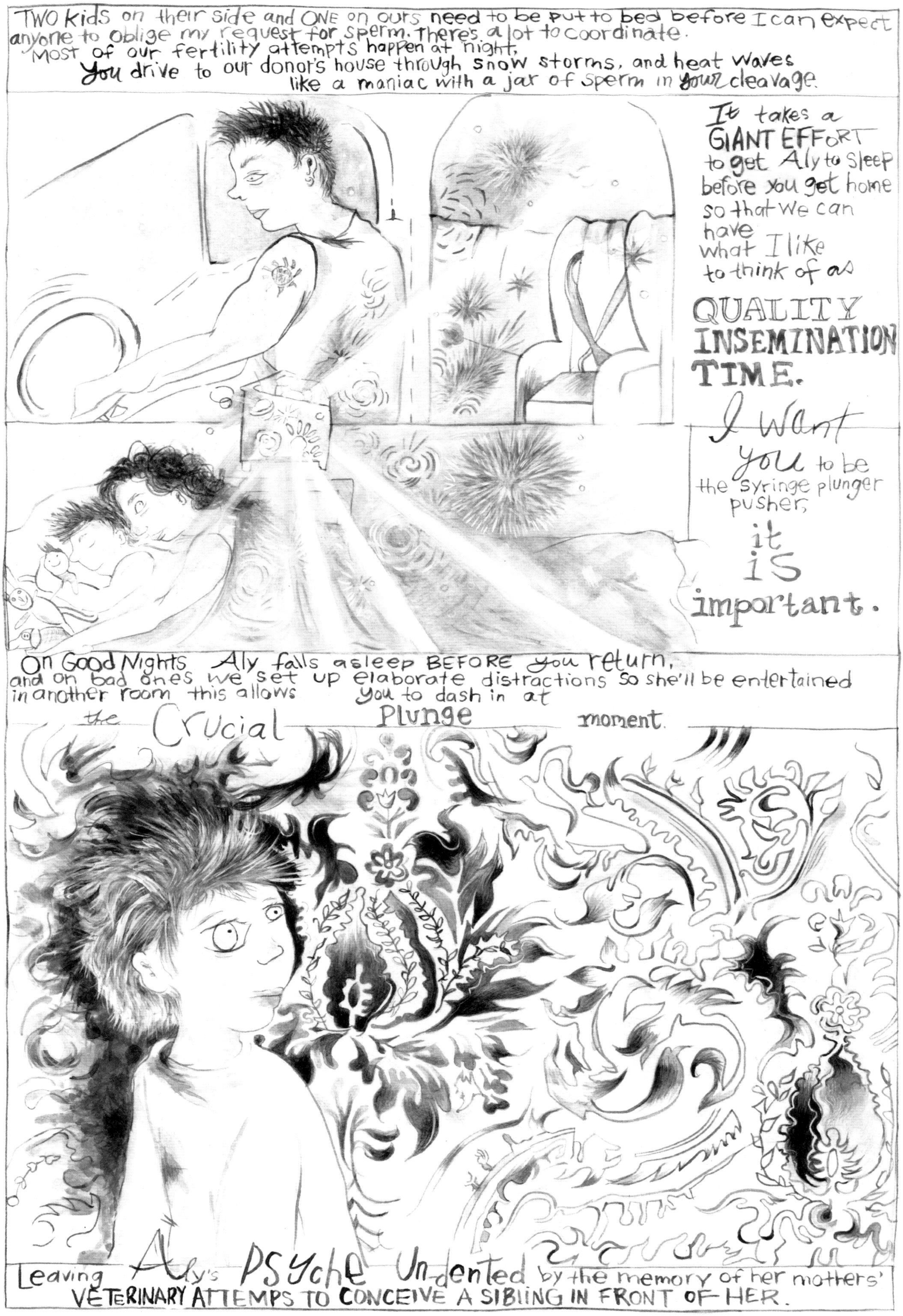
TWO kids on their side and ONE on ours need to be put to bed before I can expect anyone to oblige my request for sperm. there's a lot to coordinate.
Most of our fertility attempts happen at night,
You drive to our donor's house through snow storms, and heat waves like a maniac with a jar of sperm in your cleavage.
It takes a GIANT EFFORT to get Aly to sleep before you get home so that we can have what I like to think of as
QUALITY INSEMINATION TIME.
I want you to be the syringe plunger pusher, it is important.
On Good Nights Aly falls asleep BEFORE you return, and on bad ones we set up elaborate distractions so she'll be entertained in another room this allows you to dash in at the Crucial Plunge moment.
Leaving Aly's PSyche Un-dented by the memory of her mothers' VETERINARY ATTEMPS TO CONCEIVE A SIBLING IN FRONT OF HER.

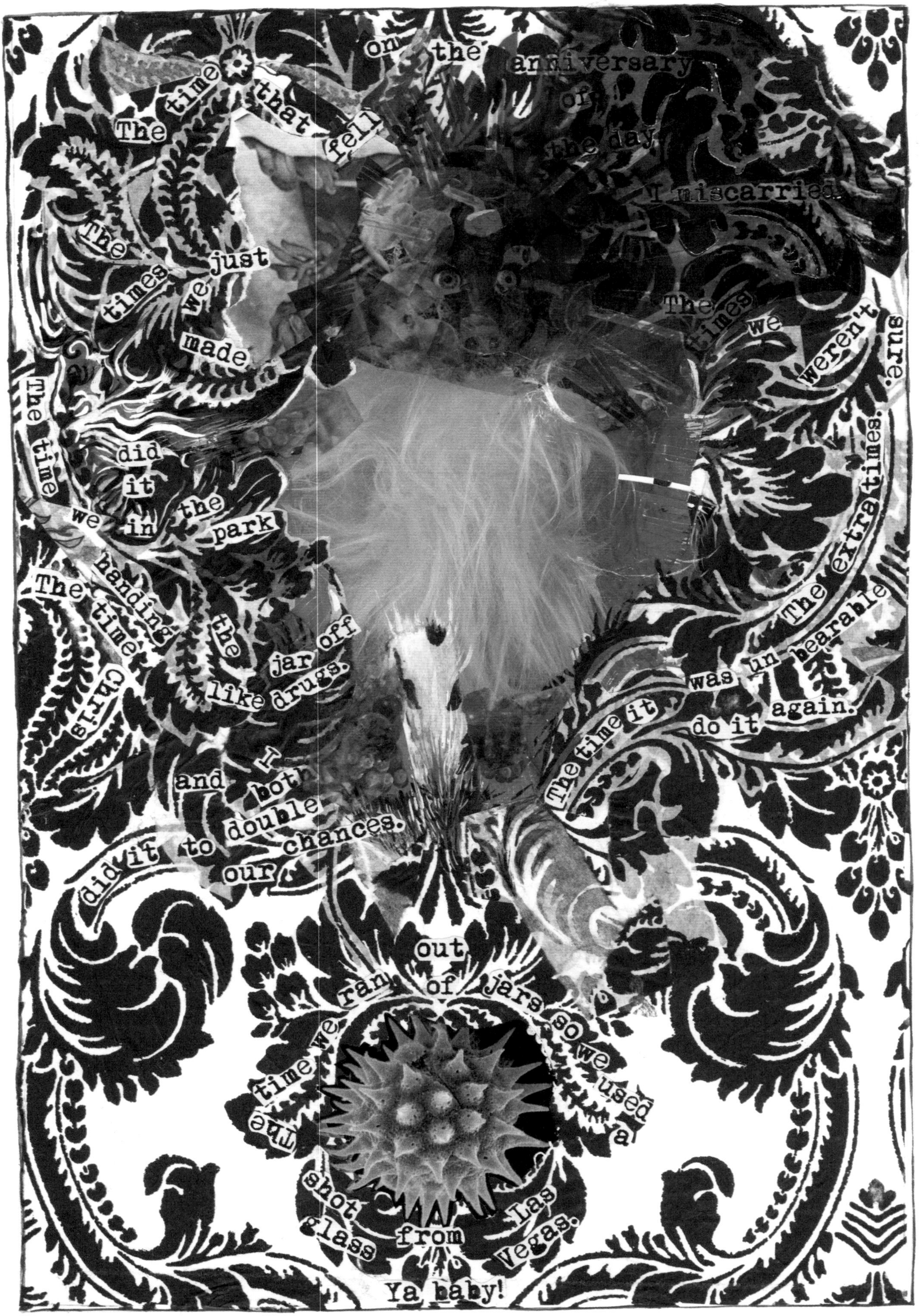
The time that I fell on the anniversary of the day I miscarried.
The times we just made.
The time we did it in the park.
The time Chris handing the jar off like drugs.
Chris and I both did it to double our chances.
The times we weren't sure.
The extra times.
The time it was un bearable do it again.
The time we ran out of jars so we used a shot glass from Las Vegas.
Ya baby!

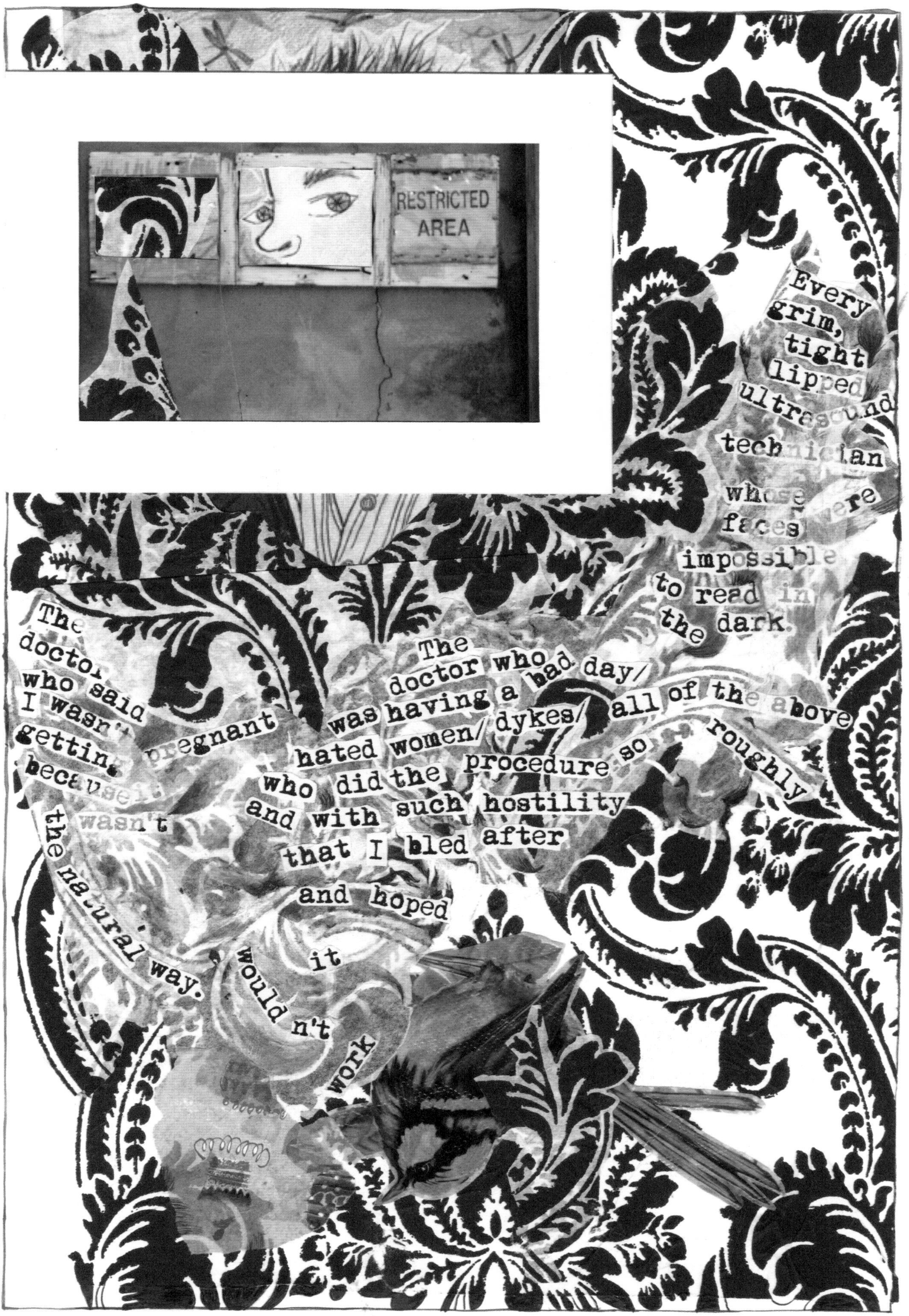
RESTRICTED AREA
Every grim, tight lipped ultrasound technician whose faces were impossible to read in the dark.
The doctor who said I wasn't pregnant getting because it wasn't the natural way.
The doctor who was having a bad day/ hated women/ dykes/ all of the above
who did the procedure so roughly and with such hostility that I bled after
and hoped it wouldn't work

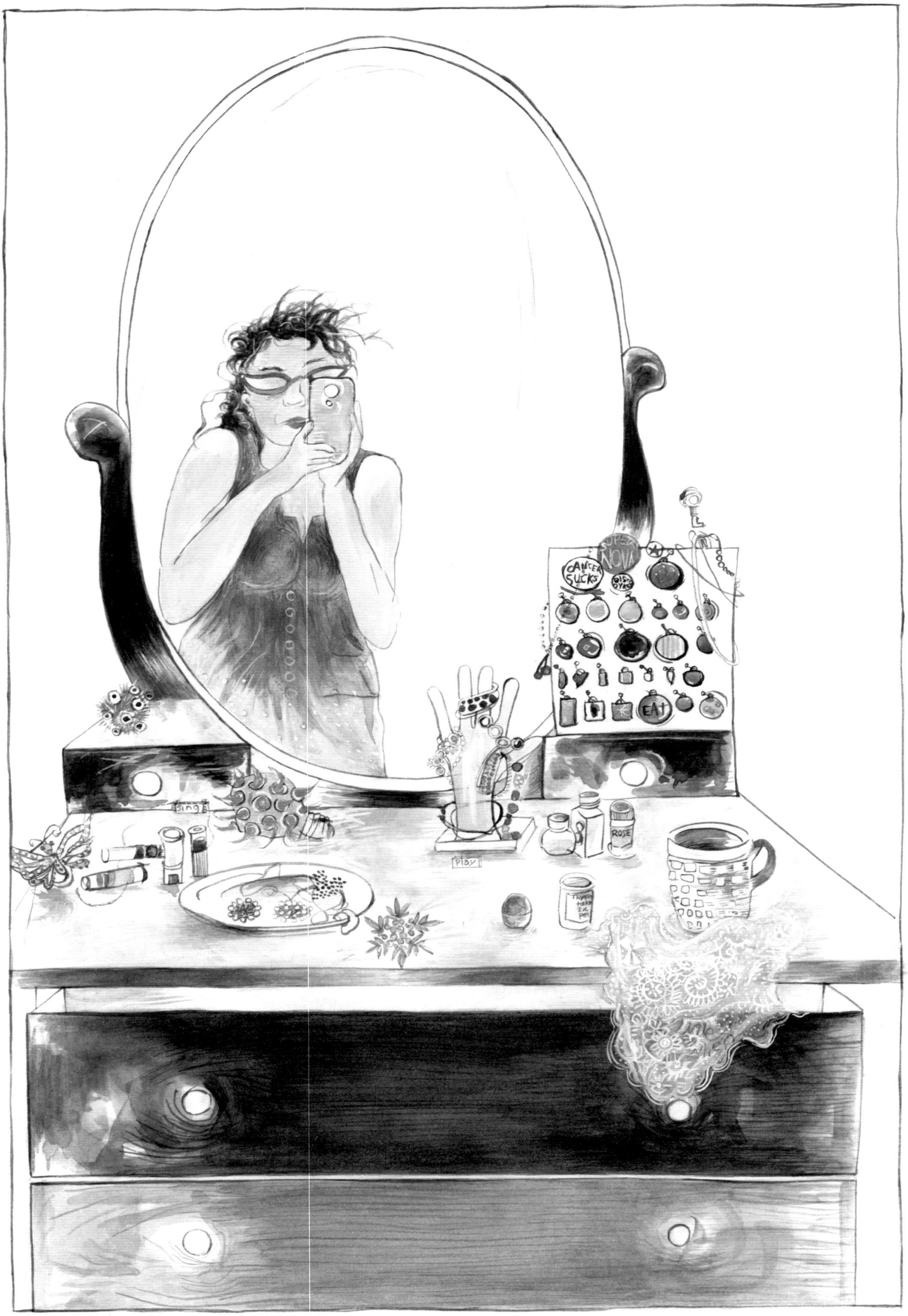
SUPER NOVA
CANCER SUCKS
EAT
sing
play
ROSE

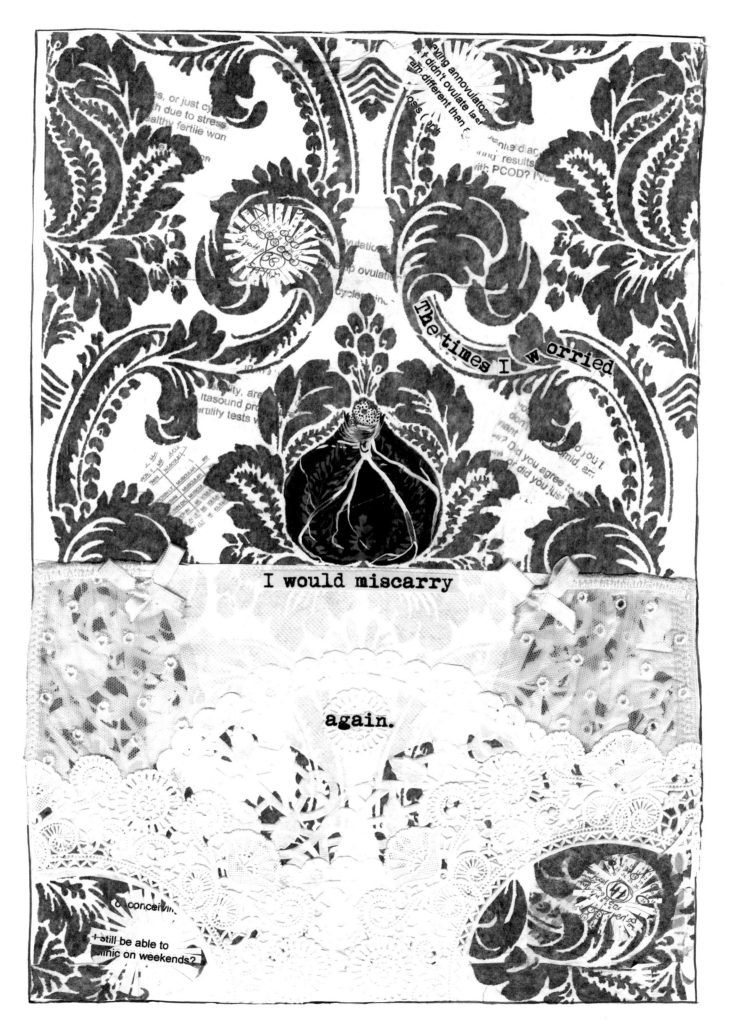

The times I worried

I would miscarry

again.

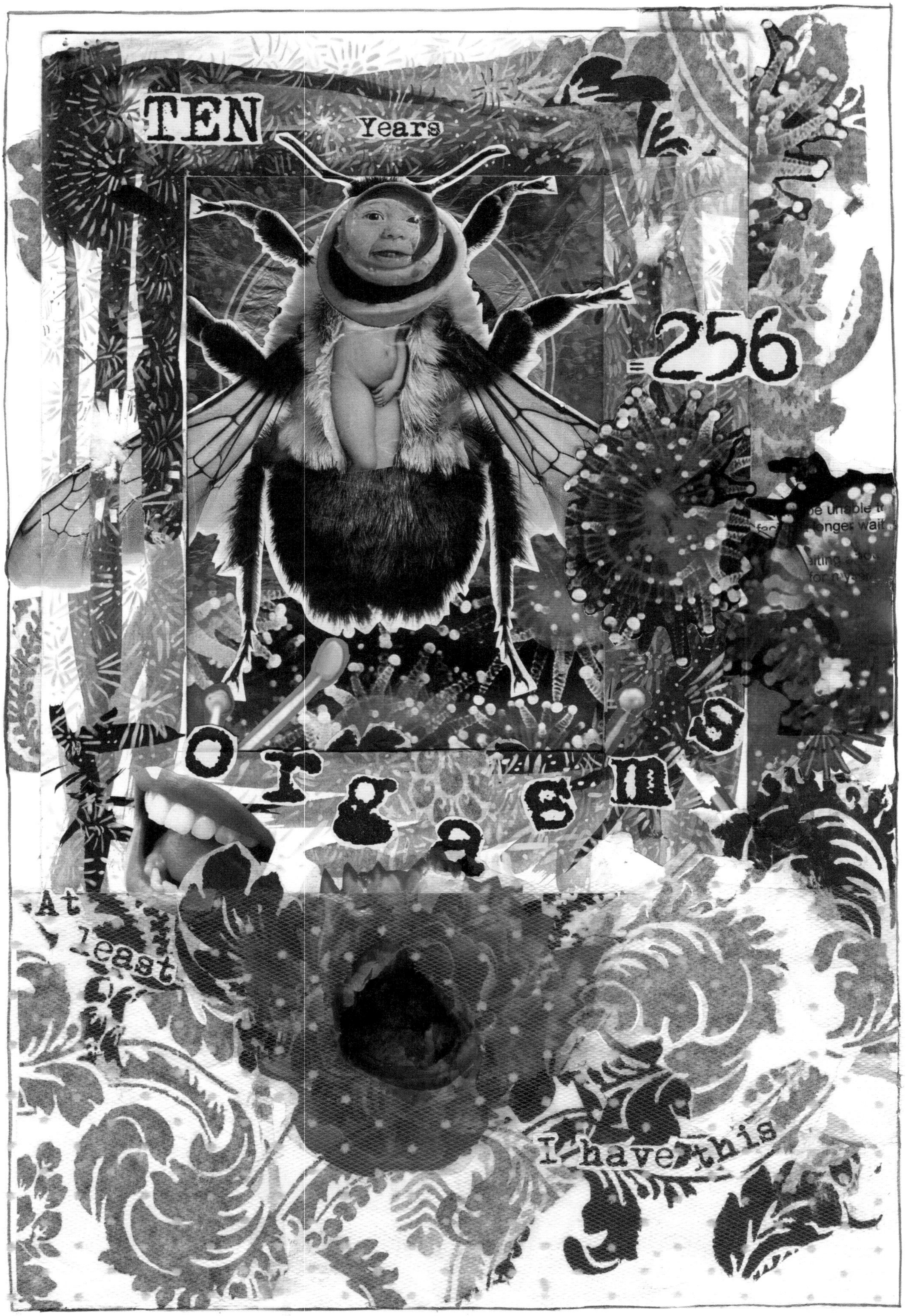
TEN
Years
256
orgasms
At least
I have this

Bluefish

and just did it when it felt like the right time.

The time I didn't use an ovulation kit

That time it was awkward.

an grey every time. Stories don't really end in fact some stories are a mile long run
in sen some stories are a prison sentence . Sometimes we are stuck living in stories long
that their usefulness

5- Sept . 2013
Babies are risky candy.
My stone is cold .Ineffective medicine as candy but it glows with a different kind of light.
The babies born are not the point. The red is the point.
s of the broken stones follow me-Let's bring our rocks back!
There are too many not top sew them on your clothes
est revealing everything, don't bother being modest
you Rabbit's wife and your god dammed stones
you see we've sucked the power right out of them?
ded them like candy but then I ate them Mrs Rabbit and I got so big now I am the tallest
tree the most enormous 5 foot woman ever to walk the earth. I am not empty because I ate
nes and all the babies they never produced. I ate them too.
tired.
ired of tired I want some candy.
a little story:
and I were sad because so much was lost. It was spring and we were broke as usual but
we decide to spend 40 dollars on seeds every kind of flower. We took a big garden store
with their doors open and birds flying in and out e ceiling. We let her go wild picking
seeds. It was fun and hopeful and also slight. And then the next weekend we
planted them all. Do you know what hap . Not a single flower from all the
seeds. Effort means nothing. You m Put down your calendar time
cancelled. All those red circles, all the blood always comes
anyway. Blood rocks I am throwin I am calling a truce
I pray to the queens of the de celled. Queen mo
of the b de children cham htly formed thin
We all love our difficult child
Some stone ill up with a nt to dig through th
slit and find the bones of y is abov the
ground above the waist
and it was ciously bi
myself.

The time we calculated when the best time was for over an hour.

The time when the nurses were mean

the time at The clinic by myself when I sneaked an orgasm.

The times I didn't.

Breakfast

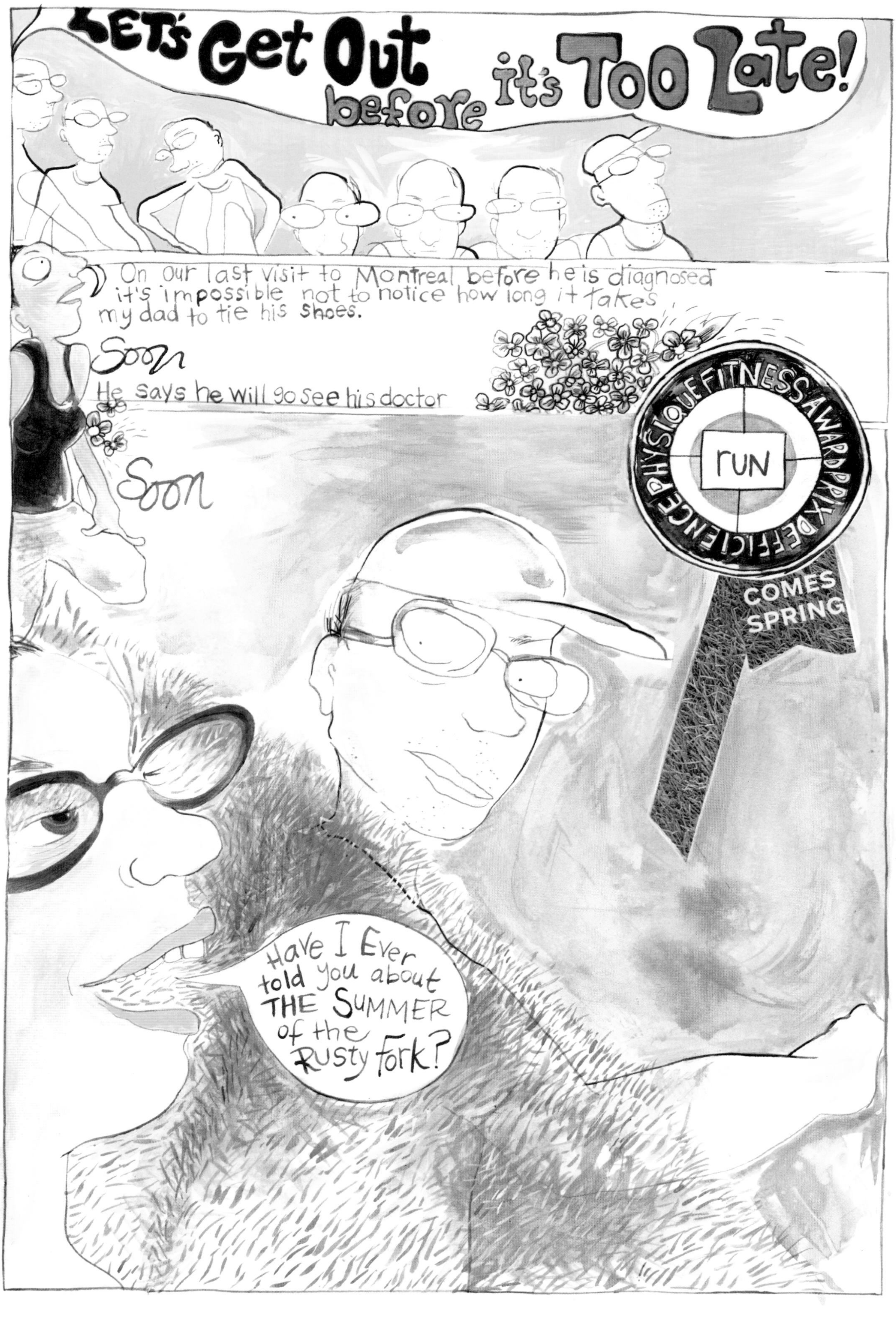
LET'S Get Out before it's TOO Late!
On our last visit to Montreal before he is diagnosed it's impossible not to notice how long it takes my dad to tie his shoes.
Soon
He says he will go see his doctor
Soon
PHYSIQUE FITNESS AWARD PRIX D'EFFICIENCE PHYSIQUE
RUN
COMES SPRING
Have I Ever told you about THE SUMMER of the RUSTY fork?

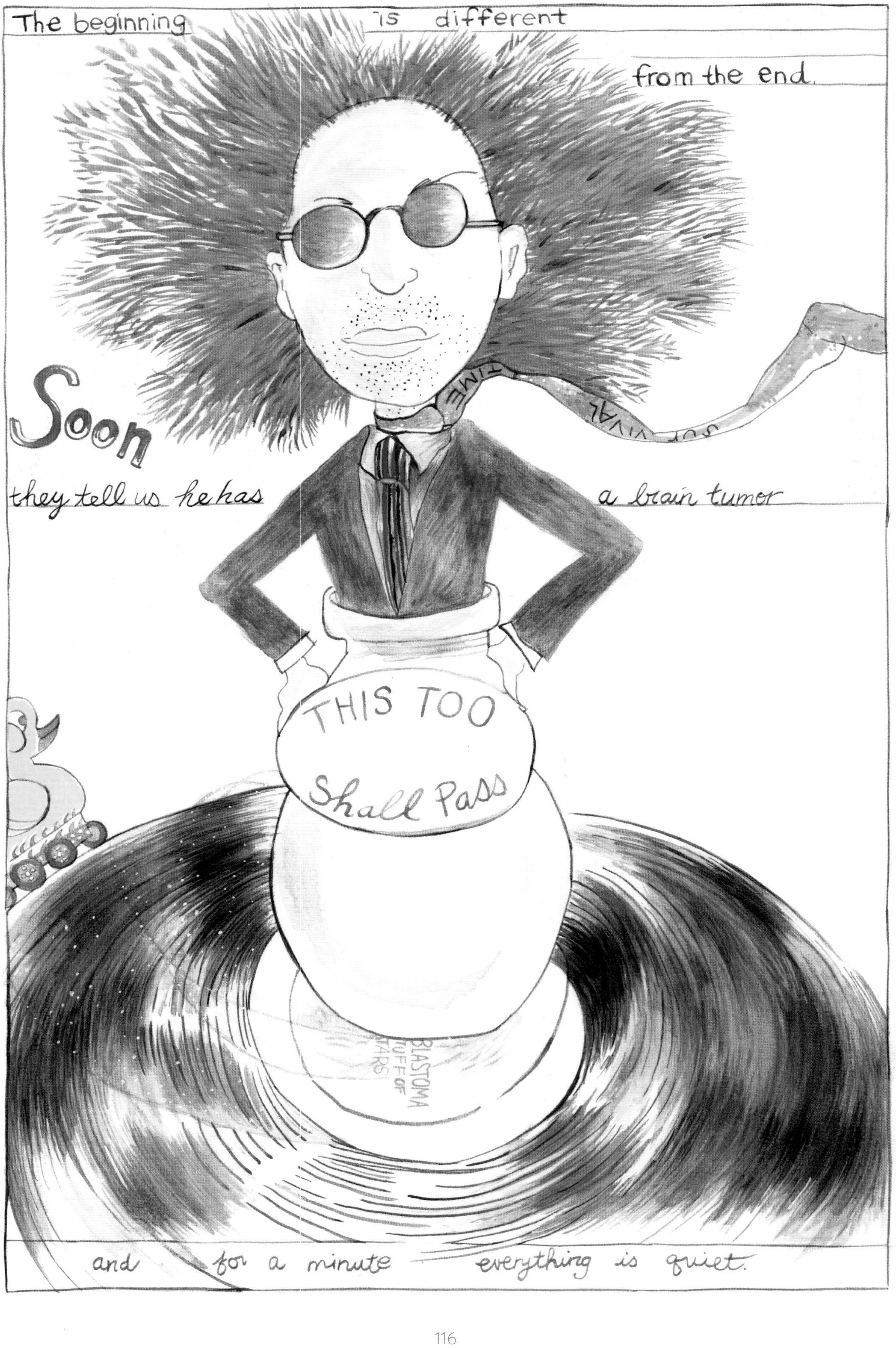
The beginning is different from the end.
Soon they tell us he has a brain tumor
TIME
THIS TOO Shall Pass
and for a minute everything is quiet.

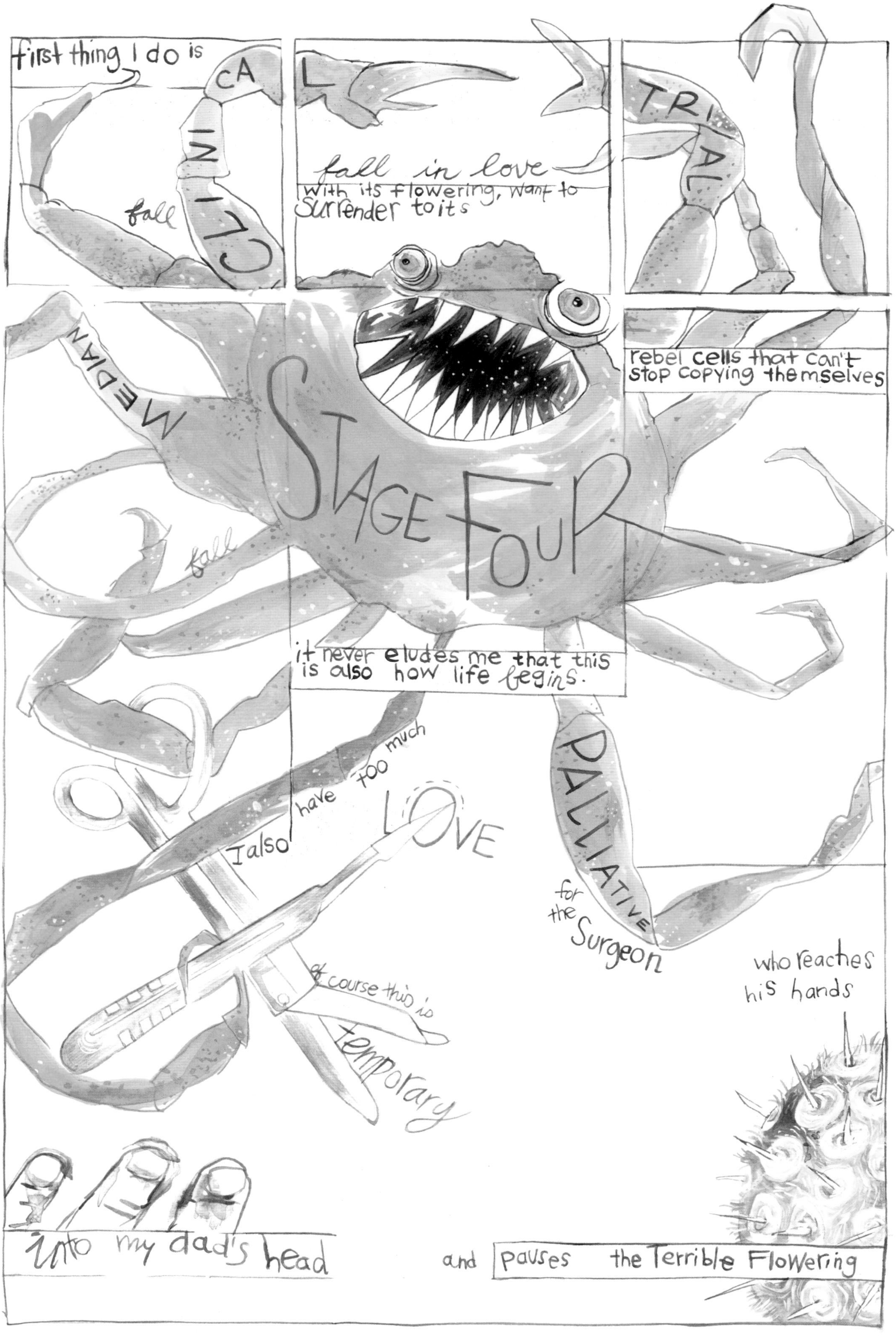

first thing I do is
CLINICAL TRIAL
fall
fall in love
with its flowering, want to surrender to its
MEDIAN
fall
STAGE FOUR
rebel cells that can't stop copying themselves
it never eludes me that this is also how life begins.
I also have too much
LOVE
PALLIATIVE
for the Surgeon
of course this is temporary
who reaches his hands
into my dad's head
and
pauses the Terrible Flowering

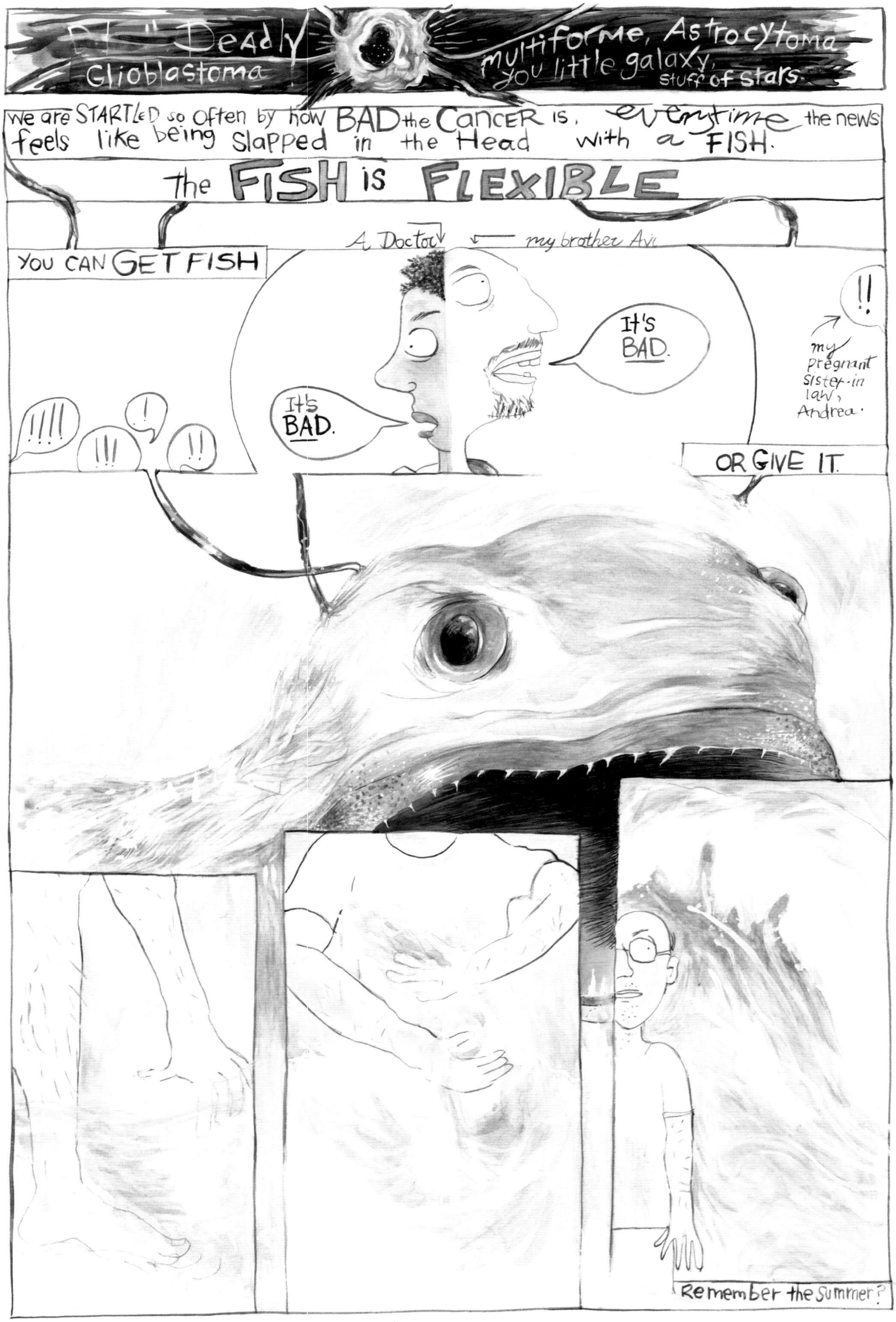
"Deadly Glioblastoma multiforme, Astrocytoma you little galaxy, stuff of stars.
We are STARTLED so often by how BAD the CANCER is, everytime the news feels like being slapped in the Head with a FISH.
The FISH is FLEXIBLE
YOU CAN GET FISH
A Doctor
my brother Avi
It's BAD.
It's BAD.
!!!!
!!!
!
!!
!!
my pregnant sister-in law, Andrea.
OR GIVE IT.
Remember the summer?

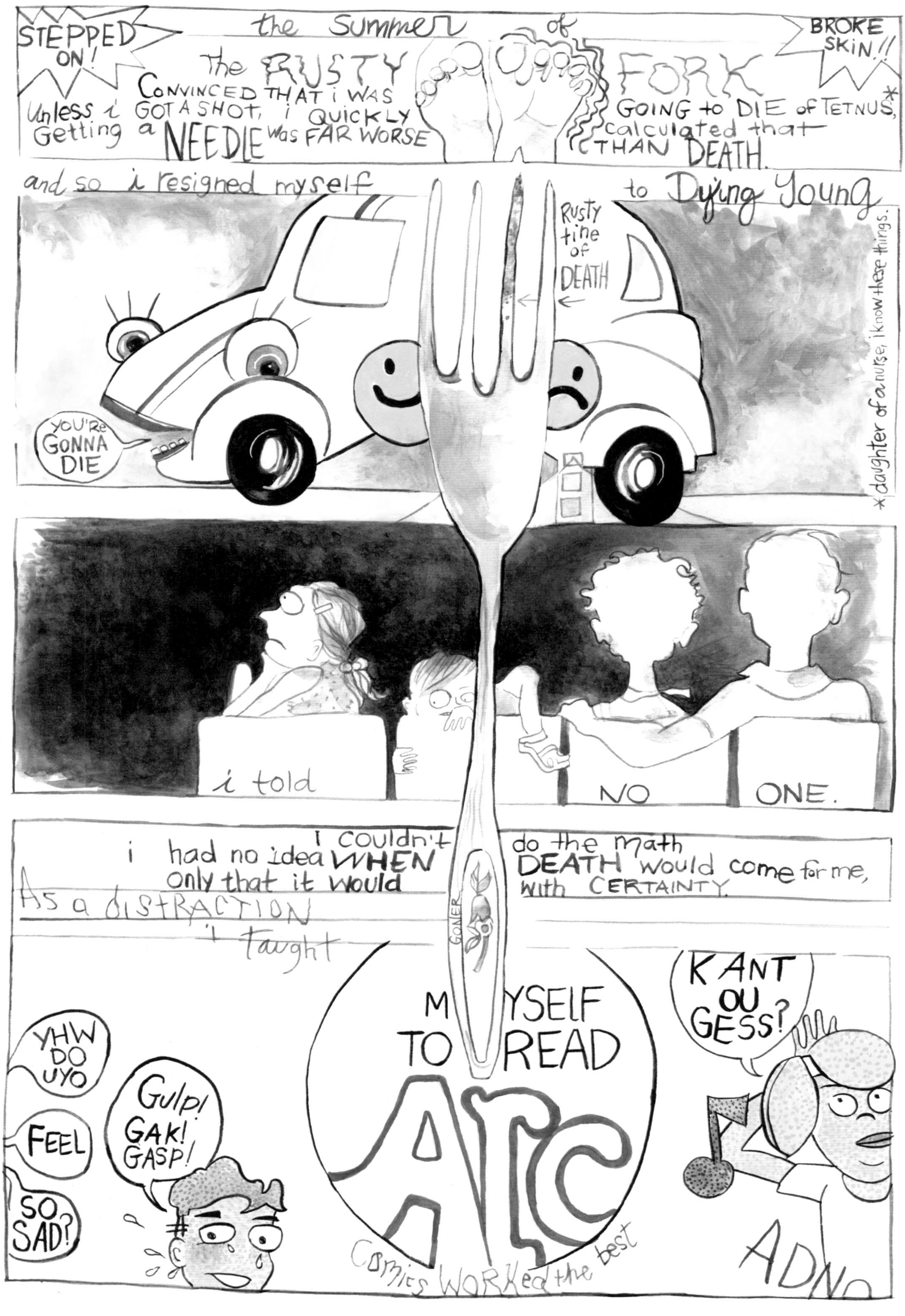

STEPPED ON!
the Summer of
the RUSTY FORK
BROKE SKIN!!
CONVINCED THAT i WAS GOING to DIE of TETNUS,*
Unless i GOT A SHOT, i QUICKLY calculated that
Getting a NEEDLE was FAR WORSE THAN DEATH.
and so i resigned myself to Dying Young
Rusty tine of DEATH
YOU'RE GONNA DIE
* daughter of a nurse, i know these things.
i told NO ONE.
i had no idea WHEN DEATH would come for me,
I couldn't do the math
only that it would with CERTAINTY.
As a DISTRACTION i taught MYSELF TO READ
GONER
YHW DO UYO FEEL SO SAD?
Gulp! GAK! GASP!
KANT OU GESS?
Comics WORKed the best
ADNO

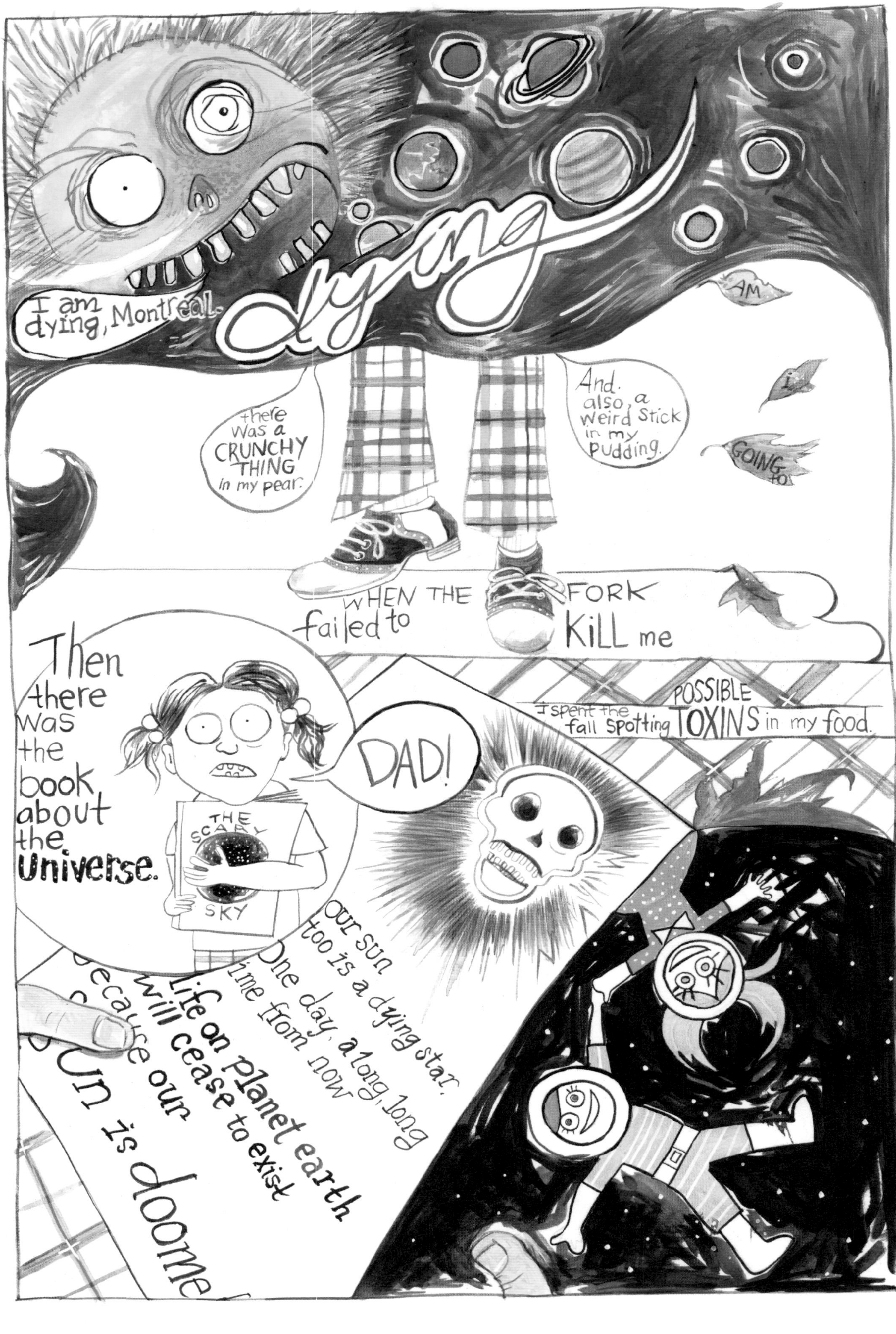

I am dying, Montreal.
dying
AM
I
GOING to
there was a CRUNCHY THING in my pear.
And also, a weird stick in my pudding.
WHEN THE FORK failed to KILL me
I spent the fall spotting POSSIBLE TOXINS in my food.
Then there was the book about the universe.
DAD!
THE SCARY SKY
Our sun too is a dying star. One day, a long, long time from now
Life on planet earth will cease to exist because our sun is doome

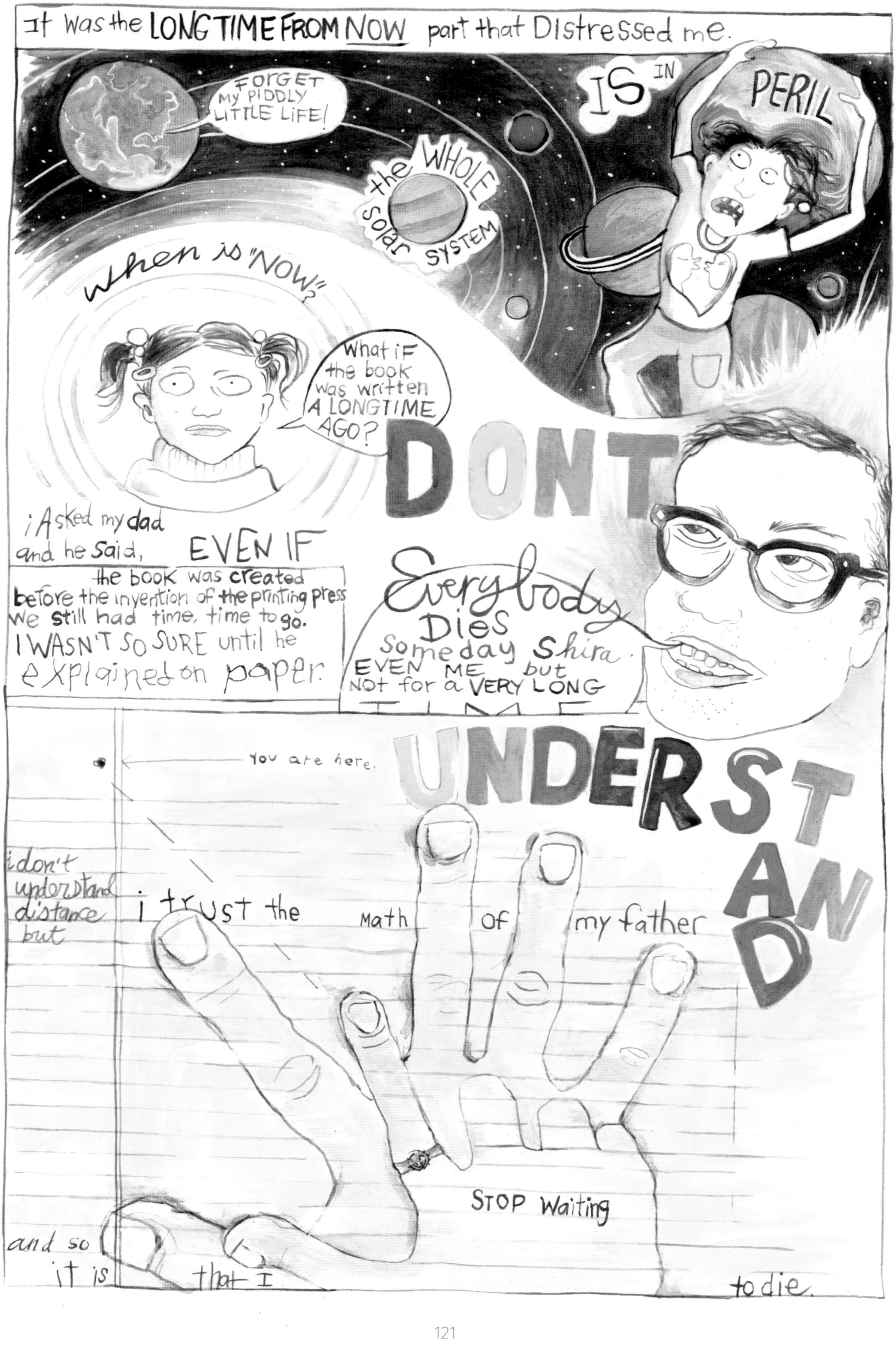
It was the LONG TIME FROM NOW part that Distressed me.
FORGET my PIDDLY LITTLE LIFE!
the WHOLE solar SYSTEM
IS IN PERIL
when is "NOW"?
What if the book was written A LONGTIME AGO?
i Asked my dad and he said, EVEN IF
the book was created before the invention of the printing press we still had time, time to go.
I WASN'T SO SURE until he explained on paper.
DONT
Everybody Dies Someday Shira. EVEN ME but NOT for a VERY LONG TIME
UNDERSTAND
you are here.
i don't understand distance but
i trust the math of my father
STOP Waiting
and so it is that I to die.

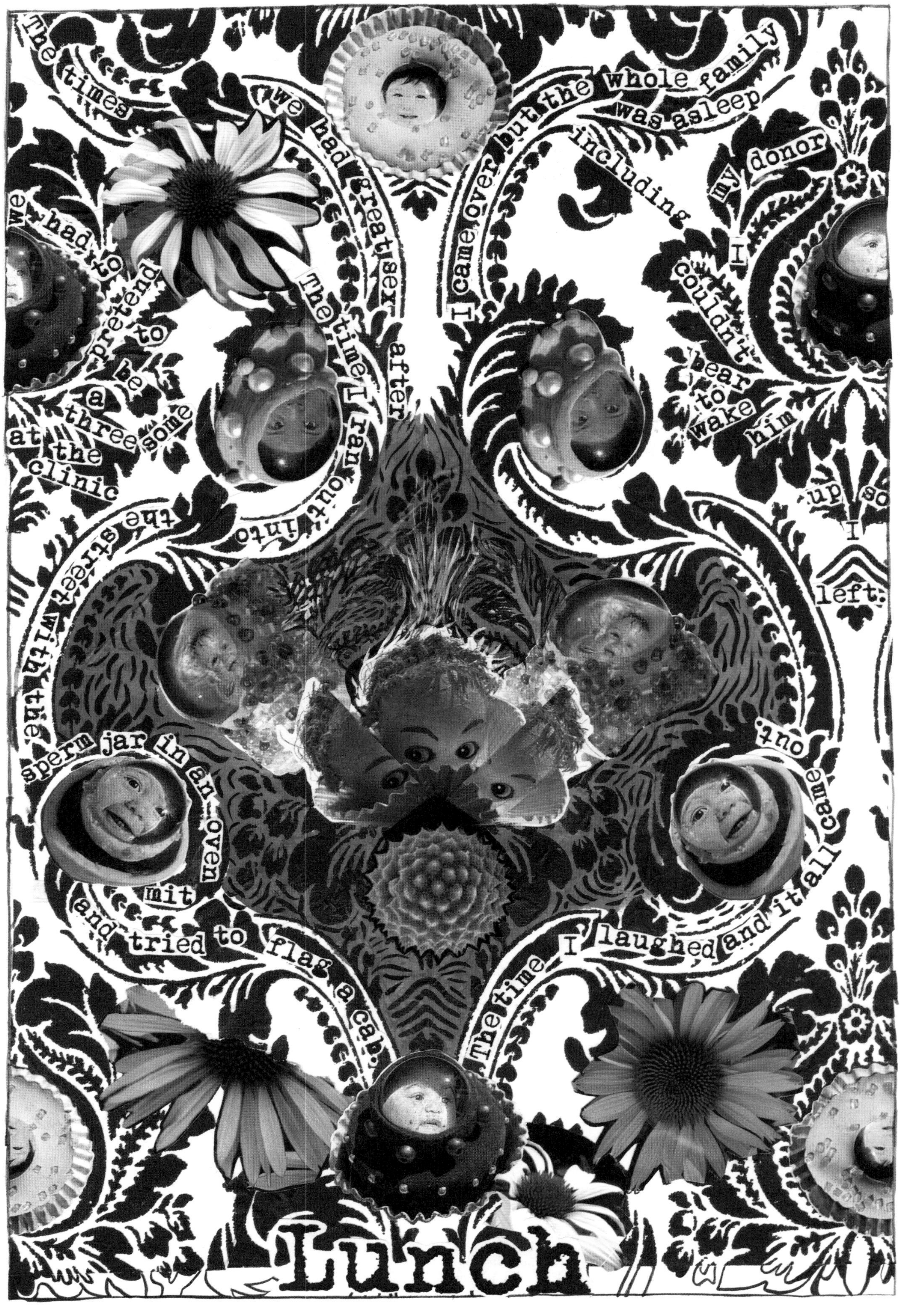

The times
we had to pretend to be a threesome at the clinic
we had great sex after
I came over but the whole family was asleep
including my donor
I couldn't bear to wake him up so I left.
The time I ran out into the street with the sperm jar in an oven mit and tried to flag a cab.
The time I laughed and it all came out.
Lunch

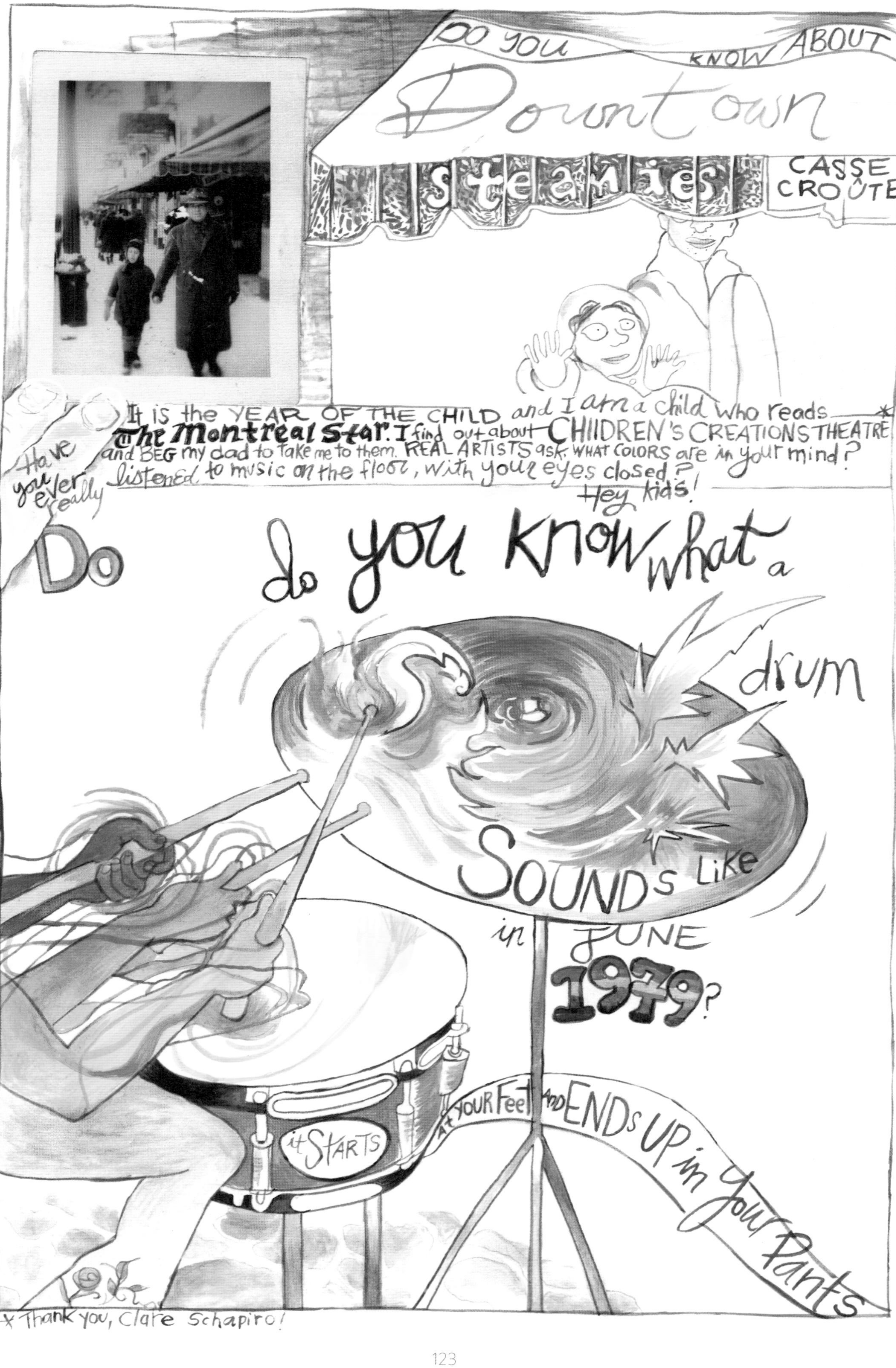
DO YOU KNOW ABOUT
Downtown
steamies
CASSE CROUTE
It is the YEAR OF THE CHILD and I am a child who reads The Montreal Star. I find out about CHILDREN'S CREATIONS THEATRE* and BEG my dad to take me to them. REAL ARTISTS ask: WHAT COLORS are in your mind?
Have you ever really listened to music on the floor, with your eyes closed?
Hey kids!
Do
do you know what a drum SOUNDs like in JUNE 1979?
it STARTS at YOUR Feet AND ENDs UP in your Pants

* Thank you, Clare Schapiro!

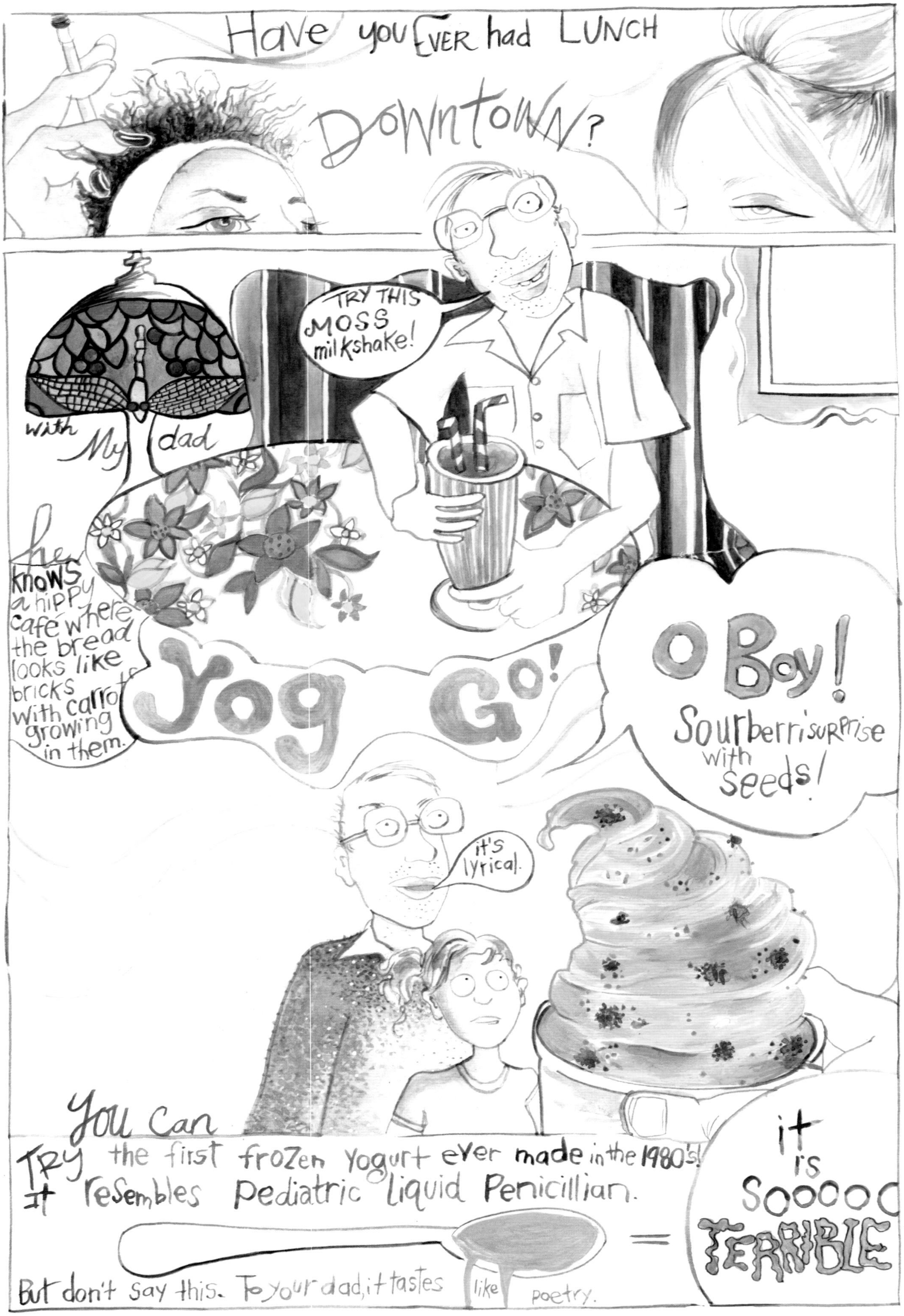
Have you EVER had LUNCH
DOWNTOWN?
TRY THIS MOSS milkshake!
with My dad
he KNOWS a hippy café where the bread looks like bricks with carrots growing in them.
Yog Go!
O Boy! Sourberrisurprise with seeds!
it's lyrical.
You can TRY the first frozen Yogurt ever made in the 1980's!
It resembles pediatric liquid Penicillian.
=
it is Sooooo TERRIBLE
But don't say this. To your dad, it tastes like poetry.

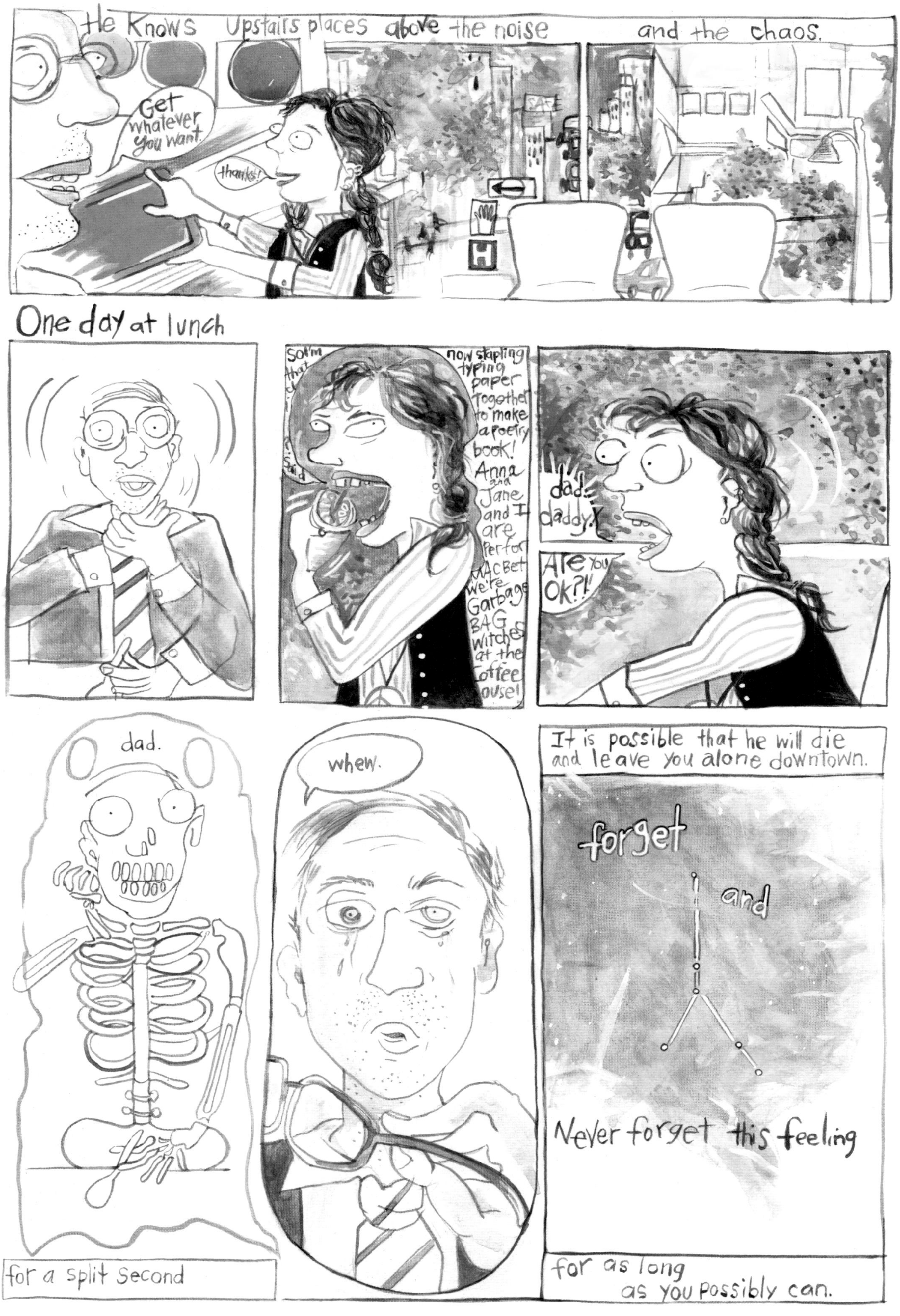
He Knows Upstairs places above the noise
and the chaos.
Get whatever you want.
thanks!
One day at lunch
So I'm
that
said
now stapling typing paper Together to make a poetry book! Anna and Jane and I are Perfor MACBet we're Garbage BAG witches at the Coffee ouse!
dad.
daddy.!
Are you OK?!
dad.
whew.
It is possible that he will die and leave you alone downtown.
forget
and
Never forget this feeling
for a split second
for as long as you possibly can.

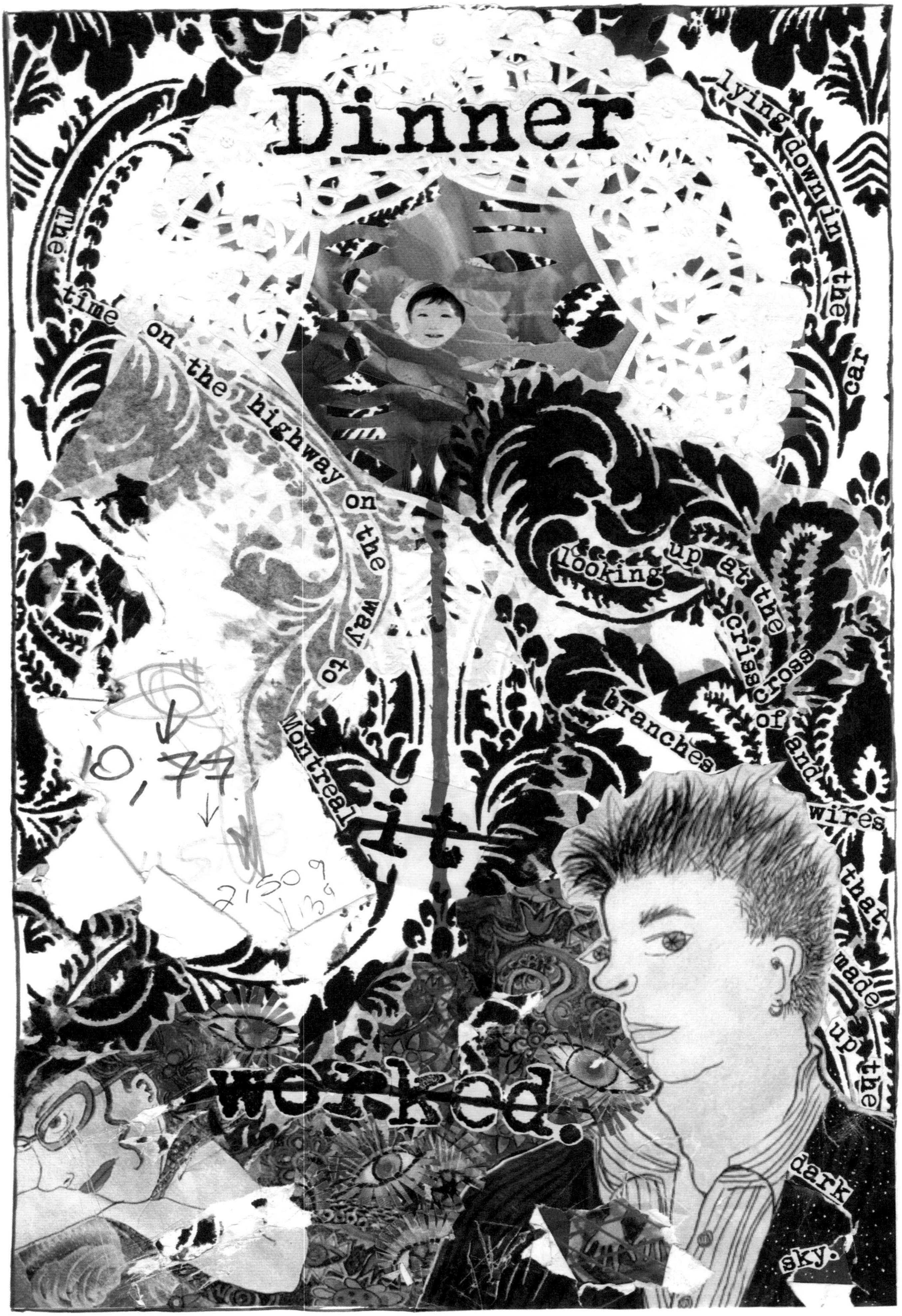

Dinner
the time on the highway on the way to Montreal
lying down in the car
looking up at the criss cross of branches and wires that made up the dark sky.
it worked.
10,77

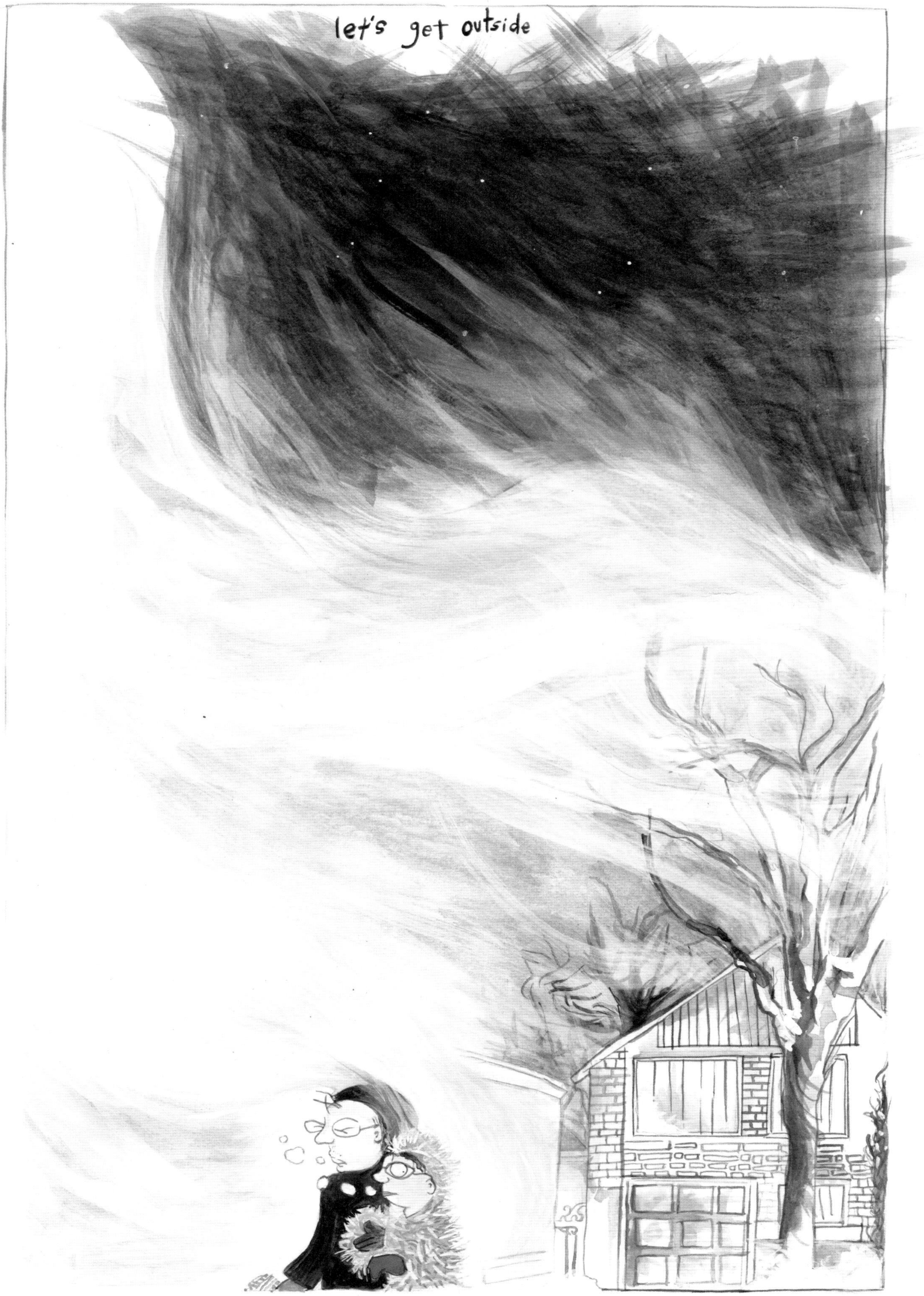
let's get outside

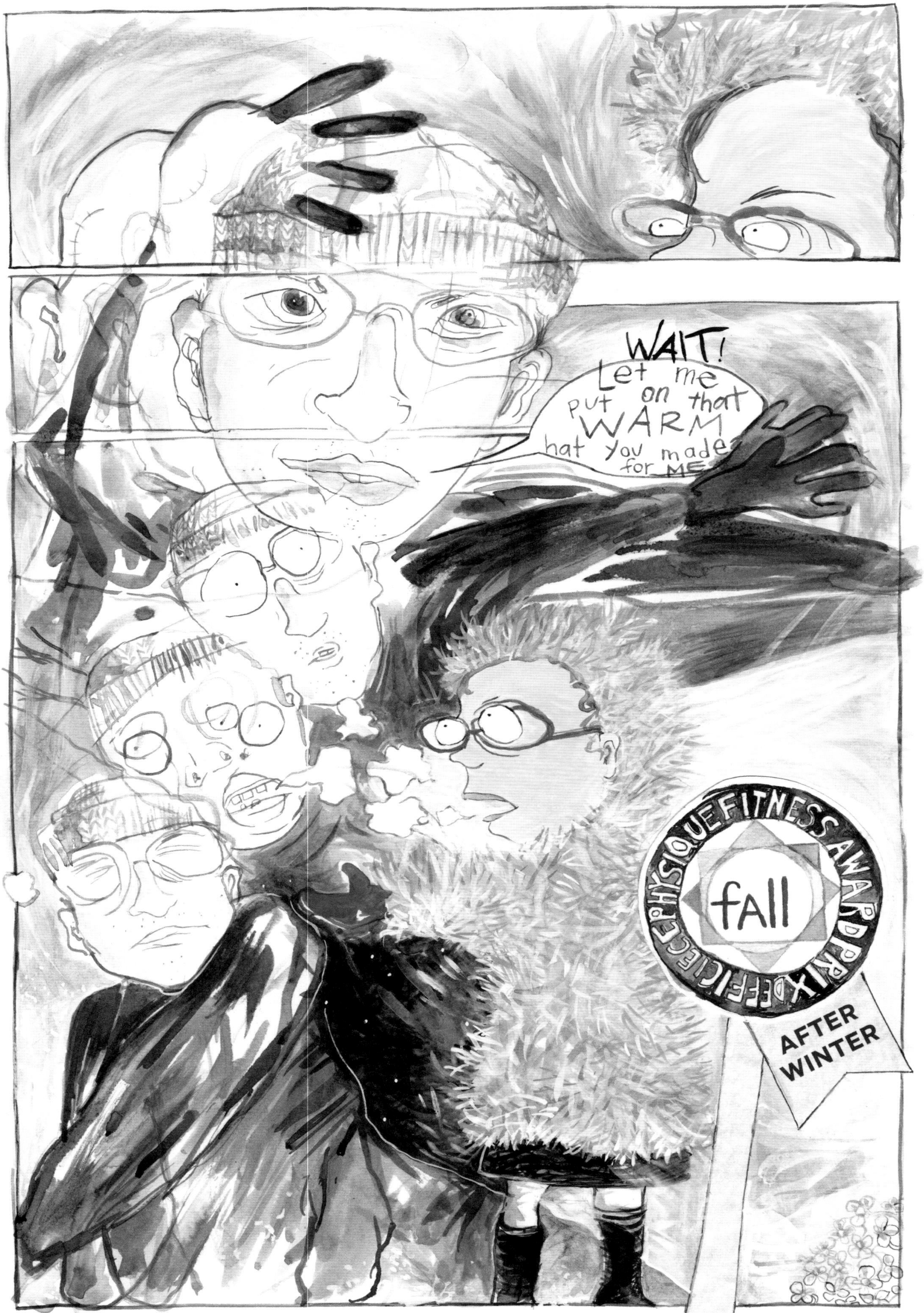
WAIT! Let me put on that WARM hat you made for ME
PHYSIQUE FITNESS AWARD PRIX DEFFICIENCE PHYSIQUE
fall
AFTER WINTER

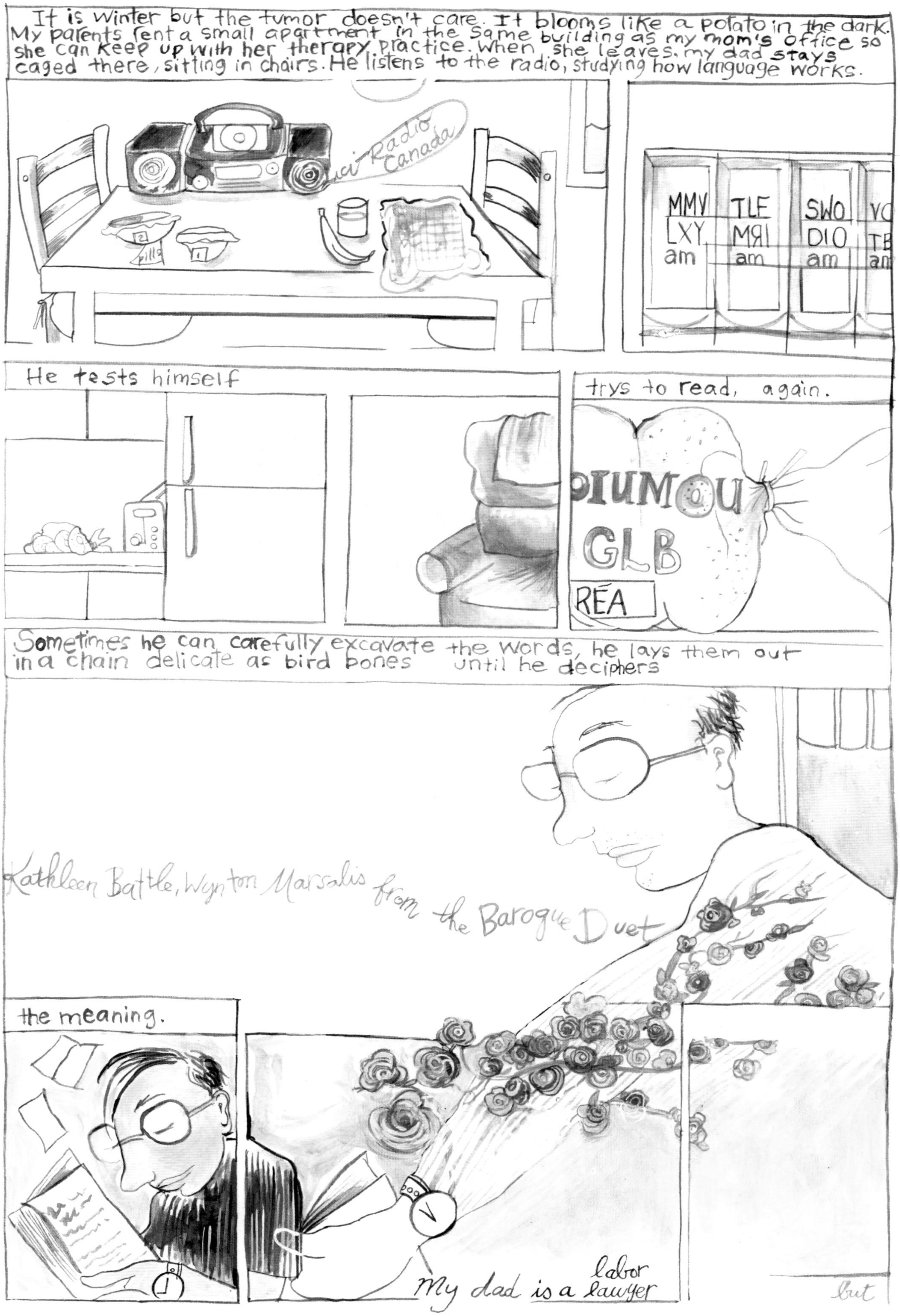
It is winter but the tumor doesn't care. It blooms like a potato in the dark. My parents rent a small apartment in the same building as my mom's office so she can keep up with her therapy practice. When she leaves, my dad stays caged there, sitting in chairs. He listens to the radio, studying how language works.
Ici Radio Canada
MMY TLF SWO
LXY MRI DIO
am am am
He tests himself
trys to read, again.
OIUMOU
GLB
RÉA
Sometimes he can carefully excavate the words, he lays them out in a chain delicate as bird bones until he deciphers
Kathleen Battle, Wynton Marsalis from the Baroque Duet
the meaning.
My dad is a labor lawyer
but

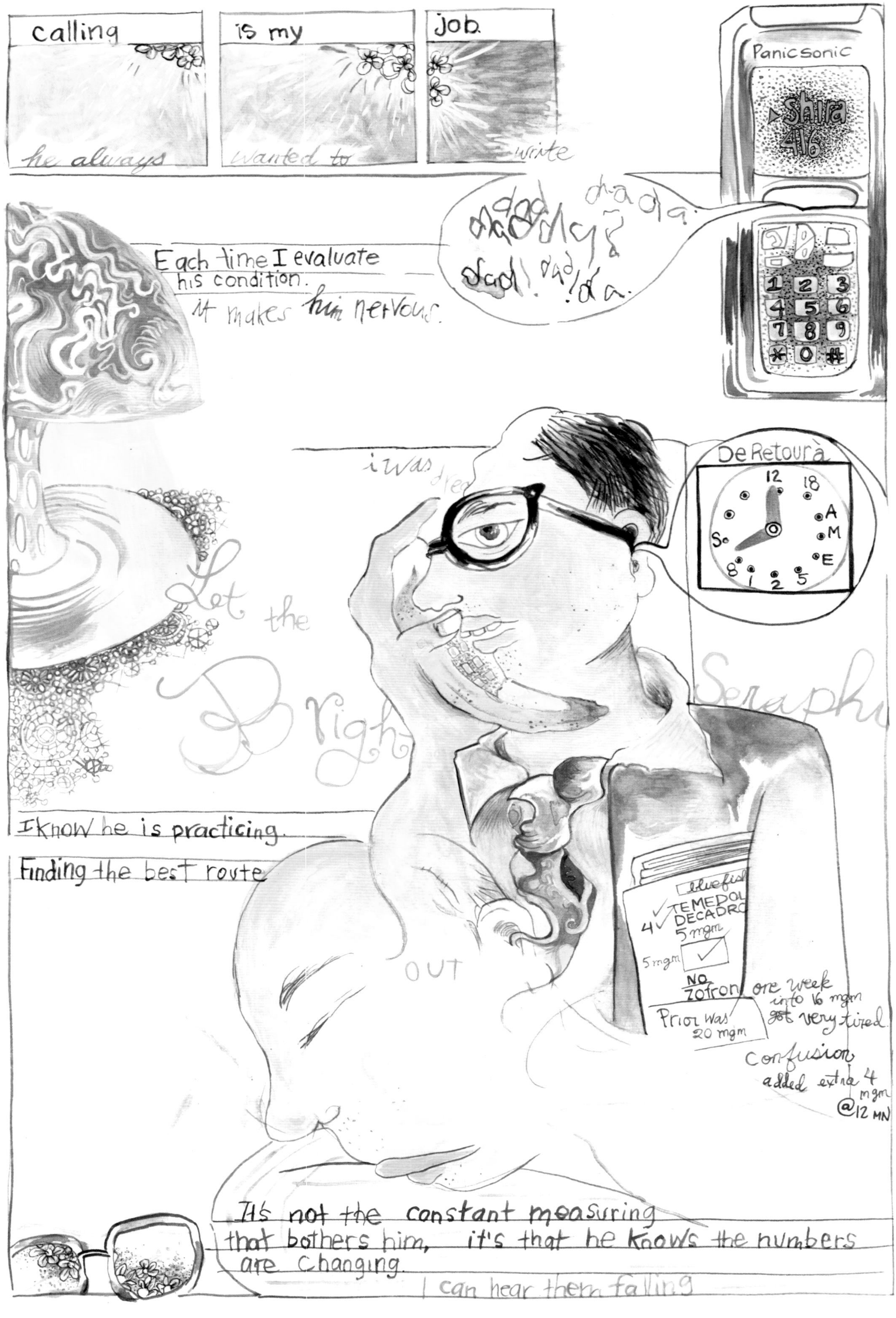
calling
is my
job.
he always
wanted to
write
Panicsonic
Shira
4/16
Each time I evaluate
his condition.
it makes him nervous.
De Retour à
i was
Let the
Bright
Seraph
I know he is practicing.
Finding the best route
OUT
bluefish
TEMEDOL
DECADRO
5 mgm
5 mgm
NO
zofron
one week
into 16 mgm
got very tired.
Prior was
20 mgm
confusion
added extra 4 mgm
@12 MN
It's not the constant measuring
that bothers him, it's that he knows the numbers
are changing.
I can hear them falling

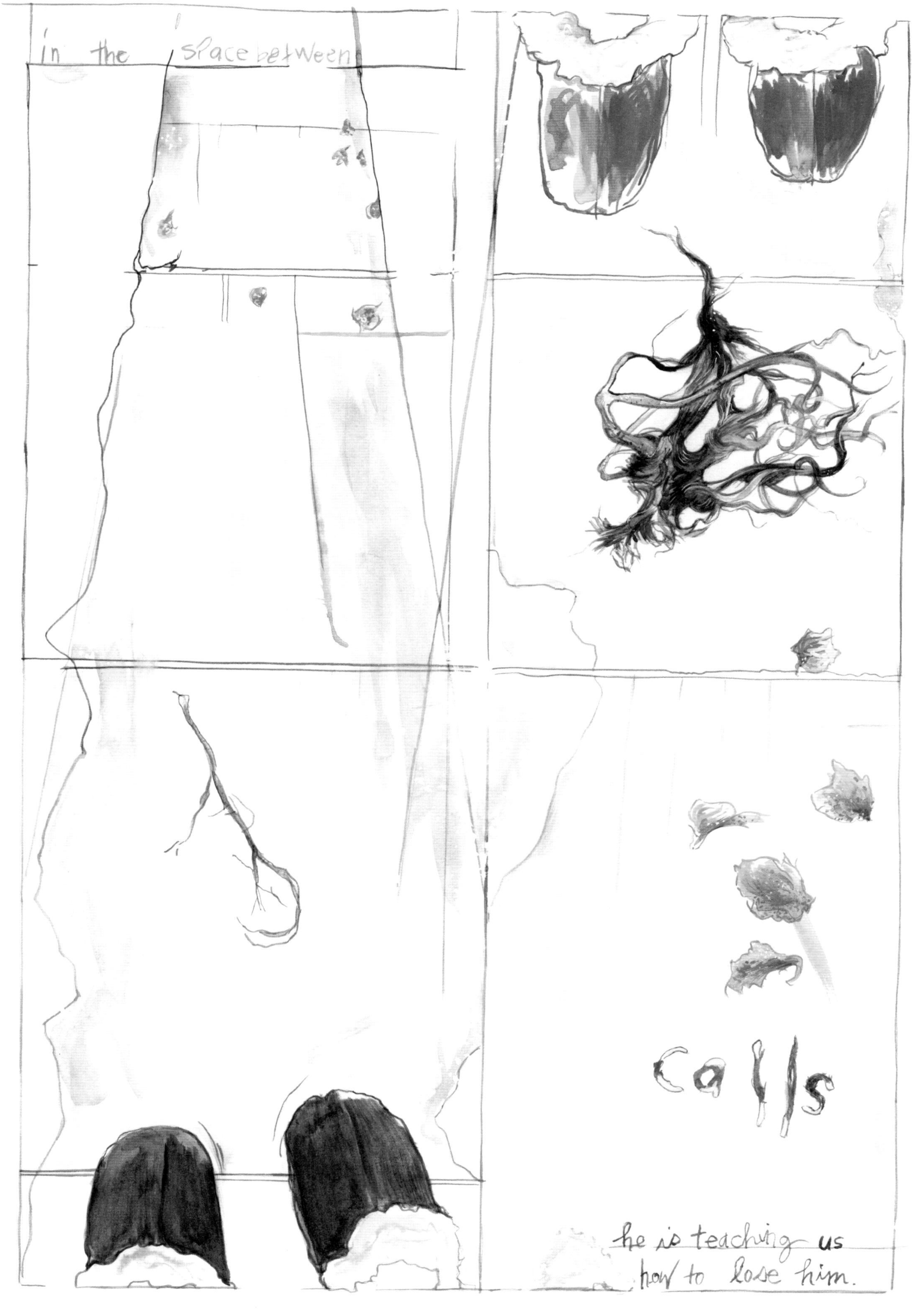
in the space between
calls
he is teaching us
how to lose him.

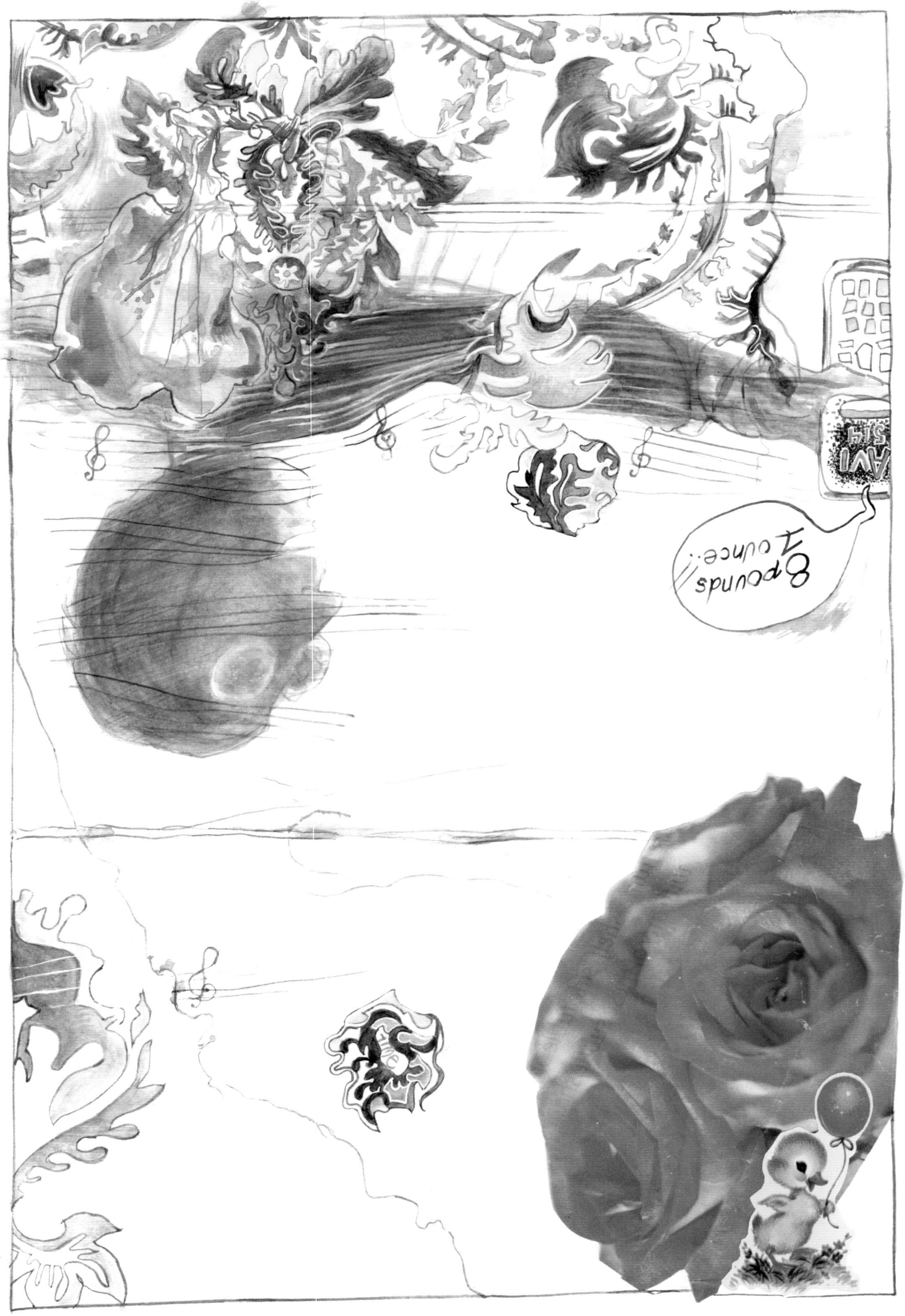
8 pounds 1 ounce...

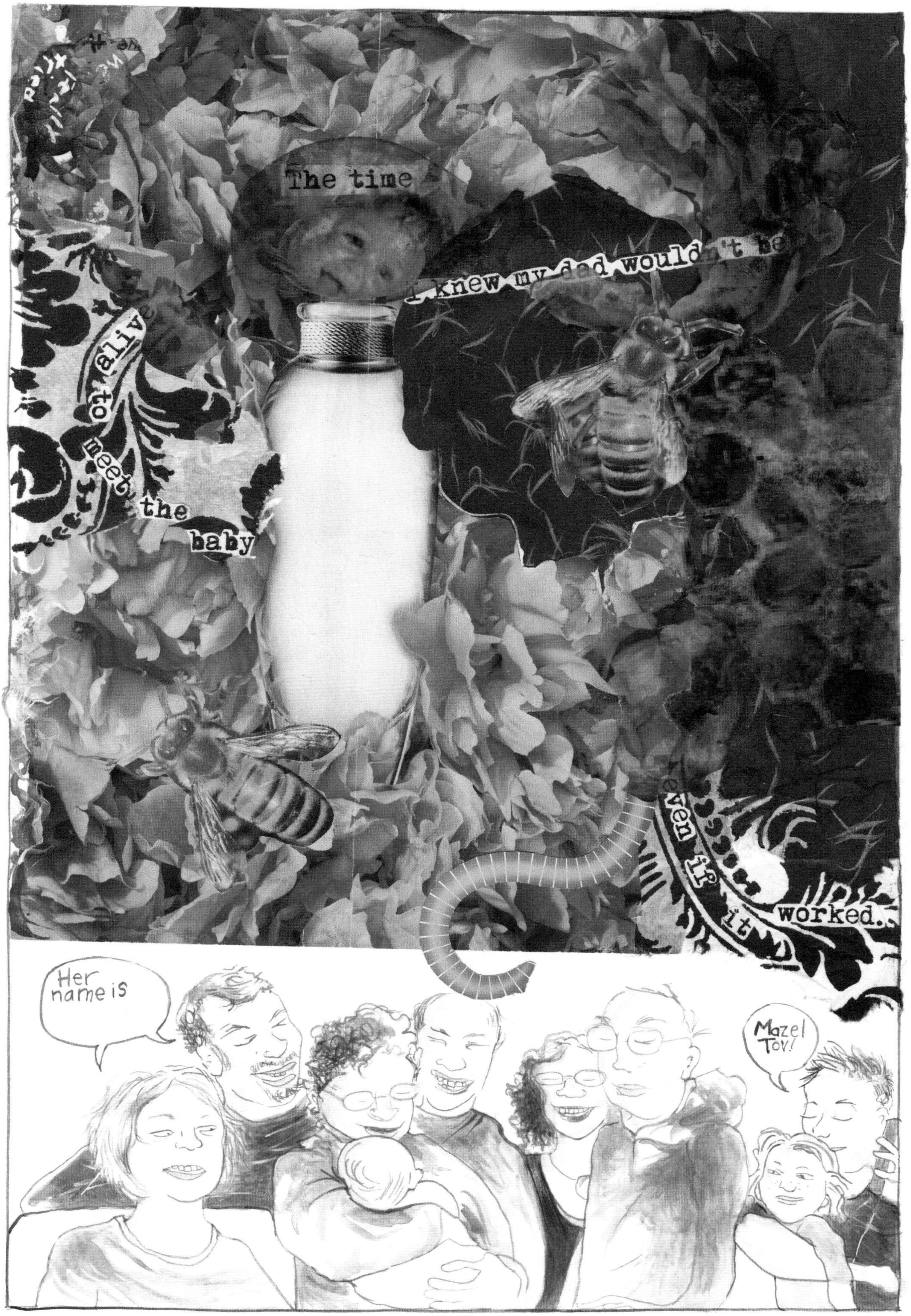
The time
I knew my dad wouldn't be
alive
to meet the
baby
even if
it
worked.
Her name is
Mazel Tov!

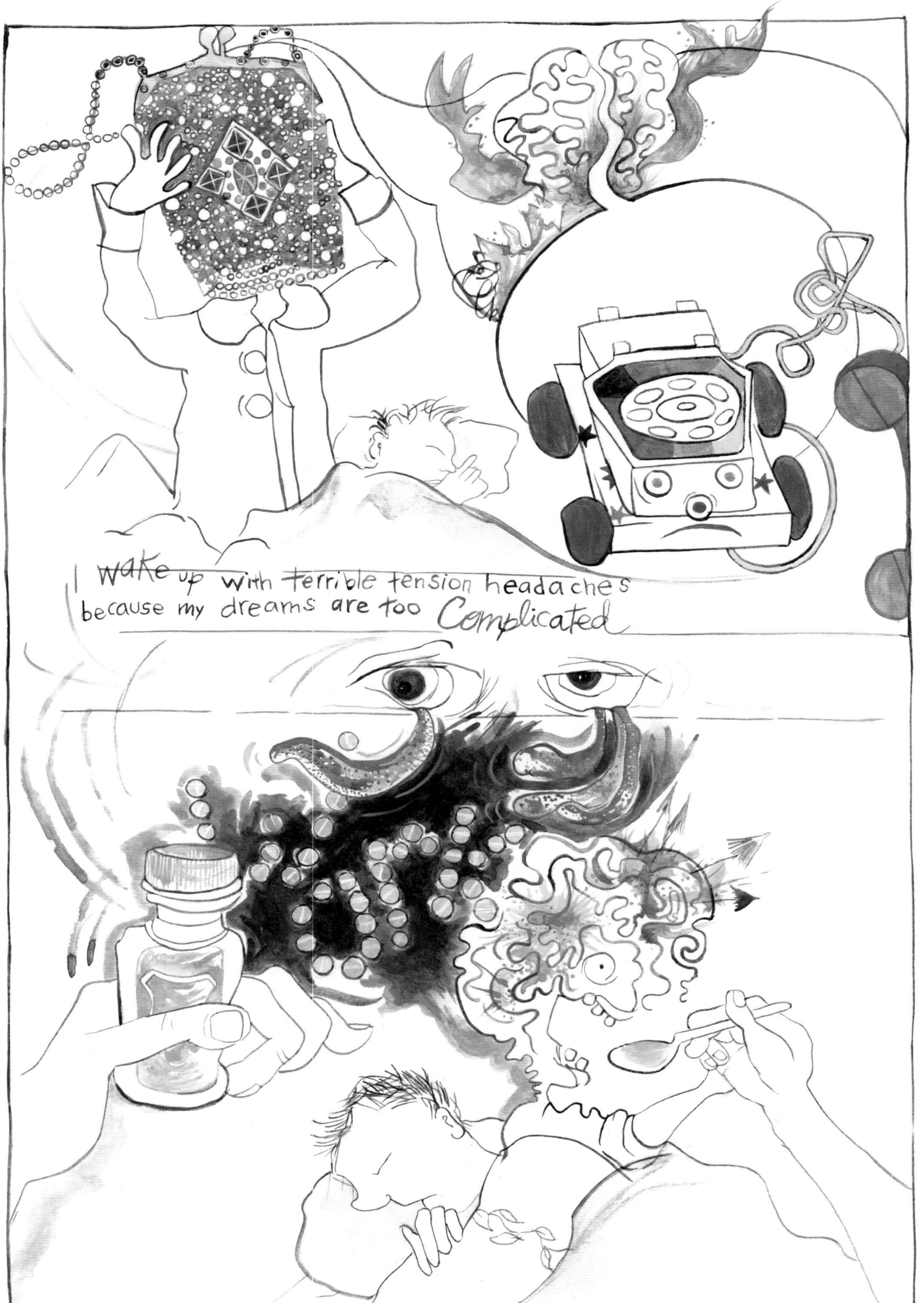
I wake up with terrible tension headaches because my dreams are too Complicated
I stumble out of bed

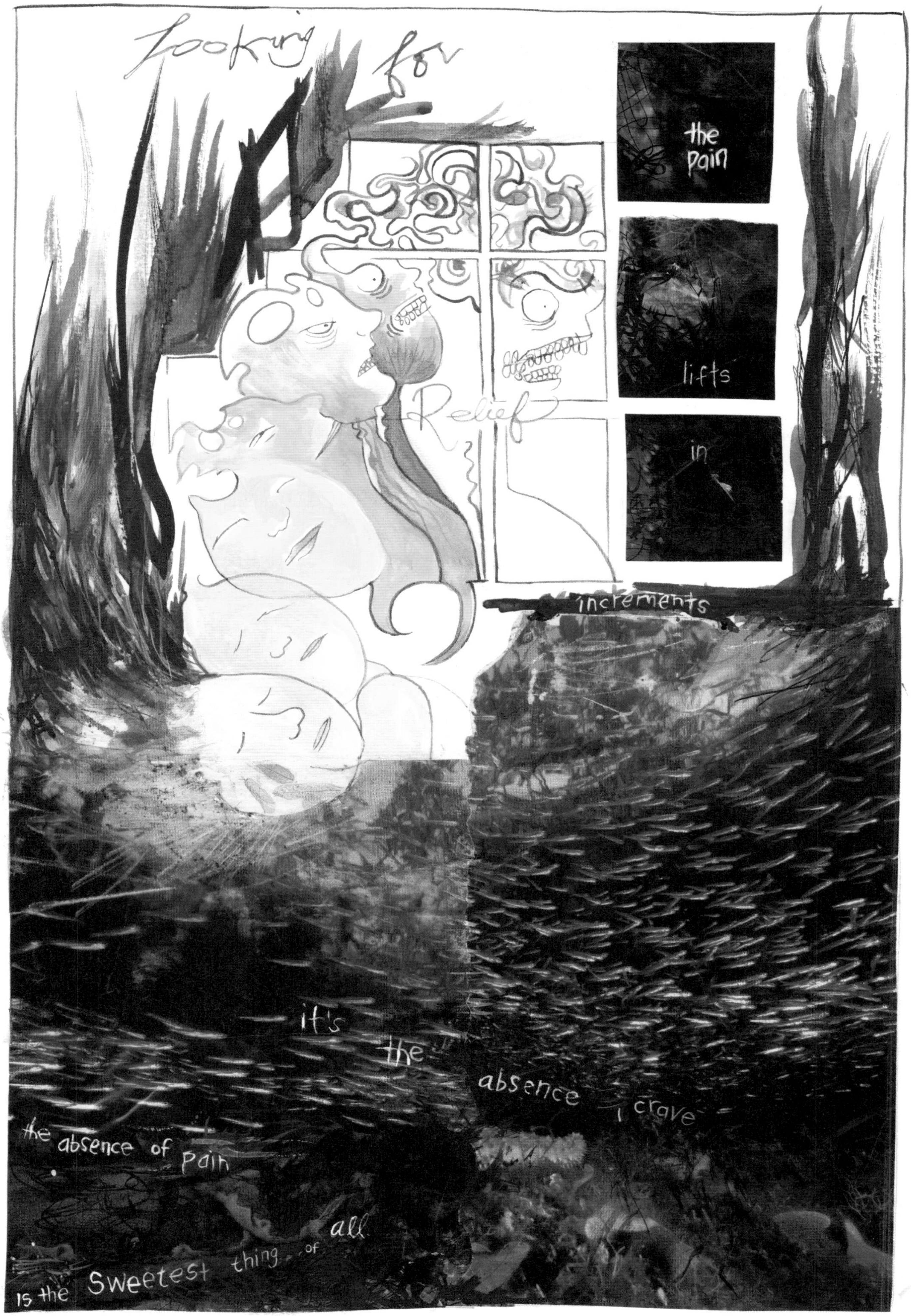
Looking for
Relief
the pain
lifts
in
increments
it's
the
absence
i crave
the absence of pain
is the Sweetest thing of all.

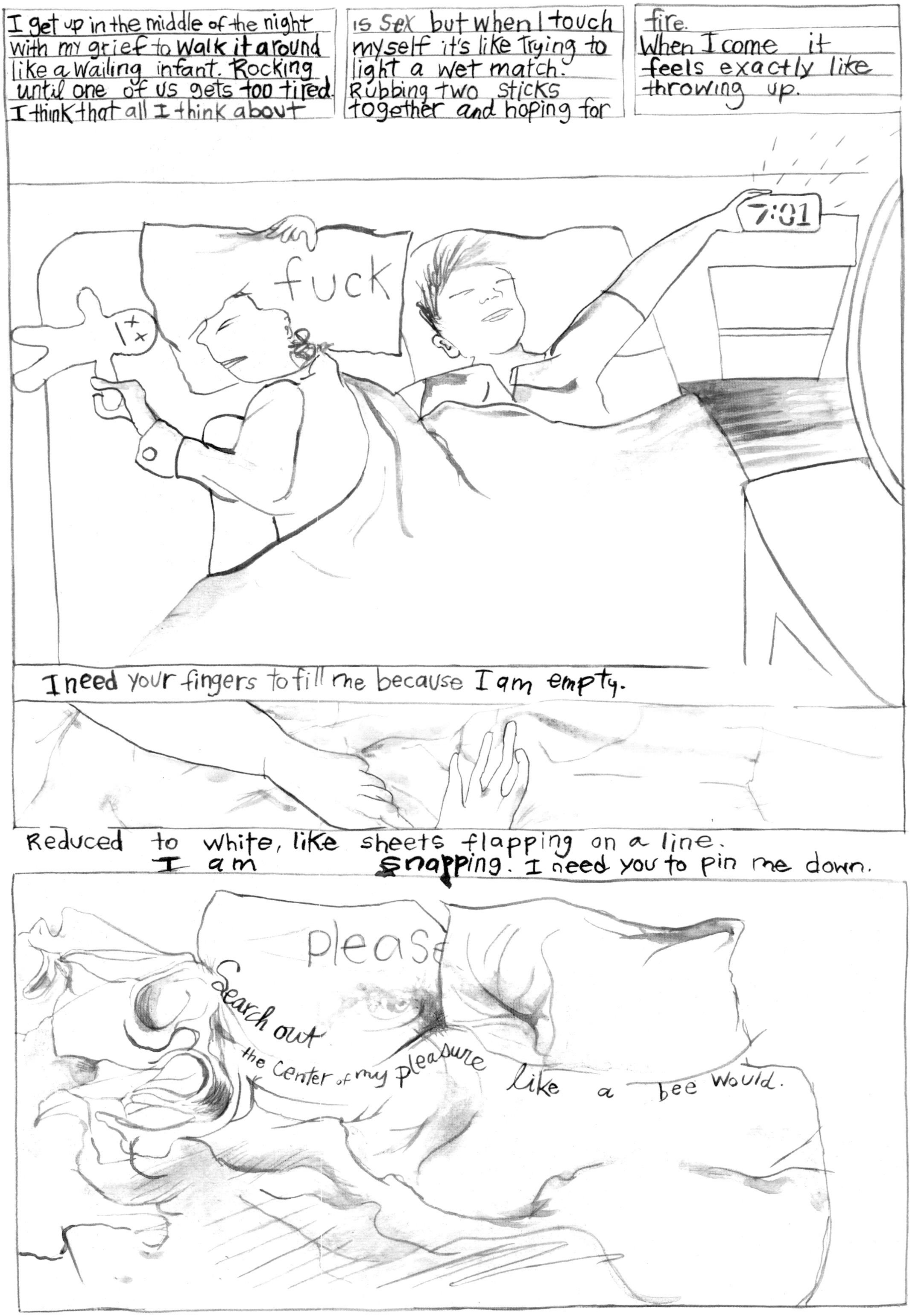
I get up in the middle of the night with my grief to walk it around like a wailing infant. Rocking until one of us gets too tired. I think that all I think about
is sex but when I touch myself it's like trying to light a wet match. Rubbing two sticks together and hoping for
fire. When I come it feels exactly like throwing up.
7:01
fuck
I need your fingers to fill me because I am empty.
Reduced to white, like sheets flapping on a line.
I am snapping. I need you to pin me down.
please
Search out the center of my pleasure like a bee would.

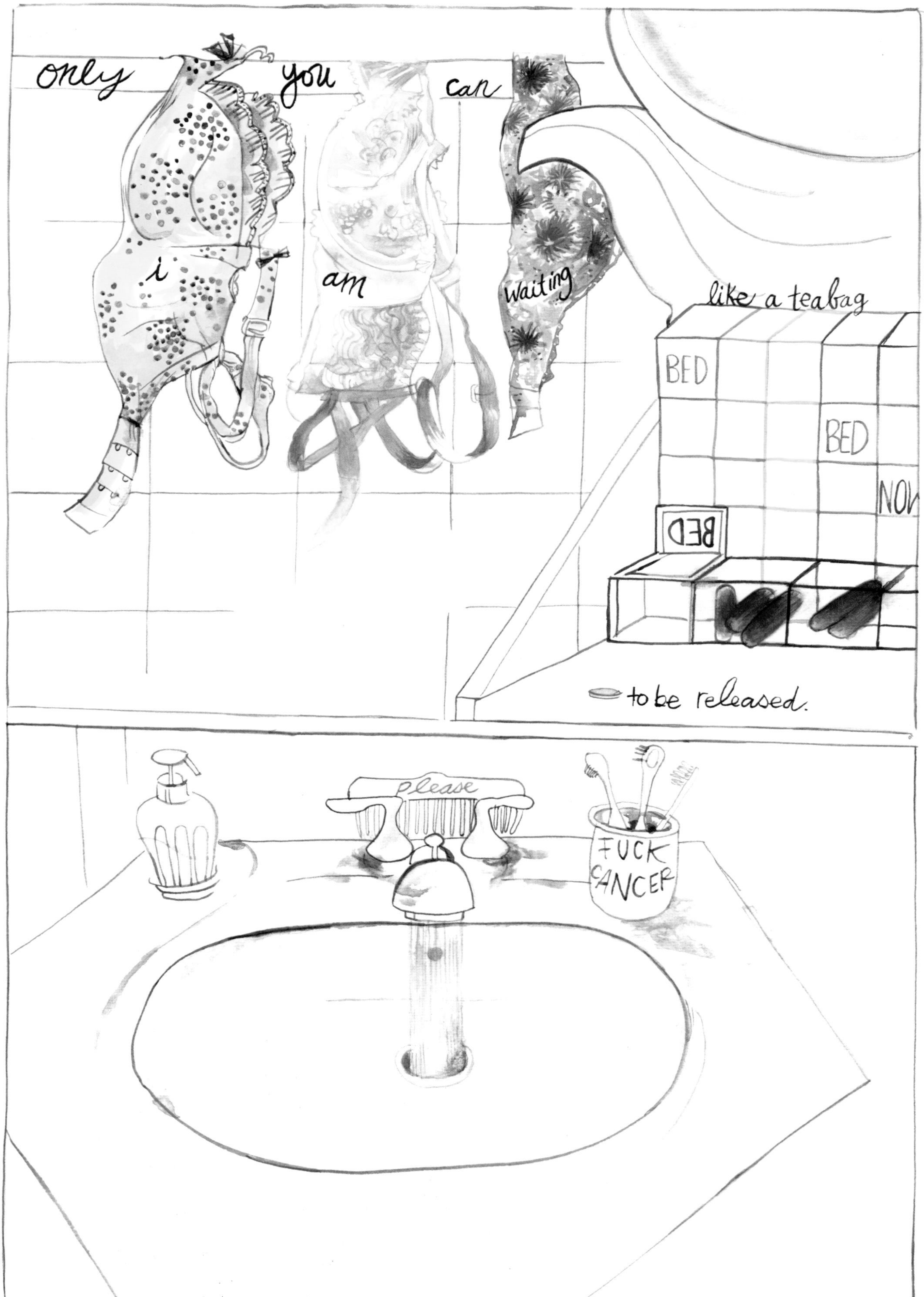
only
you
can
i
am
waiting
like a teabag
BED
BED
NOW
to be released.
please
FUCK CANCER

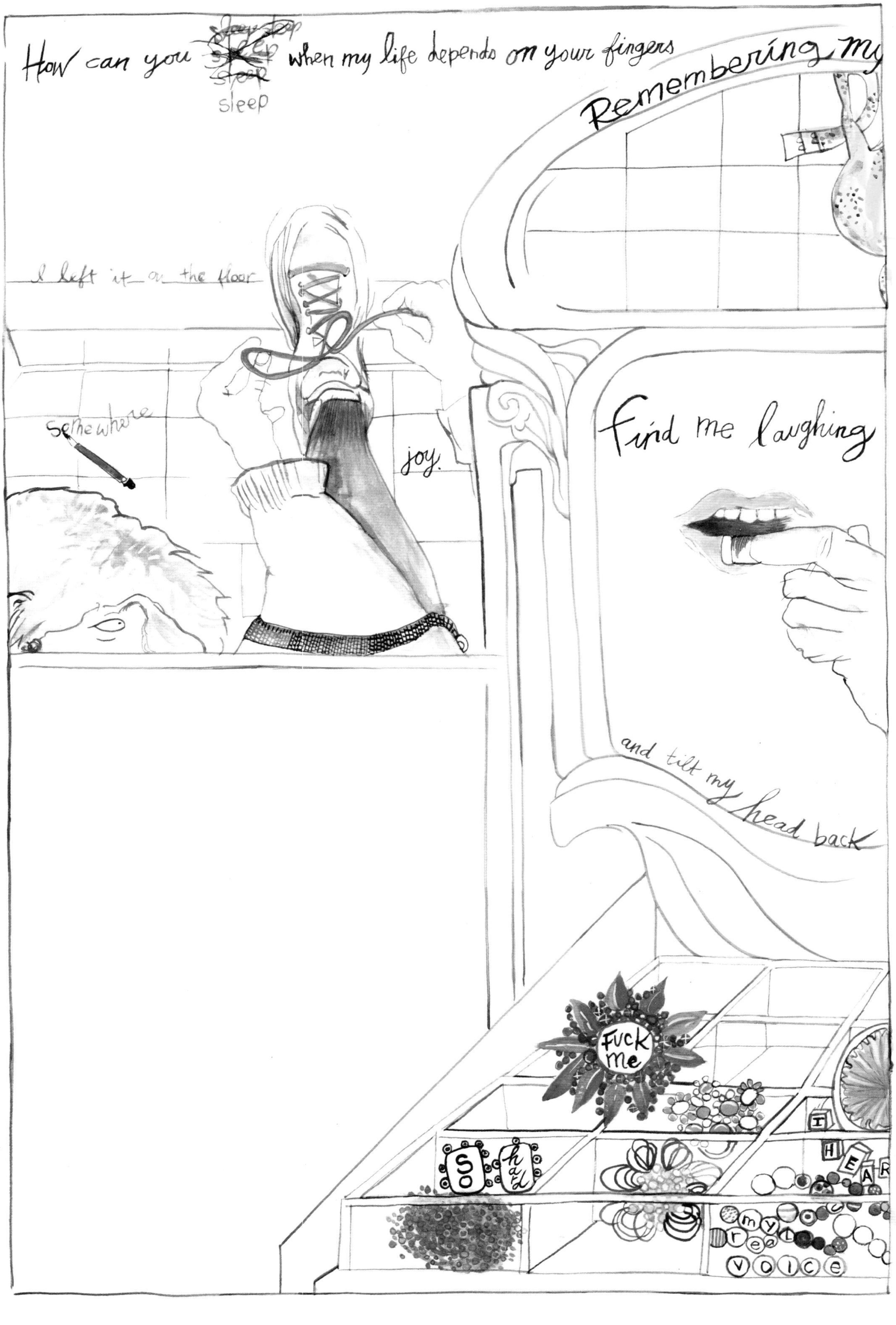
How can you sleep when my life depends on your fingers
sleep
Remembering my
I left it on the floor
Somewhere
joy.
Find me laughing
and tilt my head back
Fuck me
So hard
I HEAR
my real voice

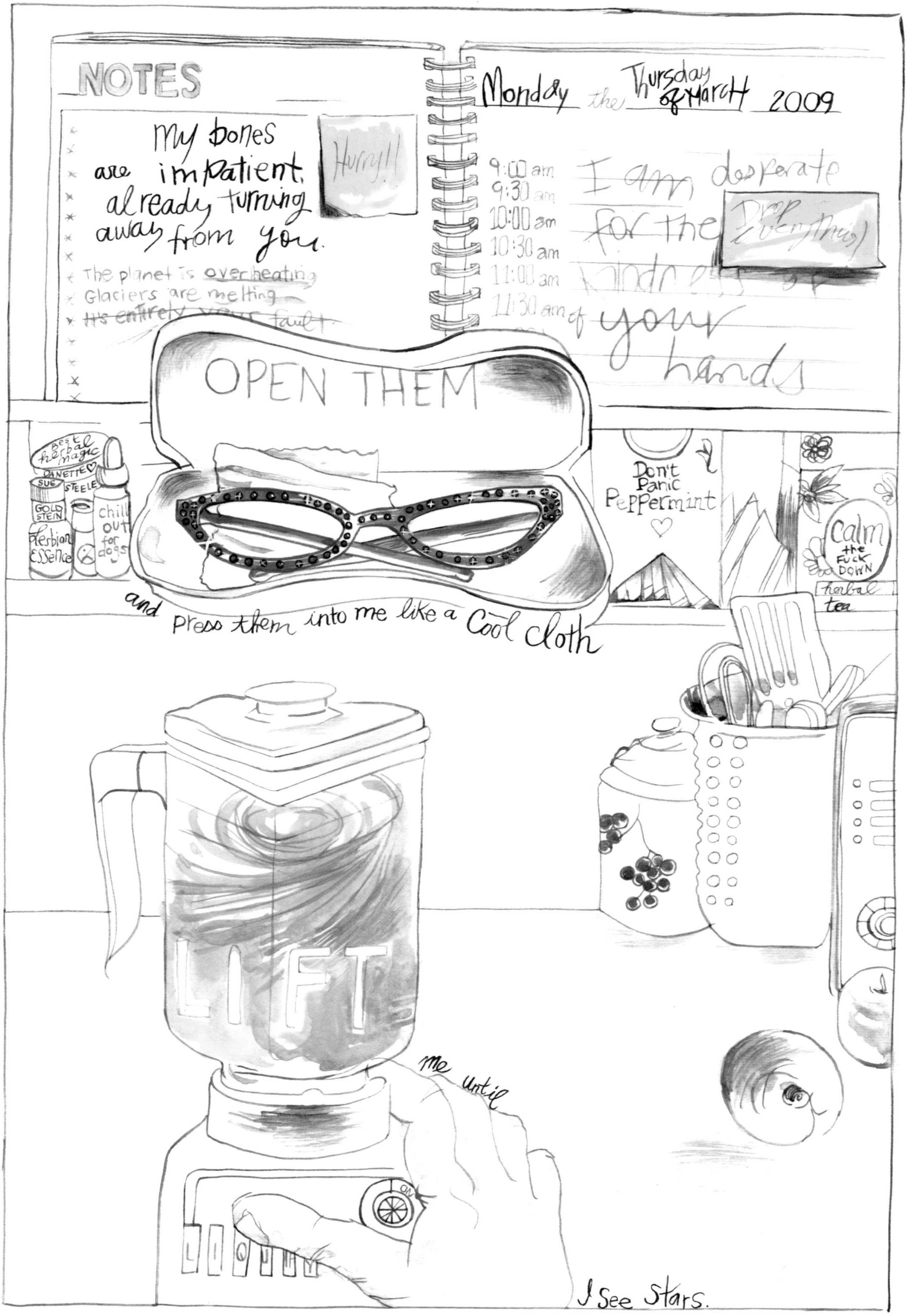
NOTES
My bones are impatient, already turning away from you.
Hurry!!
The planet is overheating
Glaciers are melting
It's entirely your fault
Monday the Thursday of March 2009
9:00 am
9:30 am
10:00 am
10:30 am
11:00 am
11:30 am
I am desperate for the kindness of your hands
OPEN THEM
and press them into me like a cool cloth
Best herbal magic
Lesbian Essence
chill out for dogs
Don't Panic Peppermint
Calm the Fuck Down
herbal tea
LIFT
me until
ON
I see stars.

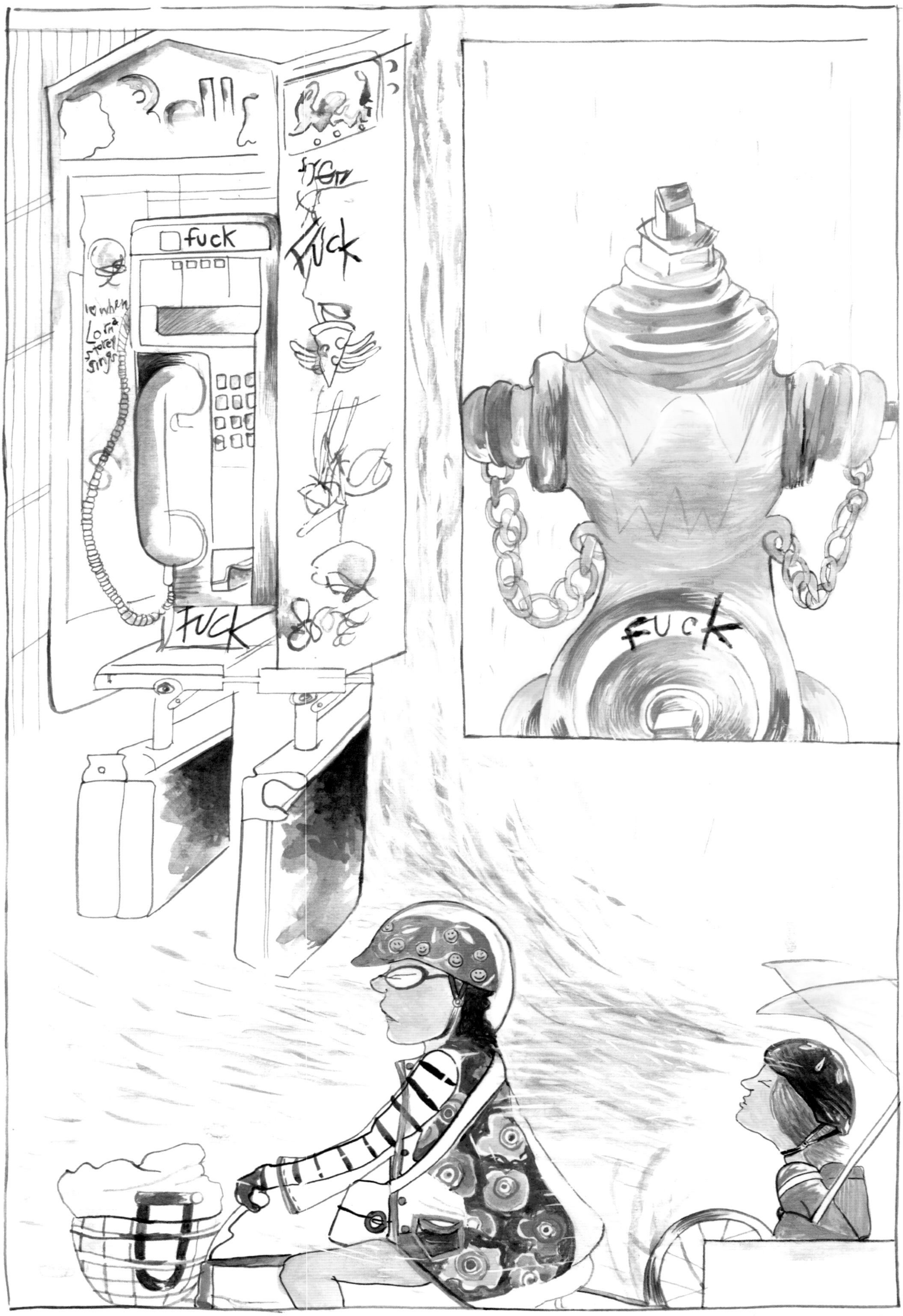
fuck
FUCK
I ♥ when Lorna storey sings
FUCK
FUCK

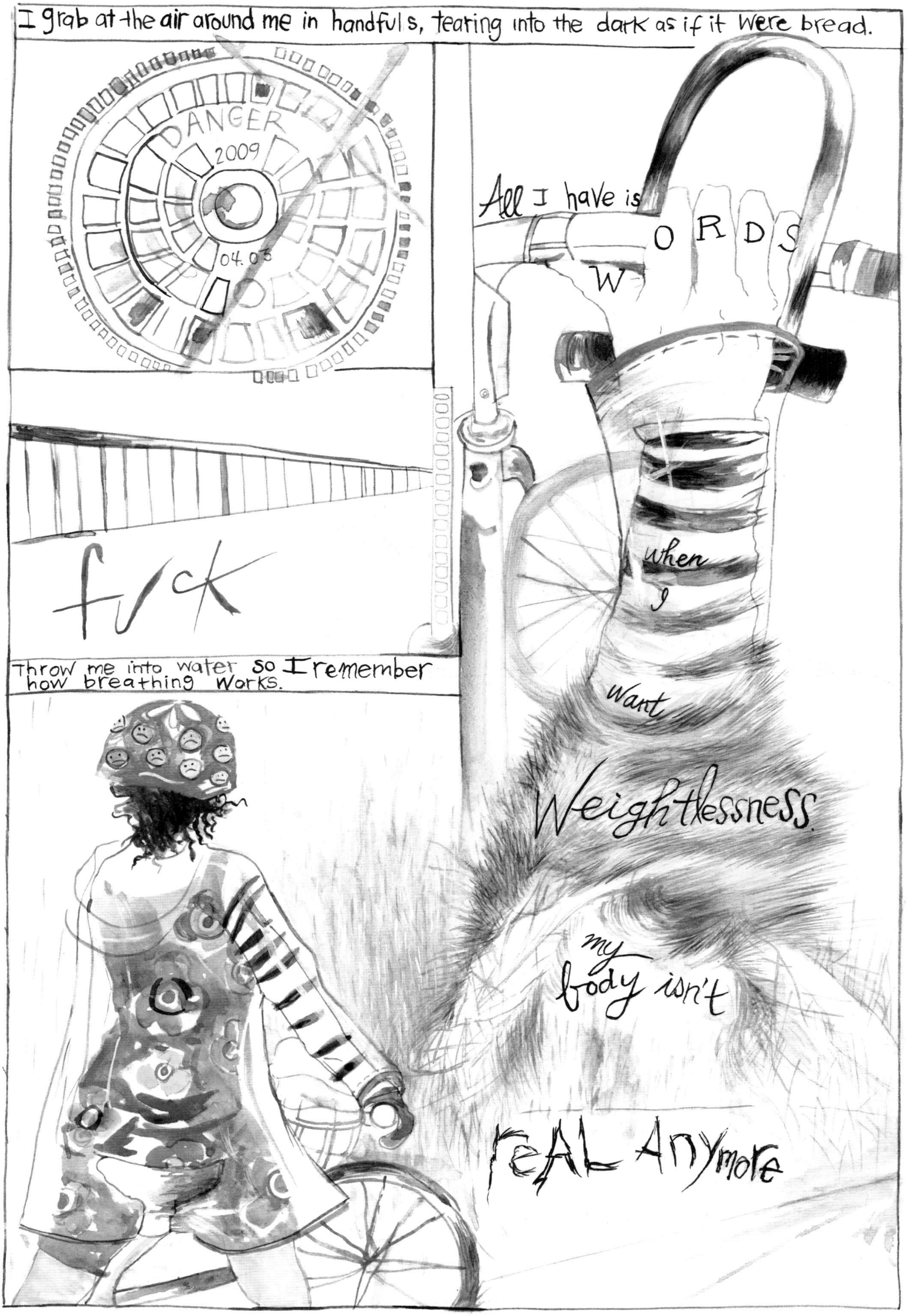
I grab at the air around me in handfuls, tearing into the dark as if it were bread.
DANGER
2009
04.05
fuck
Throw me into water so I remember how breathing works.
All I have is
WORDS
when I want
Weightlessness
my body isn't
reAL Anymore

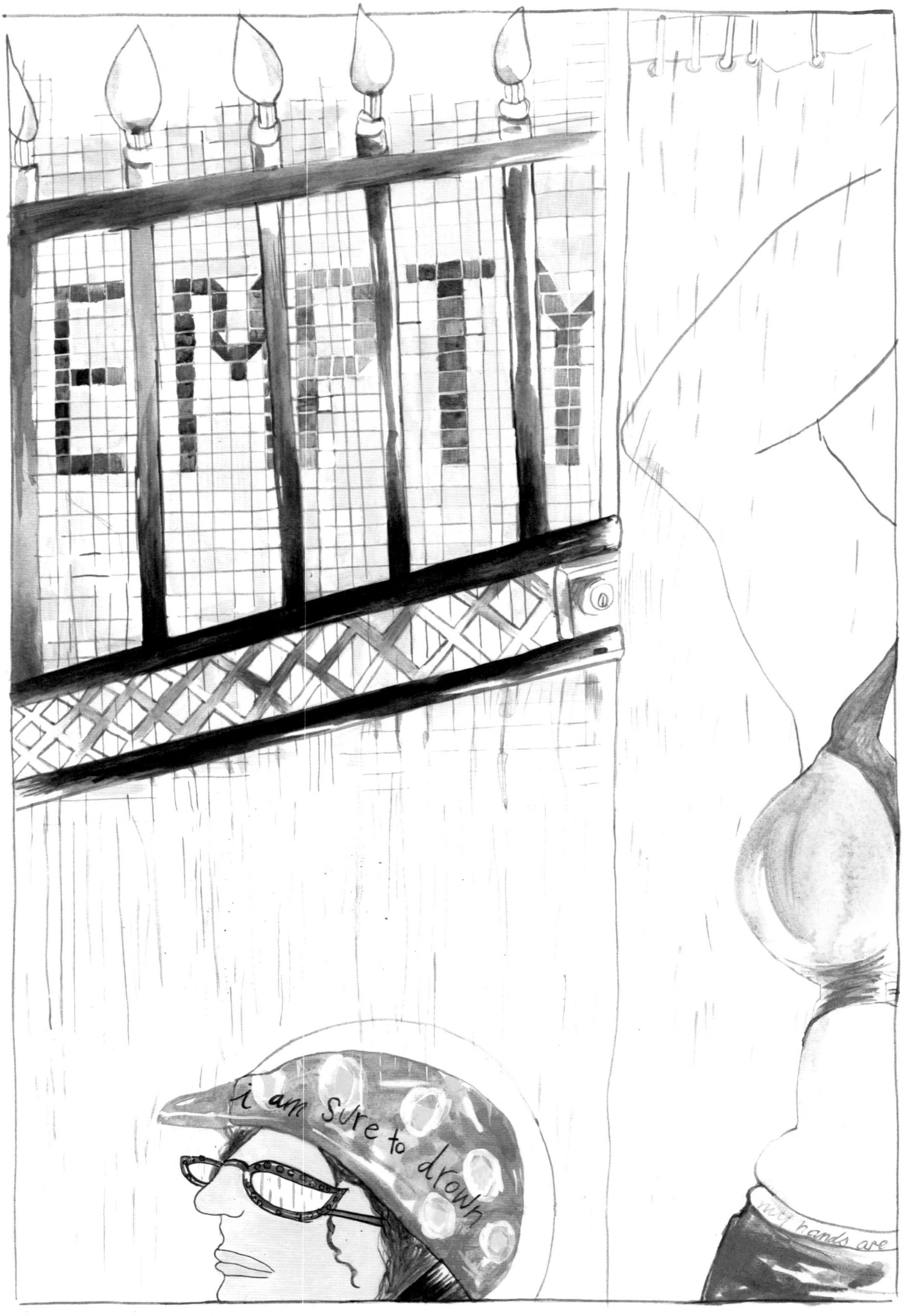
EMPTY
i am sure to drown
my hands are

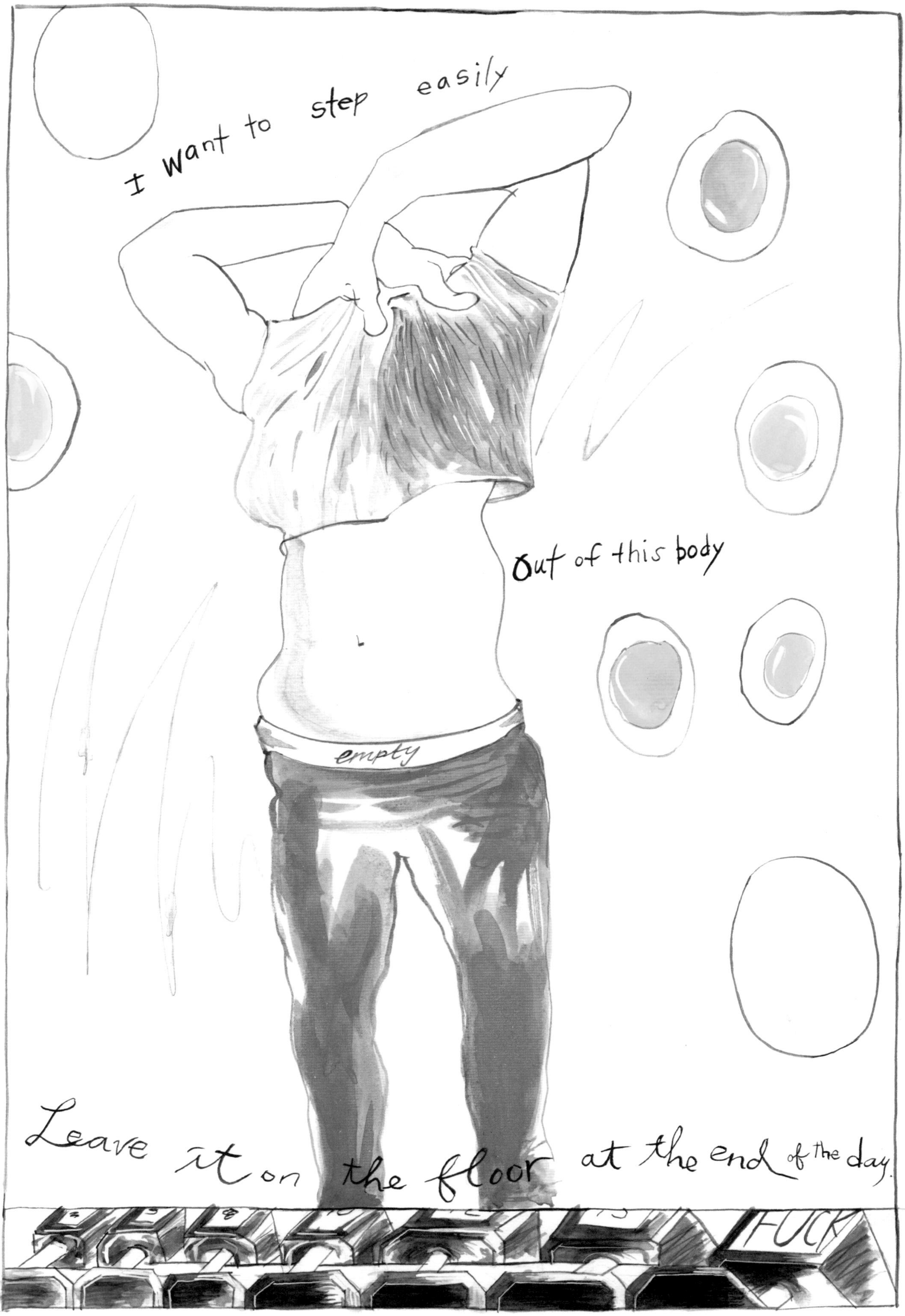
I want to step easily
Out of this body
empty
Leave it on the floor at the end of the day.
FUCK

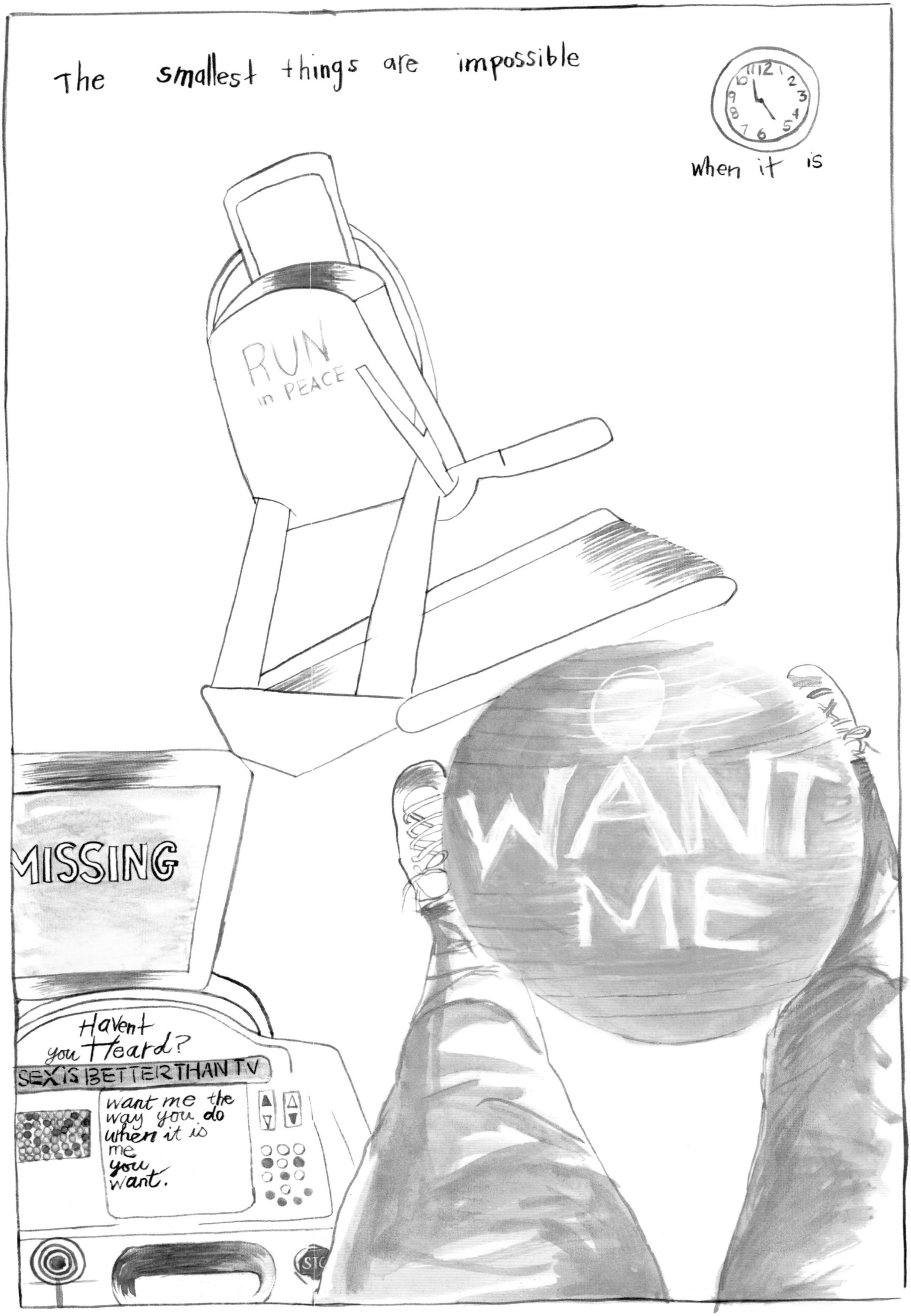
The smallest things are impossible
when it is
RUN in PEACE
MISSING
Havent you Heard?
SEX IS BETTER THAN TV
want me the way you do when it is me you want.
WANT ME

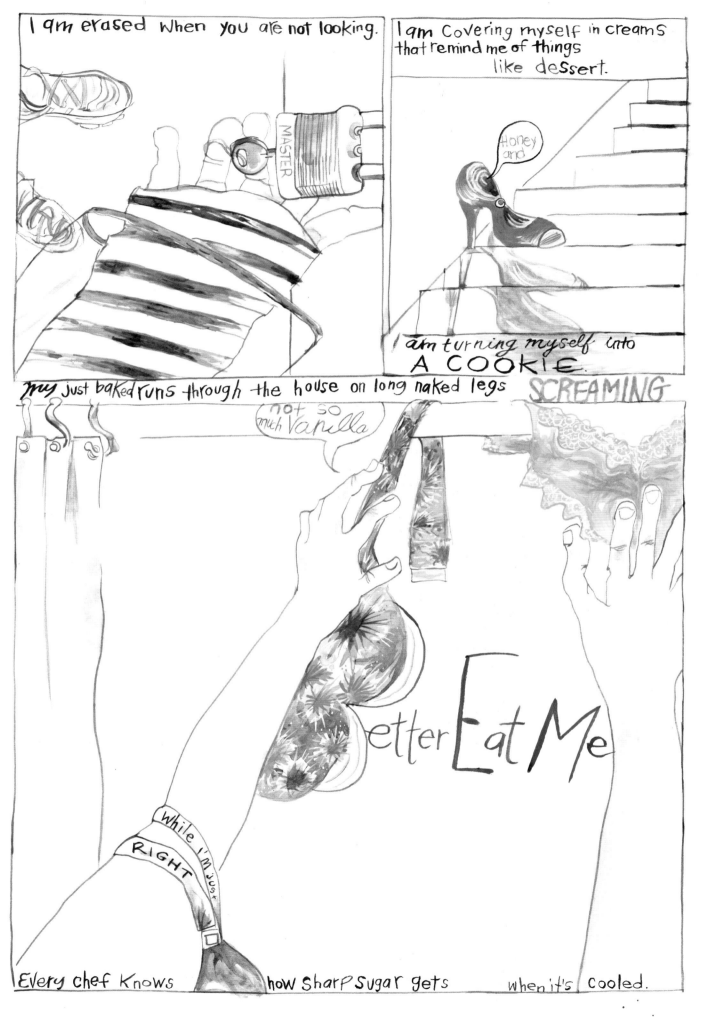

I am erased when you are not looking.

I am covering myself in creams that remind me of things like dessert.

Honey and

am turning myself into A COOKIE.

my just baked runs through the house on long naked legs SCREAMING

not so much Vanilla

Better Eat Me

while I'm
RIGHT

Every chef knows how sharp sugar gets when it's cooled.

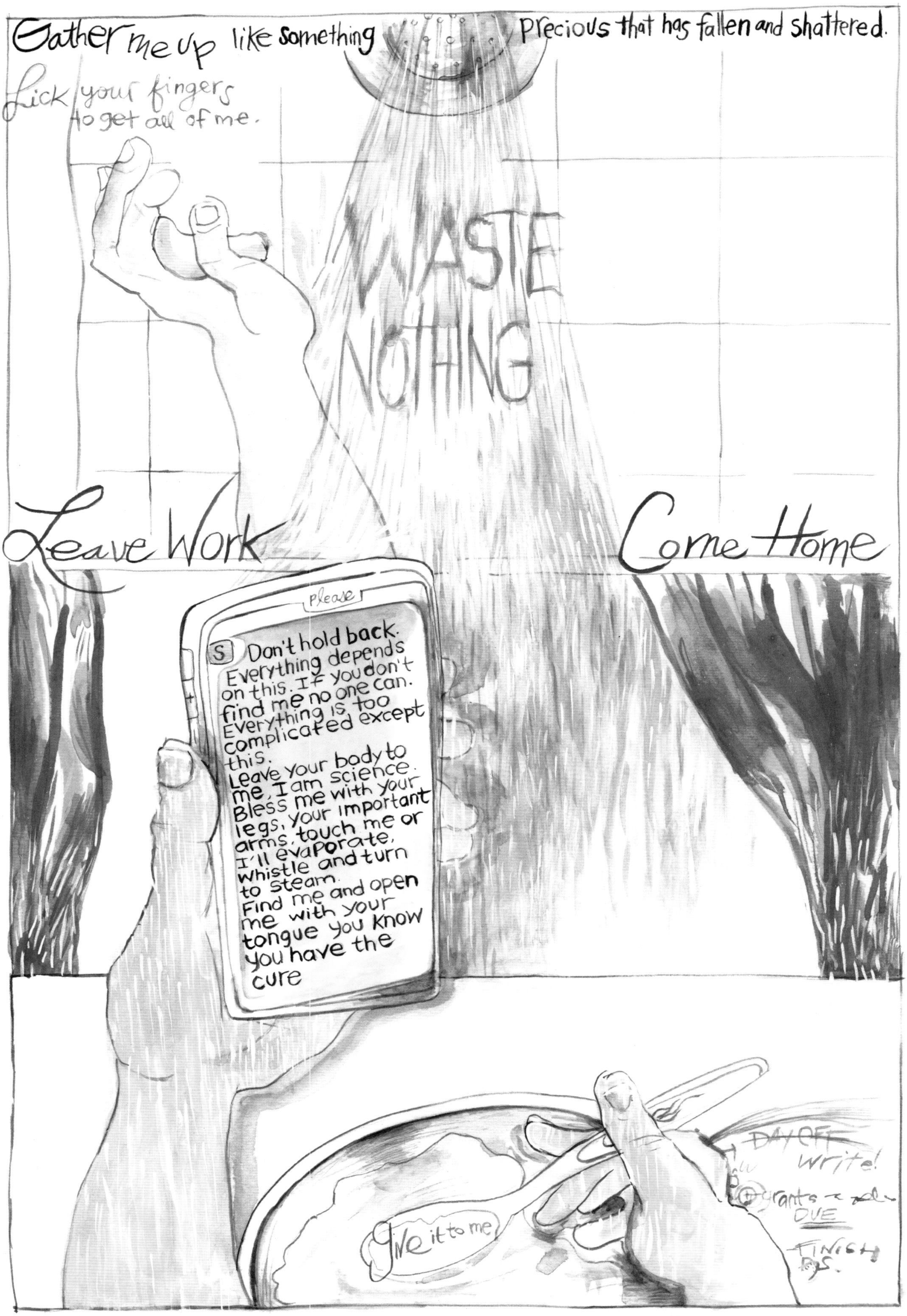
Gather me up like something precious that has fallen and shattered.
Lick your fingers to get all of me.
WASTE NOTHING
Leave Work
Come Home
Please
Don't hold back. Everything depends on this. If you don't find me no one can. Everything is too complicated except this.
Leave your body to me, I am science. Bless me with your legs, your important arms, touch me or I'll evaporate, whistle and turn to steam.
Find me and open me with your tongue you know you have the cure
DAY OFF
write!
grants
DUE
FINISH
Give it to me

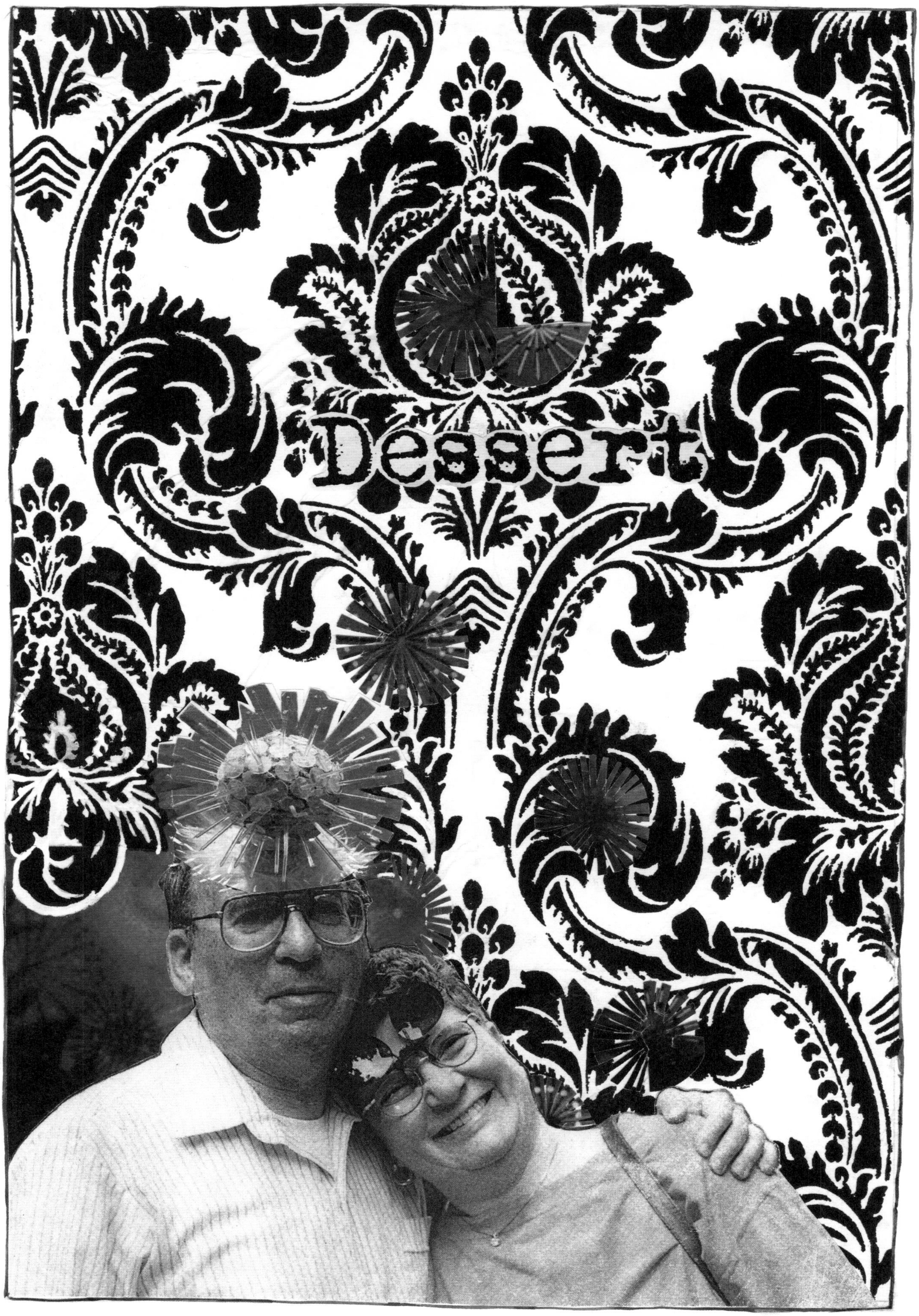
Dessert

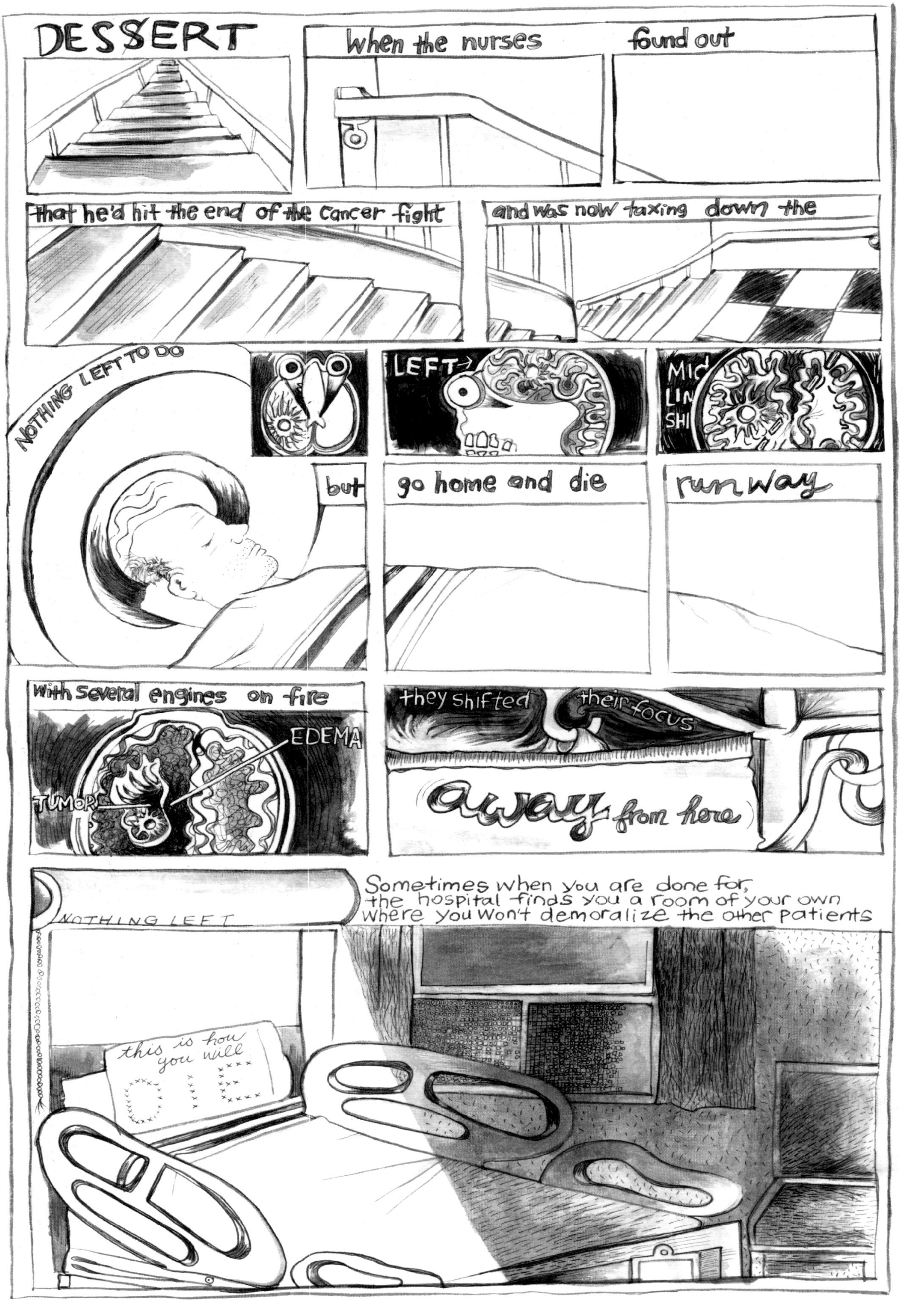
DESSERT
When the nurses
found out
that he'd hit the end of the cancer fight
and was now taxing down the
NOTHING LEFT TO DO
LEFT→
MID
LIN
SHI
but
go home and die
runway
with several engines on fire
EDEMA
TUMOR
they shifted
their focus
away from here
NOTHING LEFT
Sometimes when you are done for,
the hospital finds you a room of your own
where you won't demoralize the other patients
this is how
you will
DIE

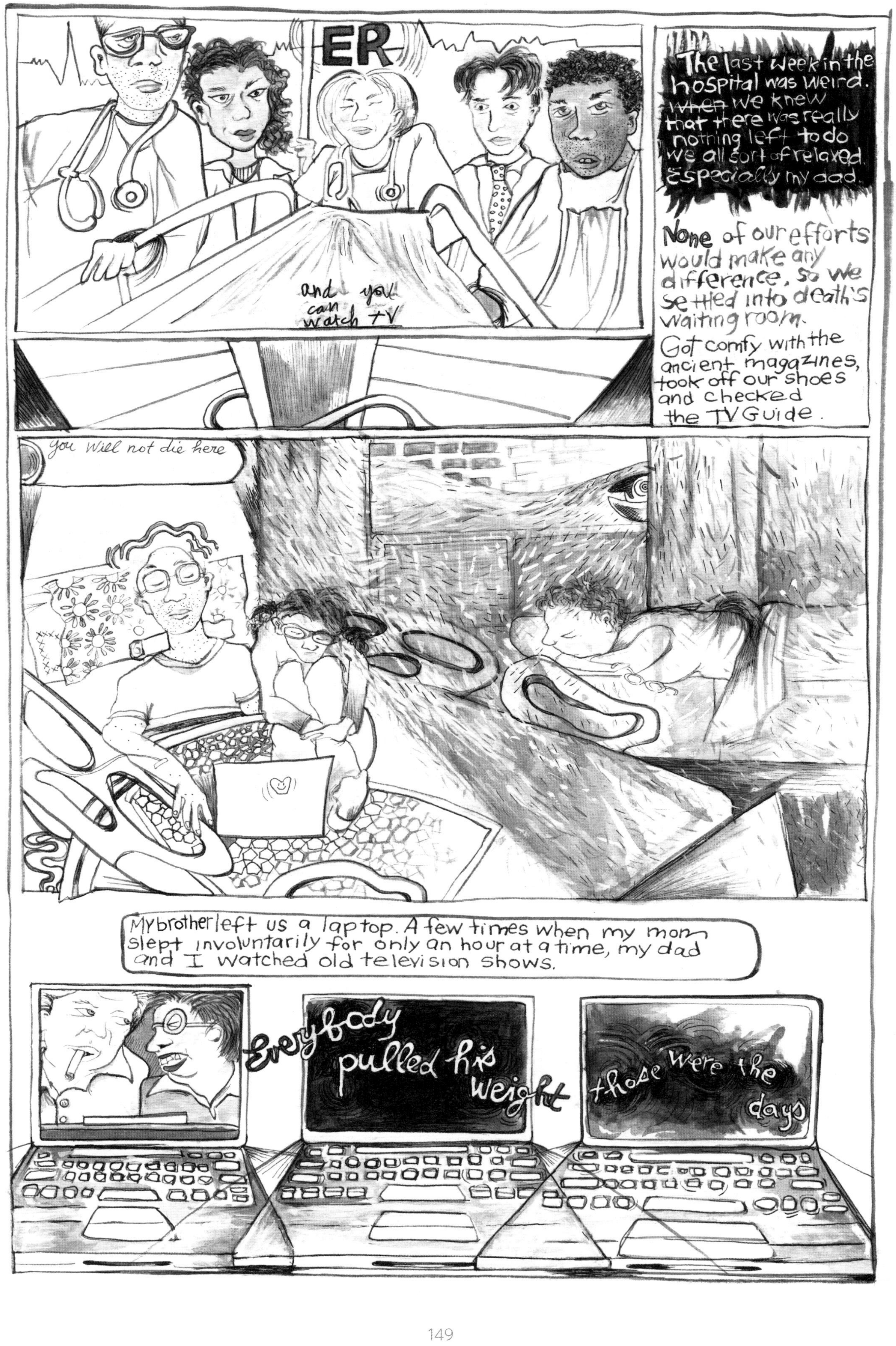
ER
and you can watch TV
The last week in the hospital was weird. When we knew that there was really nothing left to do we all sort of relaxed. Especially my dad.
None of our efforts would make any difference, so we settled into death's waiting room.
Got comfy with the ancient magazines, took off our shoes and checked the TV Guide.
You will not die here
My brother left us a laptop. A few times when my mom slept involuntarily for only an hour at a time, my dad and I watched old television shows.
Everybody pulled his weight
those were the days

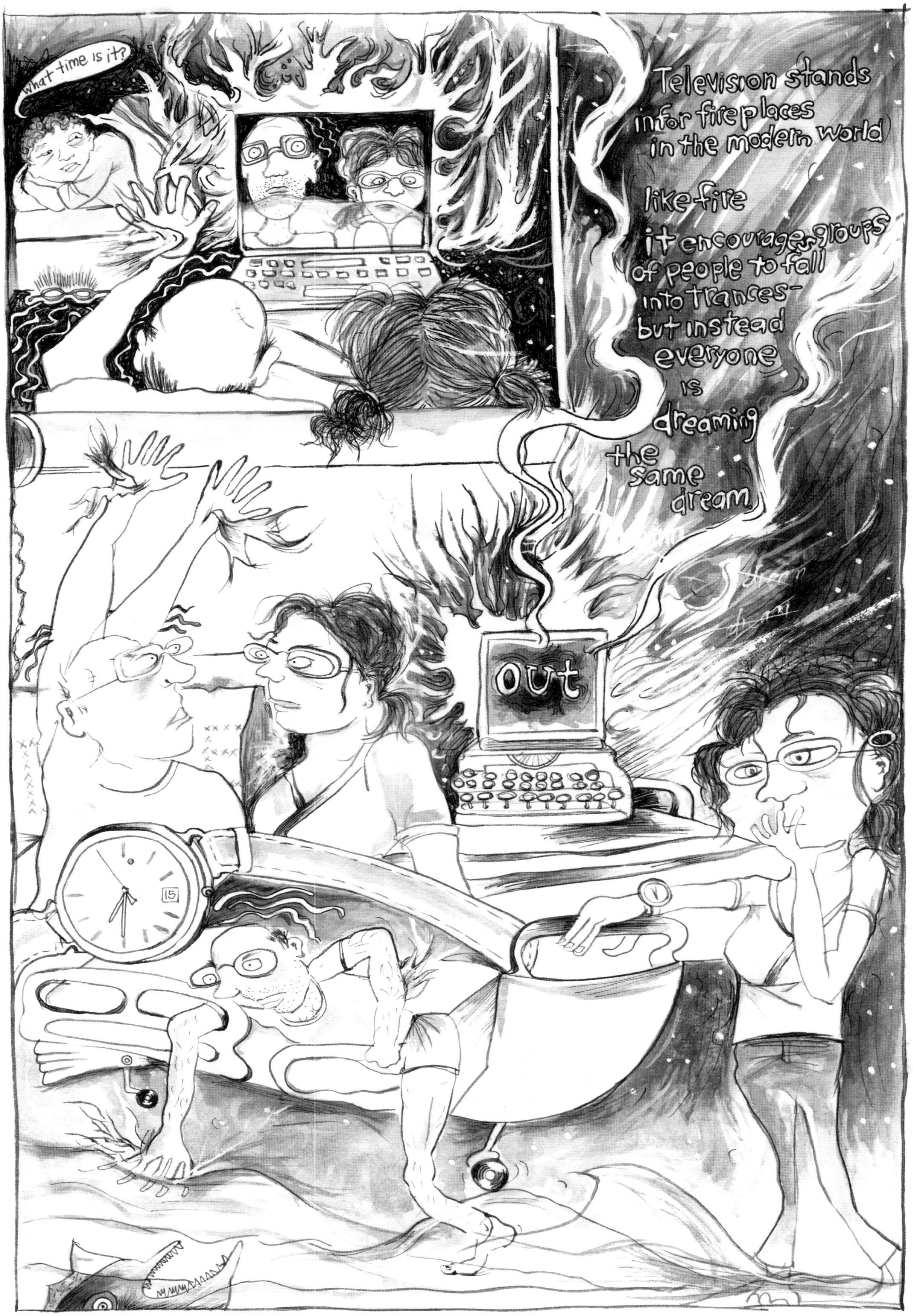
what time is it?
Television stands in for fireplaces in the modern world
like fire
it encourages groups of people to fall into trances-
but instead everyone is dreaming the same dream
OUT
15

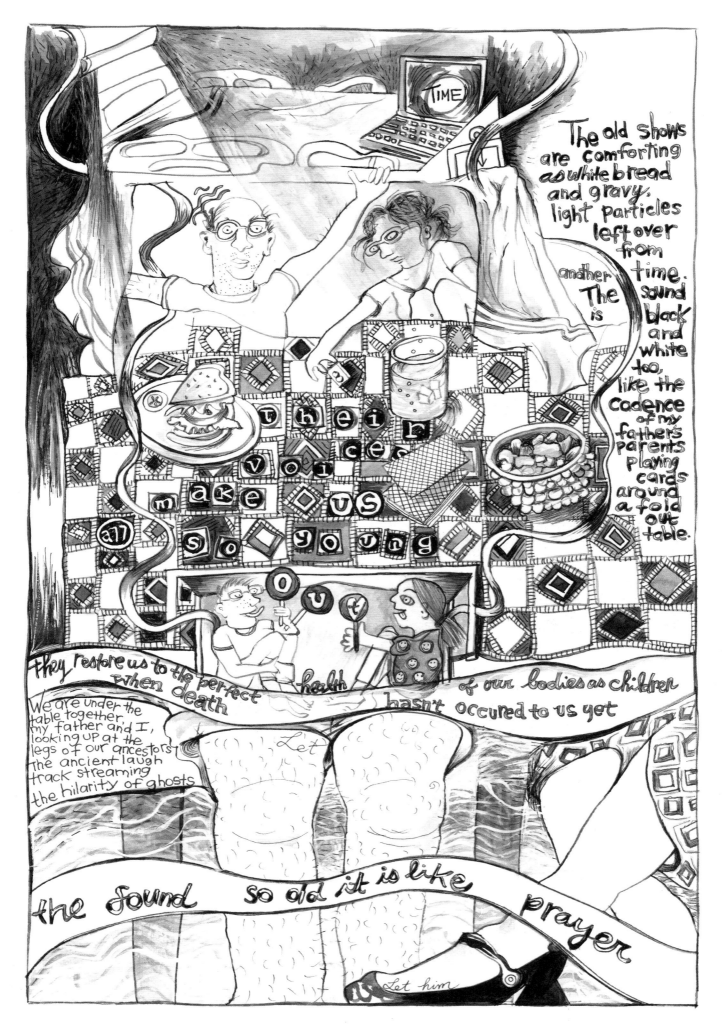

The old shows are comforting as white bread and gravy, light particles left over from time. The sound is another black and white too, like the cadence of my fathers parents playing cards around a fold out table.

TIME

Their voices make us all so young out

they restore us to the perfect health when death of our bodies as children hasn't occured to us yet

We are under the table together, my father and I, looking up at the legs of our ancestors the ancient laugh track streaming the hilarity of ghosts

Let

the sound so old it is like prayer

Let him

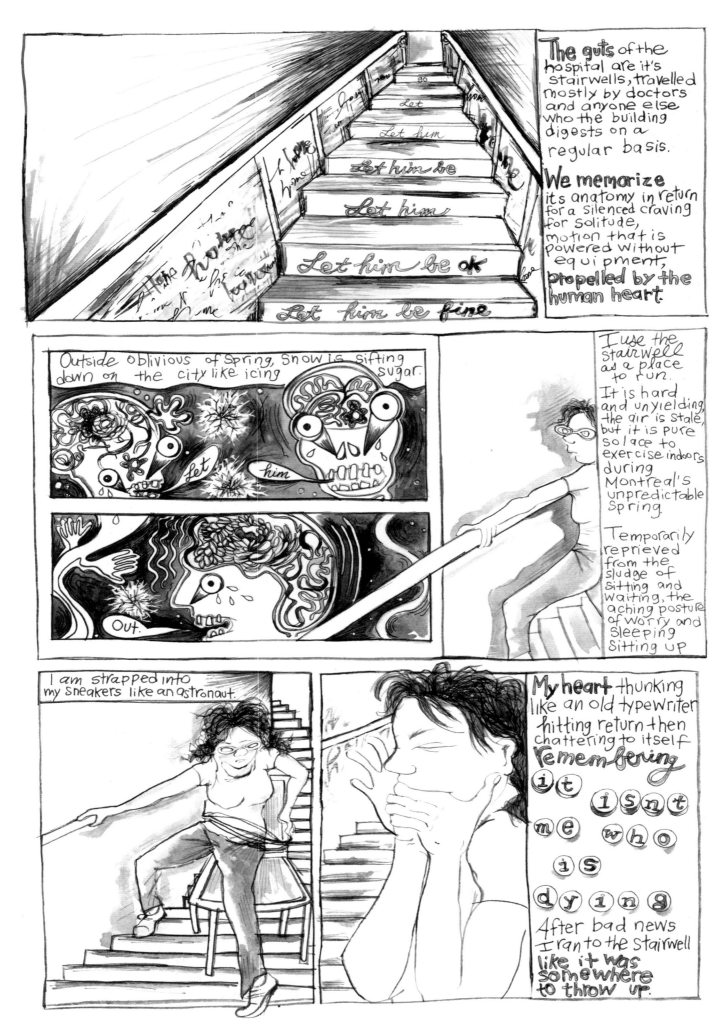

The guts of the hospital are it's stairwells, travelled mostly by doctors and anyone else who the building digests on a regular basis.

We memorize its anatomy in return for a silenced craving for solitude, motion that is powered without equipment, propelled by the human heart.

Let
Let him
Let him be
Let him
Let him be ok
Let him be fine

Outside oblivious of spring, snow is sifting down on the city like icing sugar.

Let him
Out.

I use the stairwell as a place to run.

It is hard and unyielding, the air is stale, but it is pure solace to exercise indoors during Montreal's unpredictable spring.

Temporarily reprieved from the sludge of sitting and waiting, the aching posture of worry and sleeping sitting up

I am strapped into my sneakers like an astronaut.

My heart thunking like an old typewriter hitting return then chattering to itself remembering it isnt me who is dying

After bad news I ran to the stairwell like it was somewhere to throw up.

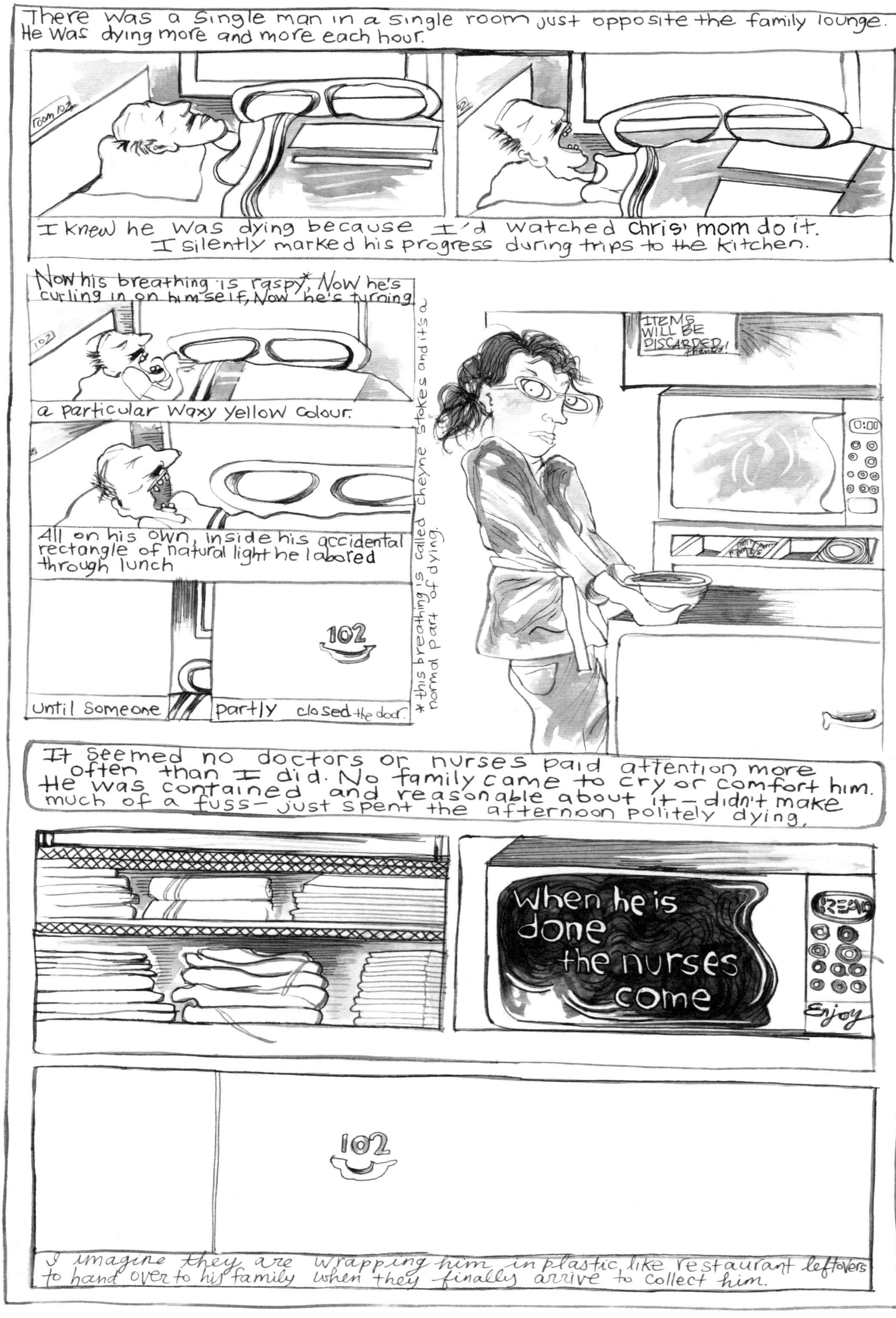
There was a single man in a single room just opposite the family lounge. He was dying more and more each hour.
room 102
102
I knew he was dying because I'd watched Chris' mom do it. I silently marked his progress during trips to the kitchen.
Now his breathing is raspy,* Now he's curling in on himself, Now he's turning
102
a particular waxy yellow colour.
All on his own, inside his accidental rectangle of natural light he labored through lunch
102
until someone partly closed the door.
* this breathing is called cheyne stokes and it's a normal part of dying.
ITEMS WILL BE DISCARDED! thanks!
0:00
It seemed no doctors or nurses paid attention more often than I did. No family came to cry or comfort him. He was contained and reasonable about it — didn't make much of a fuss — just spent the afternoon politely dying.
When he is done the nurses come
Enjoy
102
I imagine they are wrapping him in plastic like restaurant leftovers to hand over to his family when they finally arrive to collect him.

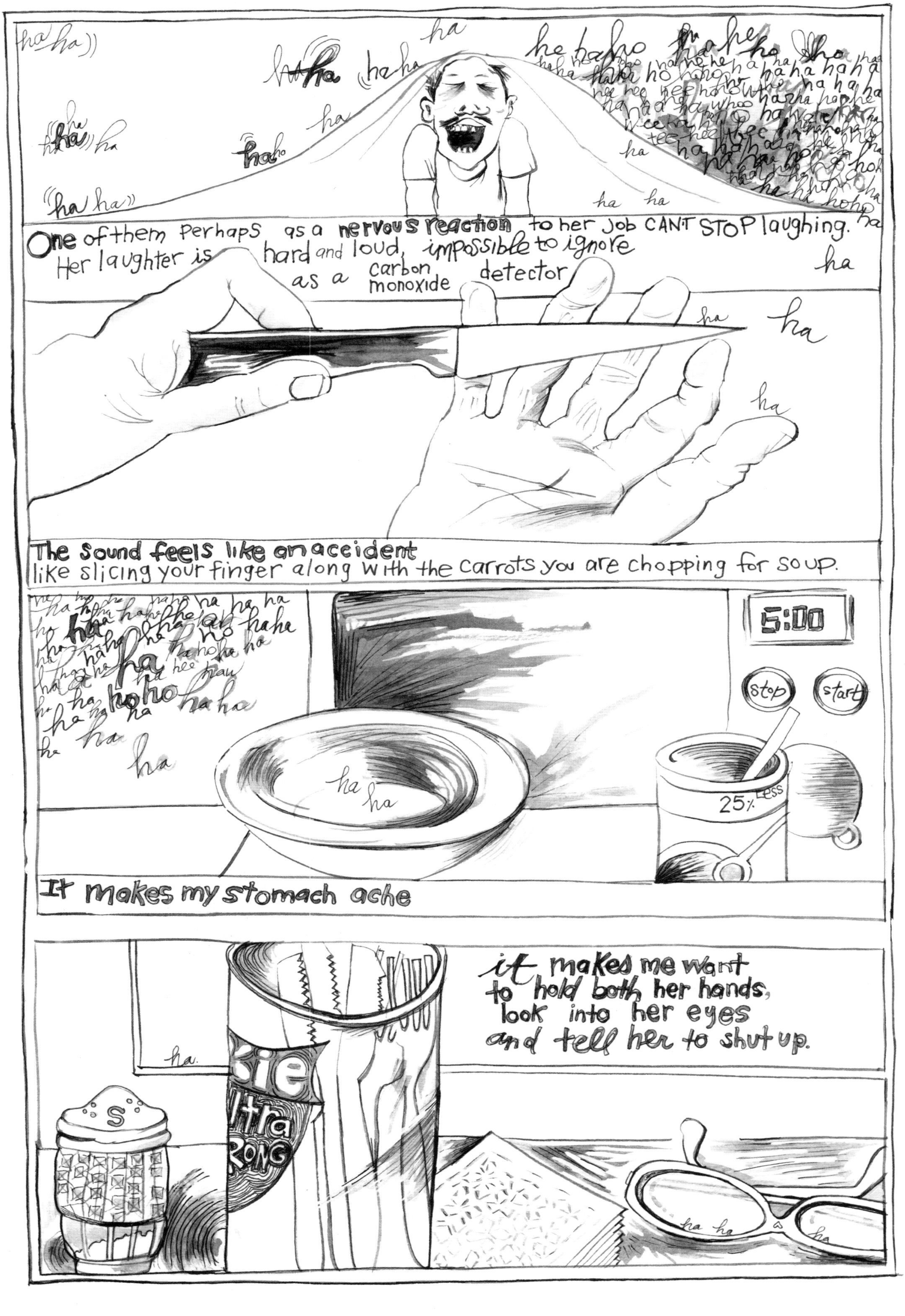
One of them perhaps as a nervous reaction to her job CAN'T STOP laughing.
Her laughter is hard and loud, impossible to ignore as a carbon monoxide detector
The sound feels like an accident
like slicing your finger along with the carrots you are chopping for soup.
5:00
stop
start
25% Less
It makes my stomach ache
it makes me want to hold both her hands, look into her eyes and tell her to shut up.

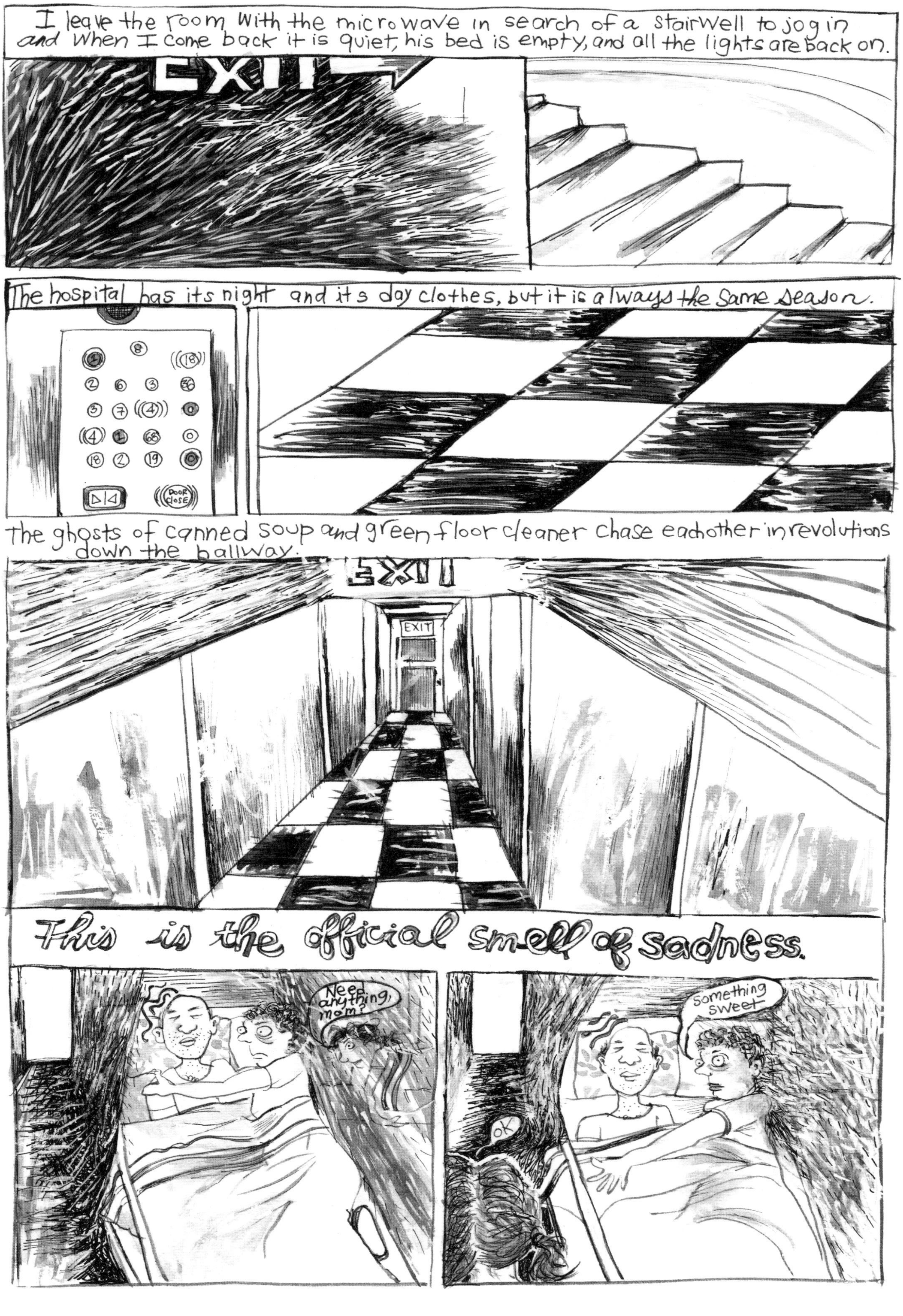
I leave the room with the microwave in search of a stairwell to jog in and when I come back it is quiet, his bed is empty, and all the lights are back on.
EXIT
The hospital has its night and its day clothes, but it is always the same season.
DOOR CLOSE
The ghosts of canned soup and green floor cleaner chase eachother in revolutions down the hallway.
EXIT
EXIT
This is the official smell of sadness.
Need anything, mom?
Something sweet
OK

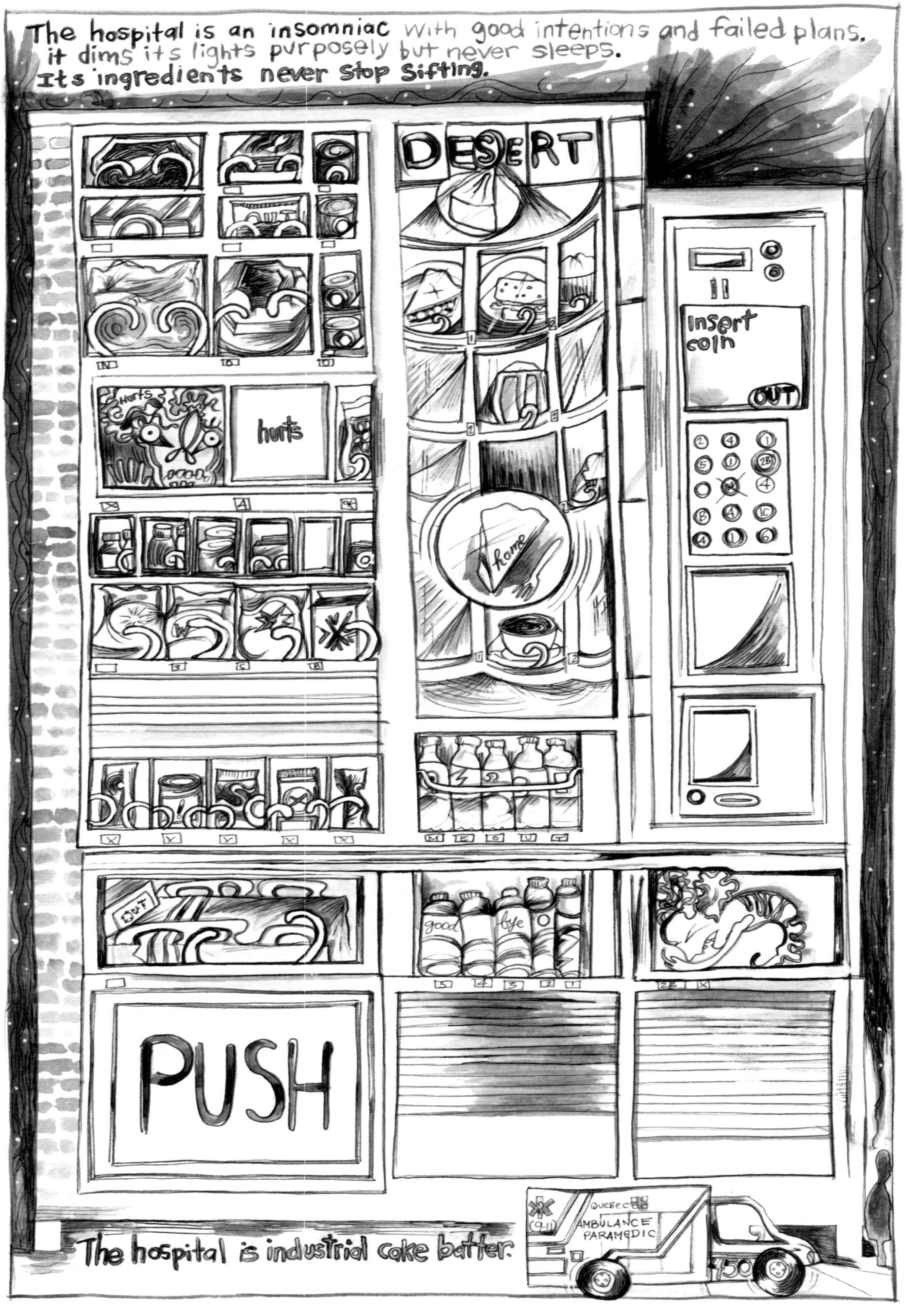

The hospital is an insomniac with good intentions and failed plans.
it dims its lights purposely but never sleeps.
Its ingredients never stop sifting.
DESERT
hurts
hurts
home
insert coin
OUT
good
bye
PUSH
QUEBEC
AMBULANCE
PARAMEDIC
The hospital is industrial cake batter.

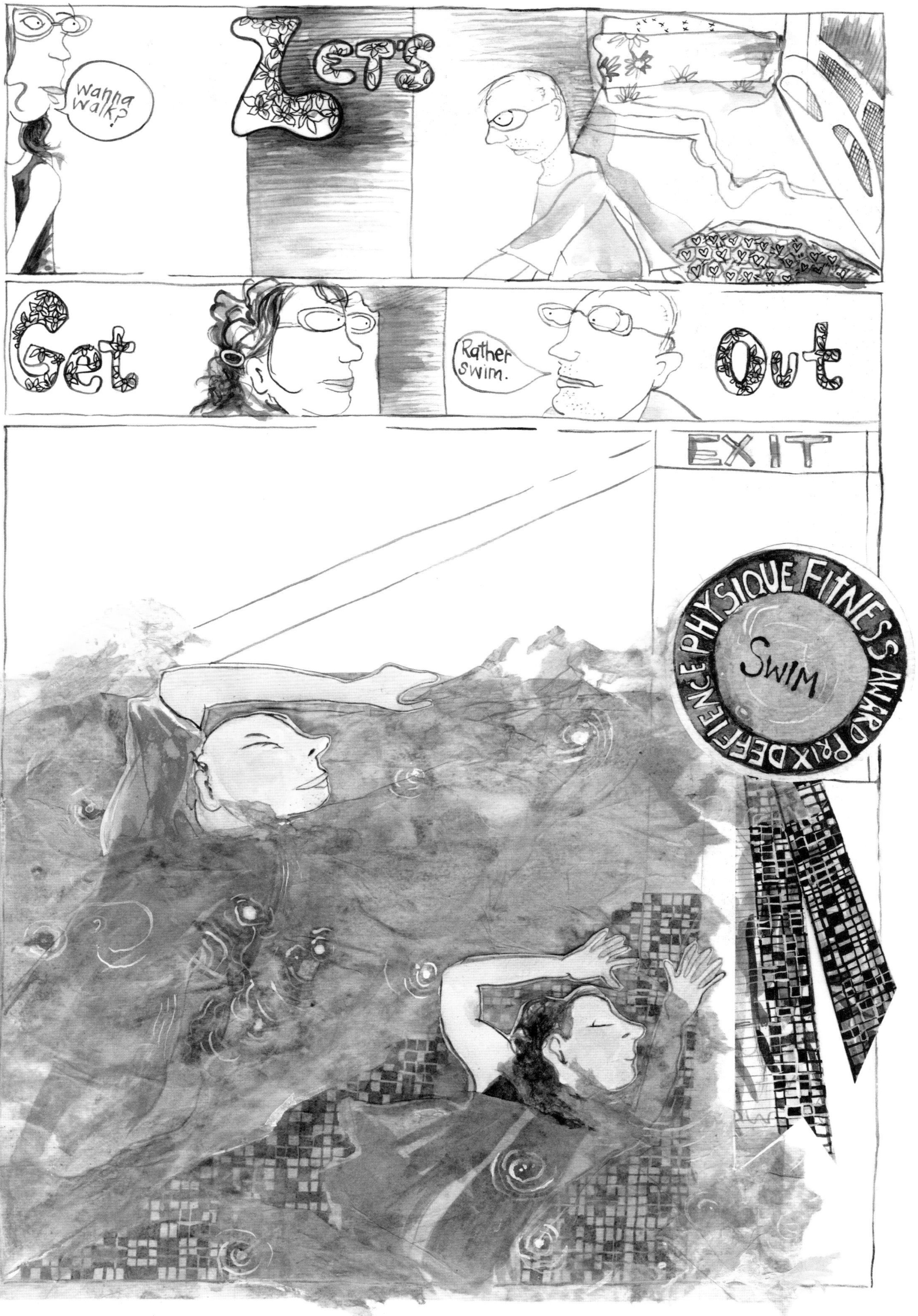

wanna walk?
Let's
Get
Rather swim.
Out
EXIT
PHYSIQUE FITNESS AWARD PRIX DEFFENCE
SWIM

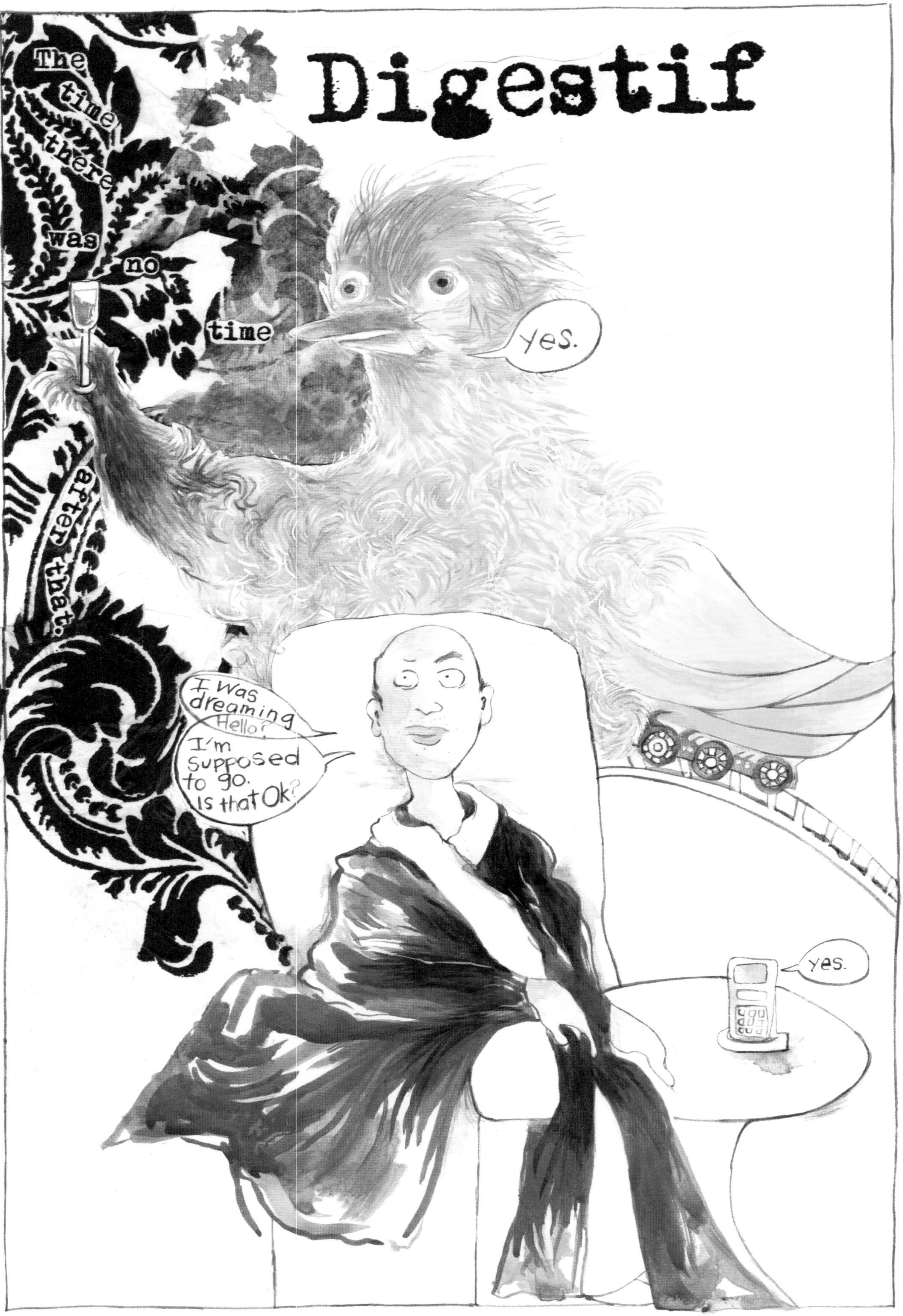
Digestif
The time there was no time after that.
yes.
I was dreaming
Hello?
I'm supposed to go. Is that Ok?
yes.

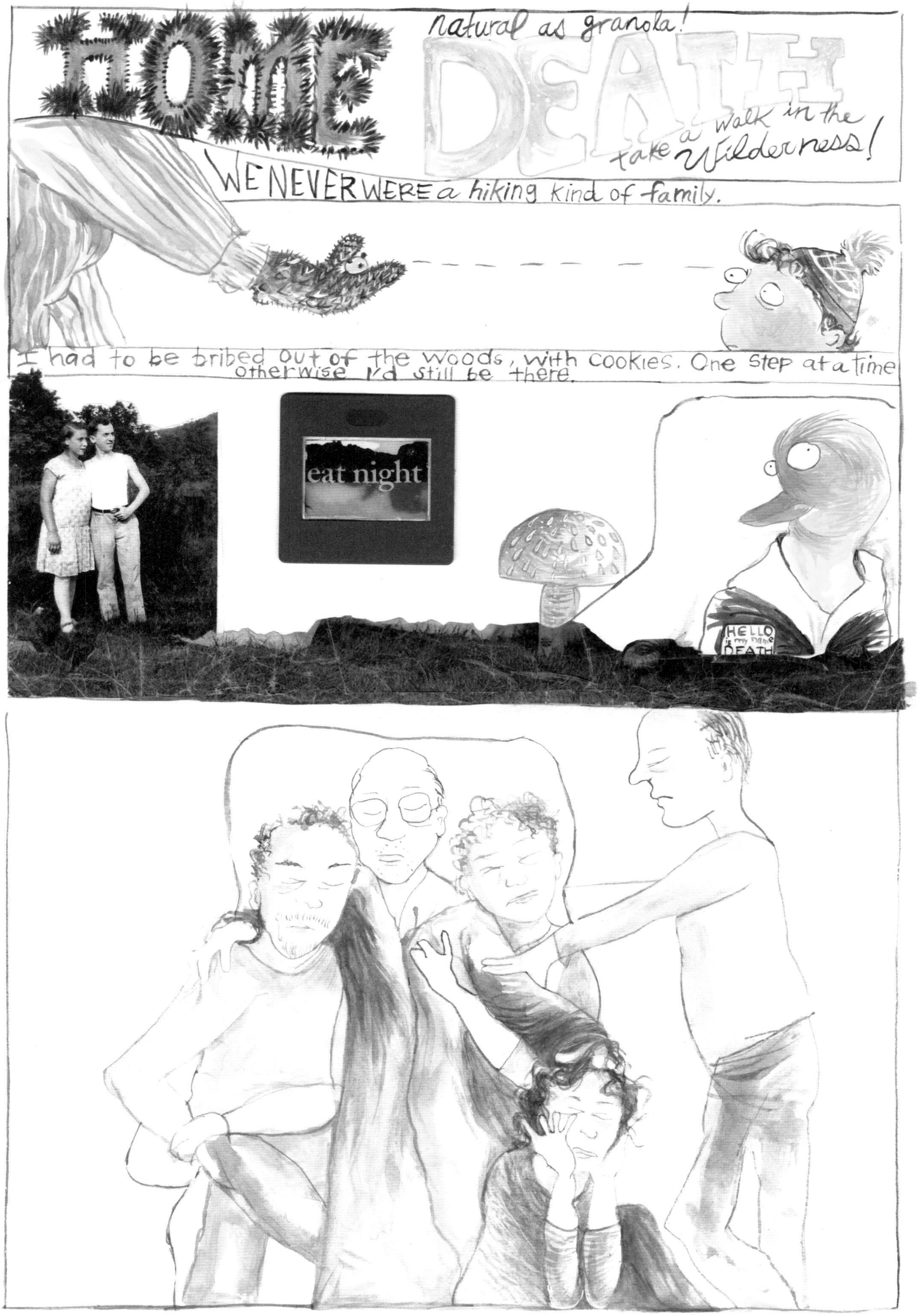
HOME DEATH
natural as granola!
take a walk in the Wilderness!
WE NEVER WERE a hiking kind of family.
I had to be bribed out of the woods, with cookies. One step at a time otherwise I'd still be there.
eat night
HELLO my name is DEATH

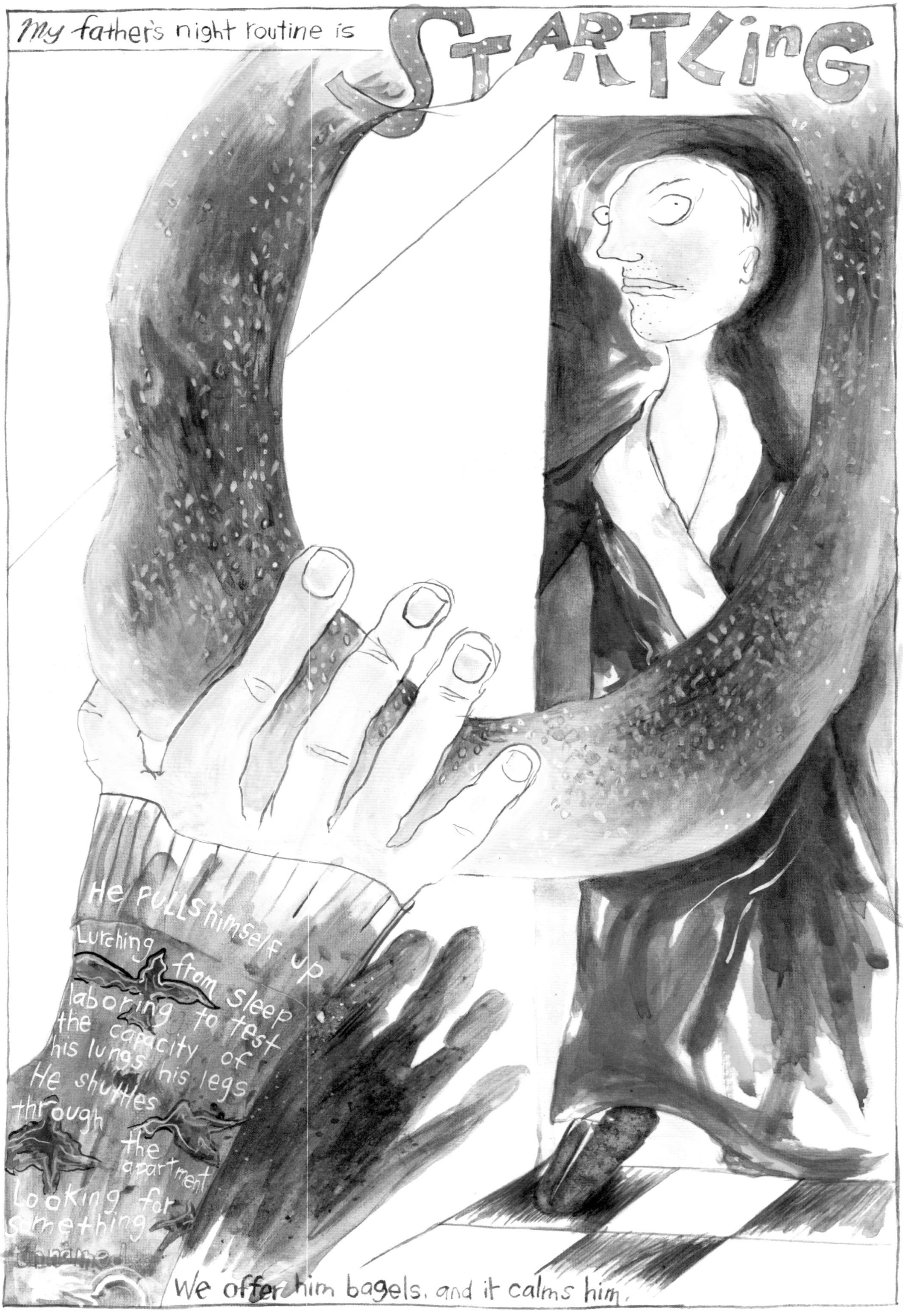
My father's night routine is
STARTLING
He PULLS himself up
Lurching from sleep
laboring to test the capacity of his lungs his legs
He shuttles through the apartment
Looking for something unnamed.
We offer him bagels. and it calms him.

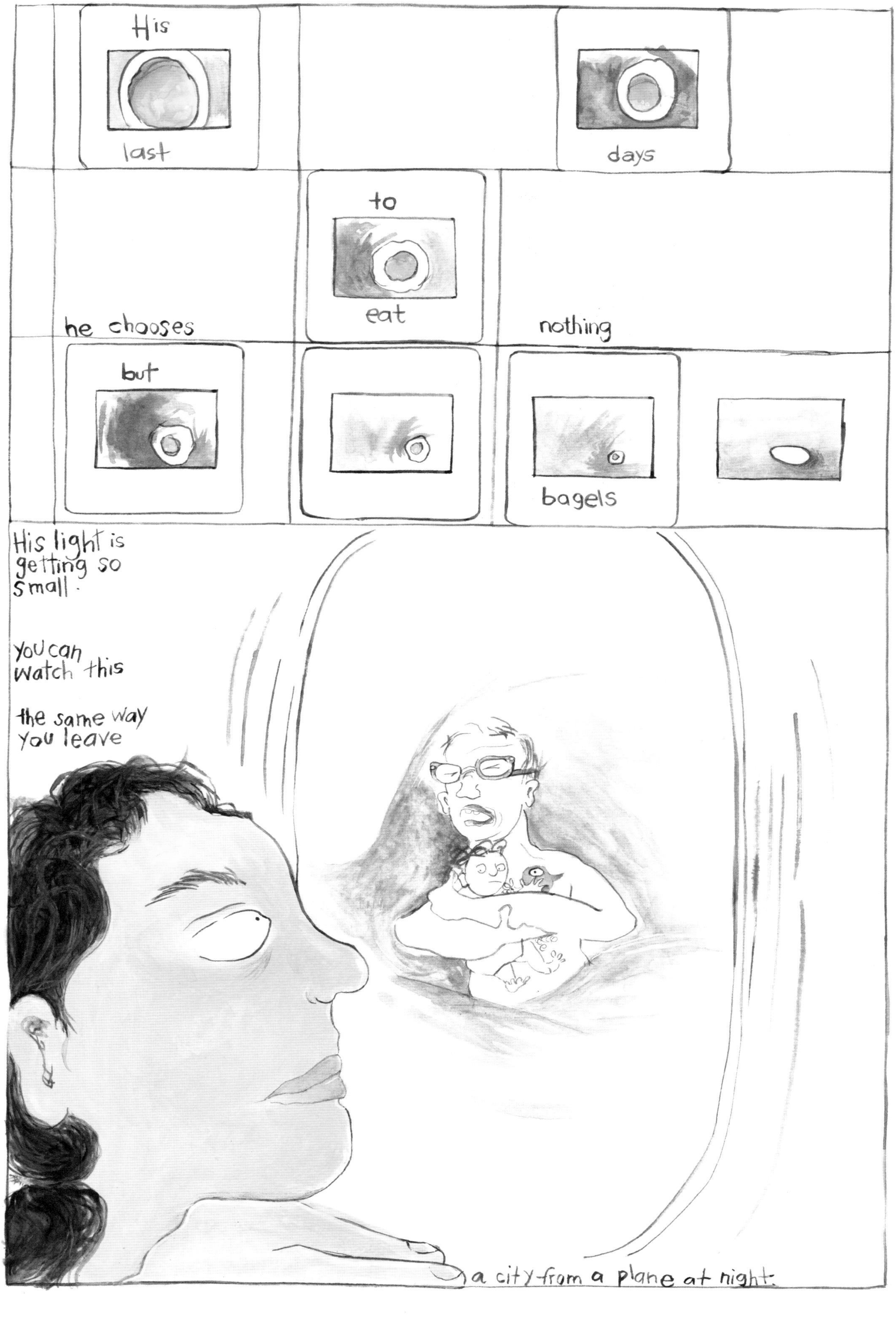
His
last
days
to
eat
he chooses
nothing
but
bagels
His light is getting so small.
You can watch this
the same way you leave
a city from a plane at night.

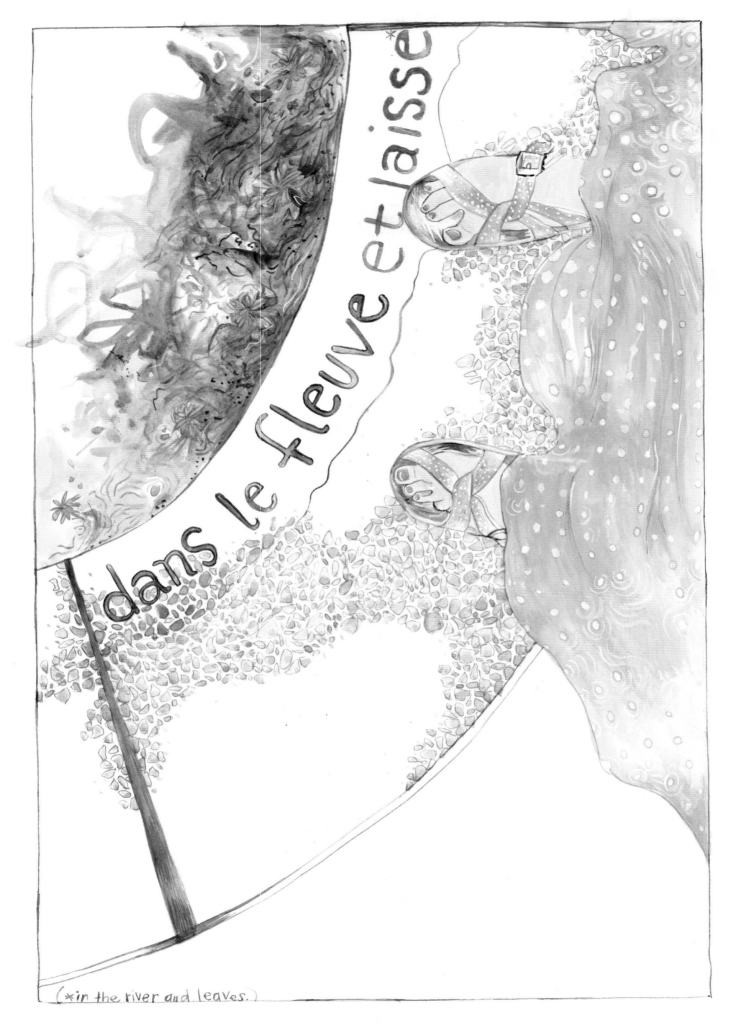

dans le fleuve et laisse*

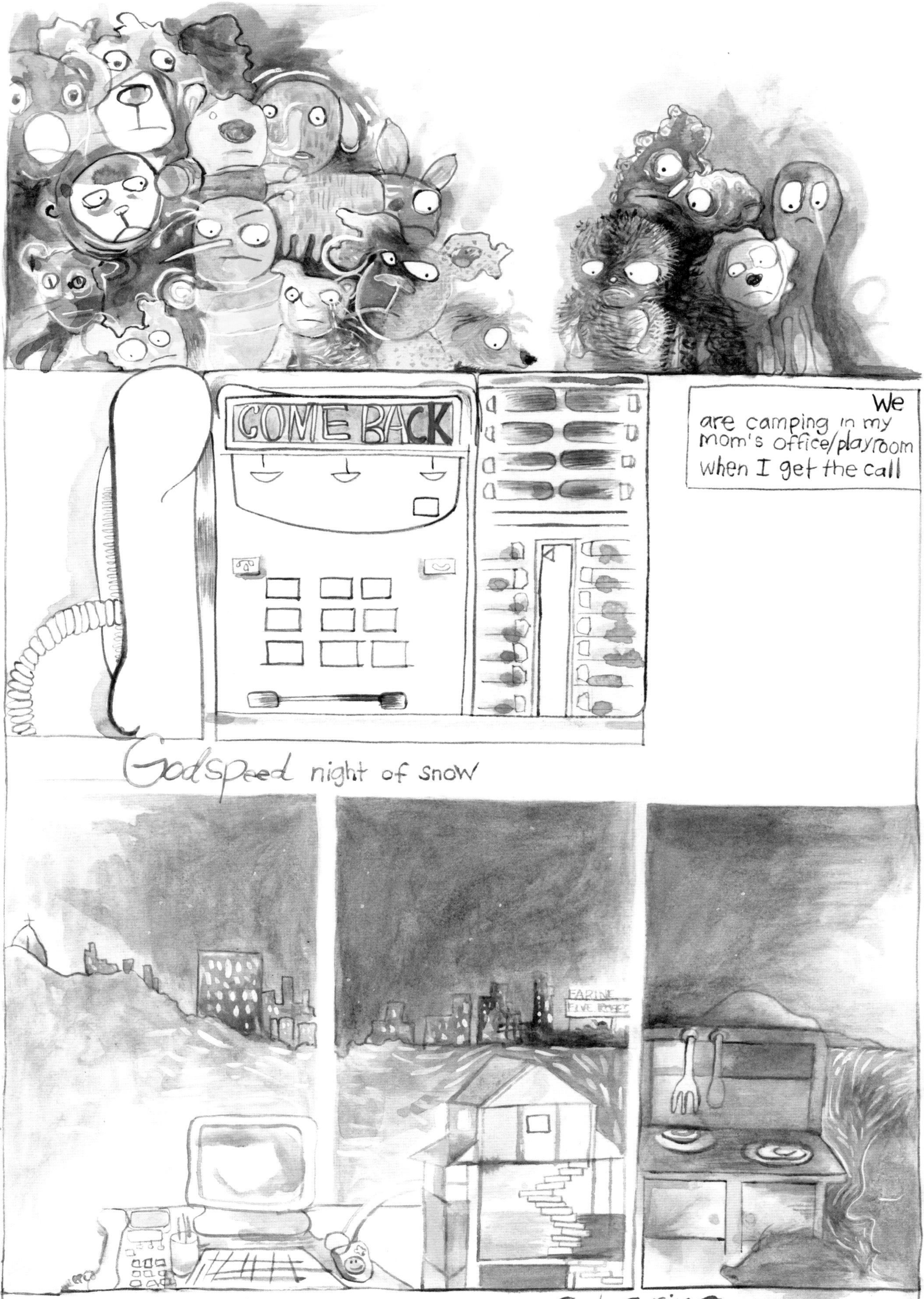
COME BACK
We are camping in my mom's office/playroom when I get the call
Godspeed night of snow
and spring

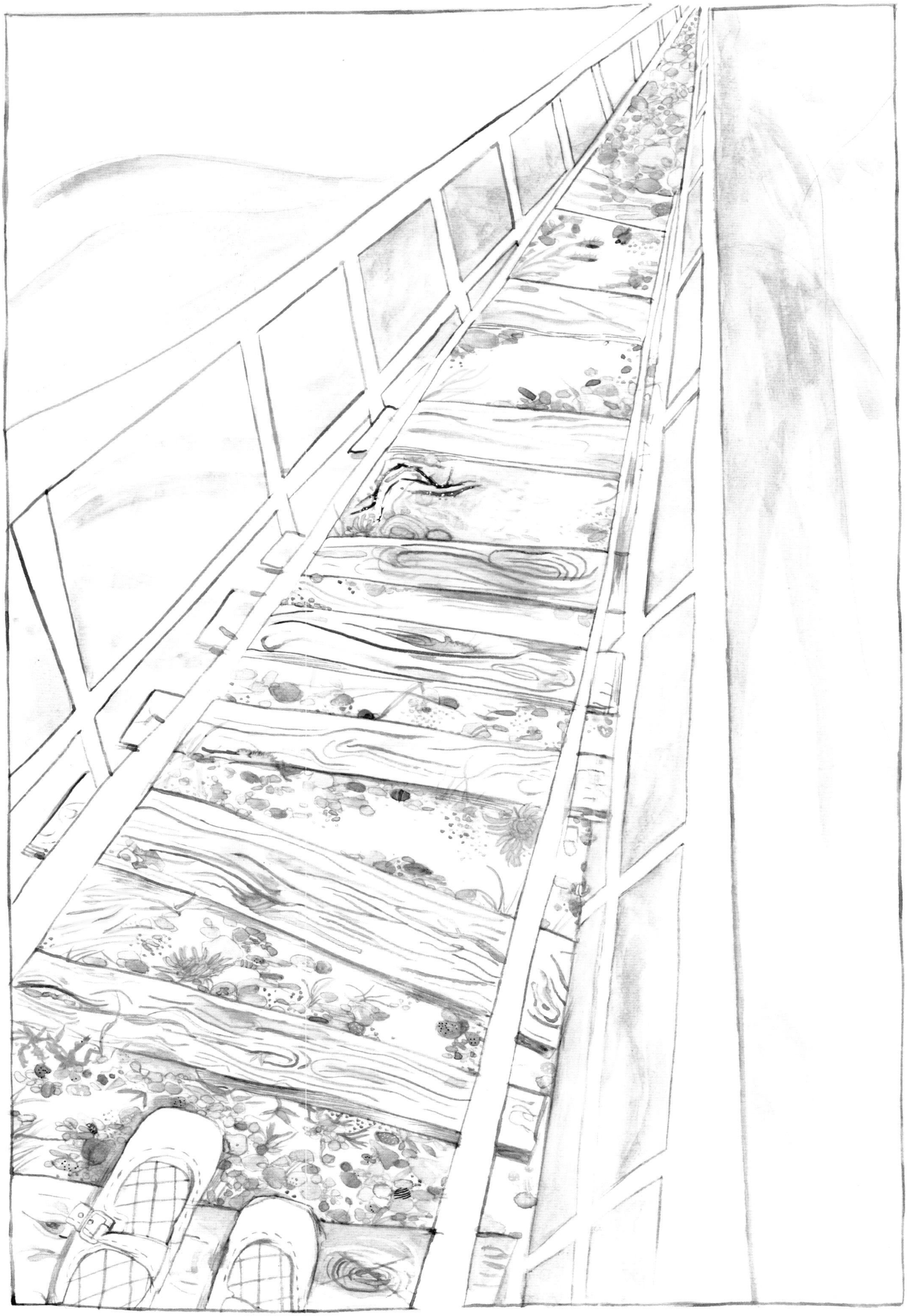

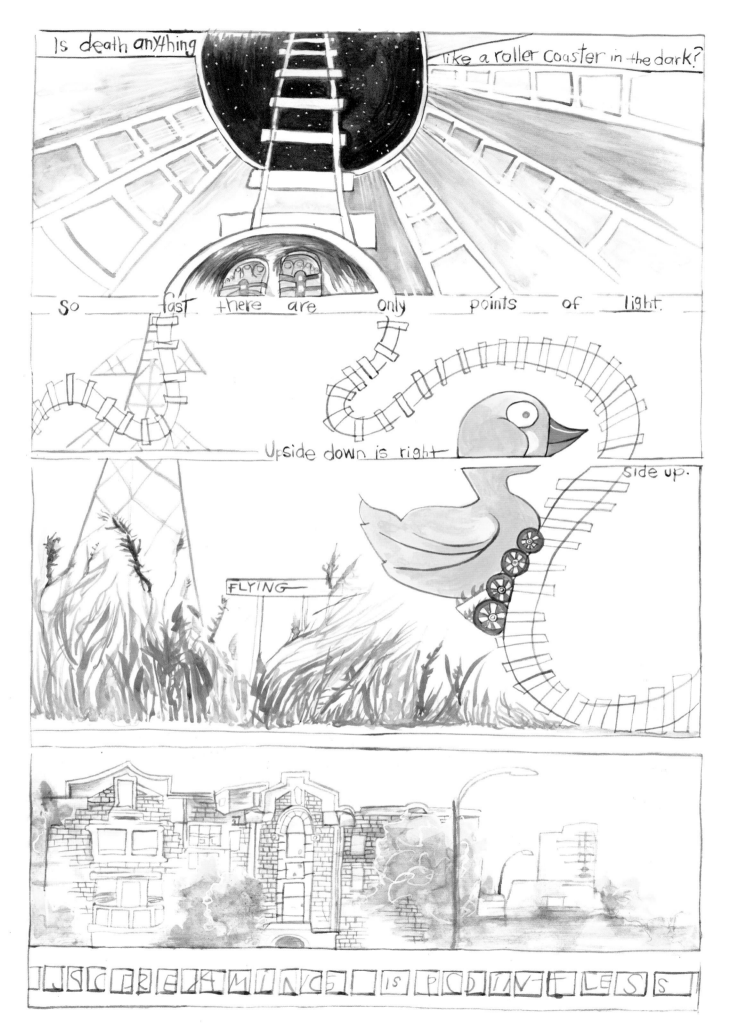

Is death anything like a roller coaster in the dark?

So fast there are only points of light.

Upside down is right side up.

FLYING

SCREAMING IS POINTLESS!

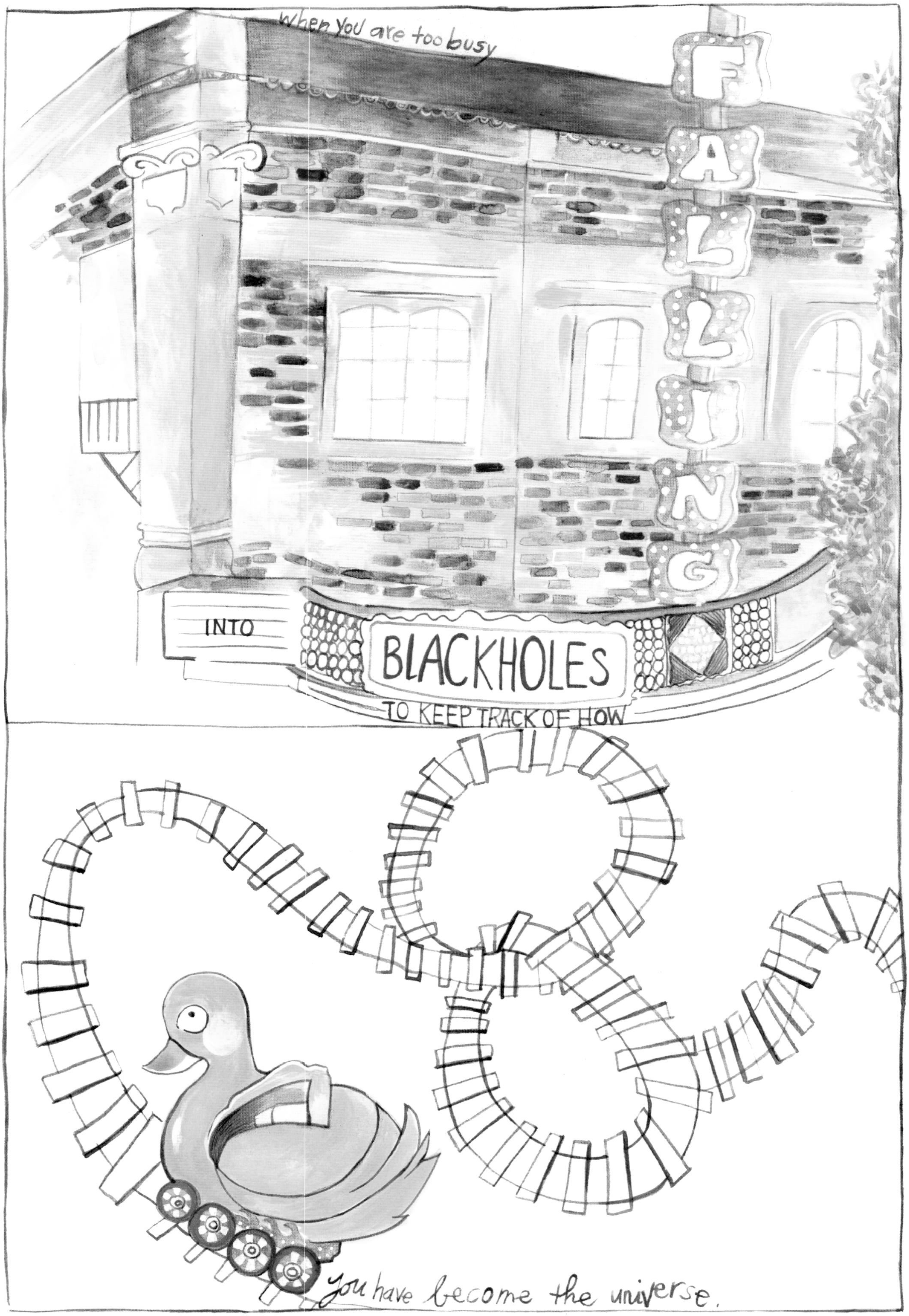

when you are too busy
FALLING
INTO
BLACKHOLES
TO KEEP TRACK OF HOW
you have become the universe.

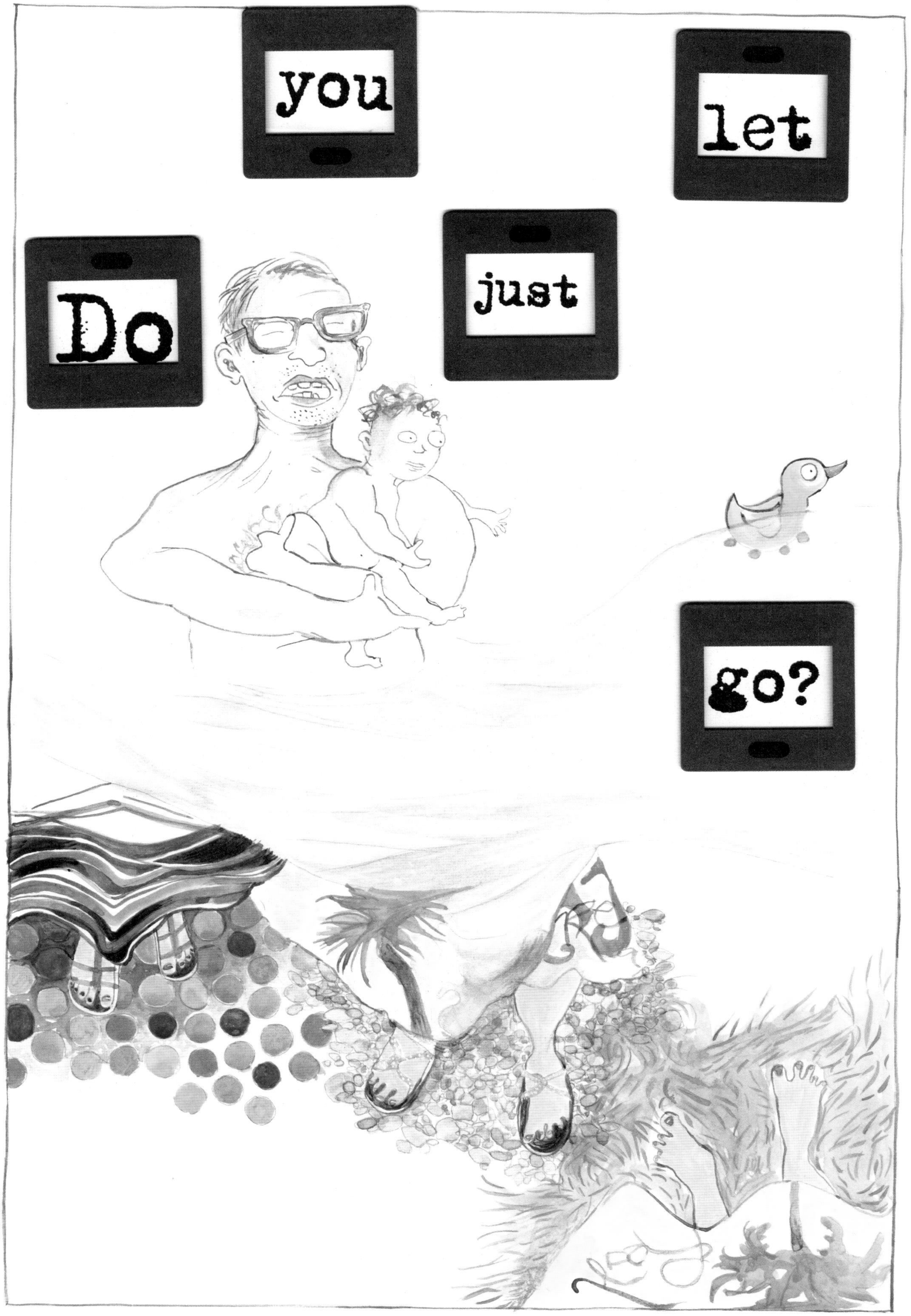
Do
you
just
let
go?

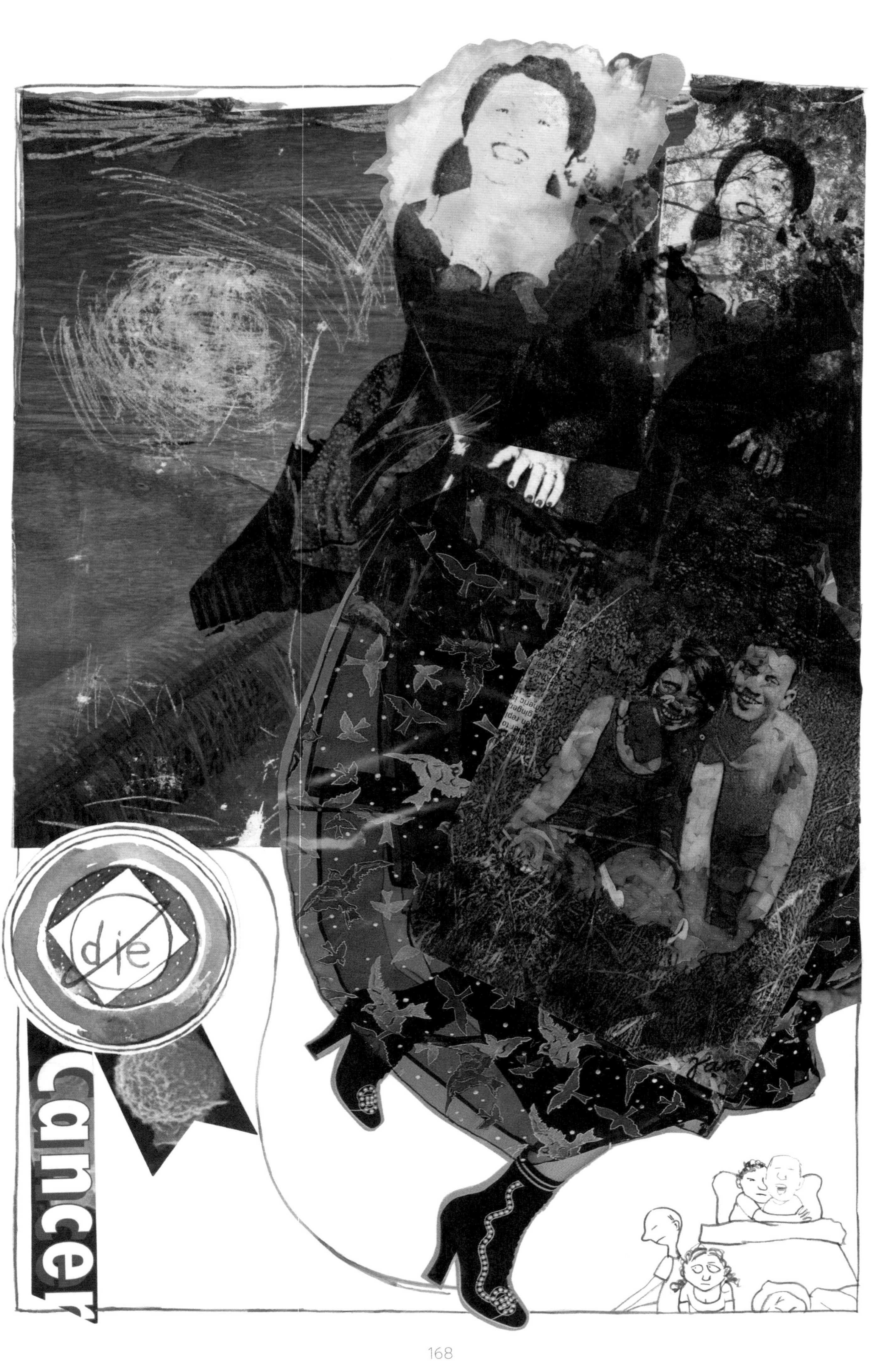
die
cancer

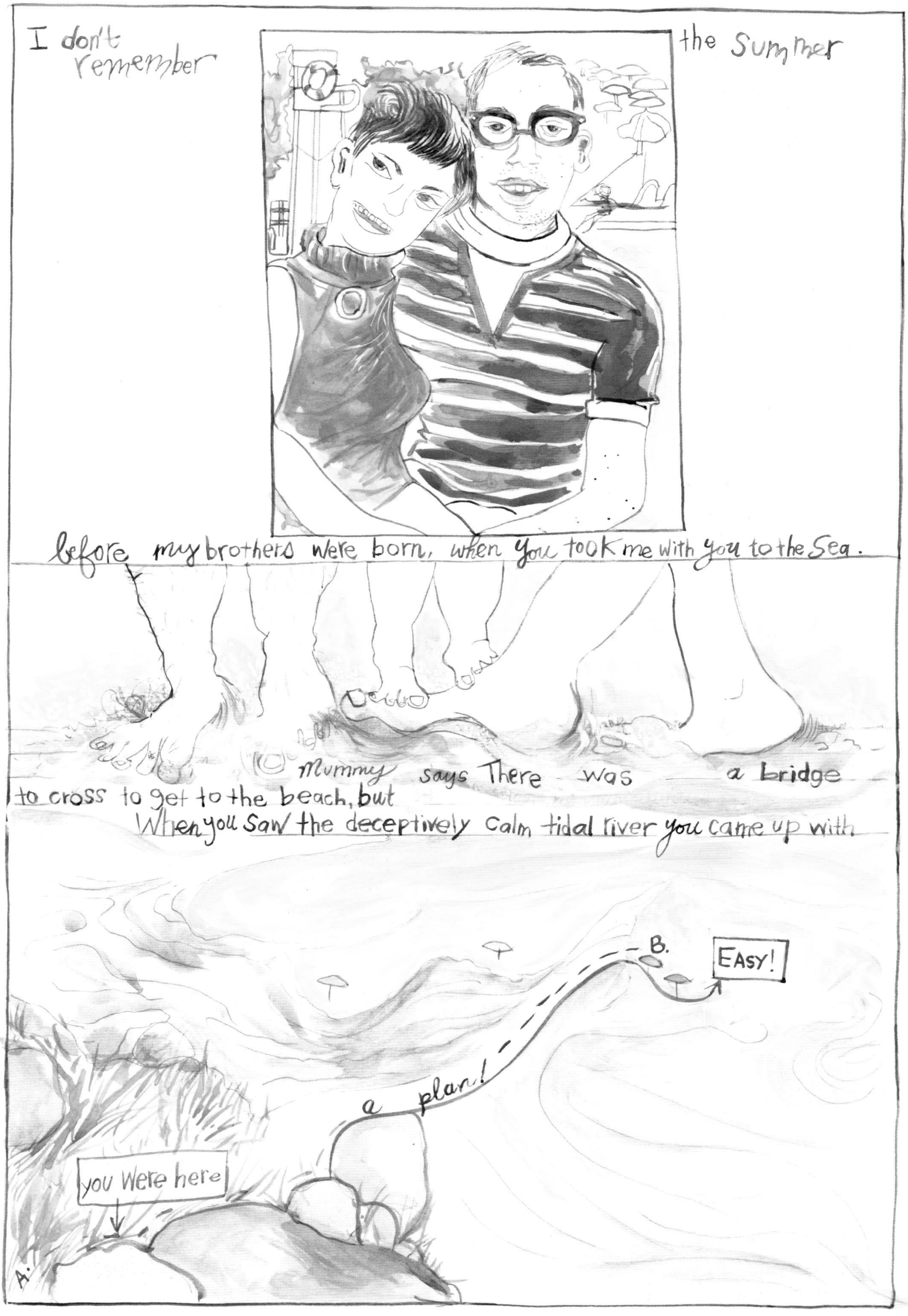
I don't remember
the Summer
before my brothers were born, when you took me with you to the Sea.
Mummy says There was a bridge to cross to get to the beach, but
When you saw the deceptively calm tidal river you came up with
a plan!
B.
EASY!
you were here
A.

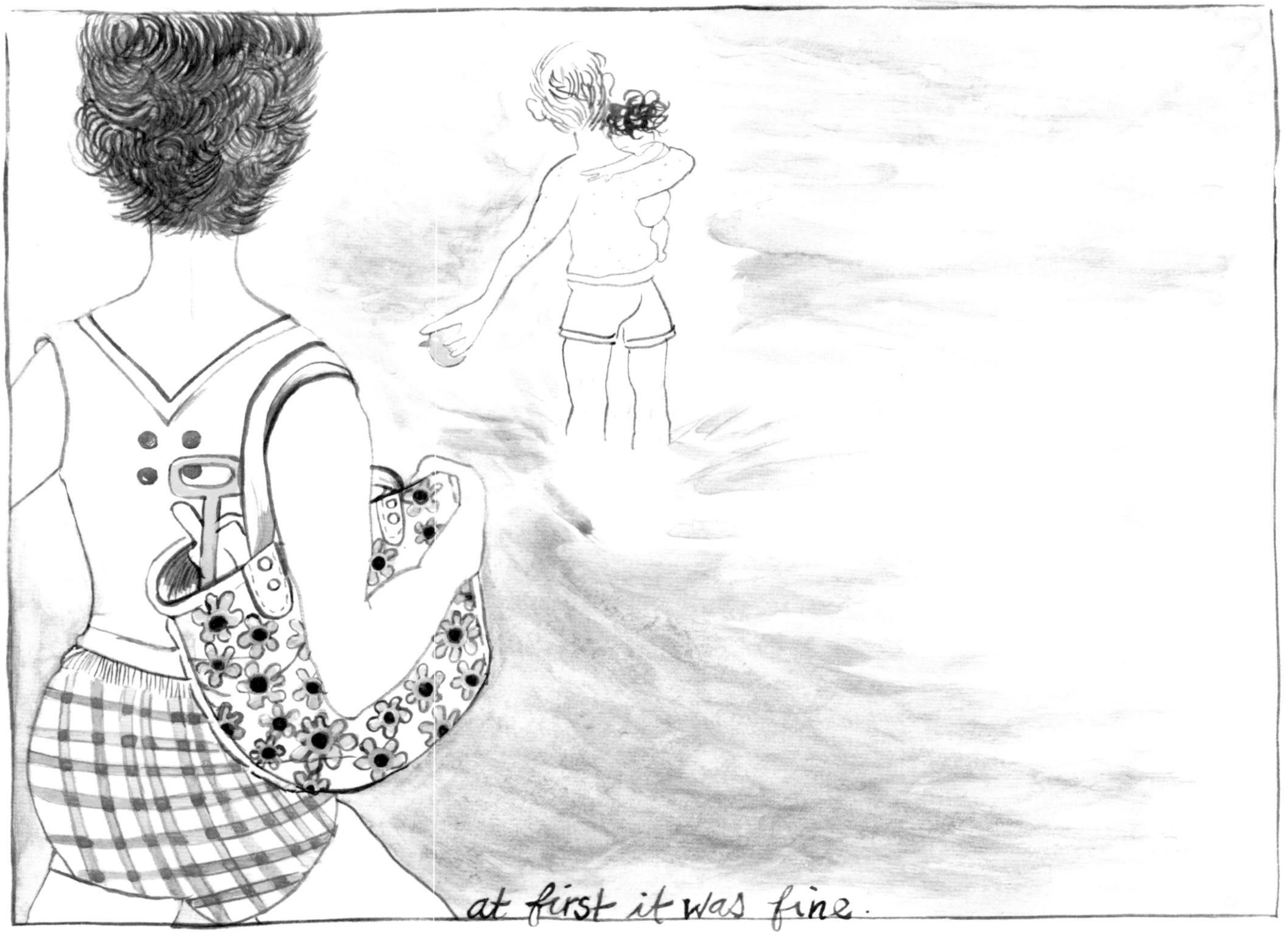
at first it was fine.

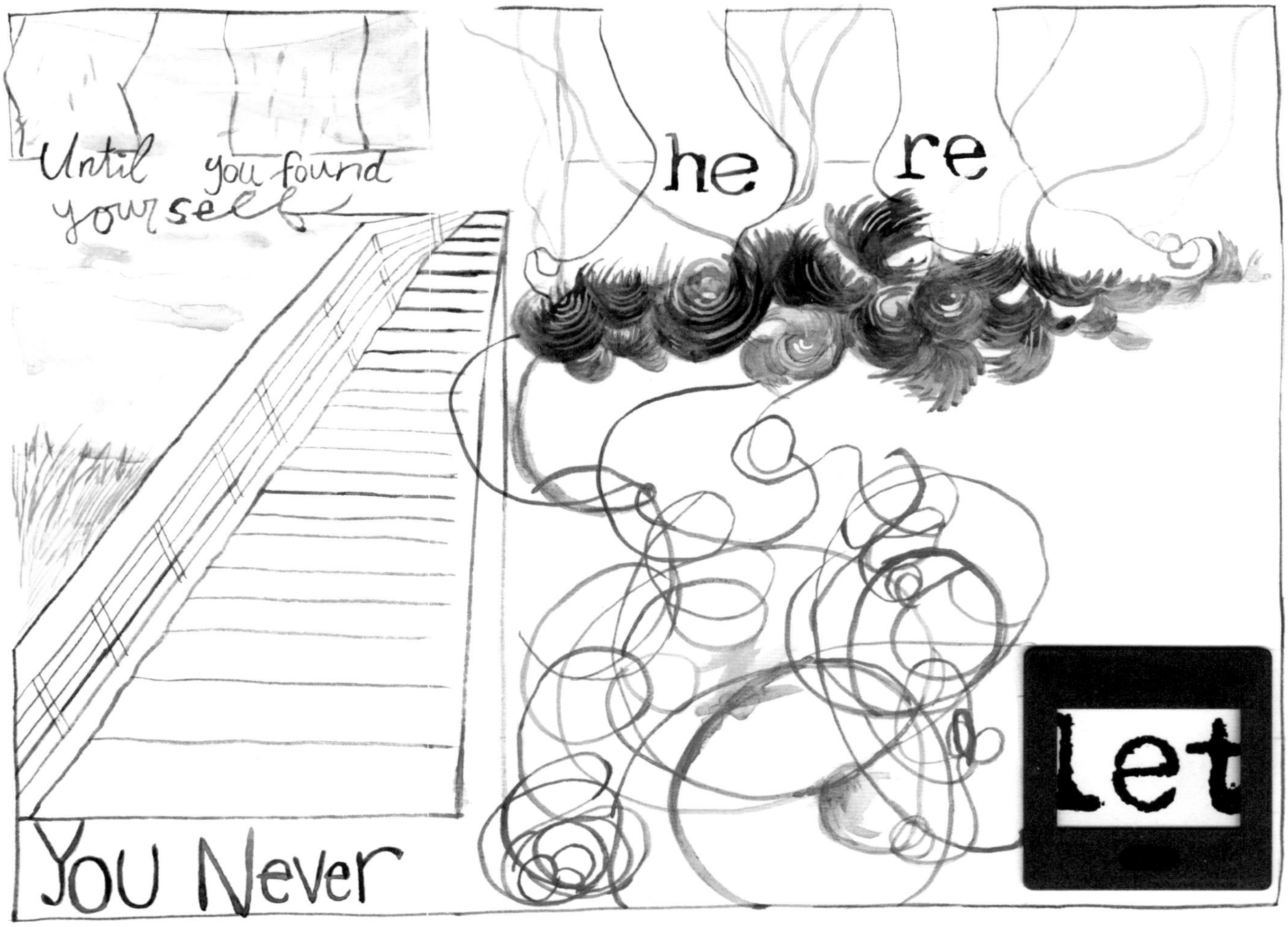
Until you found yourself
here
You Never
Let

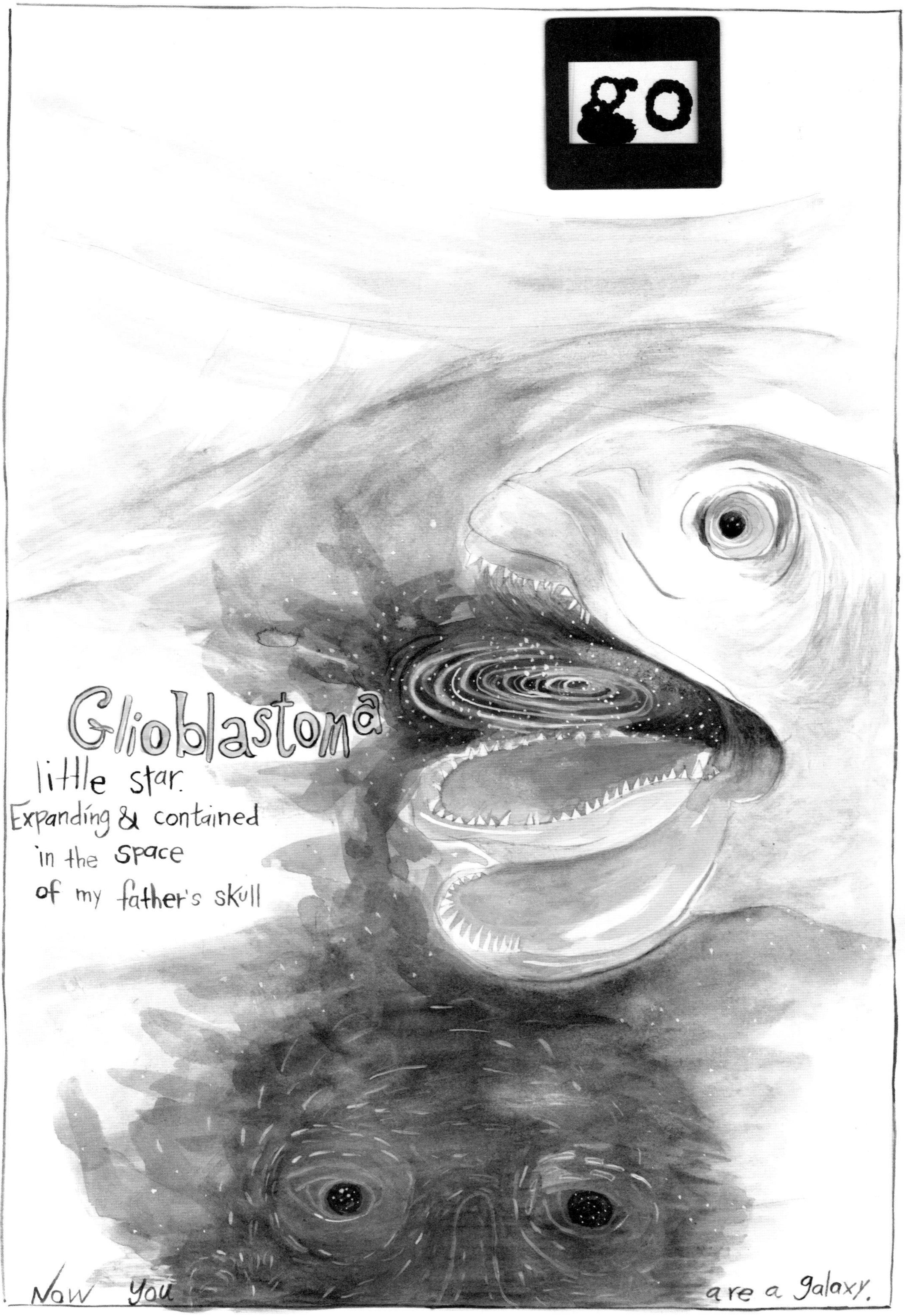
go
Glioblastoma
little star.
Expanding & contained
in the space
of my father's skull
Now you
are a galaxy.

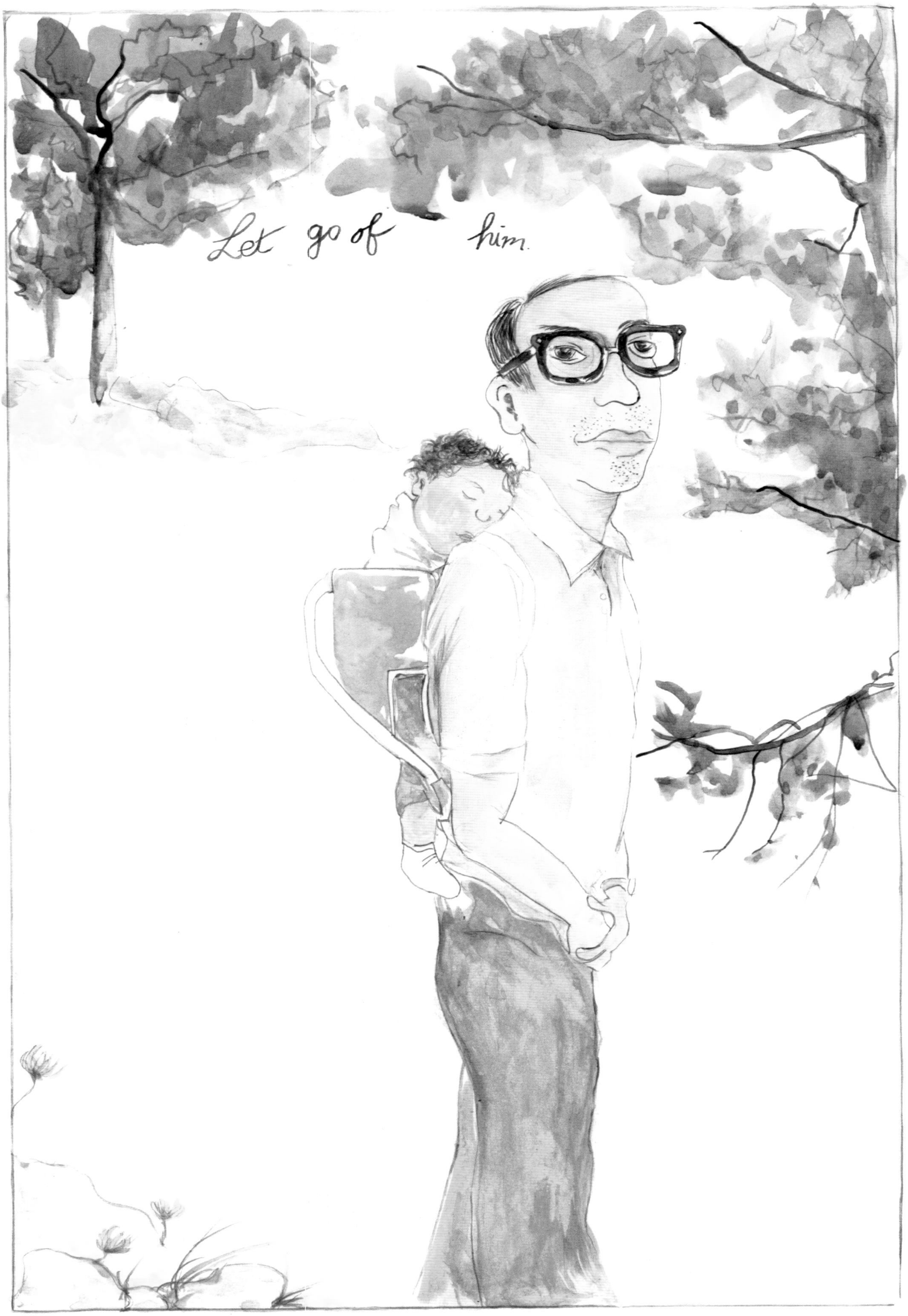
Let go of him.

Grieving
in
Fuchsia

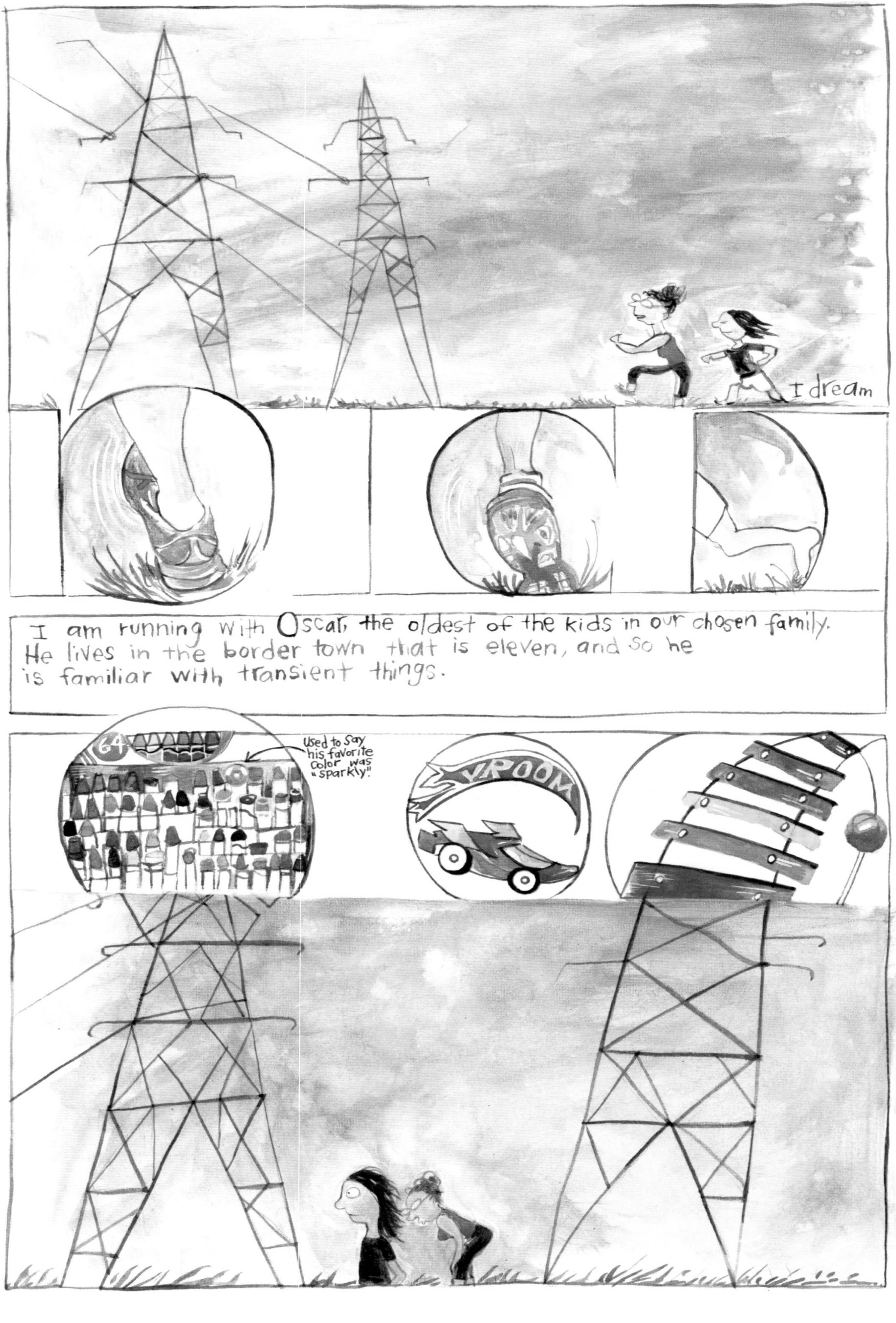
I dream
I am running with Oscar, the oldest of the kids in our chosen family. He lives in the border town that is eleven, and so he is familiar with transient things.
64
Used to say his favorite color was "sparkly".
VROOM

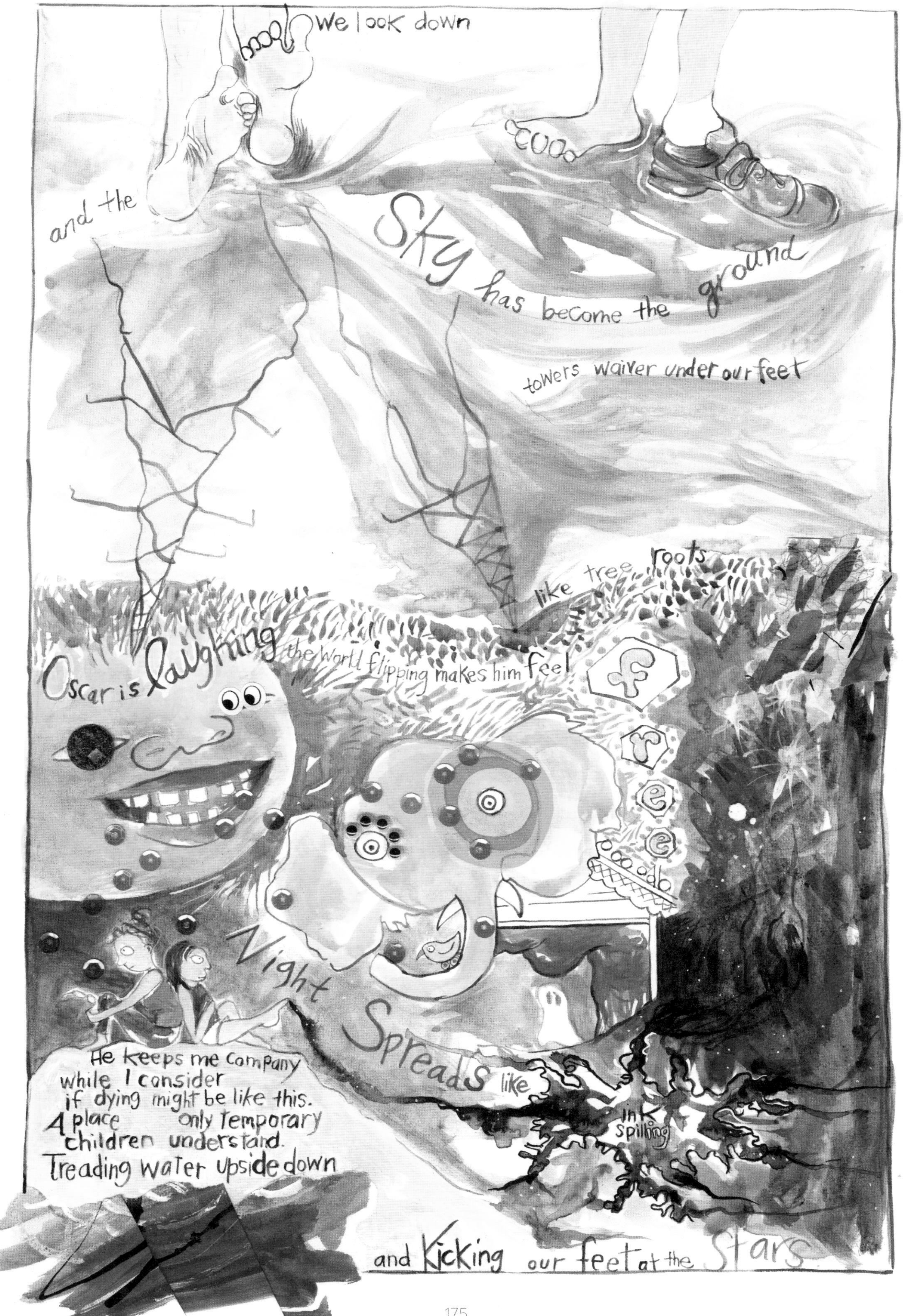

we look down
and the
Sky has become the ground
towers waiver under our feet
like tree roots
Oscar is laughing the world flipping makes him feel
f r e e
Night Spreads like ink spilling
He keeps me company
while I consider
if dying might be like this.
A place only temporary
children understand.
Treading water upside down
and Kicking our feet at the Stars

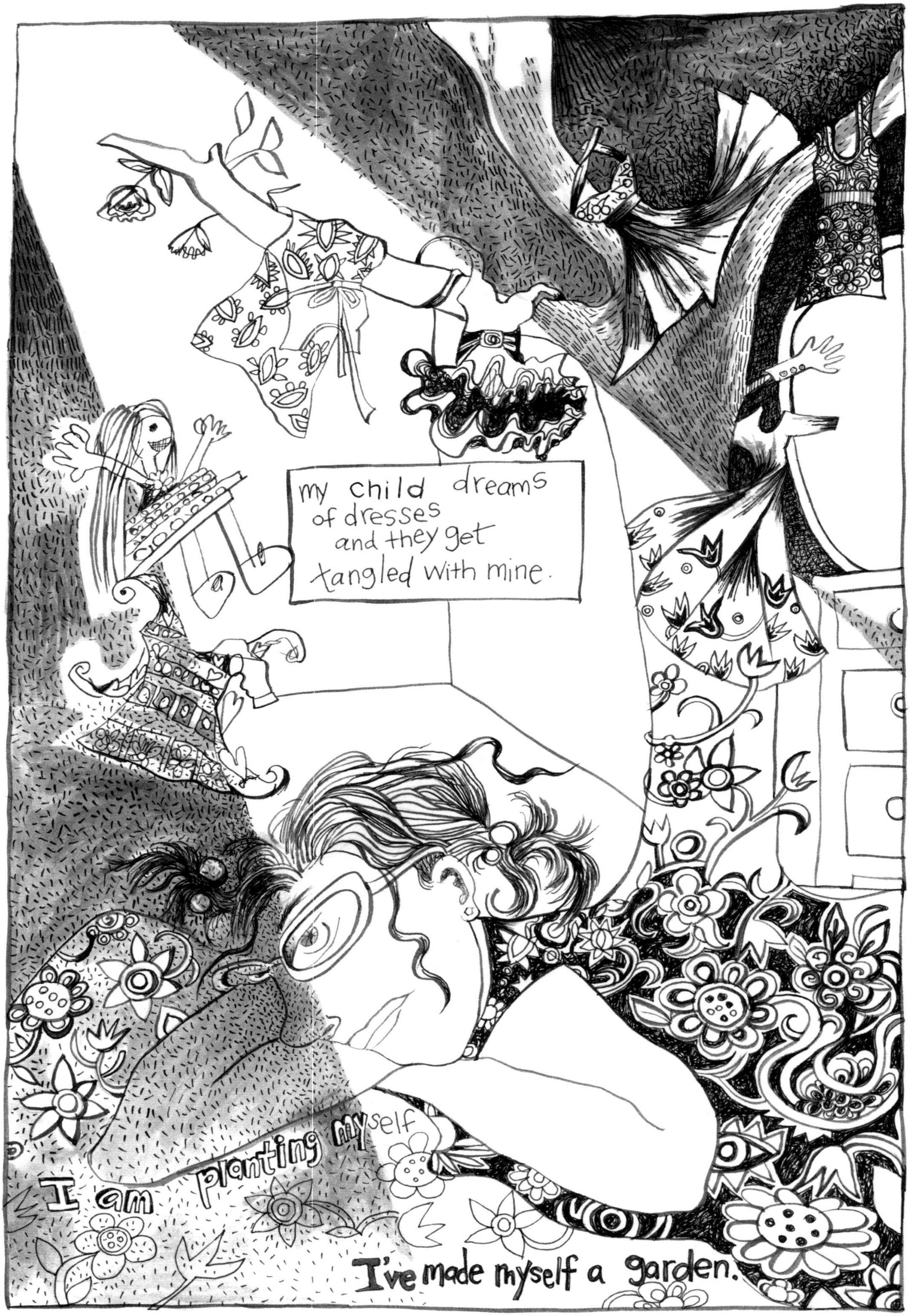
my child dreams of dresses and they get tangled with mine.
I am planting myself
I've made myself a garden.

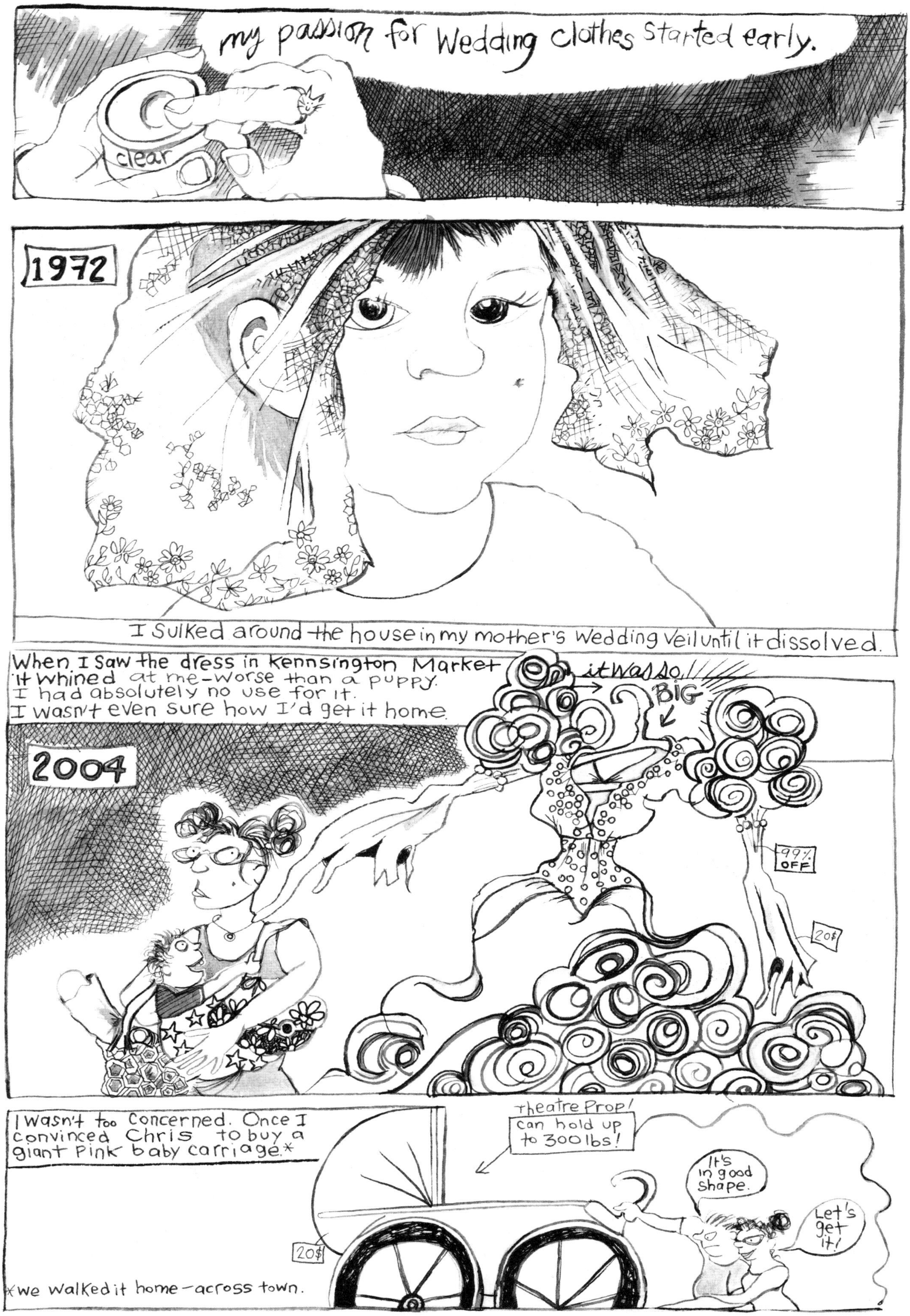
my passion for Wedding clothes Started early.
clear
1972
I sulked around the house in my mother's wedding veil until it dissolved.
When I saw the dress in Kennsington Market it whined at me—worse than a puppy.
I had absolutely no use for it.
I wasn't even sure how I'd get it home.
it was so
BIG
2004
99% OFF
20$
I wasn't too concerned. Once I convinced Chris to buy a giant Pink baby carriage.*
theatre Prop! can hold up to 300 lbs!
It's in good shape.
Let's get it!
20$
*we walked it home—across town.

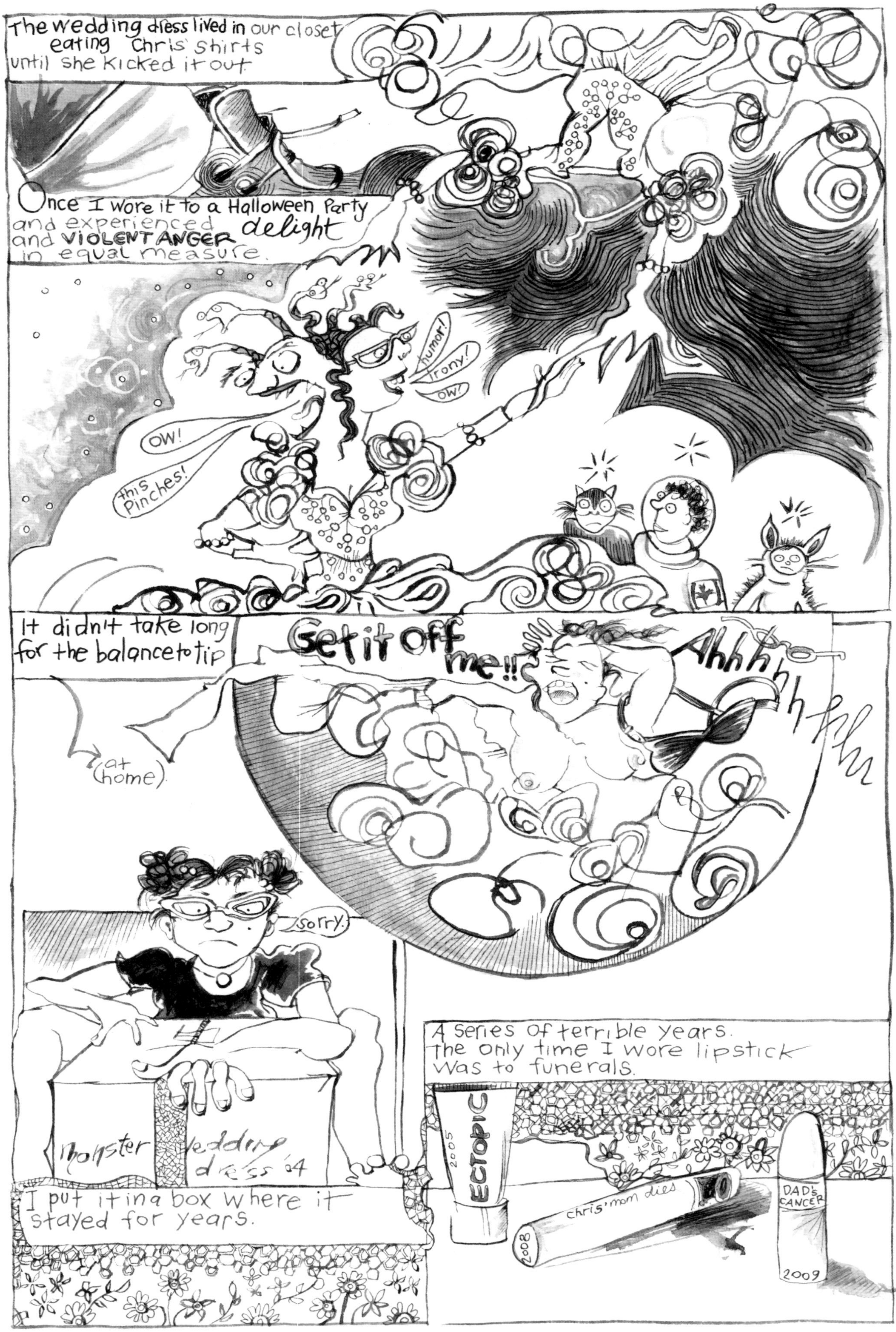

The wedding dress lived in our closet eating Chris' shirts until she kicked it out.
Once I wore it to a Halloween Party and experienced delight and VIOLENT ANGER in equal measure.
humor!
irony!
ow!
OW!
this pinches!
It didn't take long for the balance to tip
Get it off me!!
Ahhhhh
(at home)
sorry.
monster wedding dress '04
I put it in a box where it stayed for years.
A series of terrible years. The only time I wore lipstick was to funerals.
2005
ECTOPIC
2008
chris' mom dies
DAD'S CANCER
2009

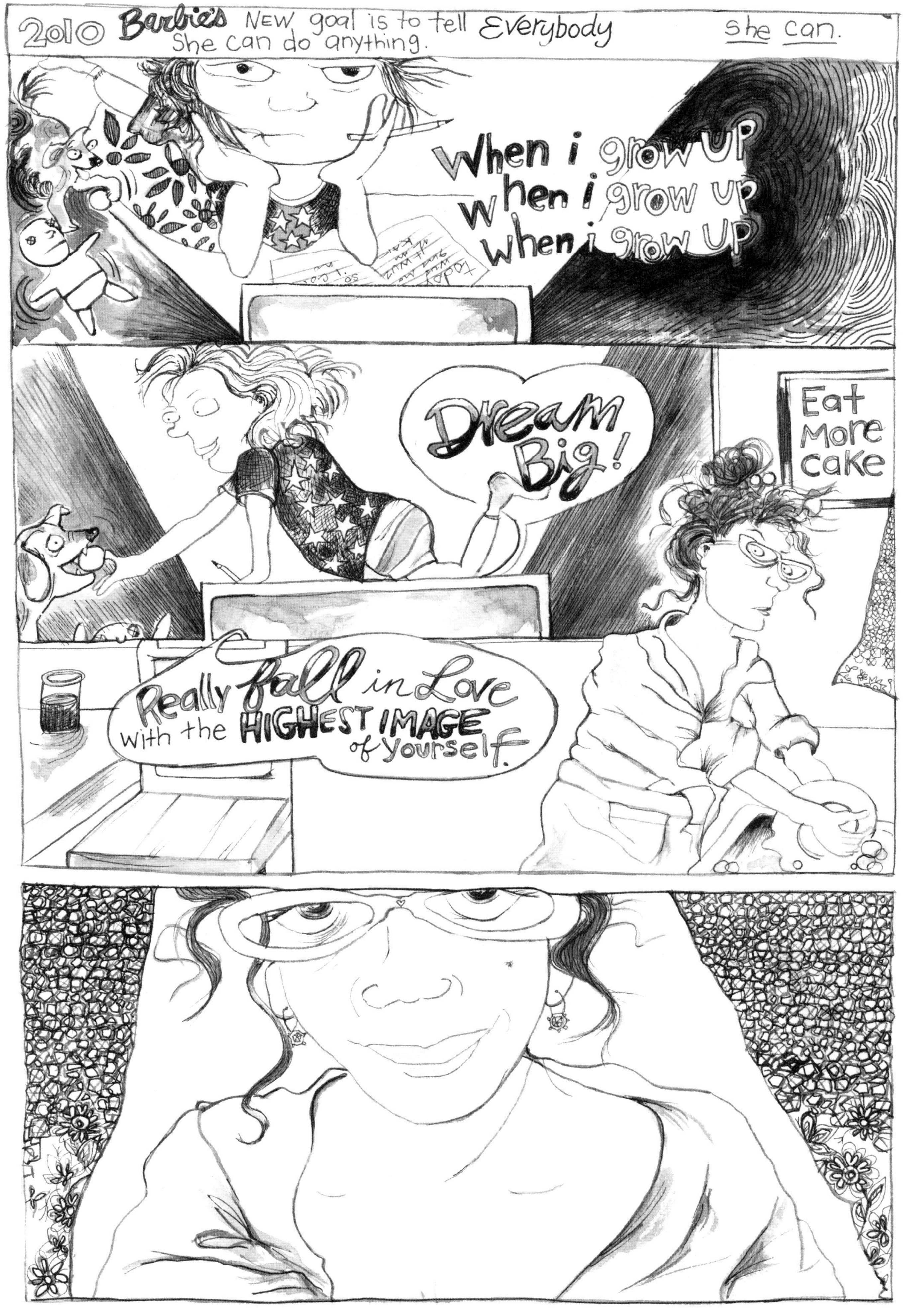
2010 Barbie's NEW goal is to tell Everybody She can do anything.
She can.
When i grow UP
when i grow up
when i grow UP
Dream Big!
Eat More cake
Really fall in Love with the HIGHEST IMAGE of yourself.

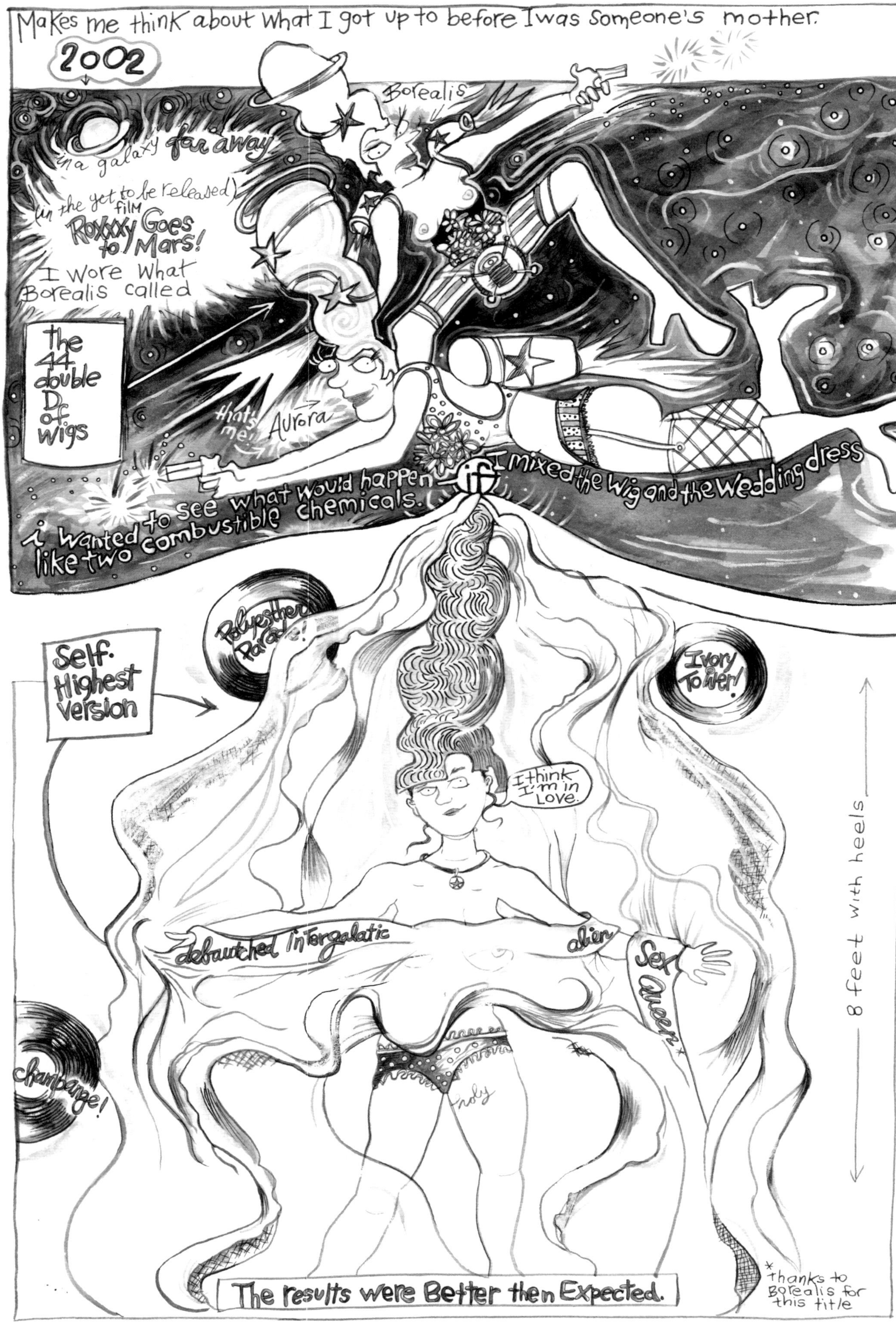
Makes me think about what I got up to before I was someone's mother.
2002
Borealis
in a galaxy far away
(in the yet to be released) film
Roxxxy Goes to Mars!
I wore what Borealis called
the 44 double D of wigs
that's me! Aurora
i wanted to see what would happen if I mixed the wig and the wedding dress
like two combustible chemicals.
Polyesther Parade!
Self. Highest version
Ivory Tower!
I think I'm in love.
debauched intergalatic alien Sex Queen*
8 feet with heels
champange!
holy
The results were Better then Expected.
*thanks to Borealis for this title

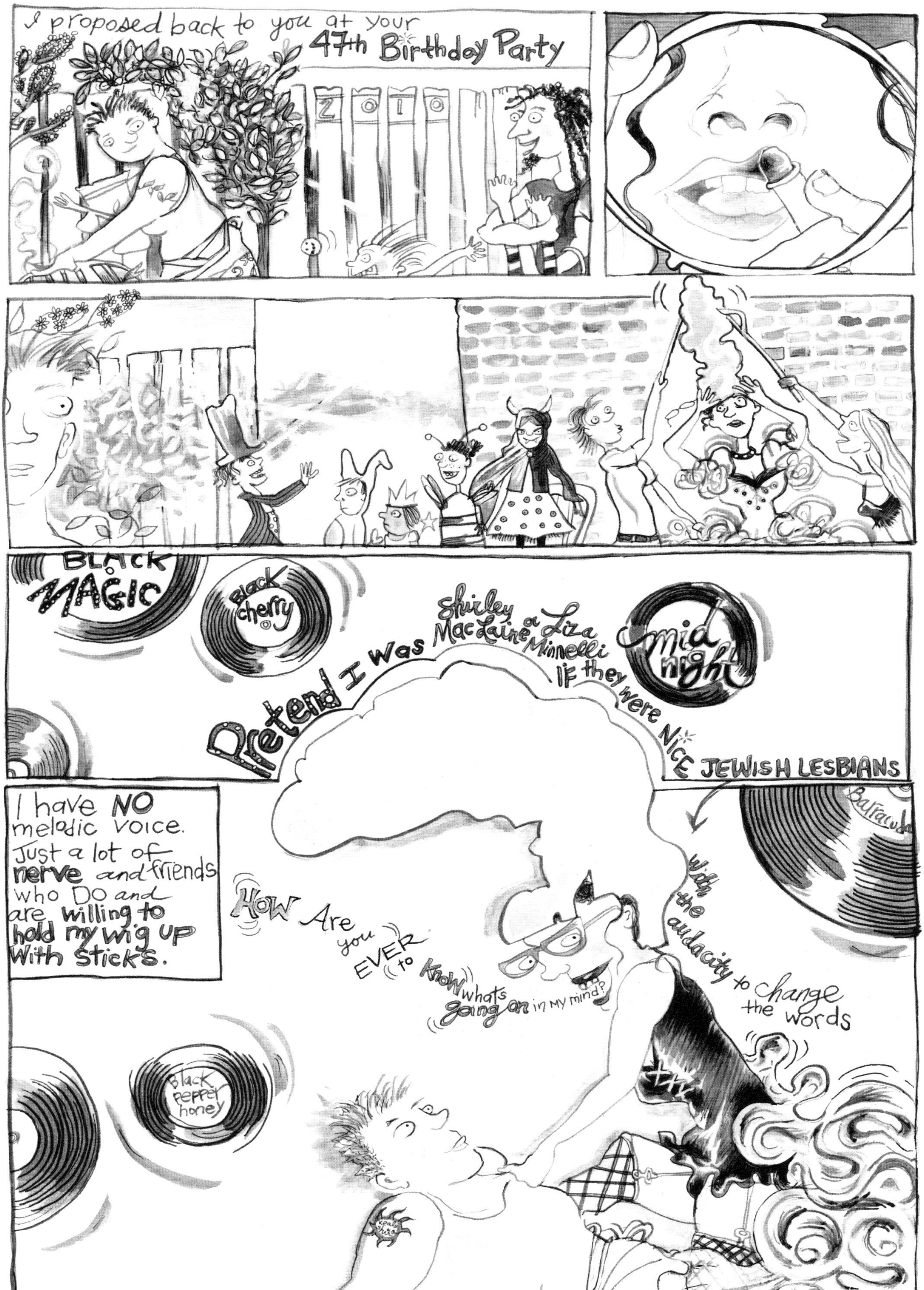
I proposed back to you at your 47th Birthday Party
2010
BLACK MAGIC
Black cherry
Pretend I was Shirley MacLaine or Liza Minnelli If they were NICE JEWISH LESBIANS
mid night
Barracuda
I have NO melodic voice. Just a lot of nerve and friends who DO and are willing to hold my wig up with sticks.
HOW Are you EVER to Know whats going on in my mind?
with the audacity to change the words
Black pepper honey

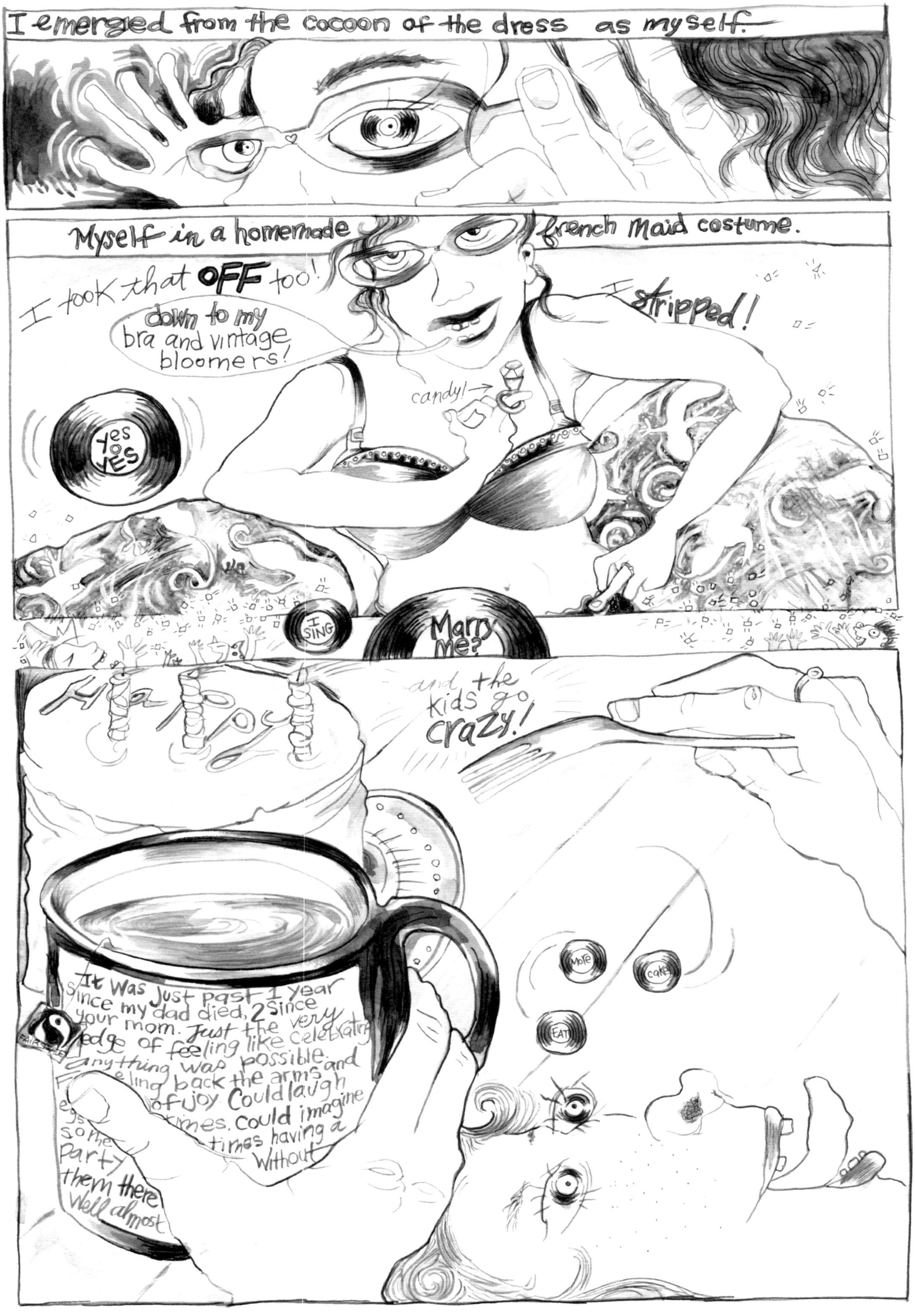
I emerged from the cocoon of the dress as myself.
Myself in a homemade french maid costume.
I took that OFF too!
down to my bra and vintage bloomers!
I stripped!
candy!
yes o YES
I SING
Marry me?
and the kids go crazy!
MORE
CAKE
EAT
It was just past 1 year
since my dad died, 2 since
your mom. Just the very
edge of feeling like celebrating
anything was possible.
F eling back the arms and
of joy. Could laugh
e times. Could imagine
some times having a
party Without
them there
Well almost

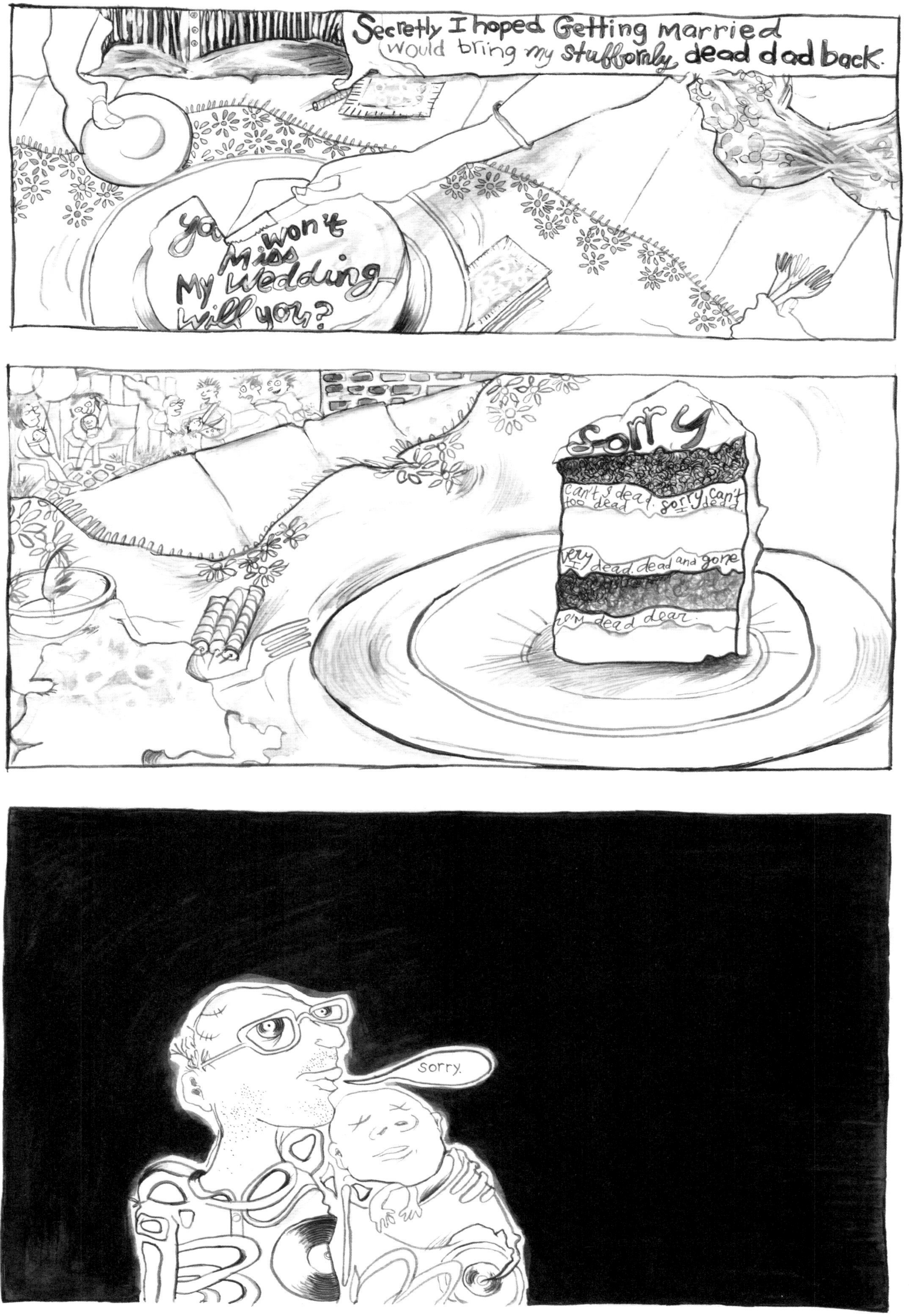
Secretly I hoped Getting married would bring my stubbornly dead dad back.
won't Miss My Wedding Will you?
sorry
can't I dead. sorry can't
too dead I dead.
very I dead. dead and gone
dead dear.
sorry.

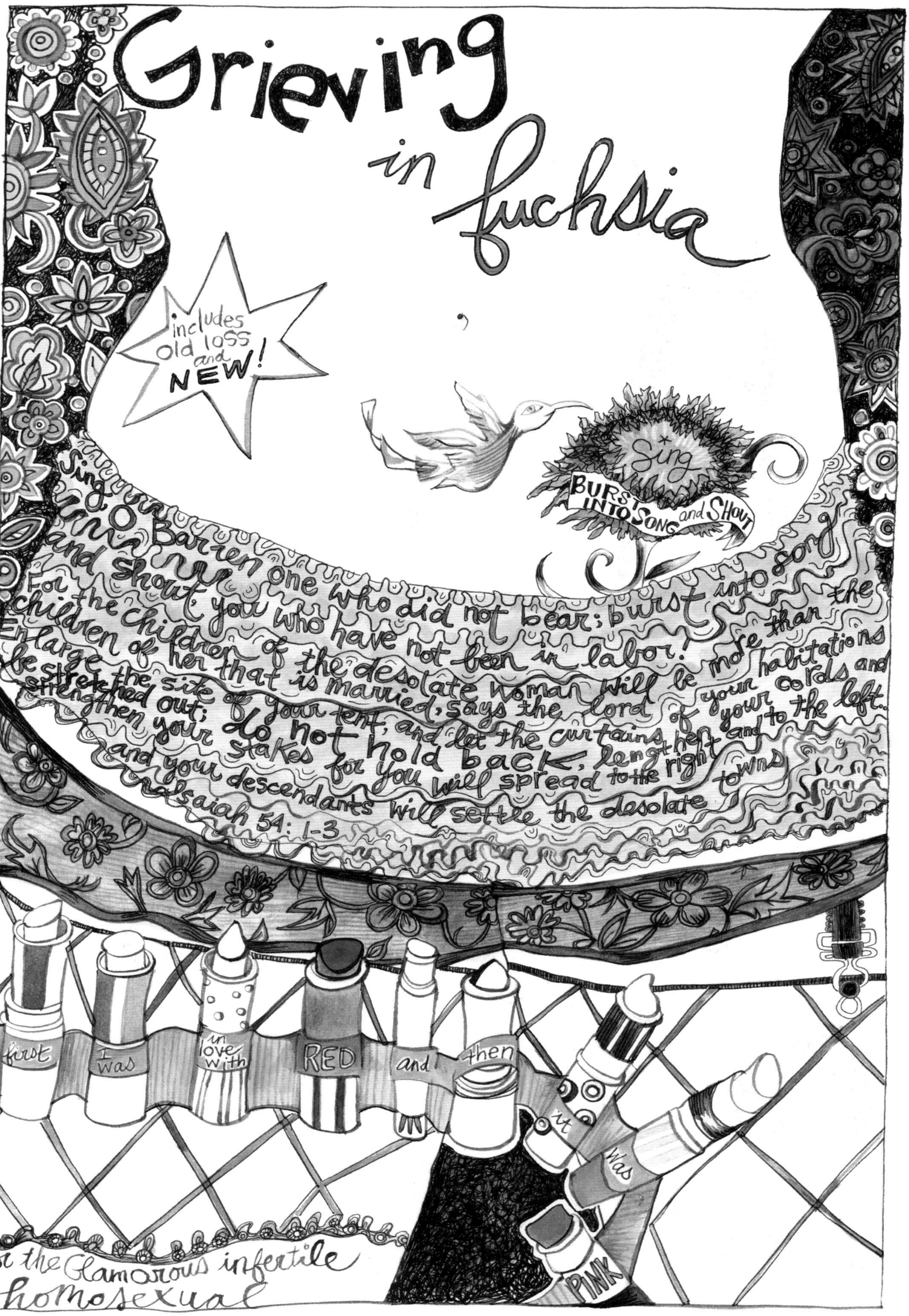
Grieving in fuchsia
includes old loss and NEW!
Sing
BURST INTO SONG and SHOUT
Sing O Barren one who did not bear; burst into song
and shout you who have not been in labor!
For the children of the desolate woman will be more than the
children of her that is married, says the lord
Enlarge the site of your tent, and let the curtains of your habitations
be stretched out; do not hold back, lengthen your cords and
strengthen your stakes for you will spread to the right and to the left.
and your descendants will settle the desolate towns
Isaiah 54: 1-3
first
I was
in love with
RED
and
then
it
was
PINK
for the Glamorous infertile homosexual

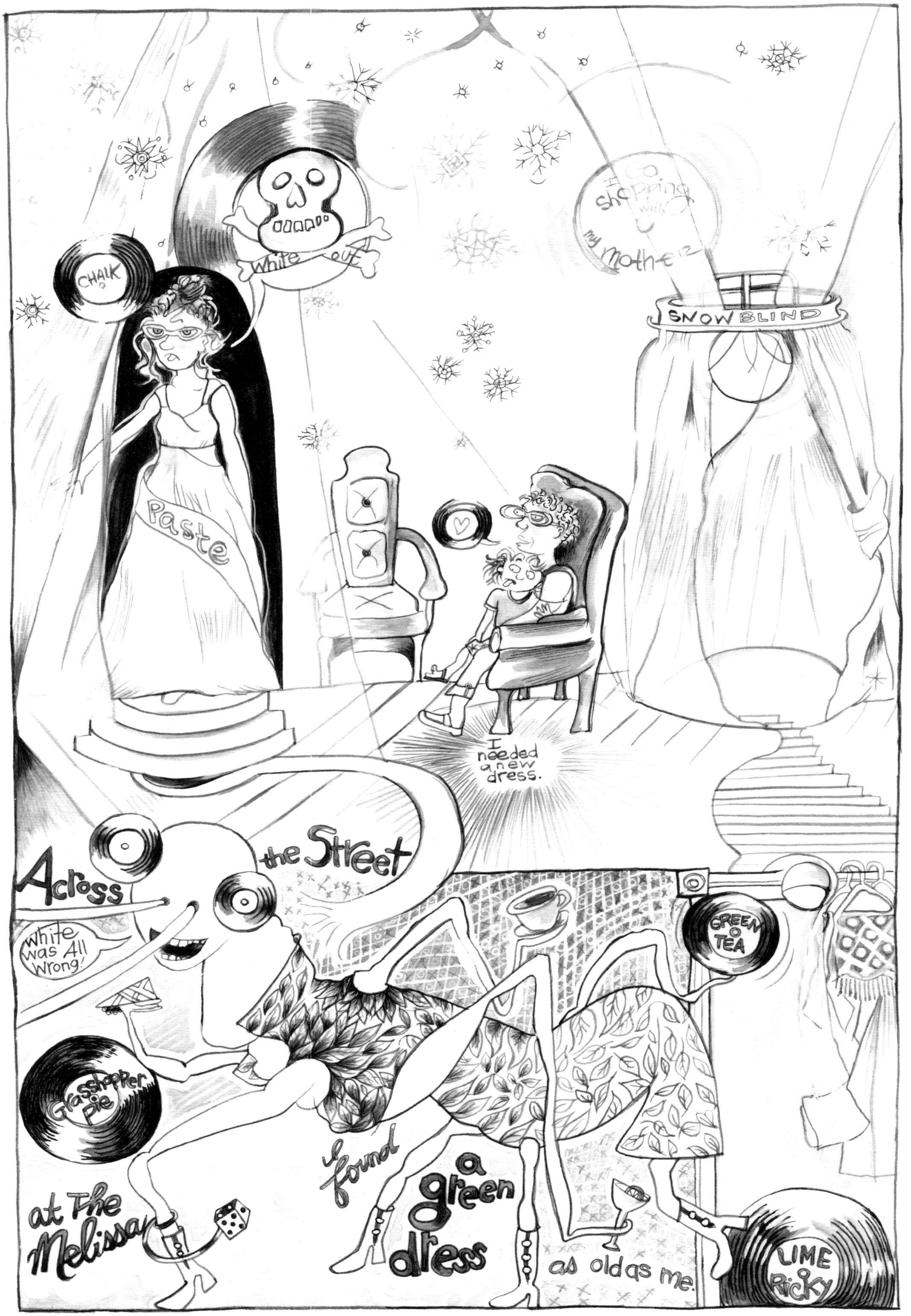
CHALK
White out
Paste
I go shopping with my mother
SNOW BLIND
I needed a new dress.
Across the Street
white was All Wrong!
GREEN TEA
Grasshopper pie
at The Melissa
I found a green dress
as old as me.
LIME RICKY

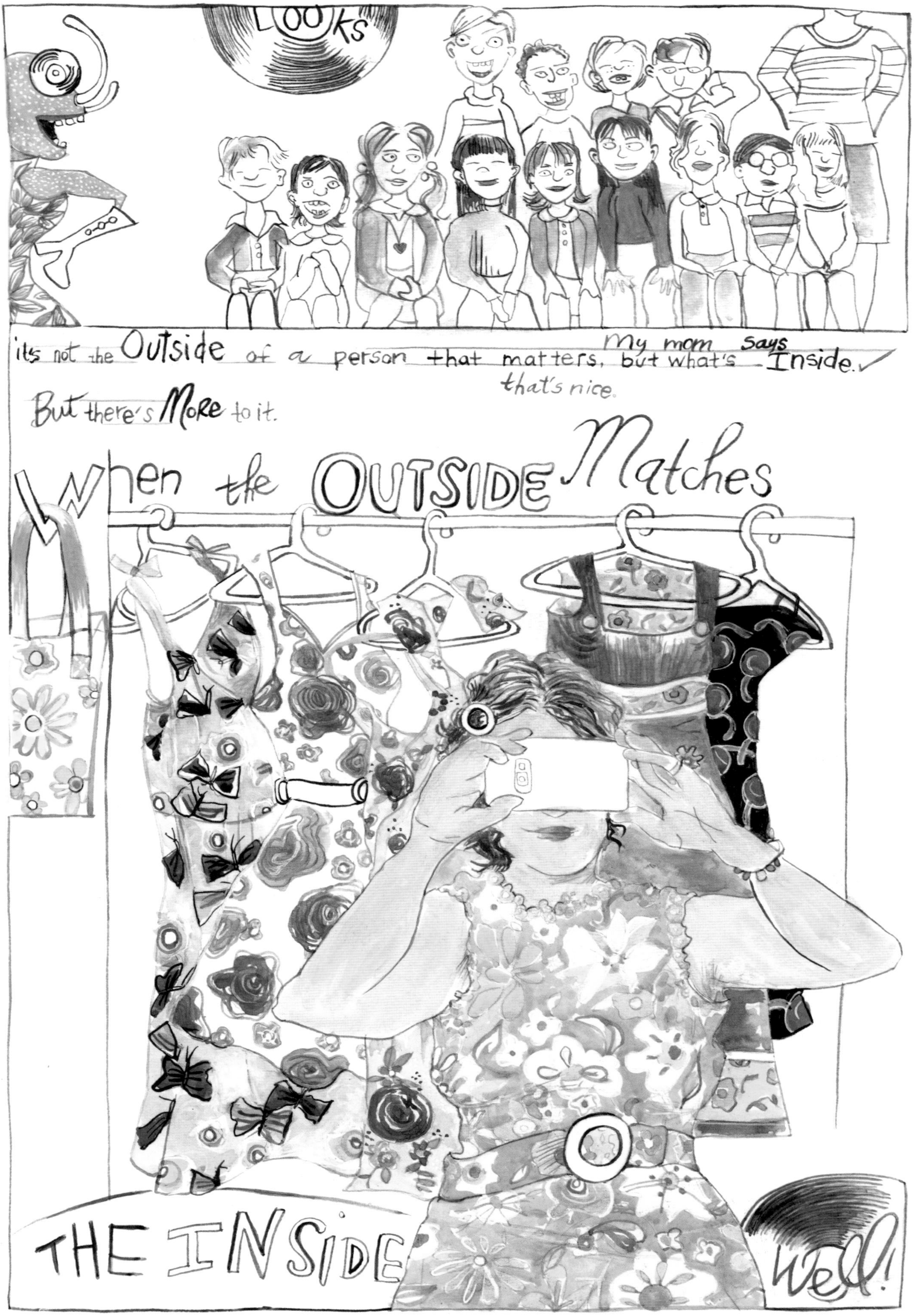
LOOKS
it's not the Outside of a person that matters, but what's Inside.
My mom says
that's nice.
But there's More to it.
When the OUTSIDE Matches
THE INSIDE
Well!

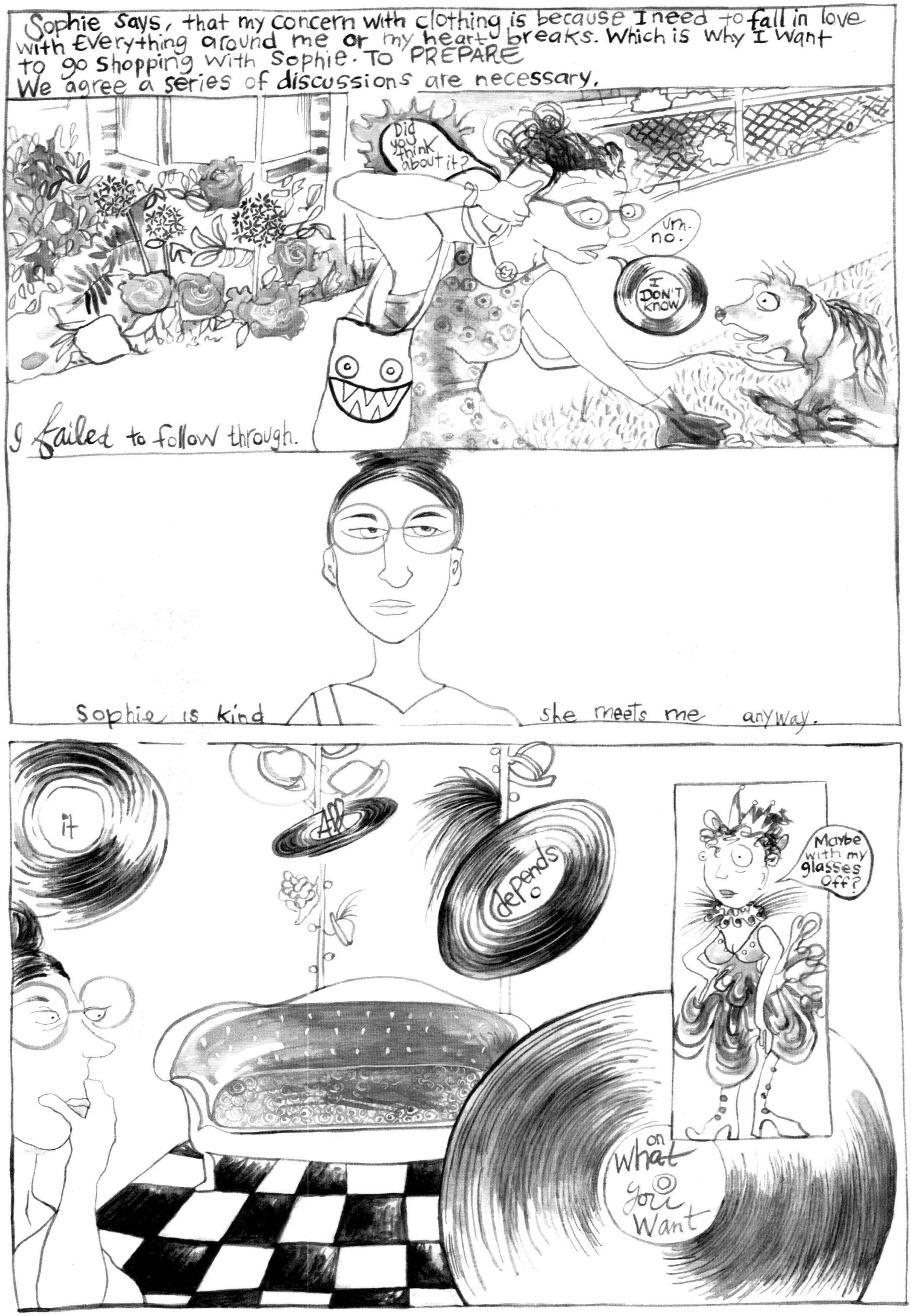
Sophie says, that my concern with clothing is because I need to fall in love with Everything around me or my heart breaks. Which is why I want to go shopping with Sophie. TO PREPARE
We agree a series of discussions are necessary.
Did you think about it?
um. no.
I DON'T KNOW
I failed to follow through.
Sophie is kind she meets me anyway.
it
All
depends
on What you Want
Maybe with my glasses off?

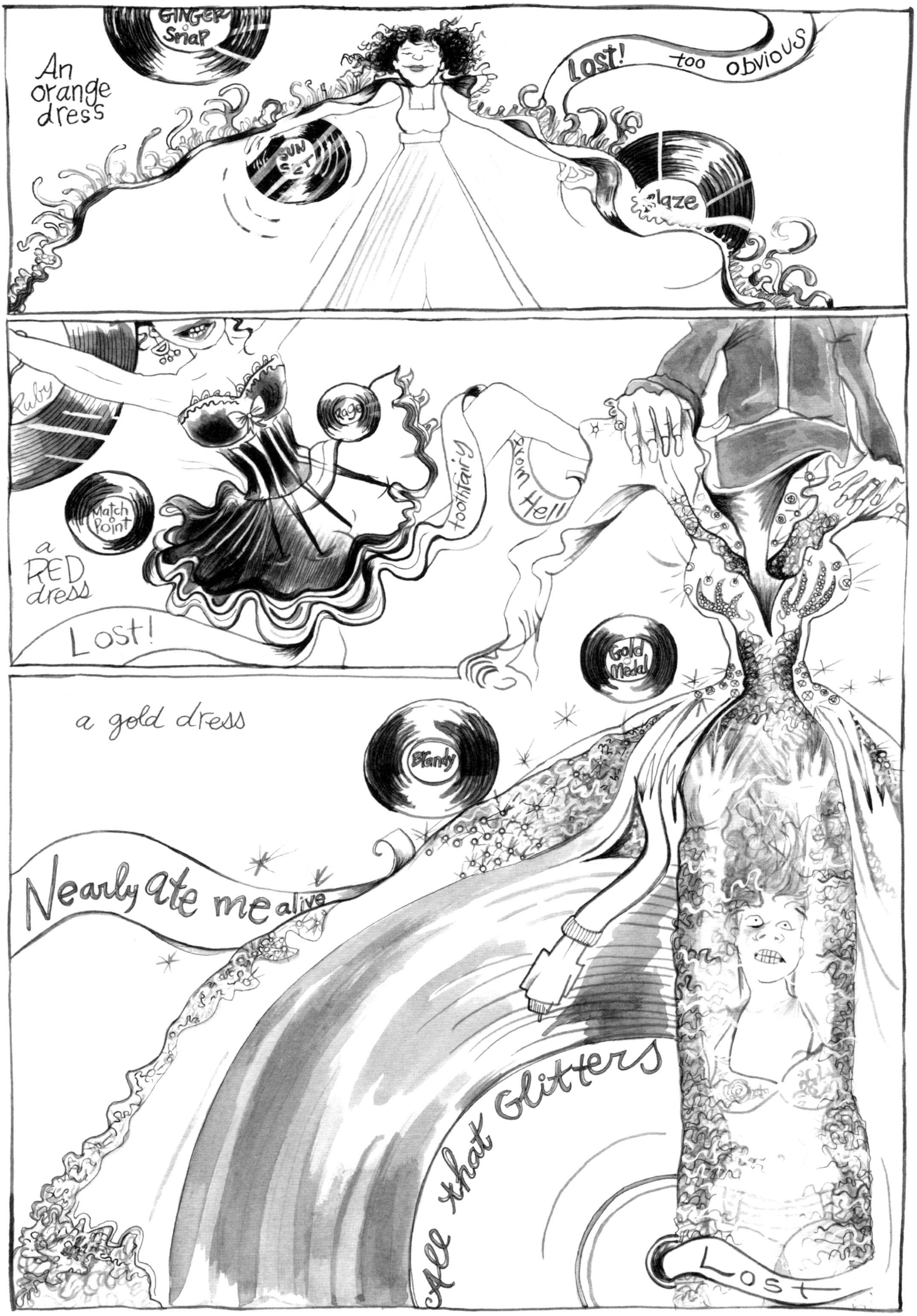
GINGER Snap
An orange dress
Lost! too obvious
SUN SET
Ruby
Rage
Match Point
toothfairy
from Hell
a RED dress
Lost!
Gold Medal
a gold dress
Brandy
Nearly ate me alive
All that Glitters
Lost

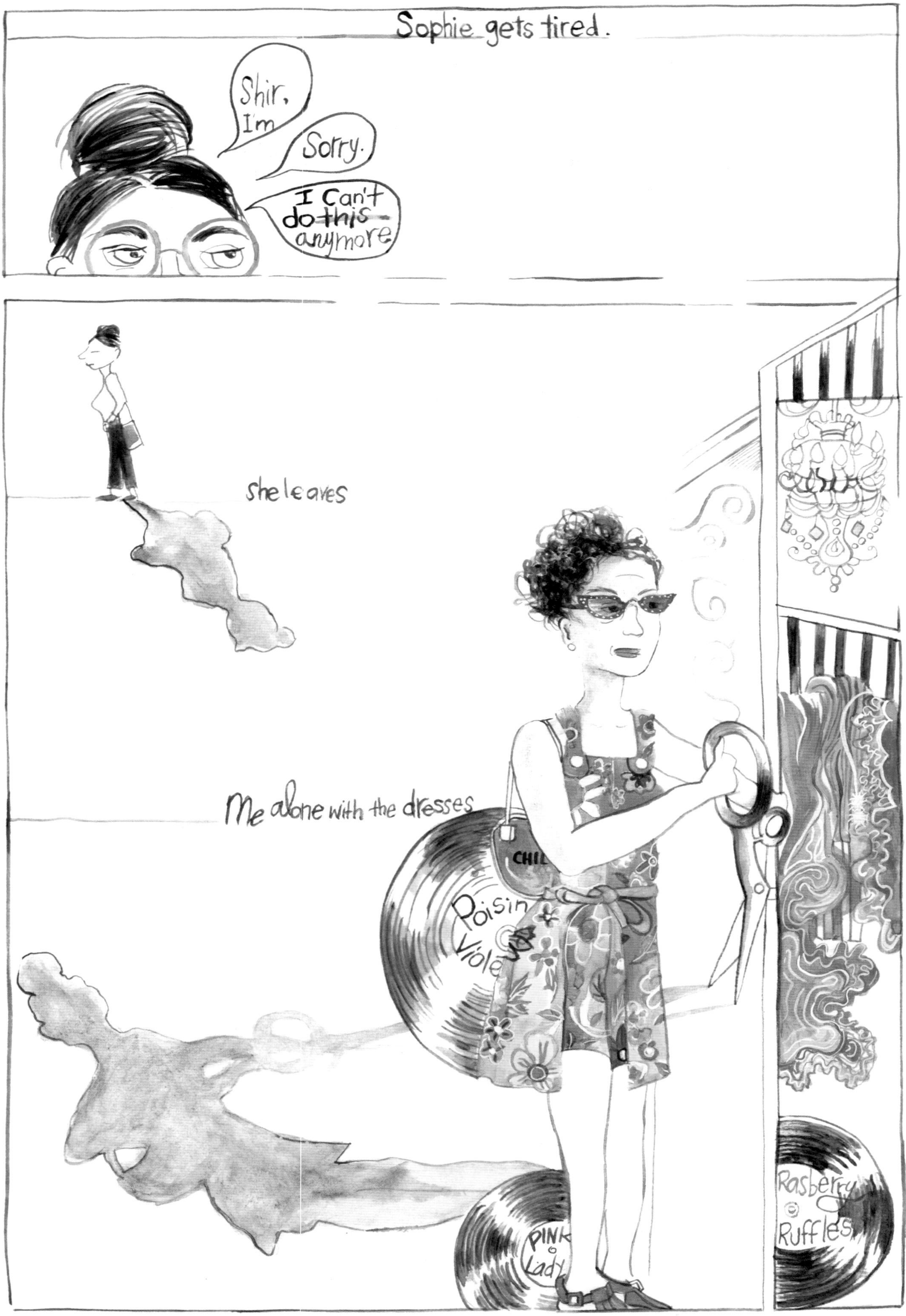
Sophie gets tired.
Shir, I'm
Sorry.
I can't do this anymore
she leaves
Me alone with the dresses
CHIL
Poisin Viole
PINK Lady
Rasberry Ruffles

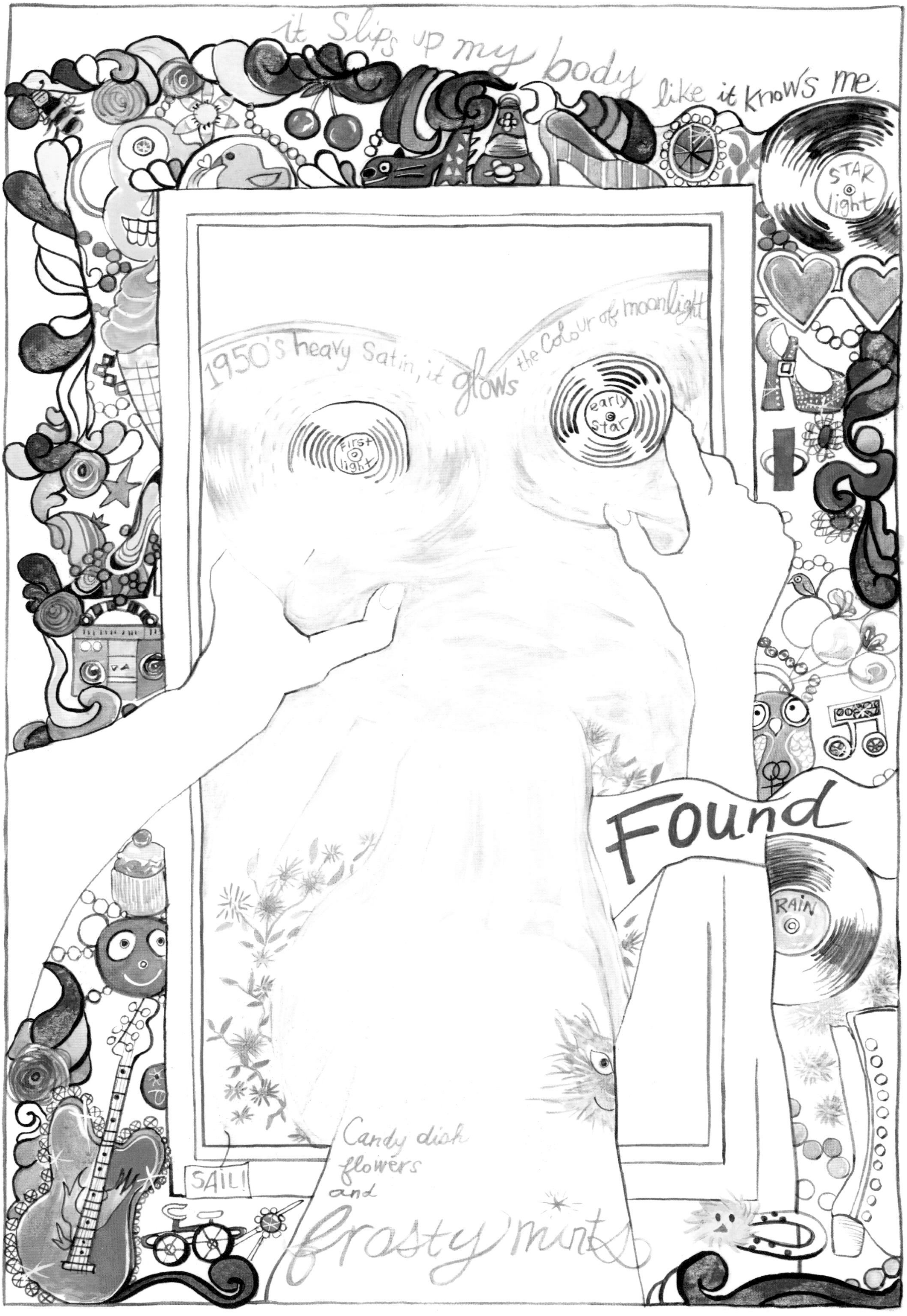
it slips up my body like it knows me.
STAR light
1950's heavy satin, it glows the colour of moonlight
first light
early star
Found
RAIN
SAIL!
Candy dish flowers and
frosty mints

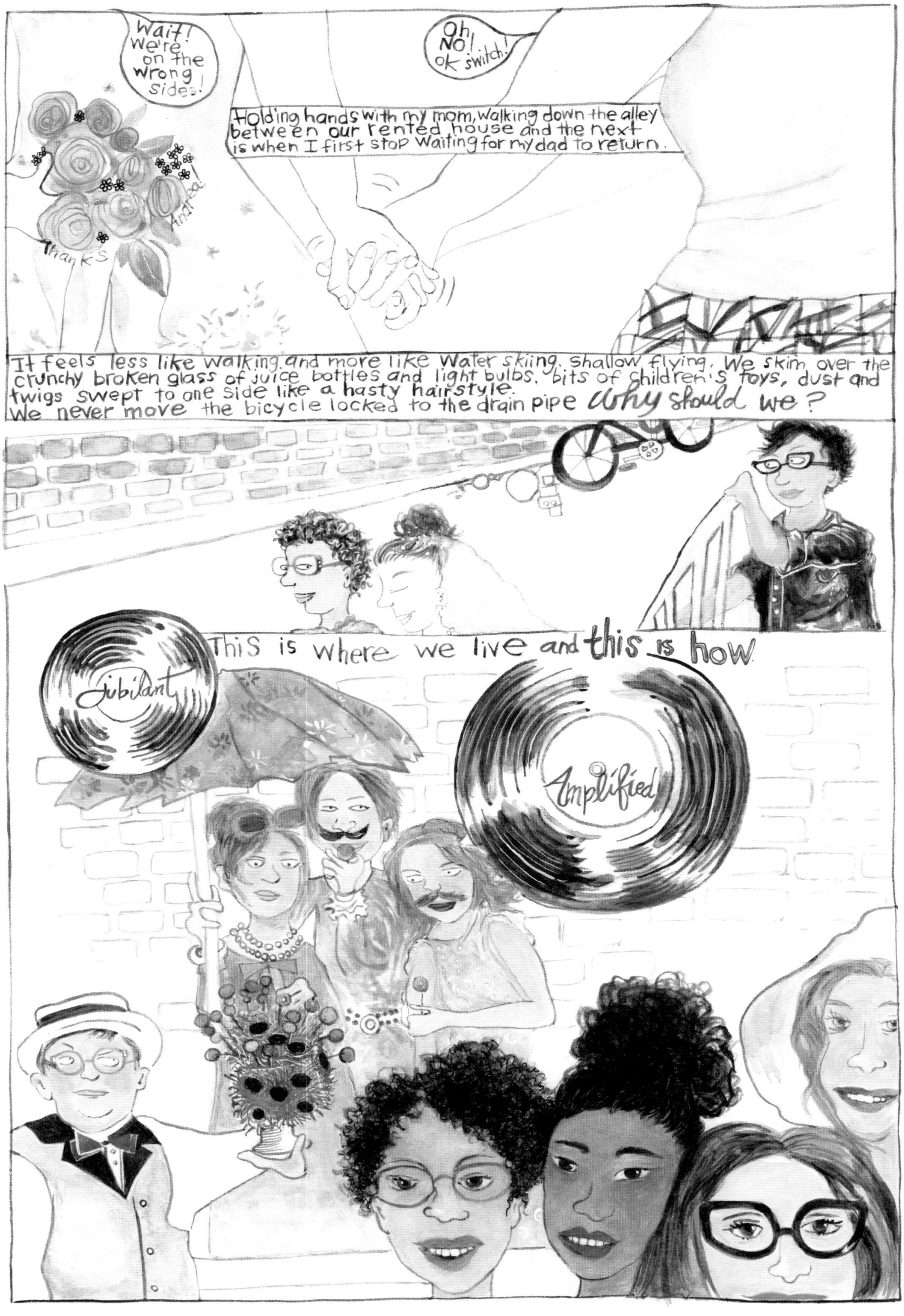
Wait! We're on the wrong sides!
Oh No! ok switch!
Holding hands with my mom, walking down the alley between our rented house and the next is when I first stop waiting for my dad to return.
Thanks Andrea!
It feels less like walking and more like water skiing, shallow flying. We skim over the crunchy broken glass of juice bottles and light bulbs, bits of children's toys, dust and twigs swept to one side like a hasty hairstyle.
We never move the bicycle locked to the drain pipe Why should we?
This is where we live and this is how
Jubilant
Amplified

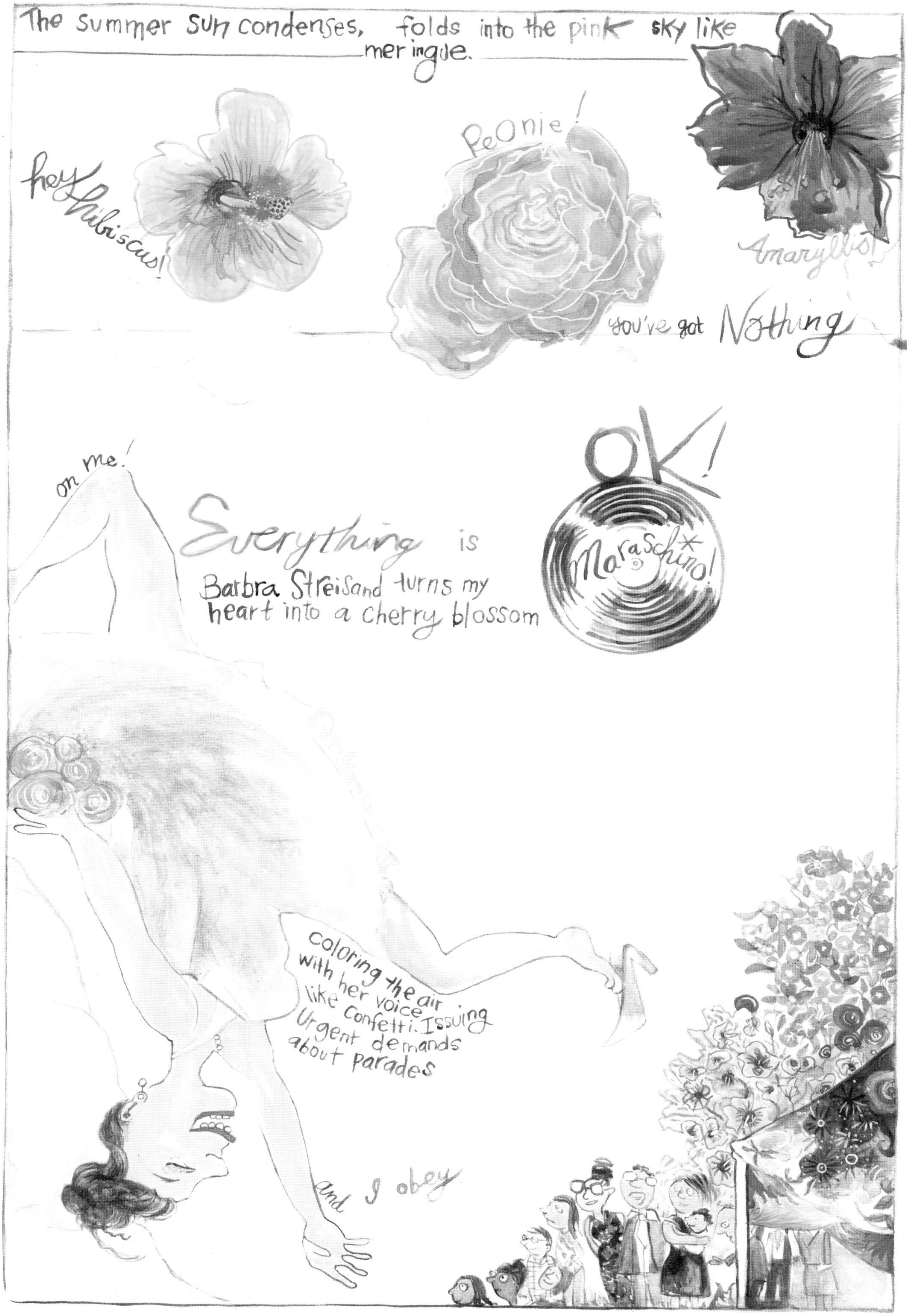
The summer sun condenses, folds into the pink sky like meringue.
hey hibiscus!
Peonie!
Amaryllis!
you've got Nothing
on me!
Everything is
OK!
Maraschino!
Barbra Streisand turns my heart into a cherry blossom
coloring the air with her voice Issuing like confetti. Urgent demands about parades
and I obey

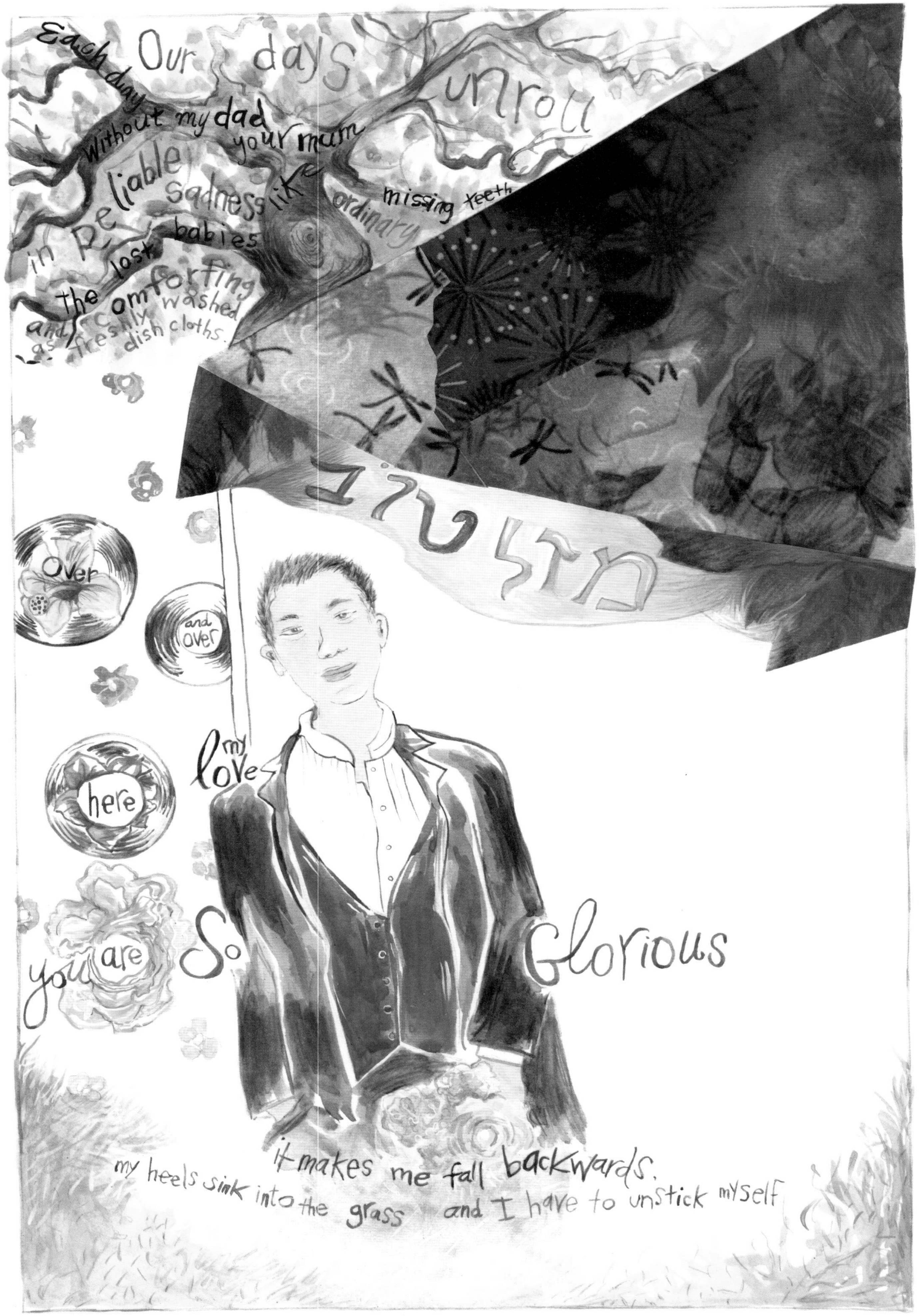
Each day
Our days unroll
without my dad
your mum
in reliable
sadness lik
missing teeth
ordinary
lost babies
the comforting
and freshly washed
as freshly dish cloths.
מזל טוב
Over
and over
my love
here
you are so Glorious
it makes me fall backwards.
my heels sink into the grass and I have to unstick myself

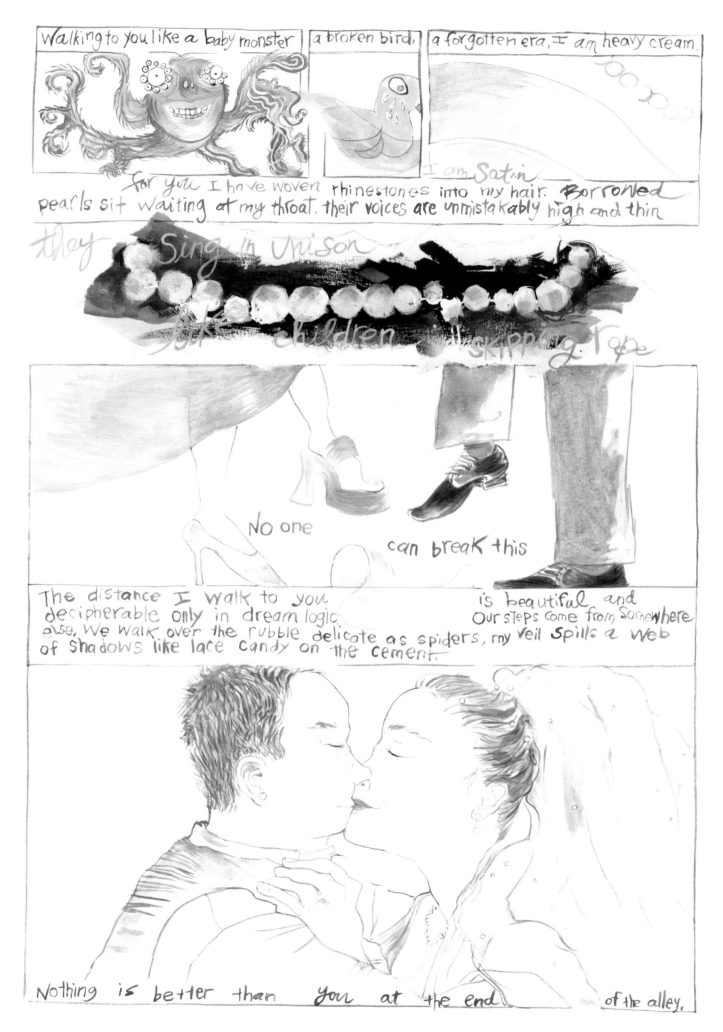

Walking to you like a baby monster, a broken bird, a forgotten era, I am heavy cream.

for you I have woven rhinestones into my hair. Borrowed pearls sit waiting at my throat. their voices are unmistakably high and thin

I am Satin

they sing in unison

like children all skipping rope

No one

can break this

The distance I walk to you, decipherable only in dream logic. is beautiful and Our steps come from Somewhere else, We walk over the rubble delicate as spiders, my veil spills a web of shadows like lace candy on the cement.

Nothing is better than you at the end of the alley.

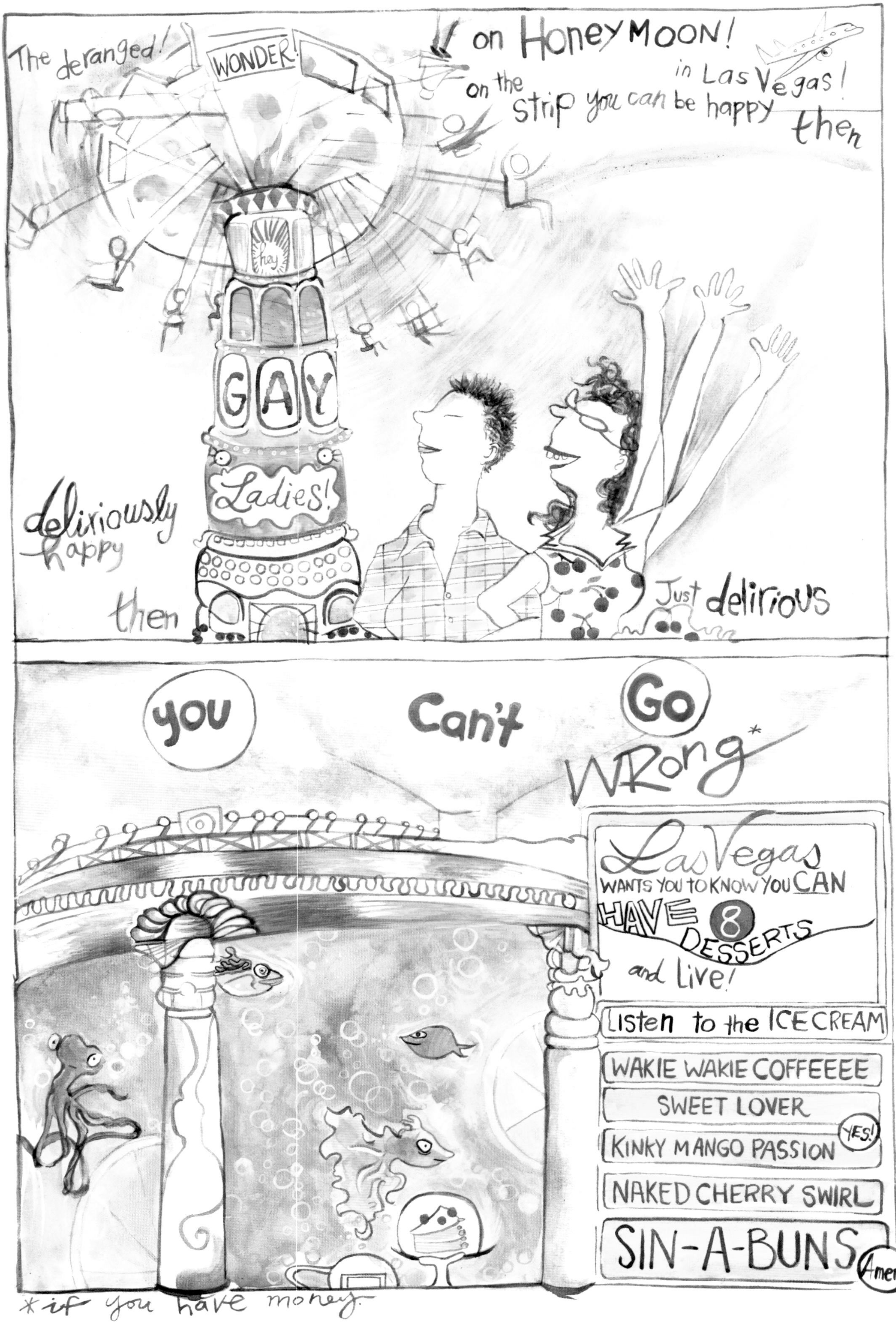
The deranged!
WONDER
on HONEYMOON!
in Las Vegas!
on the strip you can be happy
then
hay
GAY
Ladies!
deliriously happy
then
Just delirious
you
Can't
Go
WRong*
Las Vegas
WANTS YOU TO KNOW YOU CAN
HAVE 8 DESSERTS
and Live!
Listen to the ICE CREAM
WAKIE WAKIE COFFEEEE
SWEET LOVER
KINKY MANGO PASSION
YES!
NAKED CHERRY SWIRL
SIN-A-BUNS
Amen!

*if you have money.

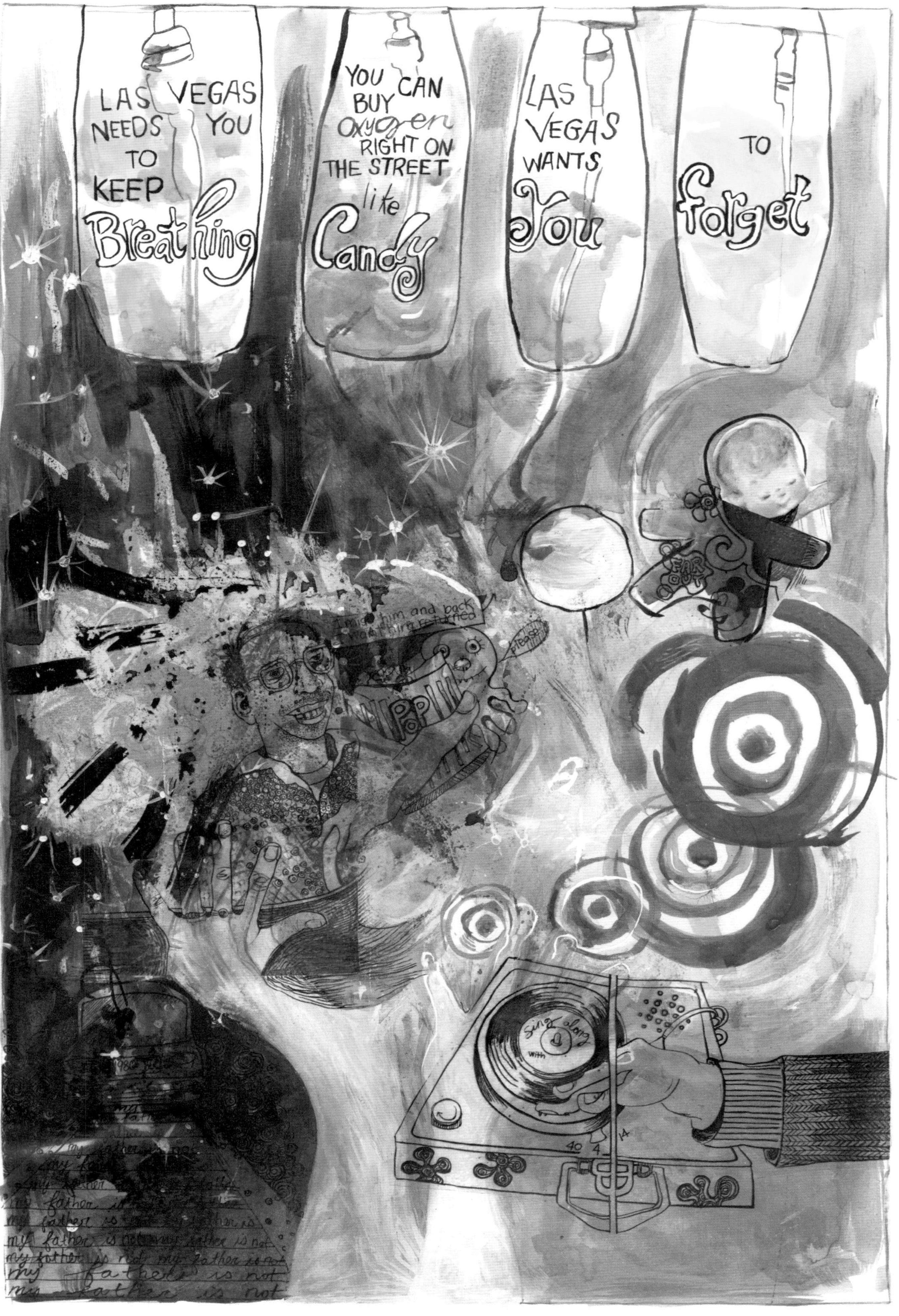
LAS VEGAS NEEDS YOU TO KEEP Breathing
YOU CAN BUY oxygen RIGHT ON THE STREET like Candy
LAS VEGAS WANTS You
TO forget
please
FAR OUT
sing along with
my father is not my father is not
my father is not
my father is not

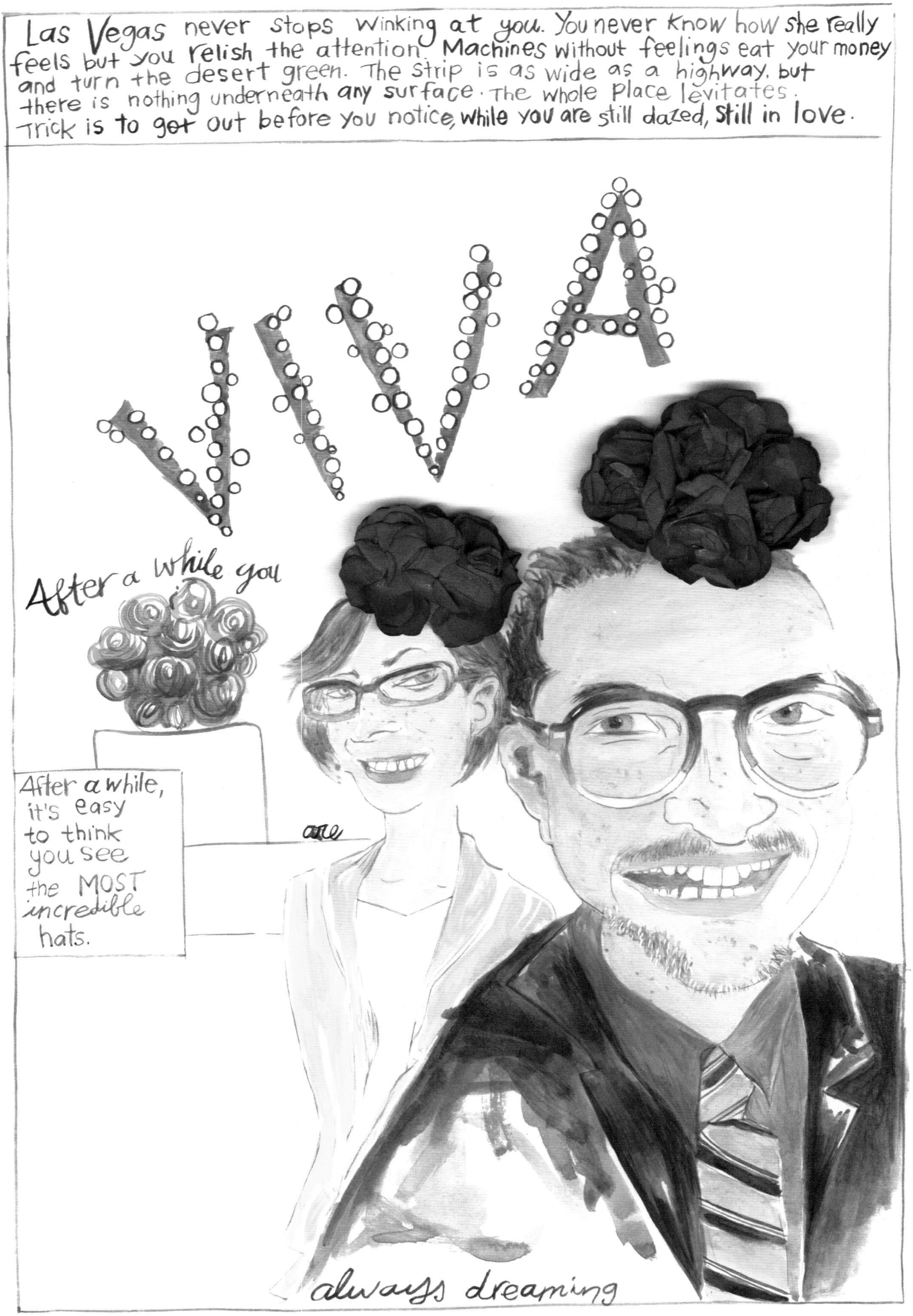
Las Vegas never stops winking at you. You never know how she really feels but you relish the attention. Machines without feelings eat your money and turn the desert green. The strip is as wide as a highway, but there is nothing underneath any surface. The whole Place levitates. Trick is to get out before you notice, while you are still dazed, Still in love.
VIVA
After a while you
After a while, it's easy to think you see the MOST incredible hats.
are
always dreaming

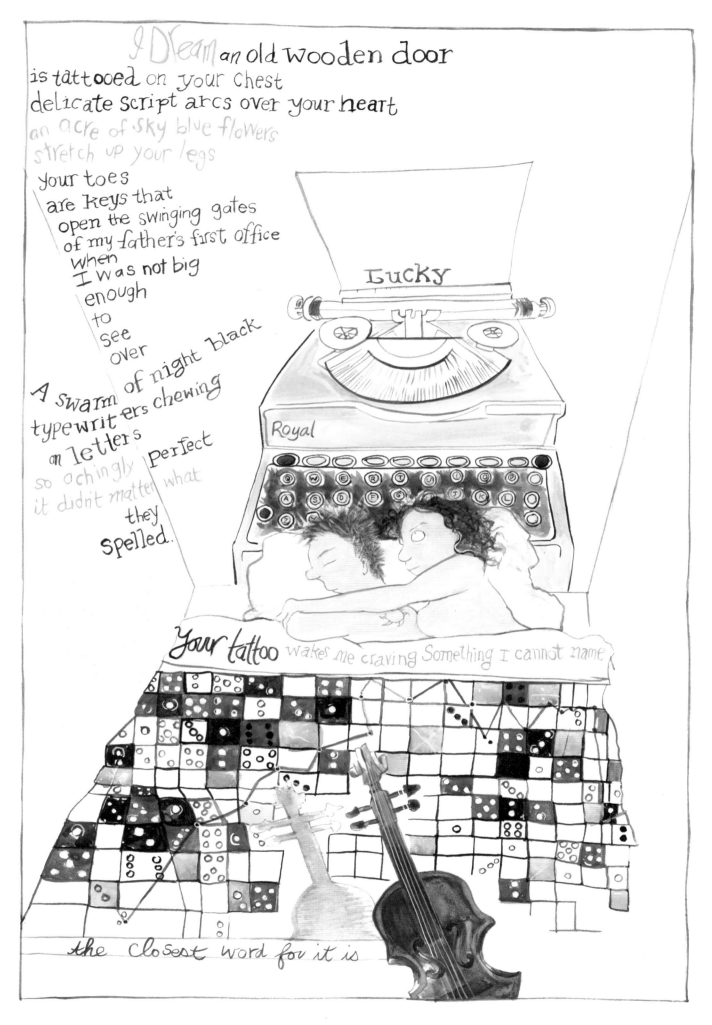

I Dream an old wooden door
is tattooed on your chest
delicate script arcs over your heart
an acre of sky blue flowers
stretch up your legs

your toes
are keys that
open the swinging gates
of my father's first office
when
I was not big
enough
to
see
over

A swarm of night black
typewriters chewing
on letters
so achingly perfect
it didn't matter what
they
spelled.

Lucky

Royal

Your tattoo wakes me craving something I cannot name

the closest word for it is

Here's a little story. Chris and I are sad because so much is lost, but it is spring! So even though we are broke we take little MAX to a big garden store.

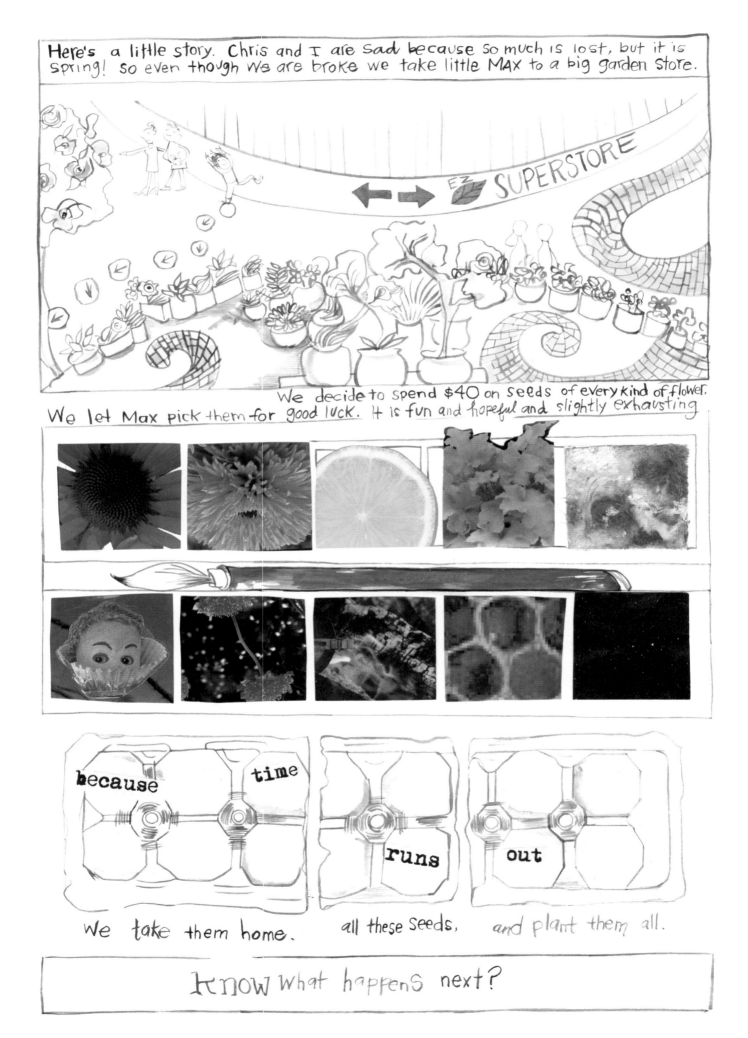

SUPERSTORE

We decide to spend $40 on seeds of every kind of flower. We let Max pick them for good luck. It is fun and hopeful and slightly exhausting

because   time

runs   out

We take them home.   all these seeds,   and plant them all.

Know what happens next?

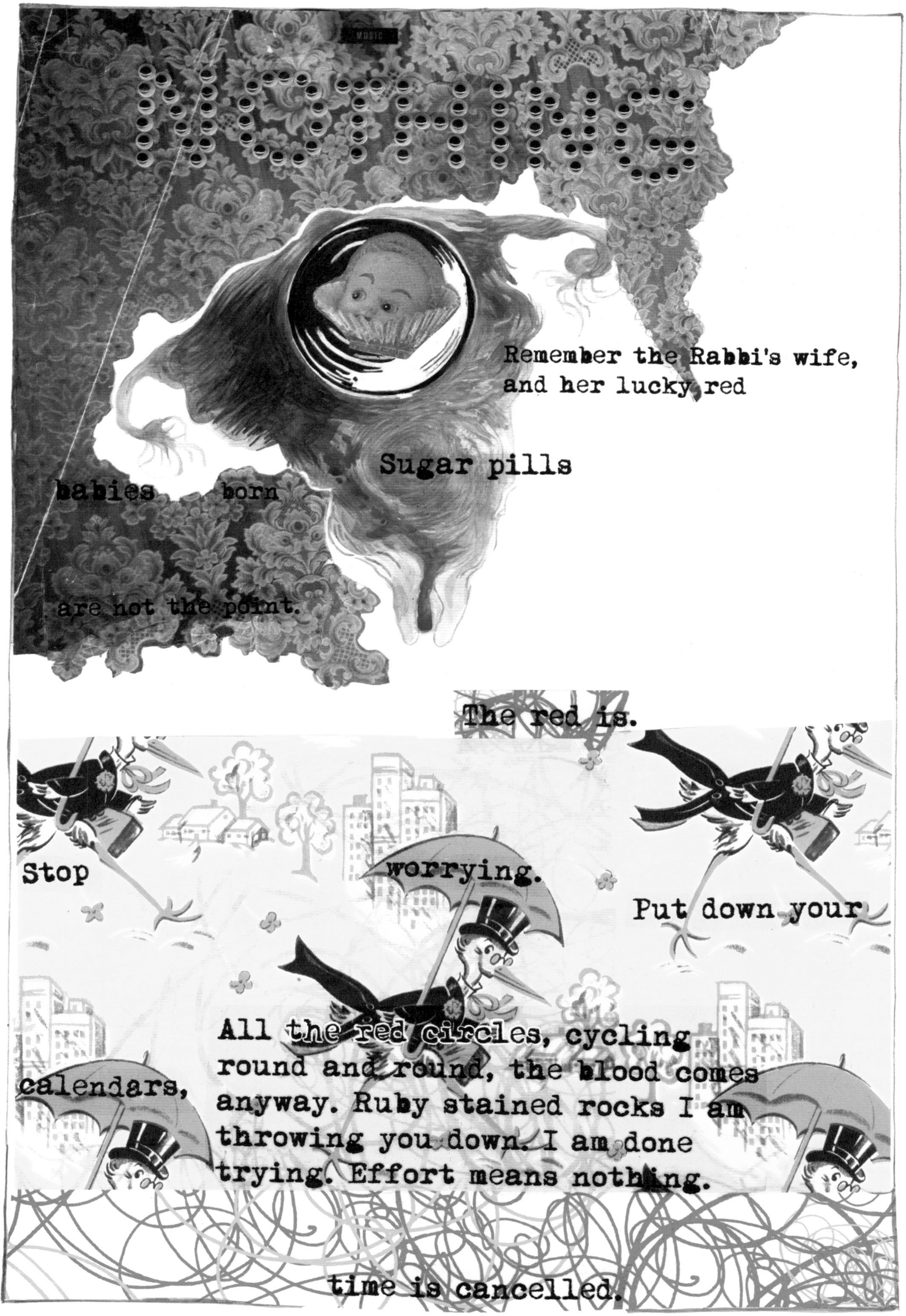
Remember the Rabbi's wife,
and her lucky red
Sugar pills
babies born
are not the point.
The red is.
Stop
worrying.
Put down your
calendars,
All the red circles, cycling
round and round, the blood comes
anyway. Ruby stained rocks I am
throwing you down. I am done
trying. Effort means nothing.
time is cancelled.

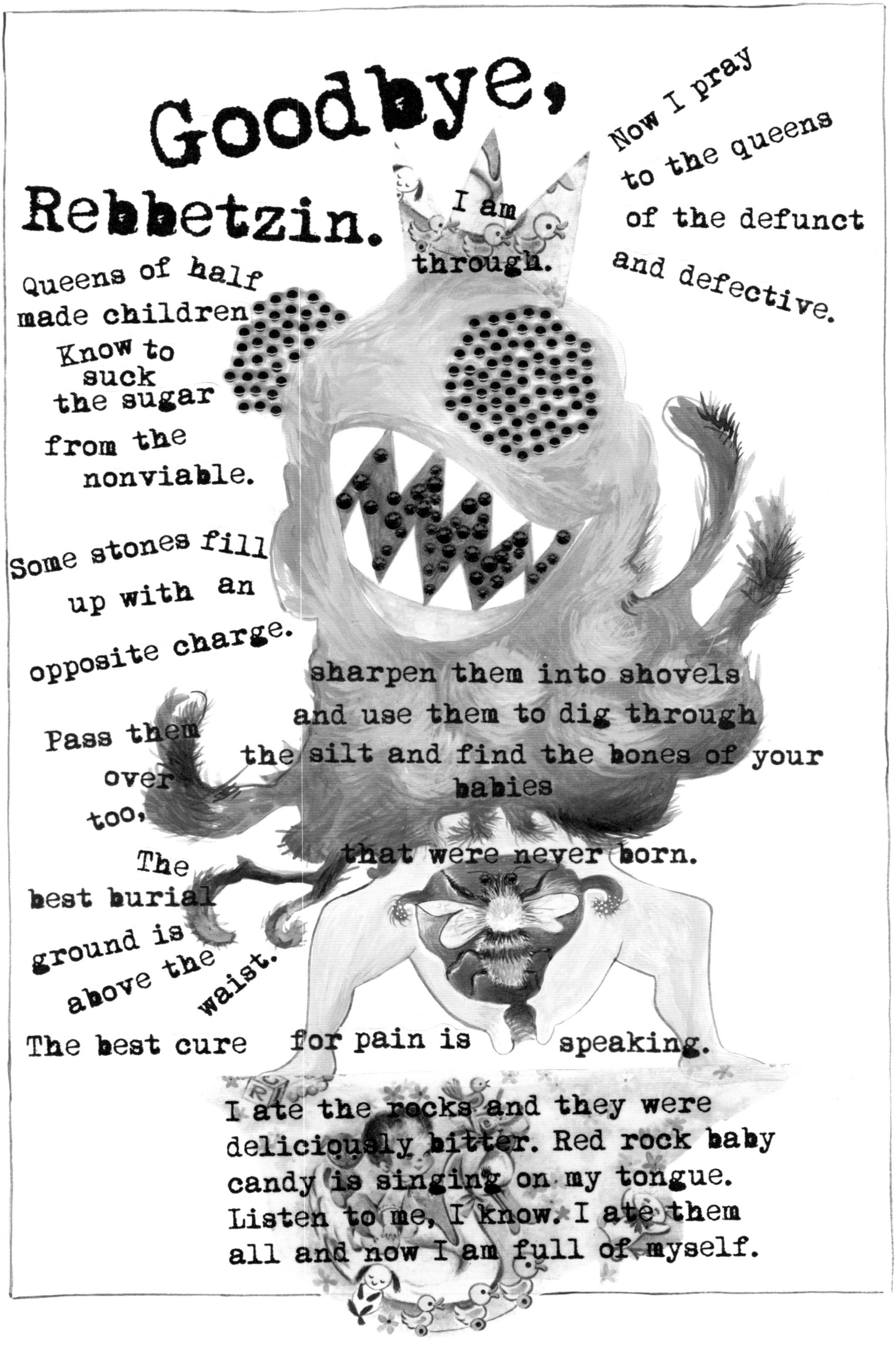
Goodbye,
Rebbetzin.
I am through.
Now I pray to the queens of the defunct and defective.
Queens of half made children Know to suck the sugar from the nonviable.
Some stones fill up with an opposite charge.
sharpen them into shovels and use them to dig through the silt and find the bones of your babies
that were never born.
Pass them over too,
The best burial ground is above the waist.
The best cure for pain is speaking.
I ate the rocks and they were deliciously bitter. Red rock baby candy is singing on my tongue. Listen to me, I know. I ate them all and now I am full of myself.

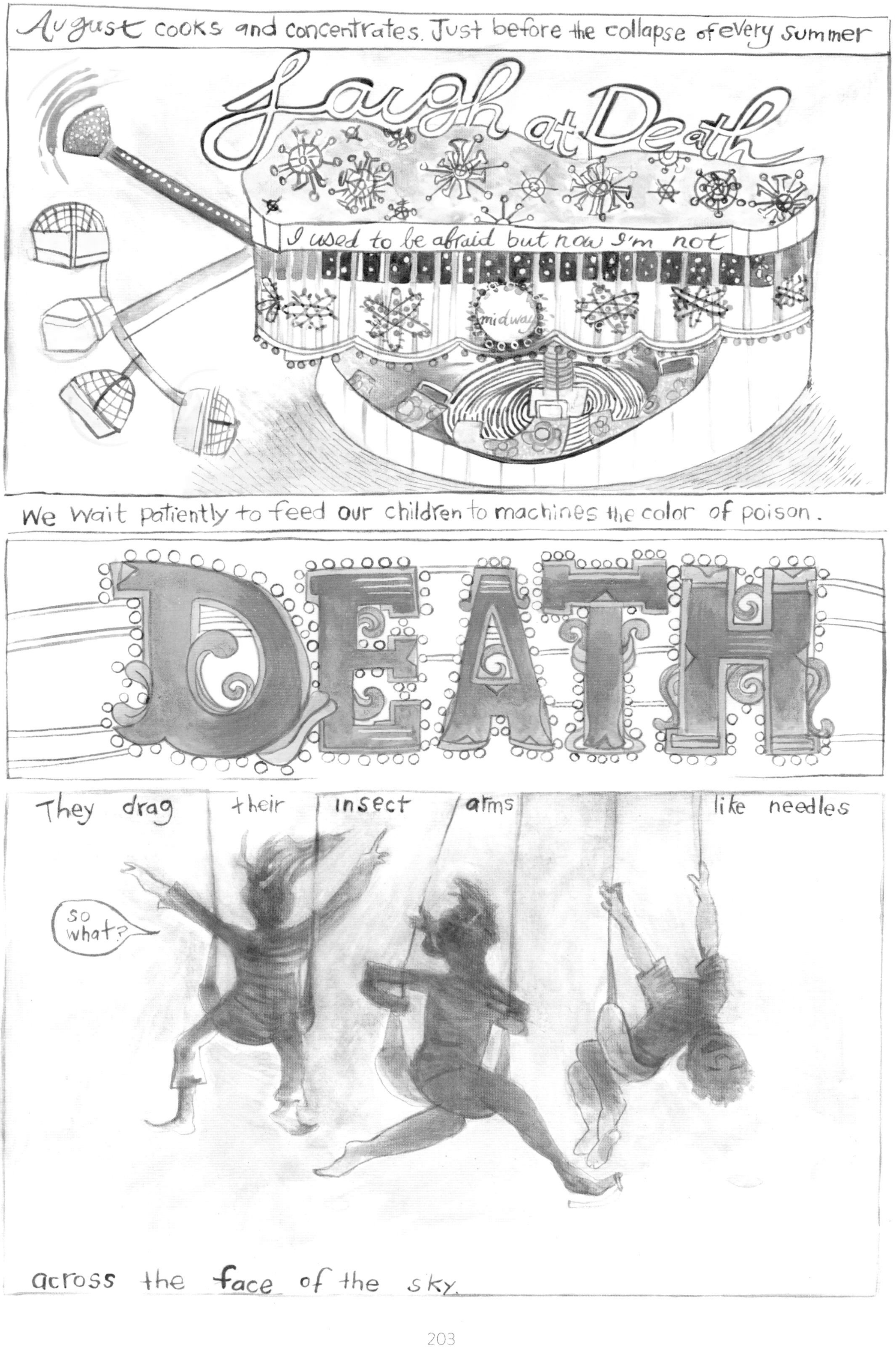
August cooks and concentrates. Just before the collapse of every summer
Laugh at Death
I used to be afraid but now I'm not
midway
We wait patiently to feed our children to machines the color of poison.
DEATH
They drag their insect arms like needles
so what?
across the face of the sky.

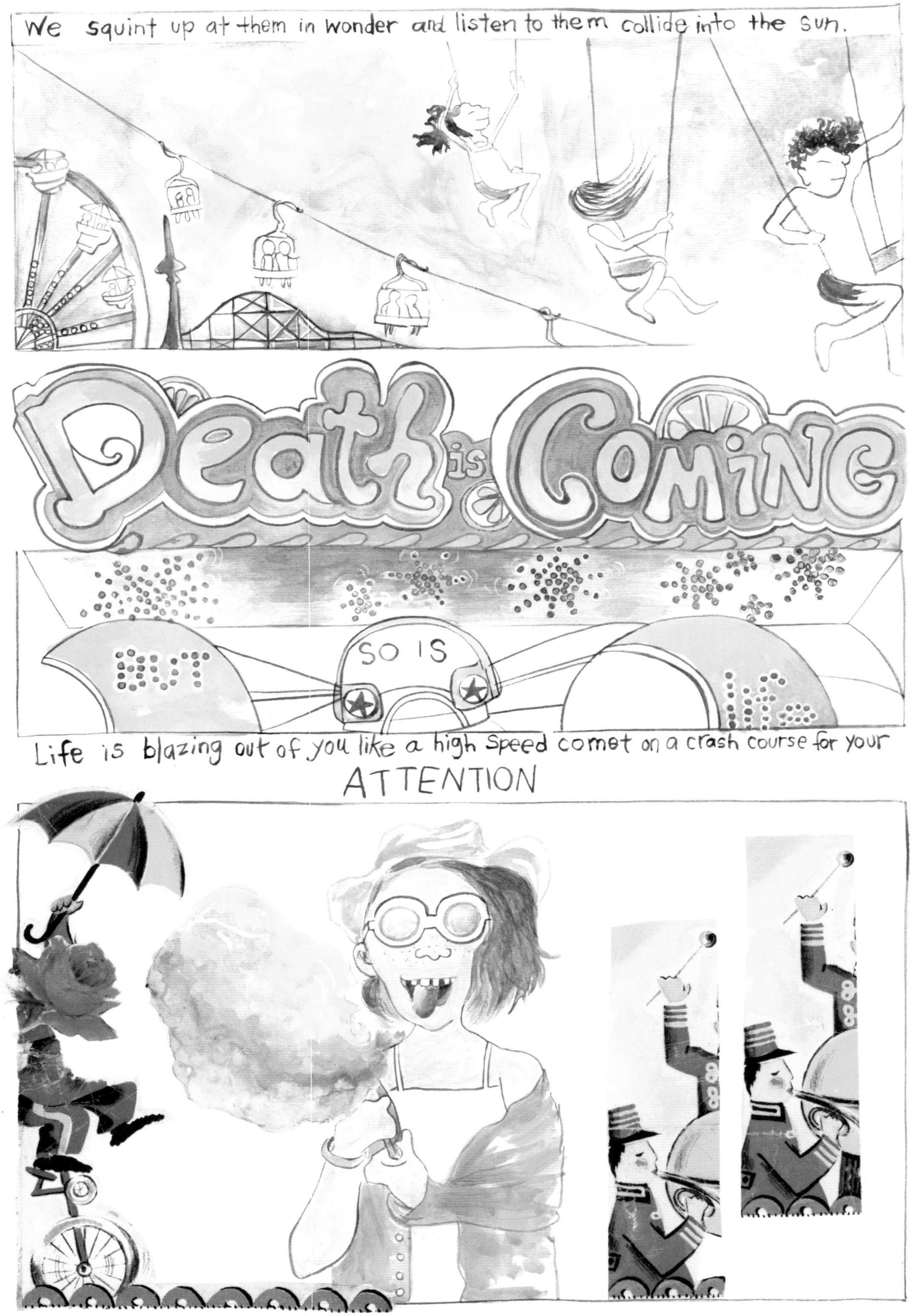
We squint up at them in wonder and listen to them collide into the sun.
Death is Coming
BUT
SO IS
life
Life is blazing out of you like a high speed comet on a crash course for your
ATTENTION

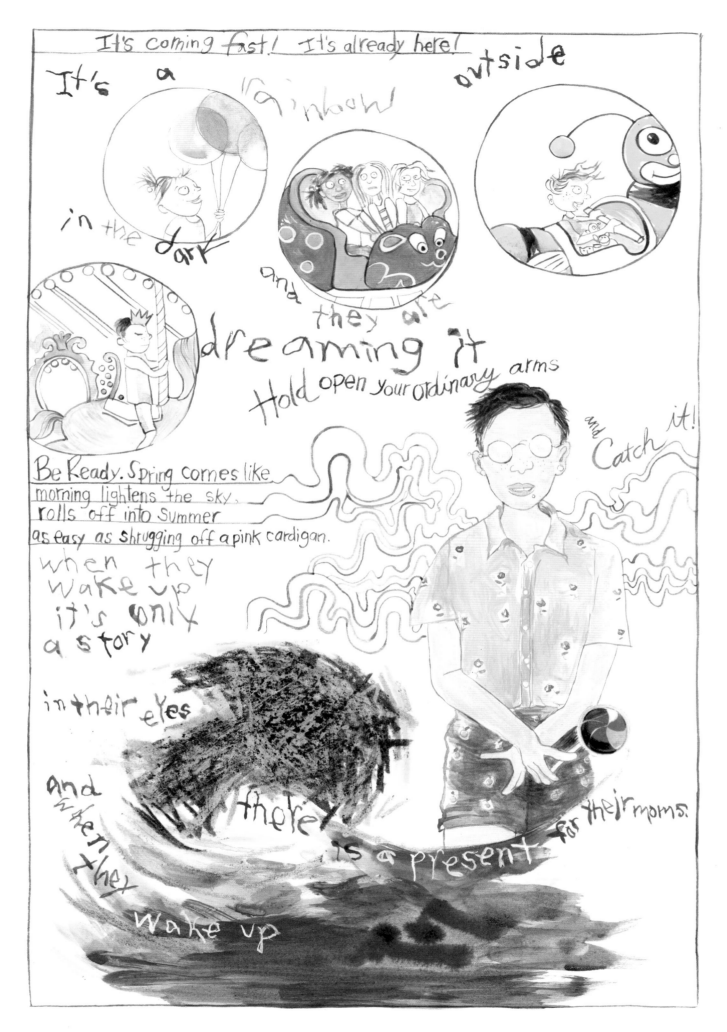

It's coming fast! It's already here!

It's a rainbow outside

in the dark

and they are

dreaming it

Hold open your ordinary arms

and Catch it!

Be Ready. Spring comes like
morning lightens the sky,
rolls off into Summer
as easy as shrugging off a pink cardigan.

when they
wake up
it's only
a story

in their eyes

and
when they

there
is a present for their moms.

wake up

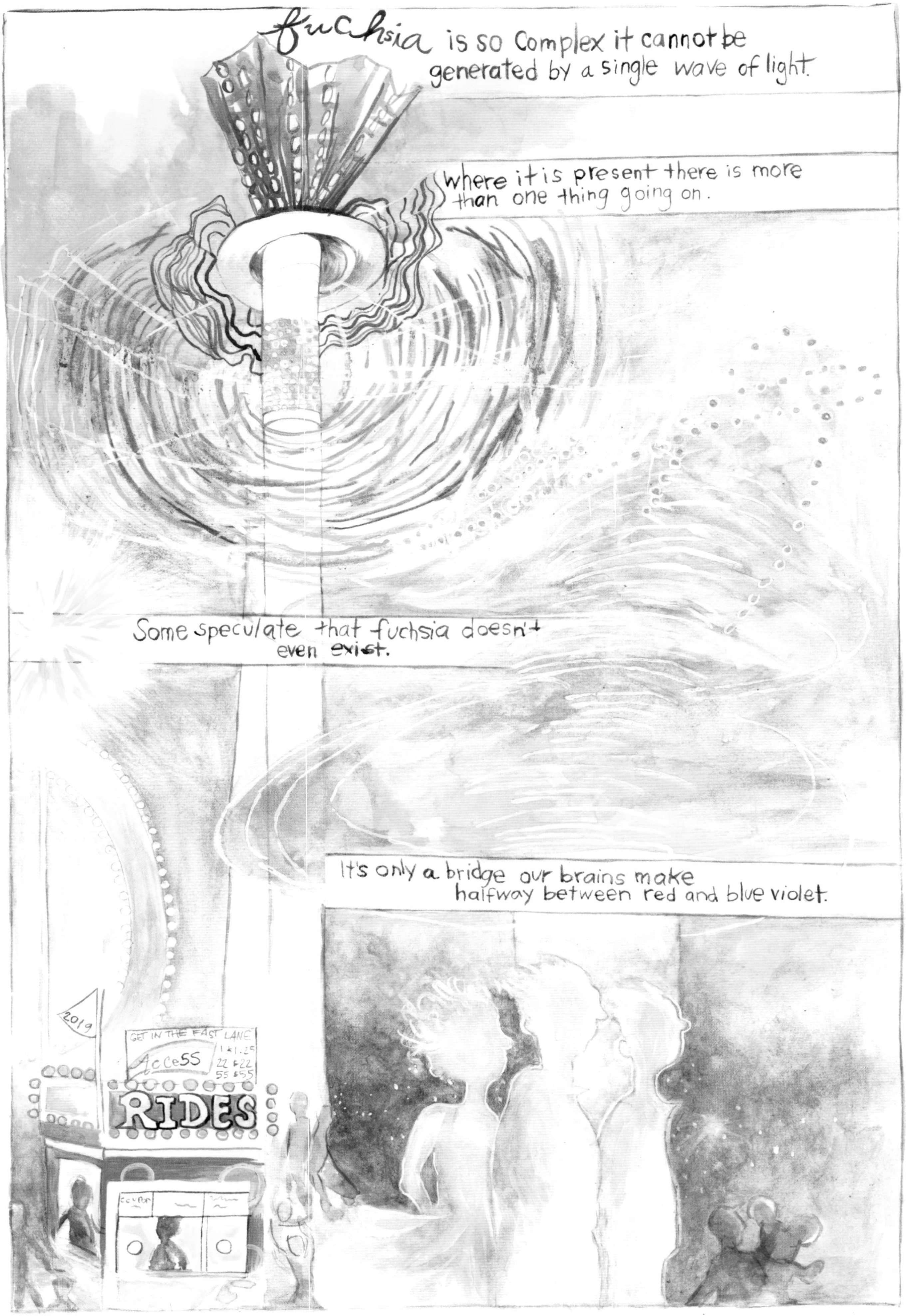
fuchsia is so complex it cannot be generated by a single wave of light.
where it is present there is more than one thing going on.
Some speculate that fuchsia doesn't even exist.
It's only a bridge our brains make halfway between red and blue violet.
2019
GET IN THE FAST LANE
Access
RIDES

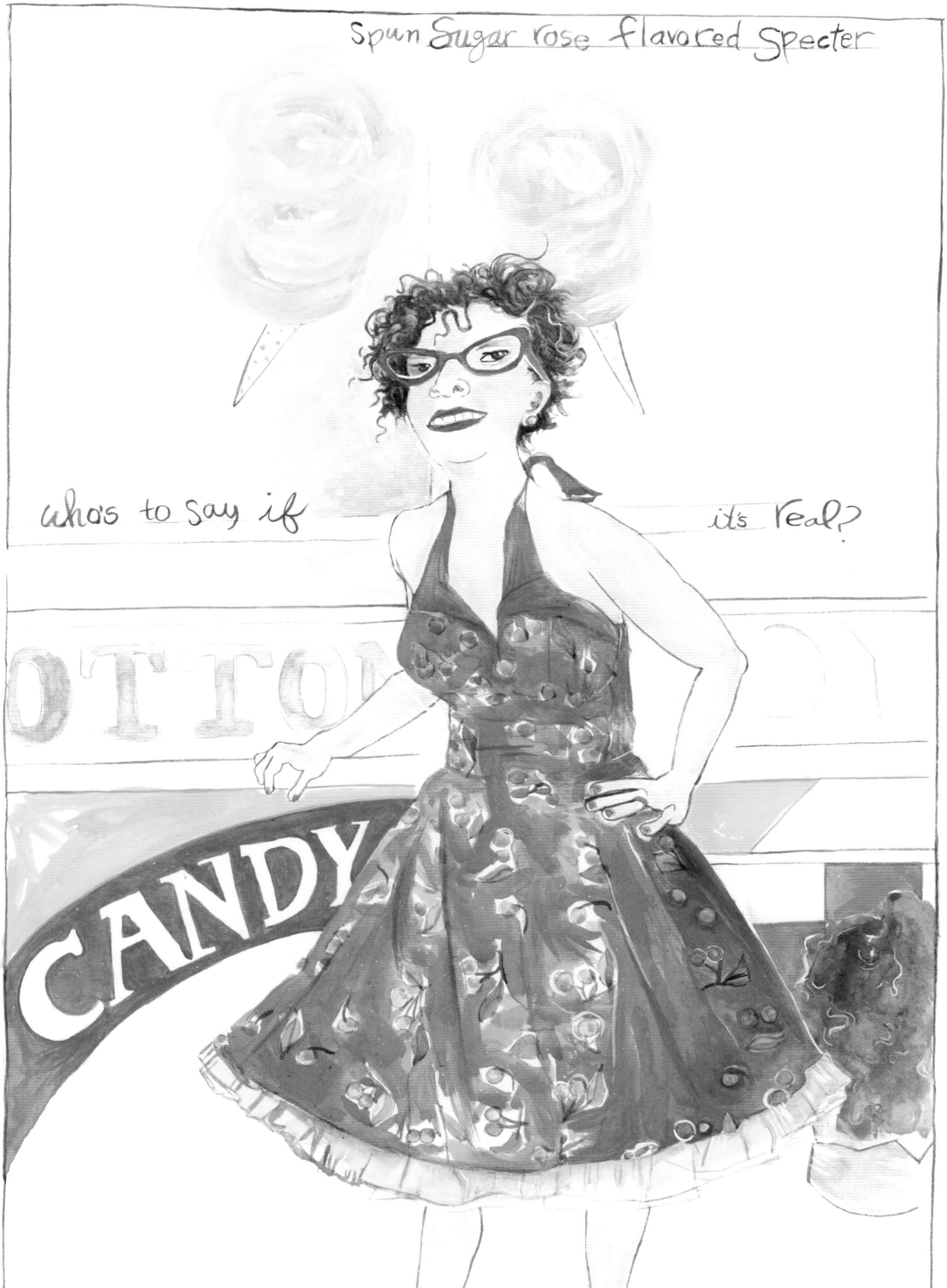
Spun Sugar rose flavored Specter
who's to say if
it's real?
OTTON
CANDY

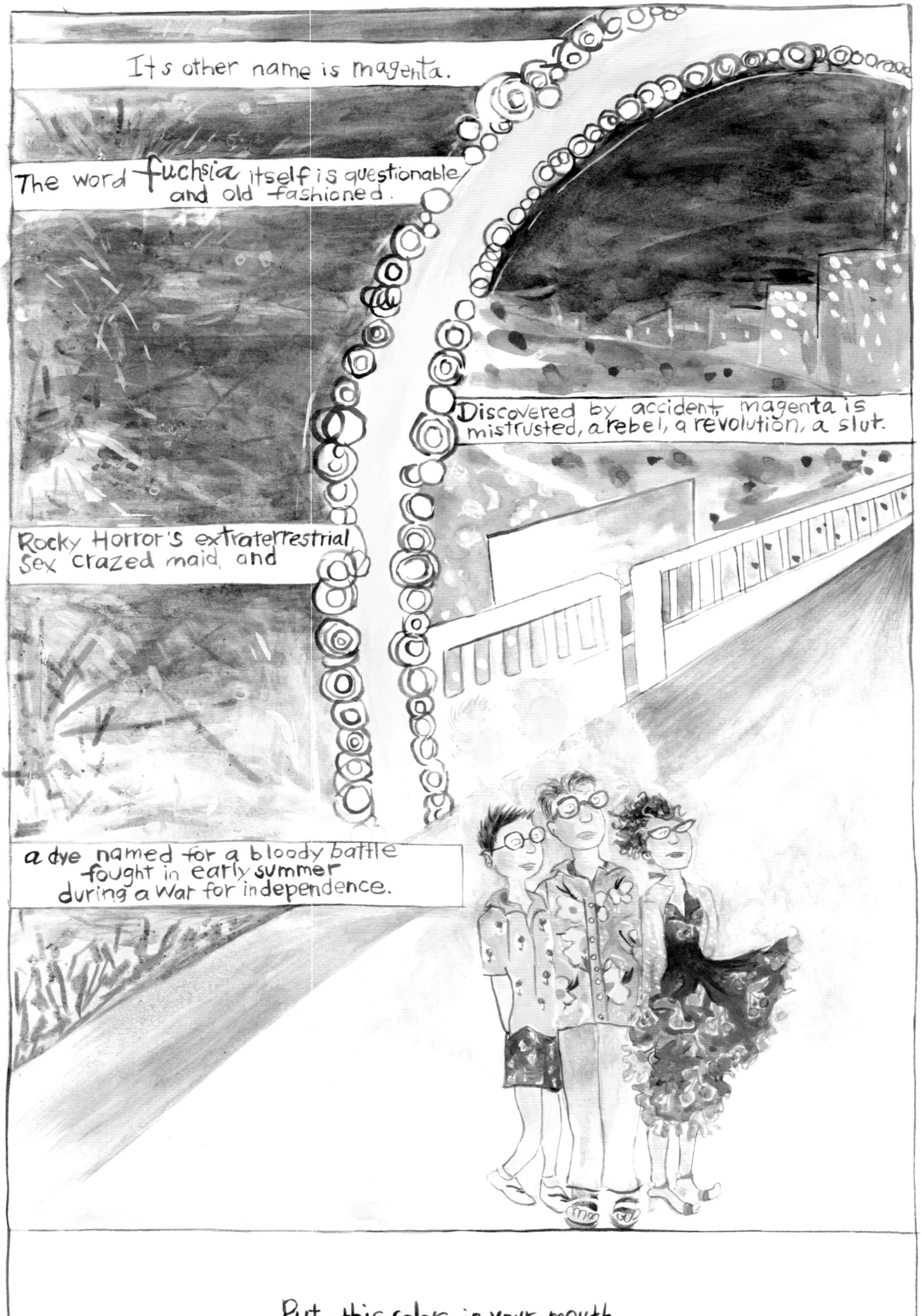

Its other name is magenta.
The word fuchsia itself is questionable and old fashioned.
Discovered by accident, magenta is mistrusted, a rebel, a revolution, a slut.
Rocky Horror's extraterrestrial sex crazed maid, and
a dye named for a bloody battle fought in early summer during a war for independence.
Put this color in your mouth.

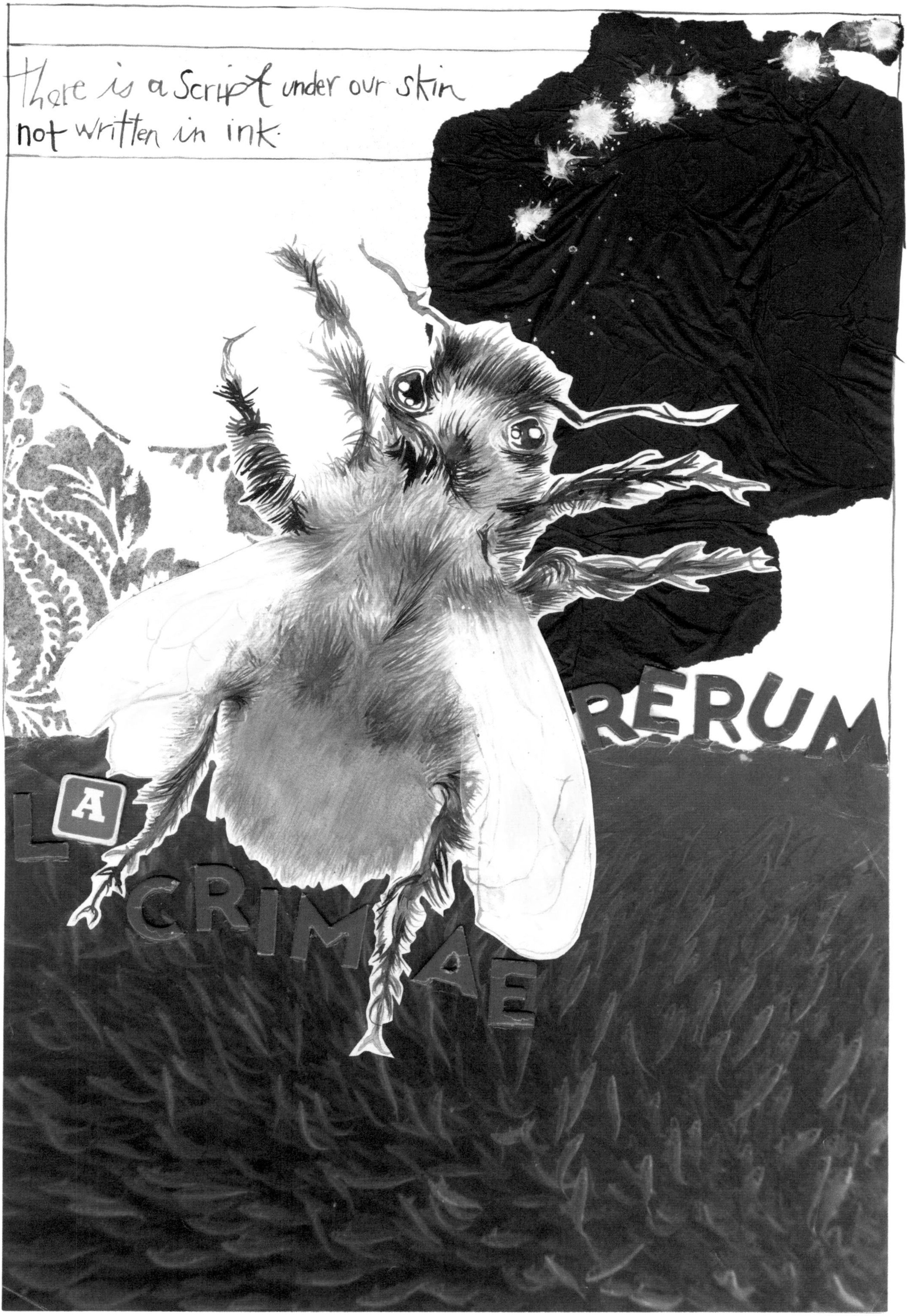
There is a Script under our skin
not written in ink.
LACRIMAE
RERUM

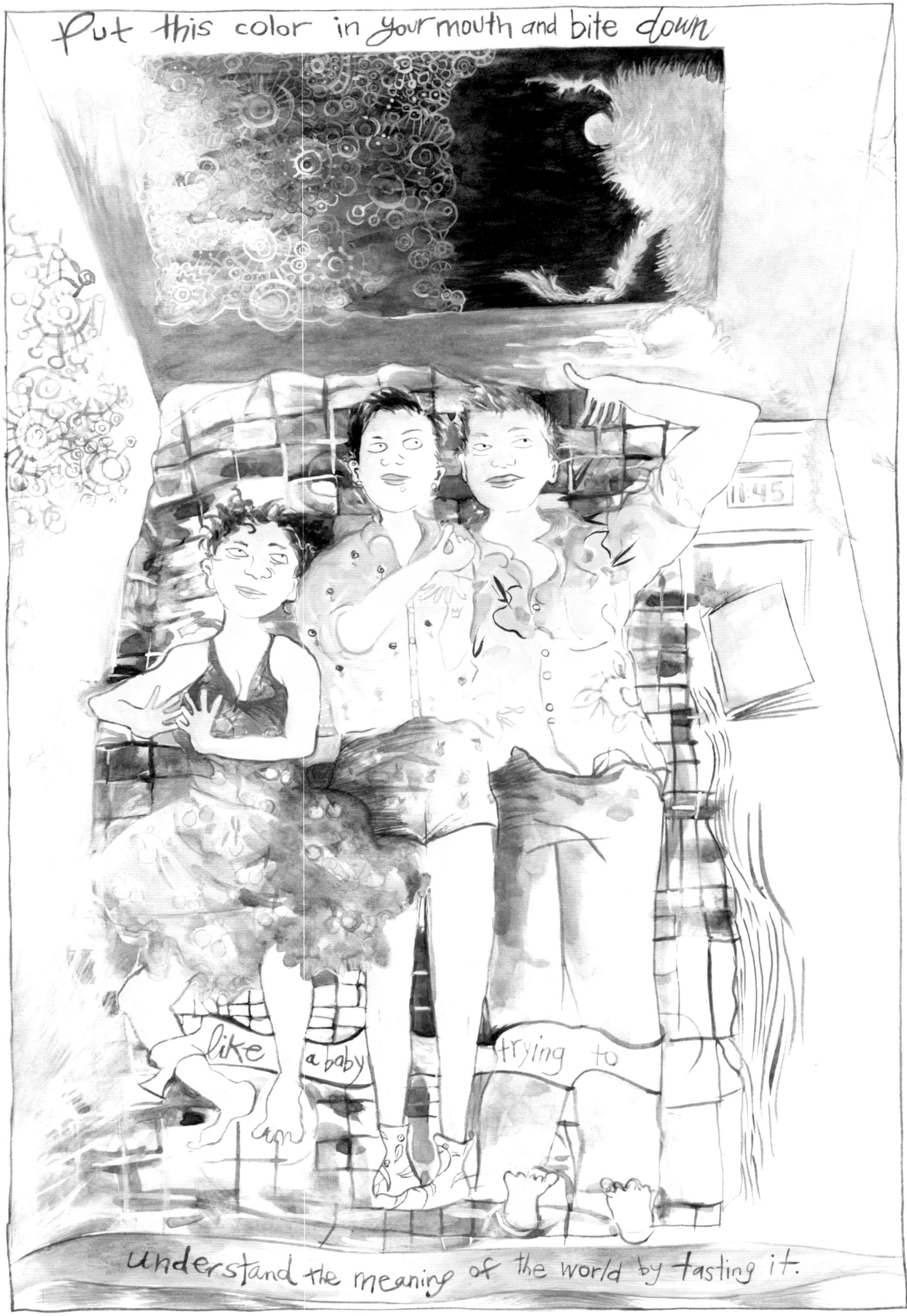
Put this color in your mouth and bite down
11:45
like a baby trying to
understand the meaning of the world by tasting it.

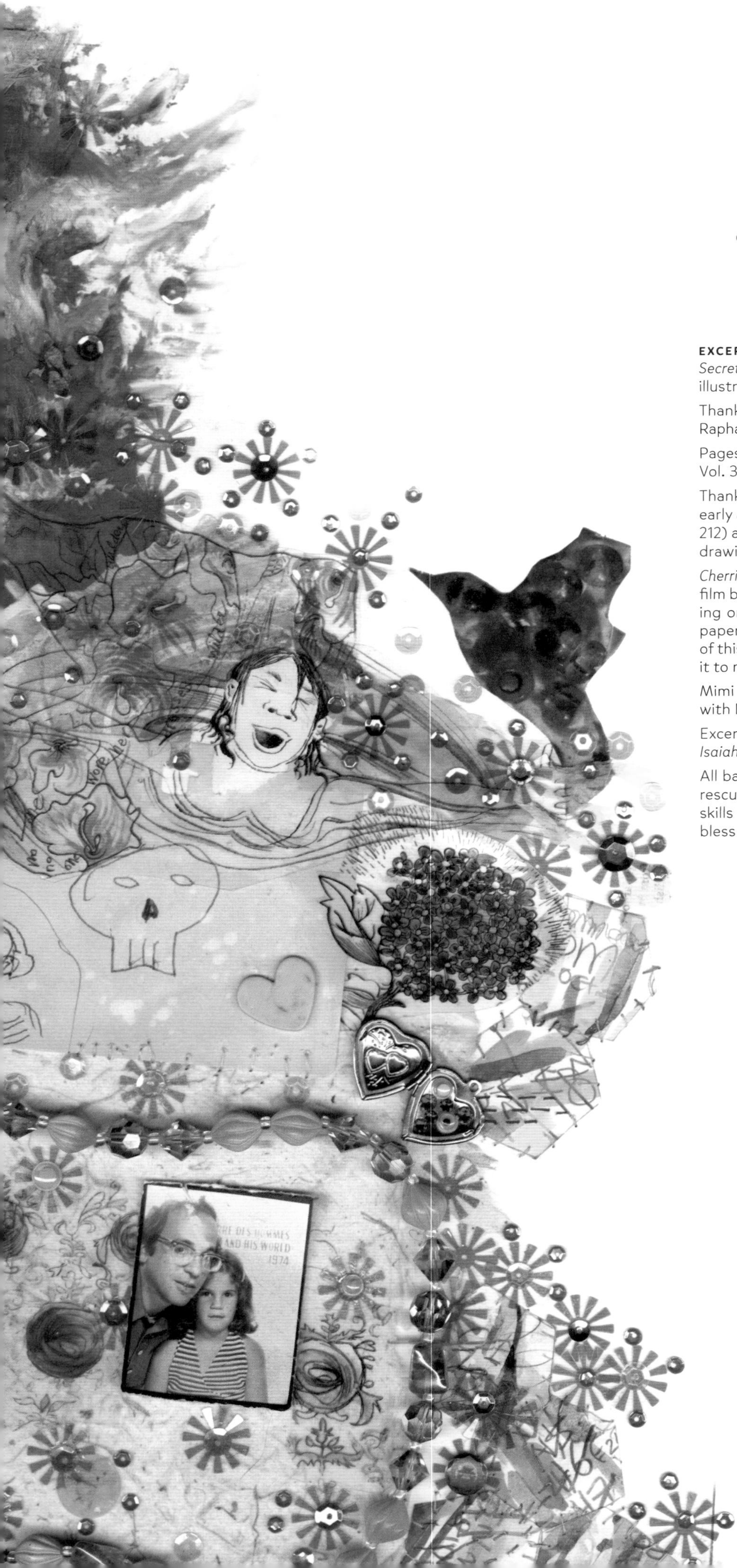
AND HIS WORLD
1974

Credits and Notations

EXCERPTS on pages 25 through 29 are from *The Secret Garden* by Frances Hodgson Burnet with illustrations by Tasha Tudor, Dell Publishing, 1962.

Thanks to Oosa and Frédérique (page 34) and to Raphael Beaulieu (page 43) for French translation.

Pages 70-80 appeared in a different form in Lilith, Vol. 34. Spring 2009.

Thanks to Sammy Winter-Spector for use of his early artwork and text (pages 16, 28, 29,173, 201, 212) and Zoë Gemelli for allowing me to base my drawing (page 203) on her photograph.

Cherries in the Snow (An Ode to Joan Nestle) a short film by the late Melissa Levin, inspired the drawing on page 105. Melissa's spectacular vintage paper collection greatly enriched the vocabulary of this book. Thanks to Nina Levitt for entrusting it to me.

Mimi Posey's bridge metaphor in conversation with Nora Jacobson is illustrated on page 162.

Excerpt on page 181 is from *The Old Testament, Isaiah*, 54:1-3.

All baby candy photos by Avi Spector, who also rescued me with his omnificent art and technical skills whenever I called. Sometimes at midnight, bless him.

Acknowledgements

I GRATEFULLY ACKNOWLEDGE support from the Canada Council for the Arts, Ontario Arts Council, Toronto Arts Council, Insomniac Press, Tightrope Books, Carousel Magazine, YYZ Gallery, Guernica Editions, Koyama Press, Sustainable Arts Foundation, and Fund the Change.

I will always be thankful to my agent Nicki Richesin whose joyful guidance and solidarity means the world to me. Admiration and gratitude to my editor, Gary Groth, for his meticulous insight, chutzpah, and sense of fun. Thanks to Jacq Cohen, Paul Baresh, Christina Chwang, Emily Silva, Chelsea Wirtz and everyone at Fantagraphics for all the love in their work.

Thanks to my teachers Bernice Rothfleisch, Sharon Erskine, Greta Hofmann Nemiroff and Régine Mainberger. Sue Goldstein's artwork is a masterclass in text as image, and I am grateful for her immense influence and support. I owe everything to Lynda Barry, Alison Bechdel, Phoebe Gloeckner, Frida Kahlo, Liza Lou, Faith Ringgold, and Wimmen's Comix.

Charlene Nero has freed me from the darkest places with vintage costumes, swing dancing and visits to french fry trucks. She is the most generous rabble rouser and bon vivant alive. Appreciation always to Sarah Fowlie and Emily Paradis for their open house and expansive love. Special thanks to Attessa Bagherpour, Peter Boullata, Catherine Cameron, Nicola Crawhall, Zio Hersh and Coworkers Without Borders for steadfast comradery and courage.

I am profoundly grateful for the company, encouragement and help of the following people: Angel Beyde, Roz Chast, Ruth Cumberbatch, Eleanor Davis, Madeleine Domingue, Anna Dow, Jen DT, Ariel Elofer, fogel fogel, Hannah Fowlie, Inge Fowlie, Frédérique, Zoë Gemelli, Caroline and Tony Grant, Deborah Goldenberg, Chantelle Grant, Joan Headley, Zen Cameron-Hersh, Zab Hobart, Nora Jacobson, Melissa Levin, Nina Levitt, Philip Lortie, Severn Lortie, Margarita Barrientos- Macdonald, Ernest Marcus, Shirley Marcus, Susan Marcus, Sandra May, Irene Mihaljek, Lynda Morris, Nick Morris, Michelle Morrison, Oosa, Alice Paradis, Oscar Paradis, Karen Pearlston, Kasey Poserina, Jake Pyne, Skya Raven, Cass Reimer, Mike Roy, Aviva Rubin, Natalie Seltzer, Andrea Simmons, Fiona Smyth, Avi Spector, Emily Spector, Mitchell Spector, Danette Steele, Lucas Crawhall-Stein, Nicci Stein, Sebastien Crawhall-Stein, Etolie Stewart, Lorna Storey, Les Tager, Jackson Tait, Esther Vise, Wendy Sherman Associates, Syrus Marcus Ware, Georgina Watts, Georgia Webber and Zoe Whittall.

Sophie Afriat has turned me to face myself since the beginning. I may have written this whole book in my head without her.

I am alive because of the persistent dreams of my ancestors; I thank them all for sticking with me.

Charles Spector taught me everything I know about kindness, poetry, and the feeling you get when you hear the overture to a musical. I am an artist because of him.

Esther Spector gifts me with every kind of support, walking with me no matter where I go. Her love and faith in me resonate through my life and the delirium of the last 70 pages of this book.

Sammy Winter-Spector, my inspiration, my light, my heart, you are the reason I tried so hard. I hope you always know you are a million times more than enough.

Rebecca Marcus, there would be no book without your brilliance and generosity. I could not surrender to the demands of this work if not for the myriad of ways you love, sustain and untangle me every single day for the past twenty years. Thank you for inventing and innovating this beautiful life with me. All I ever had to do was write it down.

Thanks to the spec that was Ruby, for choosing us and changing everything.

ONTARIO ARTS COUNCIL
CONSEIL DES ARTS DE L'ONTARIO
an Ontario government agency
un organisme du gouvernement de l'Ontario

Canada Council   Conseil des arts
for the Arts   du Canada

TORONTO **A**RTS COUNCIL | FUNDED BY THE CITY OF TORONTO

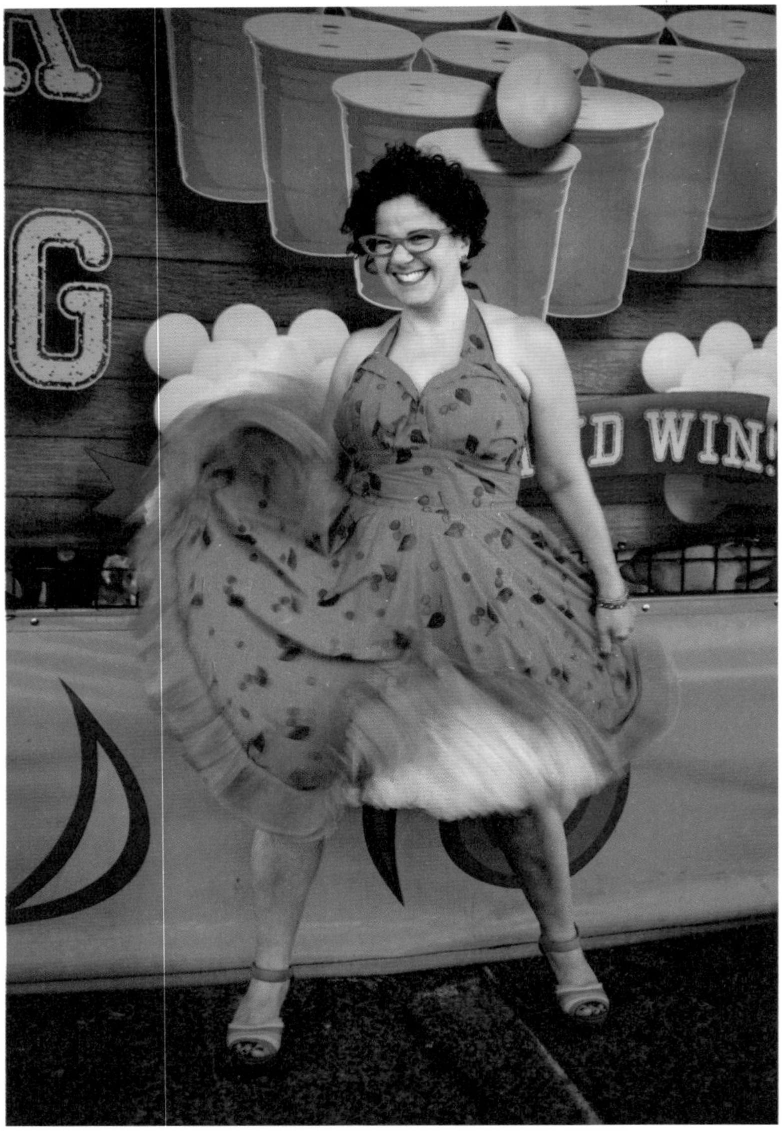

D WIN!

PHOTO: ZOË GEMELLI

SHIRA SPECTOR is a Jewish Canadian lesbian cartoonist who earned a BFA in Fibres (with Distinction) from Concordia University in Montreal. Her work has been widely anthologized and exhibited in Toronto where she is transplanted with her wife and son and a succession of rescue dogs. *Red Rock Baby Candy* is her first graphic memoir.

Spector draws inspiration from theatricality in all its forms whether found in nature or the best parts of aqua musicals. Believing that play and poetry are not luxuries, and that opportunities to embrace the fantastical belong to daily living, she accepts defying the mundane as her personal mission in life.

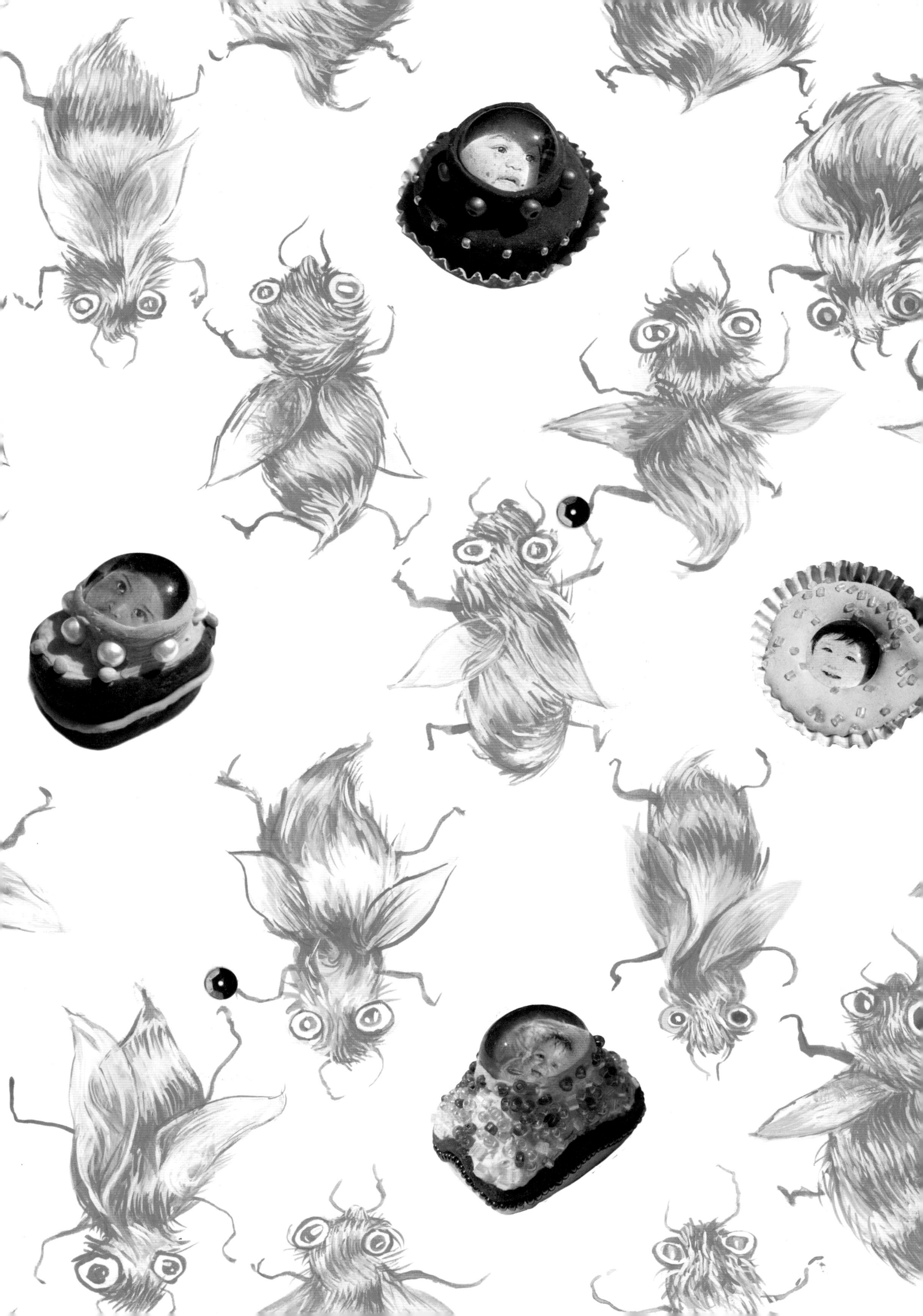

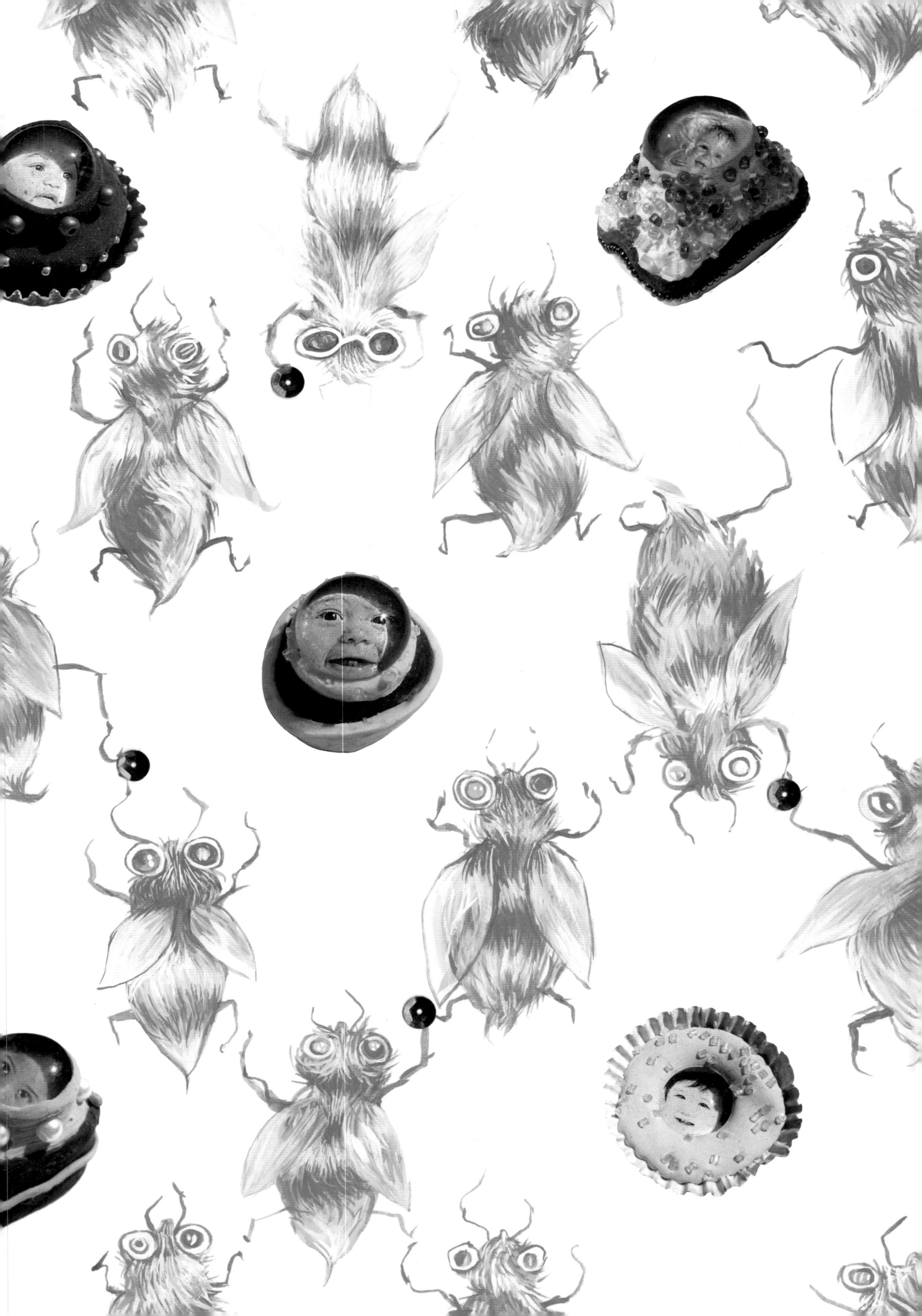